THE ILLUSTRATED

A BRIEF HISTORY OF TIME

UPDATED AND EXPANDED EDITION

THE UNIVERSE IN A NUTSHELL

STEPHEN HAWKING

BANTAM BOOKS

NEW YORK   TORONTO   LONDON   SYDNEY   AUCKLAND

Published by Bantam Dell
A Division of Random House, Inc.
New York, New York

Bantam Books and the rooster colophon are registered trademarks of Random House, Inc.

These titles were published separately: *The Illustrated A Brief History of Time, Updated and Expanded Edition,* as A Labyrinth Book,
by Bantam Books, an imprint of The Bantam Dell Publishing Group, a division of Random House, Inc., New York,
in 1996; and *The Universe in a Nutshell,* as A Book Laboratory Book, by Bantam Books, an imprint of
The Bantam Dell Publishing Group, a division of Random House, Inc., New York, in 2001.

ISBN: 978-0-307-29117-2

This 2007 hardcover edition printed in the United States of America.

2 4 6 8 10 9 7 5 3 1

THE ILLUSTRATED A BRIEF HISTORY OF TIME

CONTENTS

Looking back in time. This deepest ever optical image was taken in January 1996 by the Hubble Space Telescope. It shows the early universe, with some of the galaxies dating back to less than a billion years after the beginning of space and time. The extraordinary technological advances in the past few years are beginning to reveal the facts behind the theories of how the universe began and our position in it.

Foreword

I DIDN'T WRITE a foreword to the original edition of *A Brief History of Time*. That was done by Carl Sagan. Instead, I wrote a short piece titled "Acknowledgments" in which I was advised to thank everyone. Some of the foundations that had given me support weren't too pleased to have been mentioned however, because it led to a great increase in applications.

I don't think anyone, my publishers, my agent, or myself, expected the book to do anything like as well as it did. It was in the London *Sunday Times* best seller list for 237 weeks, longer than any other book (apparently, the Bible and Shakespeare aren't counted). It has been translated into something like forty languages and has sold about one copy for every 750 men, women, and children in the world. As Nathan Myhrvold of Microsoft (a former postdoc of mine) remarked: I have sold more books on physics than Madonna has on sex.

The success of *A Brief History* indicates that there is widespread interest in the big questions like: where did we come from? And why is the universe the way it is? However, I know that many people have found parts of the book difficult to follow. The aim in this new edition is to make it easier by including large numbers of illustrations. Even if you only look at the pictures and their captions, you should get some idea of what is going on.

I have taken the opportunity to update the book and include new theoretical and observational results obtained since the book was first published (on April Fools' Day, 1988). I have included a new chapter on wormholes and time travel. Einstein's General Theory of Relativity seems to offer the possibility that we could create and maintain wormholes, little tubes that connect different regions of space-time. If so, we might be able to use them for rapid travel around the galaxy or travel back in time. Of course, we have not seen anyone from the future (or have we?) but I discuss a possible explanation for this.

I also describe the progress that has been made recently in finding "dualities" or correspondences between apparently different theories of physics. These correspondences are a strong indication that there is a complete unified theory of physics, but they also suggest that it may not be possible to express this theory in a single fundamental formulation. Instead, we may have to use different reflections of the underlying theory in different situations. It might be like our being unable to represent the surface of the earth on a single map and having to use different maps in different regions. This would be a revolution in our view of the unification of the laws of science but it would not change the most important point: that the universe is governed by a set of rational laws that we can discover and understand.

On the observational side, by far the most important development has been the measurement of fluctuations in the cosmic microwave background radiation by COBE (the Cosmic Background Explorer satellite) and other collaborations. These fluctuations are the fingerprints of creation, tiny initial irregularities in the otherwise smooth and uniform early universe that later grew into galaxies, stars, and all the structures we see around us. Their form agrees with the predictions of the proposal that the universe has no boundaries or edges in the imaginary time direction; but further observations will be necessary to distinguish this proposal from other possible explanations for the fluctuations in the background. However, within a few years we should know whether we can believe that we live in a universe that is completely self-contained and without beginning or end.

Stephen Hawking
Cambridge, May 1996.

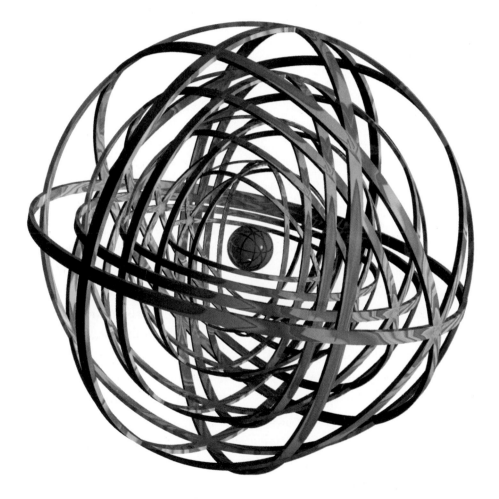

1

Our Picture of the Universe

A WELL-KNOWN SCIENTIST (some say it was Bertrand Russell) once gave a public lecture on astronomy. He described how the earth orbits around the sun and how the sun, in turn, orbits around the center of a vast collection of stars called our galaxy. At the end of the lecture, a little old lady at the back of the room got up and said: "What you have told us is rubbish. The world is really a flat plate supported on the back of a giant tortoise." The scientist gave a superior smile before replying, "What is the tortoise standing on?" "You're very clever, young man, very clever," said the old lady. "But it's turtles all the way down!"

Most people would find the picture of our universe as an infinite tower of tortoises rather ridiculous, but why do we think we know better? What do we know about the universe, and how do we know it? Where did the universe come from, and where is it going? Did the universe have a beginning, and if so, what happened *before* then? What is the nature of time? Will it ever come to an end? Can we go back in time? Recent breakthroughs in physics, made possible in part by fantastic new technologies, suggest answers to some of these longstanding questions. Someday these answers may seem as obvious to us as the earth orbiting the sun — or perhaps as ridiculous as a tower of tortoises. Only time (whatever that may be) will tell.

As long ago as 340 B.C. the Greek philosopher Aristotle, in his book *On the Heavens*, was able to put forward two good arguments for believing that the earth was a round sphere rather than a flat plate. First, he realized that eclipses of the moon were caused by the earth

To the North Star

Fig. 1.1

Opposite: *The Hindu Universe depicts the earth supported by six elephants, while the infernal regions are carried by a tortoise resting on a snake.*
Left: *Medieval depiction of the early Greek concept of a flat earth floating on water with the four elements above it.* Above: *Aristotle. Roman copy of a Greek original from the 4th century* B.C.

coming between the sun and the moon. The earth's shadow on the moon was always round, which would be true only if the earth was spherical. If the earth had been a flat disk, the shadow would have been elongated and elliptical, unless the eclipse always occurred at a time when the sun was directly under the center of the disk. Second, the Greeks knew from their travels that the North Star appeared lower in the sky when viewed in the south than it did in more northerly regions. (Since the North Star lies over the North Pole, it appears to be directly above an observer at the North Pole, but to someone looking from the equator, it appears to lie just at the horizon: Fig. 1.1.)

From the difference in the apparent position of the North Star in Egypt and Greece, Aristotle even quoted an estimate that the distance around the earth was 400,000 stadia. It is not known exactly what length a stadium was, but

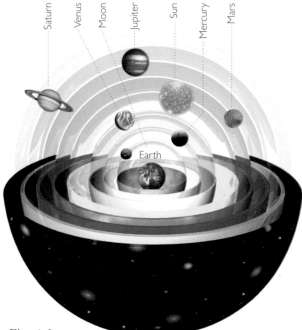

Fig. 1.2

it may have been about 200 yards, which would make Aristotle's estimate about twice the currently accepted figure. The Greeks even had a third argument that the earth must be round, for why else does one first see the sails of a ship coming over the horizon, and only later see the hull?

Aristotle thought the earth was stationary and that the sun, the moon, the planets, and the stars moved in circular orbits about the earth. He believed this because he felt, for mystical reasons, that the earth was the center of the uni-

Ptolemy using a quadrant to measure the elevation of the moon. Basle, 1508.

verse, and that circular motion was the most perfect. This idea was elaborated by Ptolemy in the second century A.D. into a complete cosmological model. The earth stood at the center, surrounded by eight spheres that carried the moon, the sun, the stars, and the five planets known at the time, Mercury, Venus, Mars, Jupiter, and Saturn (Fig. 1.2). The planets themselves moved on smaller circles attached to their respective

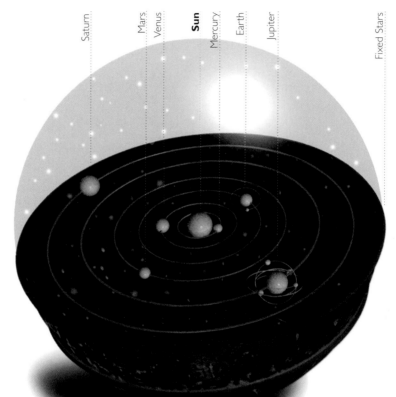

Saturn   Mars   Venus   **Sun**   Mercury   Earth   Jupiter   Fixed Stars

Fig. 1.3

spheres in order to account for their rather complicated observed paths in the sky. The outermost sphere carried the so-called fixed stars, which always stay in the same positions relative to each other but which rotate together across the sky. What lay beyond the last sphere was never made very clear, but it certainly was not part of mankind's observable universe.

Ptolemy's model provided a reasonably accurate system for predicting the positions of heav-enly bodies in the sky. But in order to predict these positions correctly, Ptolemy had to make an assumption that the moon followed a path that sometimes brought it twice as close to the earth as at other times. And that meant that the moon ought sometimes to appear twice as big as at other times! Ptolemy recognized this flaw, but nevertheless his model was generally, although not universally, accept-ed. It was adopted by the Christian church as the picture of the universe that was in accordance

N. COPERNICUS.
London Published as the Act directs April 20, 1802 by J.Wilkes

Above: *Nicholas Copernicus (1473-1543).*
Right: *Kepler's Theoretical Model linking the planetary orbits with an arrangement of concentric geometrical solids (1596).*

and the planets moved in circular orbits around the sun (Fig. 1.3). Nearly a century passed before this idea was taken seriously. Then two astronomers — the German, Johannes Kepler, and the Italian, Galileo Galilei — started publicly to support the Copernican theory, despite the fact that the orbits it predicted did not quite match the ones observed. The death blow to the Aristotelian/Ptolemaic theory came in 1609. In that year, Galileo started observing the night sky with a telescope, which had just been invented. When he looked at the planet Jupiter, Galileo found that it was accompanied by several small

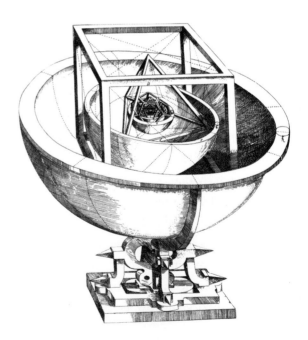

with Scripture, for it had the great advantage that it left lots of room outside the sphere of fixed stars for heaven and hell.

A simpler model, however, was proposed in 1514 by a Polish priest, Nicholas Copernicus. (At first, perhaps for fear of being branded a heretic by his church, Copernicus circulated his model anonymously.) His idea was that the sun was stationary at the center and that the earth

satellites or moons that orbited around it. This implied that everything did not have to orbit directly around the earth, as Aristotle and Ptolemy had thought. (It was, of course, still possible to believe that the earth was stationary at the center of the universe and that the moons of Jupiter moved on extremely complicated paths around the earth, giving the appearance that they orbited Jupiter. However, Copernicus's theory was much simpler.) At the same time, Johannes Kepler had modified Copernicus's theory, suggesting that the planets moved not in circles but in ellipses (an ellipse is an elongated circle). The predictions now finally matched the observations.

As far as Kepler was concerned, elliptical orbits were merely an ad hoc hypothesis, and a rather repugnant one at that, because ellipses were clearly less perfect than circles. Having discovered almost by accident that elliptical orbits fit the observations well, he could not reconcile them with his idea that the planets were made to orbit the sun by magnetic forces. An explanation was provided only much later, in 1687, when Sir Isaac Newton published his *Philosophiae Naturalis Principia Mathematica*, probably the most important single work ever published in the physical sciences. In it Newton not only put forward a theory of how bodies move in space

Galileo Galilei (1564-1642). Engraving, Padua 1744.

and time, but he also developed the complicated mathematics needed to analyze those motions. In addition, Newton postulated a law of universal gravitation according to which each body in the universe was attracted toward every other body by a force that was stronger the more massive the bodies and the closer they were to each other. It was this same force that caused objects to fall to the ground. (The story that Newton was inspired by an apple hitting his

Above: *Frontispiece of Harmonia Macrocosmica, 1708, showing Copernicus, Ptolemy and Galileo.*
Opposite: *Isaac Newton (1642-1727).*
Engraving after the portrait by Vanderbank, 1833.

head is almost certainly apocryphal. All Newton himself ever said was that the idea of gravity came to him as he sat "in a contemplative mood" and "was occasioned by the fall of an apple.") Newton went on to show that, according to his law, gravity causes the moon to move in an elliptical orbit around the earth and causes the earth and the planets to follow elliptical paths around the sun.

The Copernican model got rid of Ptolemy's celestial spheres, and with them, the idea that the universe had a natural boundary. Since "fixed stars" did not appear to change their positions apart from a rotation across the sky caused by the earth spinning on its axis, it became natural to suppose that the fixed stars were objects like our sun but very much farther away.

Newton realized that, according to his theory of gravity, the stars should attract each other, so it seemed they could not remain essentially motionless. Would they not all fall together at some point? In a letter in 1691 to Richard Bentley, another leading thinker of his day, Newton argued that this would indeed happen if there were only a finite number of stars distributed over a finite region of space. But he reasoned that if, on the other hand, there were an

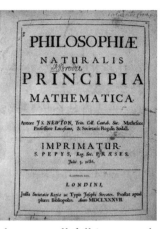

regarded as the center, because every point has an infinite number of stars on each side of it. The correct approach, it was realized only much later, is to consider the finite situation, in which the stars all fall in on each other, and then to ask how things change if one adds more stars roughly uniformly distributed outside this region. According to Newton's law, the extra stars would make no difference at all to the original ones on average, so the stars would fall in just as fast. We can add as many stars as we like, but they will still always collapse in on themselves. We now know it is impossible to have an infinite static model of the universe in which gravity is always attractive.

It is an interesting reflection on the general climate of thought before the twentieth century that no one had suggested that the universe was expanding or contracting. It was generally accepted that either the universe had existed forever in an unchanging state, or that it had been created at a finite time in the past more or less

infinite number of stars, distributed more or less uniformly over infinite space, this would not happen, because there would not be any central point for them to fall to.

This argument is an instance of the pitfalls that you can encounter in talking about infinity. In an infinite universe, every point can be

as we observe it today. In part this may have been due to people's tendency to believe in eternal truths, as well as the comfort they found in the thought that even though they may grow old and die, the universe is eternal and unchanging.

Even those who realized that Newton's theory of gravity showed that the universe could not be static did not think to suggest that it might be expanding. Instead, they attempted to modify the theory by making the gravitational force repulsive at very large distances. This did not significantly affect their predictions of the motions of the planets, but it allowed an infinite distribution of stars to remain in equilibrium — with the attractive forces between nearby stars balanced by the repulsive forces from those that were farther away. However, we now believe such an equilibrium would be unstable: if the stars in some region got only slightly nearer each other, the attractive forces between them would become stronger and dominate over the repulsive forces so that the stars would continue to fall toward each other. On the other hand, if the stars got a bit farther away from each other, the repulsive forces would dominate and drive them farther apart.

Another objection to an infinite static universe is normally ascribed to the German philosopher Heinrich Olbers, who wrote about

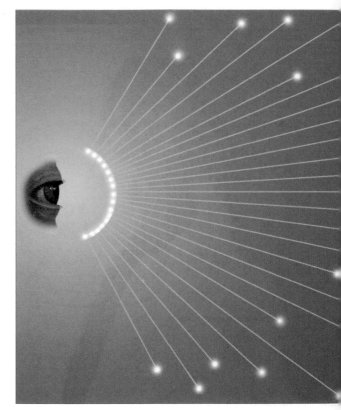

this theory in 1823. In fact, various contemporaries of Newton had raised the problem, and the Olbers article was not even the first to contain plausible arguments against it. It was, however, the first to be widely noted. The difficulty is that in an infinite static universe nearly every line of sight would end on the surface of a star (Fig. 1.4). Thus one would expect that the whole sky would be as bright as the sun, even at night. Olbers's counterargument was that the light

from distant stars would be dimmed by absorption by intervening matter. However, if that happened the intervening matter would eventually heat up until it glowed as brightly as the stars. The only way of avoiding the conclusion that the whole of the night sky should be as bright as the surface of the sun would be to assume that the stars had not been shining forever but had turned on at some finite time in the past. In that case the absorbing matter might not have heated

up yet or the light from distant stars might not yet have reached us. And that brings us to the question of what could have caused the stars to have turned on in the first place.

The beginning of the universe had, of course, been discussed long before this. According to a number of early cosmologies and the Jewish/Christian/Muslim tradition, the universe started at a finite, and not very distant, time in the past. One argument for such a beginning was the feeling that it was necessary to have "'First Cause" to explain the existence of the universe. (Within the universe, you always explained one event as being caused by some earlier event, but the existence of the universe itself could be explained in this way only if it had some beginning.) Another argument was put forward by St. Augustine in his book *The City of God*. He pointed out that civilization is progressing and we remember who performed this deed or developed that technique. Thus man, and so also perhaps the universe, could not have been around all that long. St. Augustine accepted a date of about 5000 B.C. for the Creation of the universe according to the book of Genesis. (It is interesting that this is not

Fig. 1.4 *If the universe was infinite and static, every line of sight would end in a star, making the night sky as bright as the sun.*

The Second Day of Creation
by Julius Schnorr von Carolsfeld, 1860.

so far from the end of the last Ice Age, about 10,000 B.C., which is when archaeologists tell us that civilization really began.)

Aristotle, and most of the other Greek philosophers, on the other hand, did not like the idea of a creation because it smacked too much of divine intervention. They believed, therefore, that the human race and the world around it had existed, and would exist, forever. The ancients had already considered the argument about progress described above, and answered it by saying that there had been periodic floods or other disasters that repeatedly set the human race right back to the beginning of civilization.

The questions of whether the universe had a beginning in time and whether it is limited in space were later extensively examined by the philosopher Immanuel Kant in his monumental (and very obscure) work, *Critique of Pure Reason*, published in 1781. He called these questions antinomies (that is, contradictions) of pure reason because he felt that there were equally compelling arguments for believing the thesis, that the universe had a beginning, and the antithesis, that it had existed forever. His argument for the thesis was that if the universe did not have a beginning, there would be an infinite period of time before any event, which he considered absurd. The argument for the antithesis was that

if the universe had a beginning, there would be an infinite period of time before it, so why should the universe begin at any one particular time? In fact, his cases for both the thesis and the antithesis are really the same argument. They are both based on his unspoken assumption that time continues back forever, whether or not the universe had existed forever. As we shall see, the concept of time has no meaning before the beginning of the universe. This was first pointed out by St. Augustine. When asked: "What did God do before he created the universe?" Augustine didn't reply: "He was preparing Hell for people who asked such questions." Instead, he said that time was a property of the universe that God created, and that time did not exist before the beginning of the universe.

When most people believed in an essentially static and unchanging universe, the question of whether or not it had a beginning was really one of metaphysics or theology. One could account for what was observed equally well on the theory that the universe had existed forever or on the theory that it was set in motion at some finite time in such a manner as to look as though it had existed forever. But in 1929, Edwin Hubble made the landmark observation that wherever you look, distant galaxies are moving rapidly away from us. In other words, the universe is

13

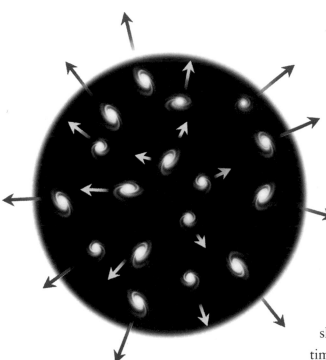

Fig. 1.5

expanding (Fig. 1.5). This means that at earlier times objects would have been closer together. In fact, it seemed that there was a time, about ten or twenty thousand million years ago, when they were all at exactly the same place and when, therefore, the density of the universe was infinite. This discovery finally brought the question of the beginning of the universe into the realm of science.

Hubble's observations suggested that there was a time, called the big bang, when the universe was infinitesimally small and infinitely dense. Under such conditions all the laws of science, and therefore all ability to predict the future, would break down. If there were events earlier than this time, then they could not affect what happens at the present time. Their existence can be ignored because it would have no observational consequences. One may say that time had a beginning at the big bang, in the sense that earlier times simply would not be defined. It should be emphasized that this beginning in time is very different from those that had been considered previously. In an unchanging universe a beginning in time is something that has to be imposed by some being outside the universe; there is no physical necessity for a beginning. One can imagine that God created the universe at literally any time in the past. On the other hand, if the universe is expanding, there may be physical reasons why there had to be a beginning. One could still imagine that God created the universe at the instant of the big bang, or even afterwards in just such a way as to make it look as though there had been a big bang, but it would be meaningless to suppose that it was created before the big bang. An expanding universe does not preclude a creator, but it does place limits on when he might have carried out his job!

In order to talk about the nature of the universe and to discuss questions such as whether it has a beginning or an end, you have to be clear about what a scientific theory is. I shall take the simpleminded view that a theory is just a model of the universe, or a restricted part of it, and a set of rules that relate quantities in the model to observations that we make. It exists only in our minds and does not have any other reality (whatever that might mean). A theory is a good theory if it satisfies two requirements. It must accurately describe a large class of observations on the basis of a model that contains only a few arbitrary elements, and it must make definite predictions about the results of future observations. For example, Aristotle's theory that everything was made out of four elements, earth, air, fire, and water, was simple enough to qualify, but it did not make any definite predictions. On the other hand, Newton's theory of gravity was based on an even simpler model, in which bodies attracted each other with a force that was proportional to a quantity called their mass and inversely proportional to the square of the distance between them. Yet it predicts the motions

Edwin Hubble (1889-1953) photographed at the Mount Wilson Observatory in 1924.

of the sun, the moon, and the planets to a high degree of accuracy.

Any physical theory is always provisional, in the sense that it is only a hypothesis: you can never prove it. No matter how many times the results of experiments agree with some theory, you can never be sure that the next time the result will not contradict the theory. On the other hand, you can disprove a theory by find-

ing even a single observation that disagrees with the predictions of the theory. As philosopher of science Karl Popper has emphasized, a good theory is characterized by the fact that it makes a number of predictions that could in principle be disproved or falsified by observation. Each time new experiments are observed to agree with the predictions the theory survives, and our confidence in it is increased; but if ever a new observation is found to disagree, we have to abandon or modify the theory.

At least that is what is supposed to happen, but you can always question the competence of the person who carried out the observation.

In practice, what often happens is that a new theory is devised that is really an extension of the previous theory. For example, very accurate observations of the planet Mercury revealed a small difference between its motion and the predictions of Newton's theory of gravity. Einstein's general theory of relativity predicted a slightly different motion from Newton's theory. The fact that Einstein's predictions matched what was seen, while Newton's did not, was one of the crucial confirmations of the new theory. However, we still use Newton's theory for all practical purposes because the difference between its predictions and those of general relativity is very small in the situations that we normally deal with. (Newton's theory also has the great advantage

that it is much simpler to work with than Einstein's!)

The eventual goal of science is to provide a single theory that describes the whole universe. However, the approach most scientists actually follow is to separate the problem into two parts. First, there are the laws that tell us how the universe changes with time. (If we know what the universe is like at any one time, these physical laws tell us how it will look at any later time.) Second, there is the question of the initial state of the universe. Some people feel that science should be concerned with only the first part; they regard the question of the initial situation as a matter for metaphysics or religion. They would say that God, being omnipotent, could have started the universe off any way he wanted. That may be so, but in that case he also could have made it develop in a completely arbitrary way. Yet it appears that he chose to make it evolve in a very regular way according to certain laws. It therefore seems equally reasonable to suppose that there are also laws governing the initial state.

It turns out to be very difficult to devise a theory to describe the universe all in one go. Instead, we break the problem up into bits and

Opposite: *Milky Way looking toward the center of the galaxy in the constellation of Sagittarius.*

invent a number of partial theories (Fig. 1.6). Each of these partial theories describes and predicts a certain limited class of observations, neglecting the effects of other quantities, or representing them by simple sets of numbers. It may be that this approach is completely wrong. If everything in the universe depends on everything else in a fundamental way, it might be impossible to get close to a full solution by investigating parts of the problem in isolation. Nevertheless, it is certainly the way that we have made progress in the past. The classic example again is the Newtonian theory of gravity, which tells us that the gravitational force between two bodies depends only on one number associated with each body, its mass, but is otherwise independent of what the bodies are made of. Thus one does not need to have a theory of the structure and constitution of the sun and the planets in order to calculate their orbits.

Today scientists describe the universe in terms of two basic partial theories — the general theory of relativity and quantum mechanics. They are the great intellectual achievements of the first half of this century. The general theory of relativity describes the force of gravity and the large-scale structure of the universe, that is, the structure on scales from only a few miles to

as large as a million million million million (1 with twenty-four zeros after it) miles, the size of the observable universe. Quantum mechanics, on the other hand, deals with phenomena on extremely small scales, such as a millionth of a millionth of an inch. Unfortunately, however, these two theories are known to be inconsistent with each other — they cannot both be correct. One of the major endeavors in physics today, and the major theme of this book, is the search for a new theory that will incorporate them both — a quantum theory of gravity. We do not yet have such a theory, and we may still be a long way from having one, but we do already know many of the properties that it must have. And we shall see, in later chapters, that we already know a fair amount about the predictions a quantum theory of gravity must make.

Now, if you believe that the universe is not arbitrary, but is governed by definite laws, you ultimately have to combine the partial theories into a complete unified theory that will describe everything in the universe. But there is a fundamental paradox in the search for such a complete unified theory. The ideas about scientific theories outlined above assume we are rational beings who are free to observe the universe as we want and to draw logical deductions from

Fig. 1.6

The Newtonian theory describes gravity in terms of force acting at a distance. It works well in the solar system but breaks down in strong gravitational fields.

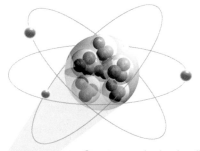

Quantum mechanics describes phenomena at the atomic level and below.

The general theory of relativity describes gravity as a warping of space-time by the mass and energy in it. Objects try to move on straight lines but their paths appear bent because space-time is curved.

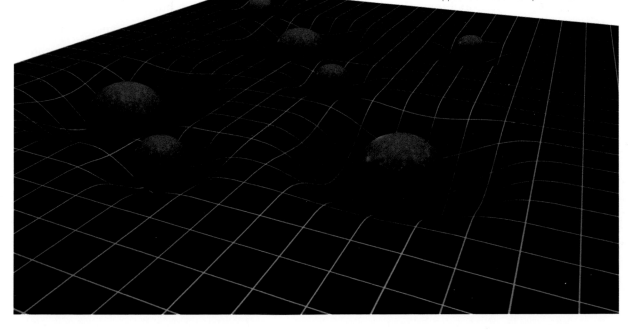

what we see. In such a scheme it is reasonable to suppose that we might progress ever closer toward the laws that govern our universe. Yet if there really is a complete unified theory, it would also presumably determine our actions. And so the theory itself would determine the

Above: *The macrocosm. Several hundred galaxies are visible in this "deepest-ever" view of the universe, called the Hubble Deep Field (HDF), made with NASA's Hubble Space Telescope.*

outcome of our search for it! And why should it

determine that we come to the right conclusions from the evidence? Might it not equally well determine that we draw the wrong conclusion? Or no conclusion at all?

The only answer that I can give to this problem is based on Darwin's principle of natural selection. The idea is that in any population of self-reproducing organisms, there will be variations in the genetic material and upbringing that different individuals have. These differences will mean that some individuals are better able than others to draw the right conclusions about the world around them and to act accordingly. These individuals will be more likely to survive and reproduce and so their pattern of behavior and thought will come to dominate. It has certainly been true in the past that what we call intelligence and scientific discovery have conveyed a survival advantage. It is not so clear that this is still the case: our scientific discoveries may well destroy us all, and even if they don't, a complete unified theory may not make much difference to our chances of survival. However, provided the universe has evolved in a regular way, we might expect that the reasoning abilities that natural selection has given us would be valid also in our search for a complete unified theory, and so would not lead us to the wrong conclusions.

Because the partial theories that we already

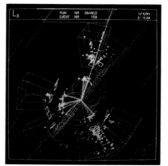

The microcosm. This computer-generated image shows an event at particle level seen on the CERN 1.3 detector screen.

have are sufficient to make accurate predictions in all but the most extreme situations, the search for the ultimate theory of the universe seems difficult to justify on practical grounds. (It is worth noting, though, that similar arguments could have been used against both relativity and quantum mechanics, and these theories have given us both nuclear energy and the microelectronics revolution!) The discovery of a complete unified theory, therefore, may not aid the survival of our species. It may not even affect our life-style. But ever since the dawn of civilization, people have not been content to see events as unconnected and inexplicable. They have craved an understanding of the underlying order in the world. Today we still yearn to know why we are here and where we came from. Humanity's deepest desire for knowledge is justification enough for our continuing quest. And our goal is nothing less than a complete description of the universe we live in.

2

Space and Time

OUR PRESENT IDEAS about the motion of bodies date back to Galileo and Newton. Before them people believed Aristotle, who said that the natural state of a body was to be at rest and that it moved only if driven by a force or impulse. It followed that a heavy body should fall faster than a light one, because it would have a greater pull toward the earth.

The Aristotelian tradition also held that one could work out all the laws that govern the universe by pure thought: it was not necessary to check by observation. So no one until Galileo bothered to see whether bodies of different weight did in fact fall at different speeds. It is said that Galileo demonstrated that Aristotle's belief was false by dropping weights from the leaning tower of Pisa. The story is almost certainly untrue, but Galileo did do something equivalent: he rolled balls of different weights down a smooth slope (Fig. 2.1). The situation is similar to that of heavy bodies falling vertically (Fig. 2.2), but it is easier to observe because the speeds are smaller. Galileo's measurements indicated that each body increased its speed at the same rate, no matter what its weight. For example, if you let go of a ball on a slope that drops by one meter for every ten meters you go along, the ball will be traveling down the slope at a speed of about one meter per second after one

Fig. 2.1

Fig. 2.2

Balls of different weights fall at the same rate

Above right: *Galileo Galilei (1564-1642), engraving by Passignani. Although Galileo's experiment from the Tower of Pisa probably never occurred, his principle of first-hand observation changed the history of science.*

second, two meters per second after two seconds, and so on, however heavy the ball. Of course a lead weight would fall faster than a feather, but that is only because a feather is slowed down by air resistance. If one drops two bodies that don't have much air resistance, such as two different lead weights, they fall at the same rate (Fig. 2.2). On the moon, where there is no air to slow things down, the astronaut David R. Scott performed the feather and lead weight experiment and found that indeed they did hit the ground at the same time (Fig. 2.3).

Galileo's measurements were used by Newton as the basis of his laws of motion. In Galileo's experiments, as a body rolled down the slope it was always acted on by the same force (its weight), and the effect was to make it constantly speed up. This showed that the real effect of a force is always to change the speed of a body, rather than just to set it moving, as was previ-

23

will accelerate, or change its speed, at a rate that is proportional to the force. (For example, the acceleration is twice as great if the force is twice as great.) The acceleration is also smaller the greater the mass (or quantity of matter) of the body. (The same force acting on a body of twice the mass will produce half the acceleration.) A familiar example is provided by a car: the more powerful the engine, the greater the acceleration, but the heavier the car, the smaller the acceleration for the same engine (Fig. 2.4). In addition to his laws of motion, Newton discovered a law to describe the force of gravity, which states that every body attracts every other body with a force that is proportional to the mass of

Above: Fig. 2.3 *On the moon, where there is no air resistance, a feather and a lead weight fall at the same speed.*
Right: Fig. 2.4 *The acceleration is larger the greater the force acting on a body, but it is smaller the greater the mass of the body to be accelerated.*

Fig. 2.4

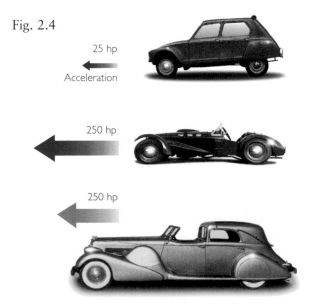

25 hp

Acceleration

250 hp

250 hp

ously thought. It also meant that whenever a body is not acted on by any force, it will keep on moving in a straight line at the same speed. This idea was first stated explicitly in Newton's *Principia Mathematica*, published in 1687, and is known as Newton's first law. What happens to a body when a force does act on it is given by Newton's second law. This states that the body

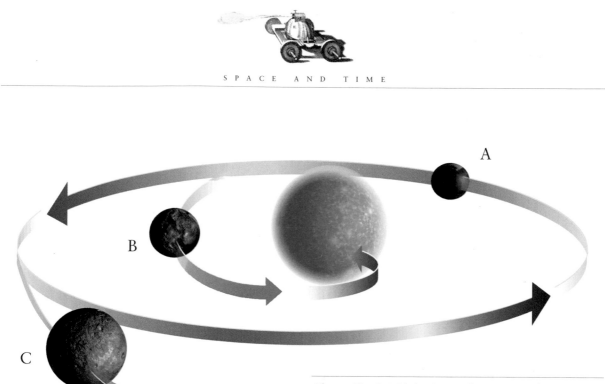

Above: Fig. 2.5 *If the force of gravity was less, or increased more rapidly with distance than Newton's theory predicts, the orbits of the planets around the sun would not be stable ellipses (A). They would either fly away from the sun (C), or spiral in (B).*

each body. Thus the force between two bodies would be twice as strong if one of the bodies (say, body A) had its mass doubled. This is what you might expect because one could think of the new body A as being made of two bodies with the original mass. Each would attract body B with the original force. Thus the total force between A and B would be twice the original force. And if, say, one of the bodies had twice the mass, and the other had three times the mass, then the force would be six times as strong. One can now see why all bodies fall at the same rate: a body of twice the weight will have twice the force of gravity pulling it down,

but it will also have twice the mass. According to Newton's second law, these two effects will exactly cancel each other, so the acceleration will be the same in all cases.

Newton's law of gravity also tells us that the farther apart the bodies, the smaller the force. Newton's law of gravity says that the gravitational attraction of a star is exactly one quarter that of a similar star at half the distance. This law predicts the orbits of the earth, the moon, and the planets with great accuracy. If the law were that the gravitational attraction of a star went down faster or increased more rapidly with distance, the orbits of the planets would

Fig. 2.6 *A tram, traveling at thirty miles an hour, passes a stationary Ping-Pong player, A. The ball on the tram appears, from the viewpoint of A, to have bounced on two spots some 13 meters apart. To the player on the tram it seems to have bounced on one spot, just as the ball bounced by A appears to do the same. Yet A is also traveling through space on the planet earth and the ball would appear to an observer within the solar system to have moved some thirty thousand meters between bounces.*

Fig. 2.7 *If B walked in a northerly direction at 5 mph while on a tram travelling south at 5 mph he would appear to be at rest to the observer on the ground (A). However, if he walked at the same speed on a tram going north (C) he would appear to the same observer to be travelling at 10 mph.*

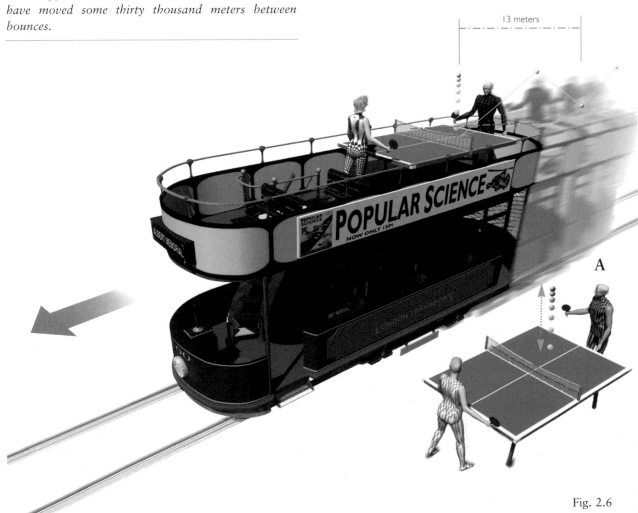

Fig. 2.6

Fig. 2.7

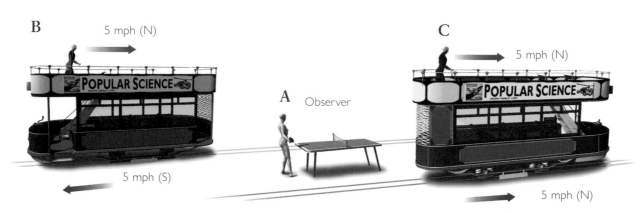

B   5 mph (N)

C   5 mph (N)

POPULAR SCIENCE

POPULAR SCIENCE

A   Observer

5 mph (S)

5 mph (N)

not be elliptical, they would either spiral in to the sun or escape from the sun (Fig. 2.5).

The big difference between the ideas of Aristotle and those of Galileo and Newton is that Aristotle believed in a preferred state of rest, which any body would take up if it were not driven by some force or impulse. In particular, he thought that the earth was at rest. But it follows from Newton's laws that there is no unique standard of rest. One could equally well say that body A was at rest and body B was moving at constant speed with respect to body A, or that body B was at rest and body A was moving. For example, if one sets aside for a moment the rotation of the earth and its orbit round the sun, one could say that the earth was at rest and that a tram on it was traveling east at thirty miles per hour or that the tram was at rest

and the earth was moving west at thirty miles per hour (Fig. 2.7). If one carried out experiments with moving bodies on the tram, all Newton's laws would still hold. For instance, playing Ping-Pong on the tram, one would find that the ball obeyed Newton's laws just like a ball on a table by the track. So there is no way to tell whether it is the tram or the earth that is moving.

The lack of an absolute standard of rest meant that one could not determine whether two events that took place at different times occurred in the same position in space. For example, suppose our Ping-Pong ball on the train bounces straight up and down, hitting the table twice on the same spot one second apart (Fig. 2.6). To someone on the track, the two bounces would seem to take place about thirteen meters apart, because the tram would have traveled that far down the track between the bounces.

The nonexistence of absolute rest therefore meant that one could not give an event an absolute position in space, as Aristotle had believed. The positions of events and the distances between them would be different for a person on the tram and one on the track, and there would be no reason to prefer one person's positions to the other's.

Newton was very worried by this lack of absolute position, or absolute space, as it was called, because it did not accord with his idea of an absolute God. In fact, he refused to accept lack of absolute space, even though it was implied by his laws. He was severely criticized for this irrational belief by many people, most notably by Bishop Berkeley, a philosopher who believed that all material objects and space and time are an illusion. When the famous Dr. Johnson was told of Berkeley's opinion, he cried, "I refute it thus!" and stubbed his toe on a large stone.

Both Aristotle and Newton believed in absolute time. That is, they believed that one could unambiguously measure the interval of time between two events, and that this time would be the same whoever measured it, pro-

vided they used a good clock. Time was completely separate from and independent of space. This is what most people would take to be the commonsense view. However, we have had to change our ideas about space and time. Although our apparently commonsense notions work well when dealing with things like apples, or planets that travel comparatively slowly, they don't work at all for things moving at or near the speed of light.

The fact that light travels at a finite, but very high, speed was first discovered in 1676 by the Danish astronomer Ole Christensen Roemer. He observed that the times at which the moons of Jupiter appeared to pass behind Jupiter were not evenly spaced, as one would expect if the moons went round Jupiter at a constant rate. As the earth and Jupiter orbit around the sun, the distance between them varies. Roemer noticed that eclipses of Jupiter's moons appeared later the farther we were from Jupiter. He argued that this was because the light from the moons took longer to reach us when we were farther away. His measurements of the variations in the distance of the earth from Jupiter were, however, not very accurate, and so his value for the speed of light was 140,000 miles per second, compared to the modern value of 186,000 miles per second. Nevertheless, Roemer's achievement, in not only proving that light travels at a finite speed, but also in measuring that speed, was remarkable — coming as it did eleven years before Newton's publication of *Principia Mathematica*.

A proper theory of the propagation of light didn't come until 1865, when the British physicist James Clerk Maxwell succeeded in unifying the partial theories that up to then had been used to describe the forces of electricity and

Opposite: *Ole Roemer's transit instrument in his Copenhagen house. Engraving from "Basis Astronomiae," 1735.*
Above: *James Clerk Maxwell (1831 1879).*

magnetism. Maxwell's equations predicted that there could be wavelike disturbances in the combined electromagnetic field, and that these would travel at a fixed speed, like ripples on a pond. If the wavelength of these waves (the distance between one wave crest and the next) is a meter or more, they are what we now call radio waves. Shorter wavelengths are known as microwaves (a few centimeters) or infrared (more than a ten thousandth of a centimeter). Visible light has a wavelength of between only forty and eighty millionths of a centimeter. Even shorter wavelengths are known as ultraviolet, X rays, and gamma rays.

Maxwell's theory predicted that radio or light waves should travel at a certain fixed speed. But Newton's theory had got rid of the idea of absolute rest, so if light was supposed to travel at a fixed speed, one would have to say what that fixed speed was to be measured relative to. It was therefore suggested that there was a substance called the "ether" that was present everywhere, even in "empty" space. Light waves should travel through the ether as sound waves travel through air, and their speed should therefore be relative to the ether. Different observers, moving relative to the ether, would see light coming toward them at different speeds, but light's speed relative to the ether would remain fixed. In particular, as the earth was moving through the ether on its orbit round the sun, the speed of light measured in the direction of the earth's motion through the ether (when we were moving toward the source of the light) should be higher than the speed of light at right angles to that motion (when we are not moving toward

the source). In 1887 Albert Michelson (who later became the first American to receive the Nobel prize for physics) and Edward Morley carried out a very careful experiment at the Case School of Applied Science in Cleveland. They compared the speed of light in the direction of the earth's motion with that at right angles to the earth's motion. To their great surprise, they found they were exactly the same!

Between 1887 and 1905 there were several attempts, most notably by the Dutch physicist Hendrik Lorentz, to explain the result of the Michelson–Morley experiment in terms of objects contracting and clocks slowing down when they moved through the ether. However, in a famous paper in 1905, a hitherto unknown clerk in the Swiss patent office, Albert Einstein, pointed out that the whole idea of an ether was

unnecessary, providing one was willing to abandon the idea of absolute time. A similar point was made a few weeks later by a leading French mathematician, Henri Poincaré. Einstein's arguments were closer to physics than those of Poincaré, who regarded this problem as mathematical. Einstein is usually given the credit for the new theory, but Poincaré is remembered by having his name attached to an important part of it.

The fundamental postulate of the theory of relativity, as it was called, was that the laws of science should be the same for all freely moving observers, no matter what their speed. This was true for Newton's laws of motion, but now the idea was extended to include Maxwell's theory and the speed of light: all observers should measure the same speed of light, no matter how fast they are moving.

Opposite left: *Albert Abraham Michelson (1852-1931).*
Opposite right: *Edward Morley (1838-1923)*
Left: *Jules Henri Poincaré (1854-1912).*
Above: *Albert Einstein (1879-1955), Germany 1920.*

This simple idea has some remarkable consequences. Perhaps the best known are the equivalence of mass and energy, summed up in Einstein's famous equation $E=mc^2$ (where E is energy, m is mass and c is the speed of light), and the law that nothing may travel faster than the

31

speed of light. Because of the equivalence of energy and mass, the energy which an object has due to its motion will add to its mass. In other words, it will make it harder to increase its speed. This effect is only really significant for objects moving at speeds close to the speed of light. For example, at 10 percent of the speed of light an object's mass is only 0.5 percent more than normal, while at 90 percent of the speed of light it would be more than twice its normal mass. As an object approaches the speed of light, its mass rises ever more quickly, so it takes more and more energy to speed it up further. It can in fact never reach the speed of light, because by then its mass would have become infinite, and by the equivalence of mass and energy, it would have taken an infinite amount of energy to get it there. For this reason, any normal object is forever confined by relativity to move at speeds slower than the speed of light. Only light, or other waves that have no intrinsic mass, can move at the speed of light.

An equally remarkable consequence of relativity is the way it has revolutionized our ideas of space and time. In Newton's theory, if a pulse of light is sent from one place to another, different observers would agree on the time that the journey took (since time is absolute), but will

not always agree on how far the light traveled (since space is not absolute). Since the speed of the light is just the distance it has traveled divided by the time it has taken, different observers would measure different speeds for the light. In relativity, on the other hand, all observers *must* agree on how fast light travels. They still, however, do not agree on the distance the light has traveled, so they must therefore now also disagree over the time it has taken. (The time taken is the distance the light has traveled — which the observers do not agree on — divided by the light's speed — which they do agree on.) In other words, the theory of relativity put an end to the idea of absolute time! It appeared that each observer must have his own measure of time, as recorded by a clock carried with him, and that identical clocks carried by different observers would not necessarily agree.

Each observer could use radar to say where and when an event took place by sending out a pulse of light or radio waves. Part of the pulse is reflected back at the event and the observer measures the time at which he receives the echo. The time of the event is then said to be the time halfway between when the pulse was sent and the time when the reflection was received back: the distance of the event is half the time taken

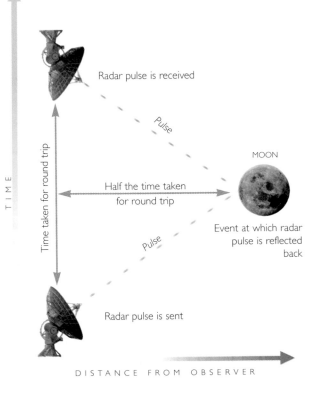

Fig. 2.8 *Time is measured vertically, and the distance from the observer is measured horizontally. The observer's path through space and time is shown as the vertical line on the left. The paths of the pulse to and from the event are the diagonal lines.*

for this round trip, multiplied by the speed of light. (An event, in this sense, is something that takes place at a single point in space, at a specified point in time.) This idea is shown in Fig. 2.8, which is an example of a space-time dia-

gram. Using this procedure, observers who are moving relative to each other will assign different times and positions to the same event. No particular observer's measurements are any more correct than any other observer's, but all the measurements are related. Any observer can work out precisely what time and position any other observer will assign to an event, provided he knows the other observer's relative velocity.

Nowadays we use just this method to measure distances precisely, because we can measure time more accurately than length. In effect, the meter is defined to be the distance traveled by light in 0.000000003335640952 seconds, as measured by a cesium clock. (The reason for that particular number is that it corresponds to the historical definition of the meter — in terms of two marks on a particular platinum bar kept in Paris.) Equally, we can use a more convenient, new unit of length called a light-second. This is simply defined as the distance that light travels in one second. In the theory of relativity, we now define distance in terms of time and the speed of light, so it follows automatically that every observer will measure light to have the same speed (by definition, 1 meter per 0.000000003335640952 seconds). There is no need to introduce the idea of an ether, whose presence anyway cannot be detected, as the Michelson–Morley experiment showed. The theory of relativity does, however, force us to change fundamentally our ideas of space and time. We must accept that time is not completely separate from and independent of space, but is combined with it to form an object called space-time.

It is a matter of common experience that one can describe the position of a point in space by three numbers, or coordinates. For instance, one can say that a point in a room is seven feet from one wall, three feet from another, and five feet above the floor. Or one could specify that a point was at a certain latitude and longitude and a certain height above sea level. One is free to use any three suitable coordinates, although they have only a limited range of validity. One would not specify the position of the moon in terms of miles north and miles west of Piccadilly Circus and feet above sea level. Instead, one might describe it in terms of distance from the sun, distance from the plane of the orbits of the planets, and the angle between the line joining the moon to the sun and the line joining the sun to a nearby star such as Alpha Centauri. Even these coordinates would not be of much use in describing the position of the sun in our galaxy

or the position of our galaxy in the local group of galaxies. In fact, one may describe the whole universe in terms of a collection of overlapping patches. In each patch, one can use a different set of three coordinates to specify the position of a point.

An event is something that happens at a particular point in space and at a particular time. So one can specify it by four numbers or coordinates. Again, the choice of coordinates is arbitrary; one can use any three well-defined spatial coordinates and any measure of time. In relativity, there is no real distinction between the space and time coordinates, just as there is no real difference between any two space coordinates. One could choose a new set of coordinates in which, say, the first space coordinate was a combination of the old first and second space coordinates. For instance, instead of measuring the position of a point on the earth in miles north of Piccadilly and miles west of Piccadilly, one could use miles northeast of Piccadilly, and miles northwest of Piccadilly. Similarly, in relativity, one could use a new time coordinate that was the old time (in seconds) plus the distance (in light-seconds) north of Piccadilly.

It is often helpful to think of the four coordinates of an event as specifying its position in a four-dimensional space called space-time. It is impossible to imagine a four-dimensional space. I personally find it hard enough to visualize three-dimensional space! However, it is easy to draw diagrams of two-dimensional spaces, such as the surface of the earth. (The surface of the earth is two-dimensional because the position of a point can be specified by two coordinates, latitude and longitude.) I shall generally use diagrams in which time increases upward and one of the spatial dimensions is shown horizontally. The other two spatial dimensions are ignored or, sometimes, one of them is indicated by perspective. (These are called space-time diagrams, like Fig. 2.8.) For example, in Fig. 2.9 time is measured upwards in years and the distance along the line from the sun to Alpha Centauri is measured horizontally in miles. The paths of the sun and of Alpha Centauri through space-time are shown as the vertical lines on the left and right of the diagram. A ray of light from the sun follows the diagonal line, and takes four years to get from the sun to Alpha Centauri.

Fig. 2.9 *Space-time diagram showing a light signal (diagonal line) going from the sun to Alpha Centauri. The paths of the sun and Alpha Centauri through space-time are straight lines.*

As we have seen, Maxwell's equations predicted that the speed of light should be the same whatever the speed of the source, and this has been confirmed by accurate measurements. It follows from this that if a pulse of light is emitted at a particular time at a particular point in space, then as time goes on it will spread out as a sphere of light whose size and position are independent of the speed of the source. After one millionth of a second the light will have spread out to form a sphere with a radius of 300 meters; after two millionths of a second, the

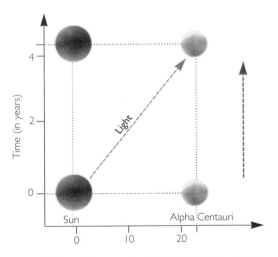

Expanding ripples

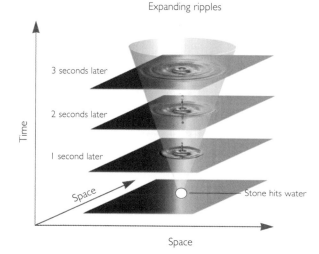

Fig. 2.10

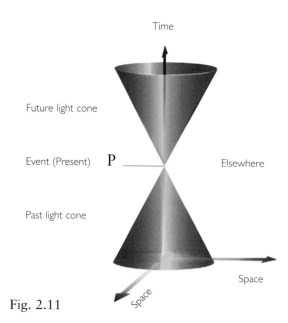

Fig. 2.11

radius will be 600 meters; and so on. It will be like the ripples that spread out on the surface of a pond when a stone is thrown in. The ripples spread out as a circle that gets bigger as time goes on. If one stacks snapshots of the ripples at different times one above the other, the expanding circle of ripples will mark out a cone whose tip is at the place and time at which the stone hit the water (Fig. 2.10). Similarly, the light spreading out from an event forms a (three-dimensional) cone in (the four-dimensional) space-time. This cone is called the future light cone of the event. In the same way we can draw another cone, called the past light cone, which is the set of events from which a pulse of light is able to reach the given event (Fig. 2.11).

Given an event P, one can divide the other events in the universe into three classes. Those

Above: Fig. 2.10 *A space-time diagram showing ripples spreading on the surface of a pond. The expanding circle of ripples makes a cone in space-time of two space directions and one time direction.*

Below: Fig. 2.11 *The path of a pulse of light from an event P forms a cone in space-time called "the future light cone of P." Similarly, "the past light cone of P" is the path of rays of light that will pass through the event P. The two light cones divide space-time into the future, the past and the elsewhere of P.*

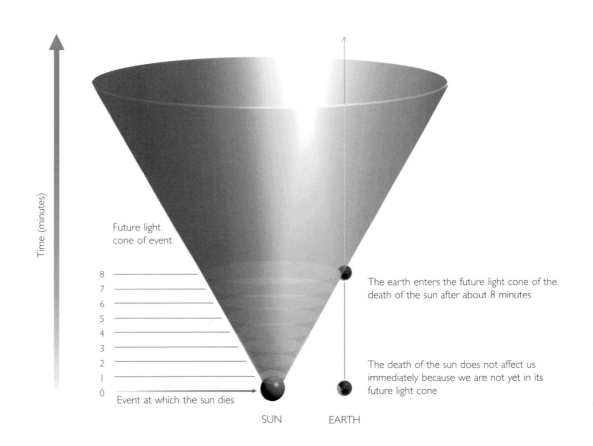

Time (minutes)

Future light
cone of event

8
7
6
5
4
3
2
1
0

Event at which the sun dies

SUN

EARTH

The earth enters the future light cone of the
death of the sun after about 8 minutes

The death of the sun does not affect us
immediately because we are not yet in its
future light cone

events that can be reached from the event P by a particle or wave traveling at or below the speed of light are said to be in the future of P. They will lie within or on the expanding sphere of light emitted from the event P. Thus they will lie within or on the future light cone of P in the space-time diagram. Only events in the future of P can be affected by what happens at P because nothing can travel faster than light.

Above: Fig. 2.12 *Space-time diagram showing how long we would have to wait to know that the sun has died.*

Similarly, the past of P can be defined as the set of all events from which it is possible to reach the event P traveling at or below the speed of light. It is thus the set of events that can affect what happens at P. The events that do not lie in the future or past of P are said to lie in the

Fig. 2.13

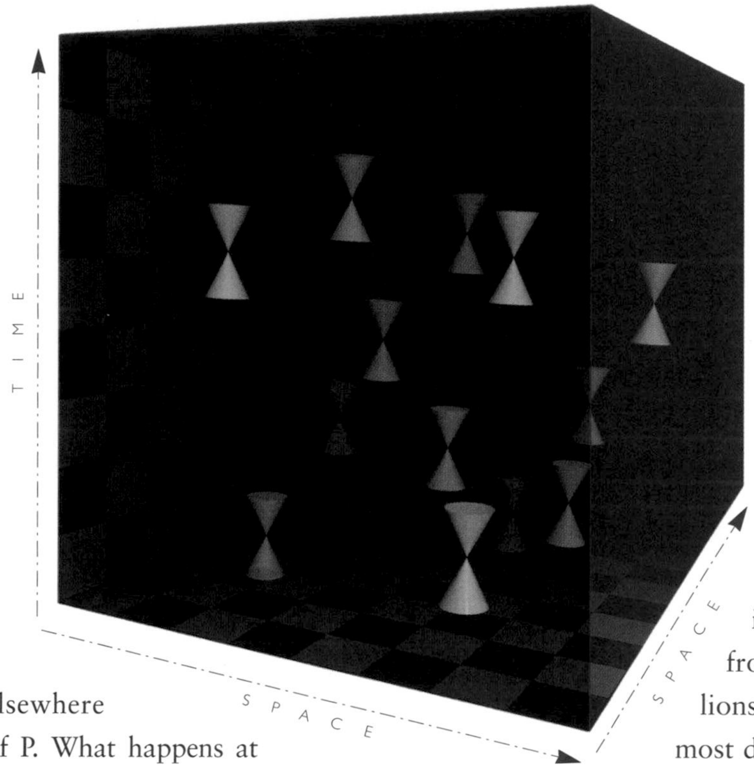

TIME

SPACE

SPACE

Fig. 2.13 *When the effects of gravity are neglected, the light cones of all events all point in the same direction.*

elsewhere of P. What happens at such events can neither affect nor be affected by what happens at P. For example, if the sun were to cease to shine at this very moment, it would not affect things on earth at the present time because they would be in the elsewhere of the event when the sun went out (Fig. 2.12). We would know about it only after eight minutes, the time it takes light to reach us from the sun. Only then would events on earth lie in the future light cone of the event at which the sun went out. Similarly, we do not know what is happening at the moment farther away

in the universe: the light that we see from distant galaxies left them millions of years ago, and in the case of the most distant object that we have seen, the light left some eight thousand million years ago. Thus, when we look at the universe, we are seeing it as it was in the past.

If one neglects gravitational effects, as Einstein and Poincaré did in 1905, one has what is called the special theory of relativity. For every event in space-time we may construct a light cone (the set of all possible paths of light in space-time emitted at that event), and since the speed of light is the same at every event and in every direction, all the light cones will be identical and will all point in the same direction

38

Fig. 2.14

Fig. 2.15

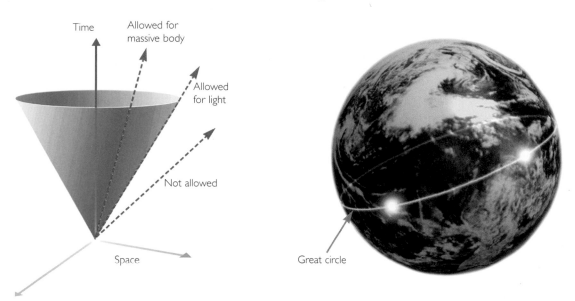

Fig. 2.14 *Bodies with a mass of their own move slower than the speed of light. Thus their paths lie within the future light cone.*

Fig. 2.15 *On the earth, a geodesic is the shortest route between two points on what is called a great circle.*

(Fig. 2.13). The theory also tells us that nothing can travel faster than light. This means that the path of any object through space and time must be represented by a line that lies within the light cone at each event on it (Fig. 2.14). The special theory of relativity was very successful in explaining that the speed of light appears the same to all observers (as shown by the Michelson–Morley experiment) and in describ-ing what happens when things move at speeds close to the speed of light. However, it was inconsistent with the Newtonian theory of grav-ity, which said that objects attracted each other with a force that depended on the distance between them. This meant that if one moved one of the objects, the force on the other one would change instantaneously. Or in other words, gravitational effects should travel with infinite velocity, instead of at or below the speed of light, as the special theory of relativity required. Einstein made a number of unsuccess-ful attempts between 1908 and 1914 to find a theory of gravity that was consistent with special

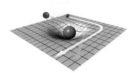

Above: *Solar disc as seen during the total solar eclipse in 1991.* Opposite: Fig. 2.16 *The mass of the sun (A) distorts the space-time near it. This deflects light from a distant star (B) passing near the sun so that it appears on Earth (C) to have come from a different direction (D).*

relativity. Finally, in 1915, he proposed what we now call the general theory of relativity.

Einstein made the revolutionary suggestion that gravity is not a force like other forces, but is a consequence of the fact that space-time is not flat, as had been previously assumed: it is curved, or "warped," by the distribution of mass and energy in it. Bodies like the earth are not made to move on curved orbits by a force called gravity; instead, they follow the nearest thing to a straight path in a curved space, which is called a geodesic. A geodesic is the shortest (or

longest) path between two nearby points. For example, the surface of the earth is a two-dimensional curved space. A geodesic on the earth is called a great circle, and is the shortest route between two points (Fig 2.15). As the geodesic is the shortest path between any two airports, this is the route an airline navigator will tell the pilot to fly along. In general relativity, bodies always follow straight lines in four-dimensional space-time, but they nevertheless appear to us to move along curved paths in our three-dimensional space. (This is rather like watching an airplane flying over hilly ground. Although it follows a straight line in three-dimensional space, its shadow follows a curved path on the two-dimensional ground.)

The mass of the sun curves space-time in such a way that although the earth follows a straight path in four-dimensional space-time, it appears to us to move along a circular orbit in three-dimensional space. In fact, the orbits of the planets predicted by general relativity are almost exactly the same as those predicted by the Newtonian theory of gravity. However, in the case of Mercury, which, being the nearest planet to the sun, feels the strongest gravitational effects, and has a rather elongated orbit, general relativity predicts that the long axis of the

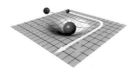

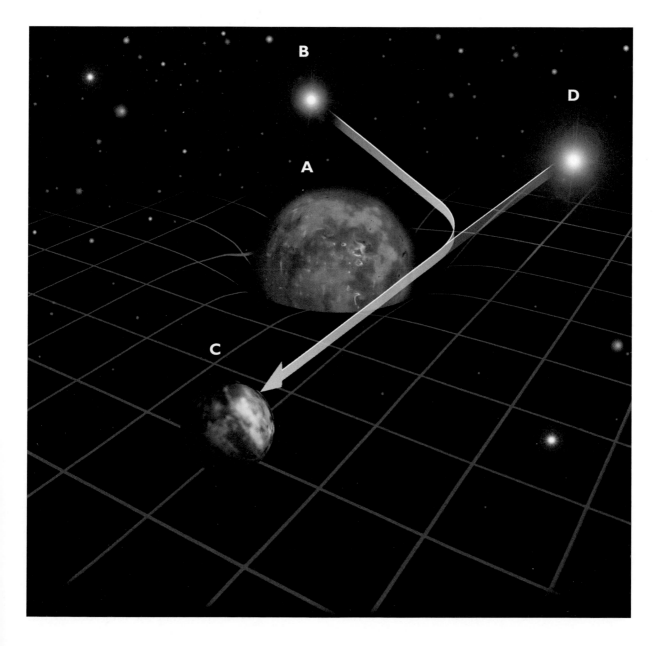

ellipse should rotate about the sun at a rate of about one degree in ten thousand years. Small though this effect is, it had been noticed before 1915 and served as one of the first confirmations of Einstein's theory. In recent years the even smaller deviations of the orbits of the other planets from the Newtonian predictions have been measured by radar and found to agree with the predictions of general relativity.

Light rays too must follow geodesics in space-time. Again, the fact that space is curved means that light no longer appears to travel in straight lines in space. So general relativity predicts that light should be bent by gravitational fields. For example, the theory predicts that the light cones of points near the sun would be slightly bent inward, on account of the mass of the sun. This means that light from a distant star that happened to pass near the sun would be deflected through a small angle, causing the star to appear in a different position to an observer on the earth (Fig. 2.16). Of course, if the light from the star always passed close to the sun, we would not be able to tell whether the light was being deflected or if instead the star was really where we see it. However, as the earth orbits around the sun, different stars appear to pass

behind the sun and have their light deflected. They therefore change their apparent position relative to other stars.

It is normally very difficult to see this effect, because the light from the sun makes it impossible to observe stars that appear near to the sun in the sky. However, it is possible to do so during an eclipse of the sun, when the sun's light is blocked out by the moon. Einstein's prediction of light deflection could not be tested immediately in 1915, because the First World War was in progress, and it was not until 1919 that a British expedition, observing an eclipse from West Africa, showed that light was indeed deflected by the sun, just as predicted by the theory. This proof of a German theory by British scientists was hailed as a great act of reconciliation between the two countries after the war. It is ironic, therefore, that later examination of the photographs taken on that expedition showed the errors were as great as the effect they were trying to measure. Their measurement had been sheer luck, or a case of knowing the result they wanted to get, not an uncommon occurrence in science. The light deflection has, however, been accurately confirmed by a number of later observations.

Above: Fig. 2.17 *The clock at the base of the tower, nearer to the earth, is found to run slower than the one at the top.*

Another prediction of general relativity is that time should appear to run slower near a massive body like the earth. This is because there is a relation between the energy of light and its frequency (that is, the number of waves of light per second): the greater the energy, the higher the frequency. As light travels upward in the earth's gravitational field, it loses energy, and so its frequency goes down. (This means that the length of time between one wave crest and the next goes up.) To someone high up, it would appear that everything down below was taking longer to happen. This prediction was tested in 1962, using a pair of very accurate clocks mounted at the top and bottom of a water tower (Fig. 2.17). The clock at the bottom, which was nearer the earth, was found to run slower, in exact agreement with general relativity. The difference in the speed of clocks at different heights above the earth is now of considerable practical importance, with the advent of very accurate navigation systems based on signals from satellites. If one ignored the predictions of general relativity, the position that one calculated would be wrong by several miles!

Newton's laws of motion put an end to the idea of absolute position in space. The theory of relativity gets rid of absolute time. Consider a pair of twins. Suppose that one twin goes to live on the top of a mountain while the other stays at sea level. The first twin would age faster than the second. Thus, if they met again, one would be older than the other. In this case, the difference in ages would be very small, but it would be much larger if one of the twins went for a long trip in a spaceship at nearly the speed of light. When he returned, he would be much younger than the one who stayed on earth. This is known as the twins paradox, but it is a paradox only if one has the idea of absolute time at the back of one's mind. In the theory of relativity there is no unique absolute time, but instead each individual has his own personal measure of time that depends on where he is and how he is moving.

Before 1915, space and time were thought of as a fixed arena in which events took place, but which was not affected by what happened in it. This was true even of the special theory of relativity. Bodies moved, forces attracted and repelled, but time and space simply continued, unaffected. It was natural to think that space and time went on forever.

The situation, however, is quite different in the general theory of relativity. Space and time are now dynamic quantities: when a body moves, or a force acts, it affects the curvature of space and time — and in turn the structure of space-time affects the way in which bodies move and forces act. Space and time not only affect but also are affected by everything that happens in the universe. Just as one cannot talk about events in the universe without the notions of space and time, so in general relativity it became meaningless to talk about space and time outside the limits of the universe.

In the following decades this new understanding of space and time was to revolutionize our view of the universe. The old idea of an essentially unchanging universe that could have existed, and could continue to exist, forever was replaced by the notion of a dynamic, expanding universe that seemed to have begun a finite time ago, and that might end at a finite time in the future. That revolution forms the subject of the next chapter. And years later, it was also to be the starting point for my work in theoretical physics. Roger Penrose and I showed that Einstein's general theory of relativity implied that the universe must have a beginning and, possibly, an end.

Time and space are now seen as dynamic quantities with each individual particle, or planet, having its own unique measure of time depending on where and how each is moving.

3

The Expanding Universe

I F ONE LOOKS AT THE SKY on a clear, moonless night, the brightest objects one sees are likely to be the planets Venus, Mars, Jupiter, and Saturn. There will also be a very large number of stars, which are just like our own sun but much farther from us. Some of these fixed stars do, in fact, appear to change very slightly their positions relative to each other as the earth orbits around the sun: they are not really fixed at all! This is because they are comparatively near to us. As the earth goes round the sun, we see them from different positions against the background of more distant stars (Fig. 3.1). This is fortunate, because it enables us to measure directly the distance of these stars from us: the nearer they are, the more they appear to move. The nearest star, called Proxima Centauri, is found to be about four light-years away (the light from it takes about four years to reach earth), or about twenty-three million million miles. Most of the other stars that are visible to the naked eye lie within a few hundred light-years of us. Our sun, for comparison, is a mere eight light-minutes away! The visible stars appear spread all over the night sky, but are particularly concentrated in one band, which we call the Milky Way. As long ago as 1750, some astronomers were suggesting that the appearance of the Milky Way could be explained if most of the visible stars lie in a single disklike configuration, one example of what we now call a spiral galaxy. Only a few decades later, the astronomer Sir William Herschel confirmed this idea by painstakingly cataloging the positions and distances of vast numbers of stars. Even so, the idea gained complete acceptance only early this century.

Our modern picture of the universe dates back to only 1924, when the American astronomer Edwin Hubble demonstrated that ours

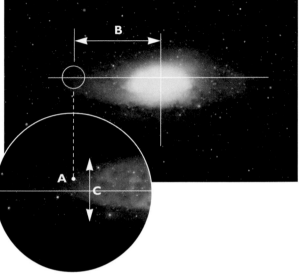

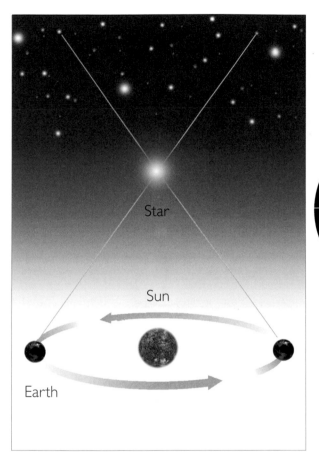

Star

Sun

Earth

Left: Fig. 3.1 *As the earth orbits the sun, the position of a nearby star appears to move against the background of more distant stars.*

Above: Fig. 3.2 *Astronomers agree that our sun (A) lies about 25,000 light-years from the center (B) and 68 light-years from the galactic plane, in the outer disk, which is about 1300 light-years thick in our vicinity (C).*

Opposite: *Whirlpool Galaxy — M51. Our own galaxy is thought to resemble such a stellar spiral.*

was not the only galaxy. There were in fact many others, with vast tracts of empty space between them. In order to prove this, he needed to determine the distances to these other galaxies, which are so far away that, unlike nearby stars, they really do appear fixed. Hubble was forced, therefore, to use indirect methods to measure the distances. Now, the apparent brightness of a star depends on two factors: how much light it radiates (its luminosity), and how far it is from us. For nearby stars, we can measure their apparent brightness and their distance, and so we can work out their luminosity. Conversely, if we knew the luminosity of stars in other galaxies, we could work out their distance by measuring their apparent brightness. Hubble noted that certain types of stars always have the same luminosity when they are near enough for

Solar System

Our galaxy

Local Group

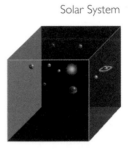  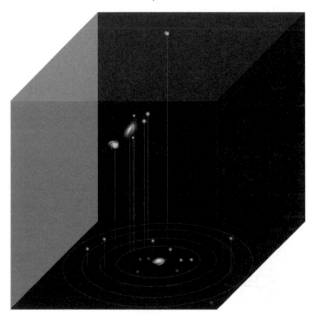

us to measure; therefore, he argued, if we found such stars in another galaxy, we could assume that they had the same luminosity — and so calculate the distance to that galaxy. If we could do this for a number of stars in the same galaxy, and our calculations always gave the same distance, we could be fairly confident of our estimate.

In this way, Edwin Hubble worked out the distances to nine different galaxies. We now know that our galaxy is only one of some hundred thousand million that can be seen using modern telescopes, each galaxy itself containing some hundred thousand million stars (Fig. 3.3). The inset on page 46 shows a picture of one spiral galaxy that is similar to what we think ours must look like to someone living in another galaxy. We live in a galaxy that is about one hundred thousand light-years across and is slowly rotating; the stars in its spiral arms orbit around its center about once every several hun-

Fig. 3.3. From the left: *Our sun is just one of the one hundred thousand million stars that make up our galaxy, the Milky Way. The Milky Way is only one of the many galaxies in the Local Group. The Local Group, in turn, is just one of the thousands of groups and clusters of galaxies which form the largest known structures of our universe.*

dred million years. Our sun is just an ordinary, average-sized, yellow star, near the inner edge of one of the spiral arms (Fig. 3.2). We have certainly come a long way since Aristotle and Ptolemy, when we thought that the earth was the center of the universe!

Clusters of galaxies

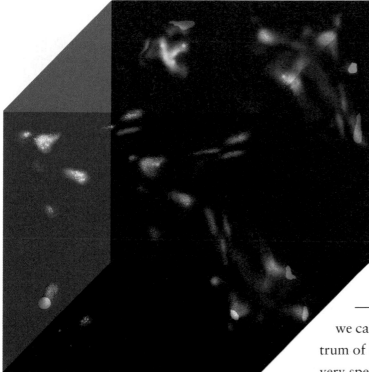

colors (its spectrum) as in a rainbow. By focusing a telescope on an individual star or galaxy, one can similarly observe the spectrum of the light from that star or galaxy. Different stars have different spectra, but the relative brightness of the different colors is always exactly what one would expect to find in the light emitted by an object that is glowing red hot. (In fact, the light emitted by any opaque object that is glowing red hot has a characteristic spectrum that depends only on its temperature — a thermal spectrum. This means that we can tell a star's temperature from the spectrum of its light.) Moreover, we find that certain very specific colors are missing from stars' spectra, and these missing colors may vary from star to star. Since we know that each chemical element absorbs a characteristic set of very specific colors, by matching these to those that are missing from a star's spectrum, we can determine exactly which elements are present in the star's atmosphere.

In the 1920s, when astronomers began to look at the spectra of stars in other galaxies, they found something most peculiar: there were

Stars are so far away that they appear to us to be just pinpoints of light. We cannot see their size or shape. So how can we tell different types of stars apart? For the vast majority of stars, there is only one characteristic feature that we can observe — the color of their light. Newton discovered that if light from the sun passes through a triangular-shaped piece of glass, called a prism, it breaks up into its component

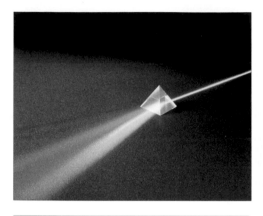

Isaac Newton used a prism to break white light into a spectrum.

the same characteristic sets of missing colors as for stars in our own galaxy, but they were all shifted by the same relative amount toward the red end of the spectrum. To understand the implications of this, we must first understand the Doppler effect. As we have seen, visible light consists of fluctuations, or waves, in the electromagnetic field. The wavelength (or distance from one wave crest to the next) of light is extremely small, ranging from four to seven tenmillionths of a metre. The different wavelengths of light are what the human eye sees as different colors, with the longest wavelengths appearing at the red end of the spectrum and the shortest wavelengths at the blue end. Now imagine a source of light at a constant distance from us, such as a star, emitting waves of light at a constant wavelength (Fig. 3.4a). Obviously the

wavelength of the waves we receive will be the same as the wavelength at which they are emitted (the gravitational field of the galaxy will not be large enough to have a significant effect). Suppose now that the source starts moving toward us. When the source emits the next wave crest it will be nearer to us, so the distance between wave crests will be smaller than when the star was stationary. This means that the wavelength of the waves we receive is shorter, than when the star was stationary. Correspondingly, if the source is moving away from us, the wavelength of the waves we receive will be longer. In the case of light, therefore, this means that stars moving away from us will have their spectra shifted toward the red end of the spectrum (red-shifted) and those moving toward us will have their spectra blue-shifted. This rela-

Fig. 3.4a

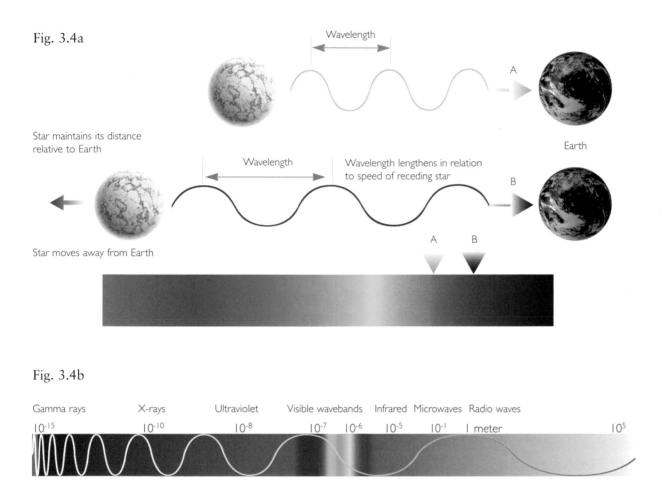

Star maintains its distance relative to Earth

Star moves away from Earth

Fig. 3.4b

Gamma rays	X-rays	Ultraviolet	Visible wavebands	Infrared	Microwaves	Radio waves
10^{-15}	10^{-10}	10^{-8}	10^{-7} 10^{-6}	10^{-5}	10^{-1} 1 meter	10^{5}

tionship between wavelength and speed, which is called the Doppler effect, is an everyday experience. Listen to a car passing on the road: as the car is approaching, its engine sounds at a higher pitch (corresponding to a shorter wavelength and higher frequency of sound waves), and when it passes and goes away, it sounds at a lower pitch (Fig. 3.5). The behavior of light or

Fig. 3.4a *A star that is stationary with respect to the earth radiates light at a fixed wavelength — the same wavelength that we observe. If the star is moving away from us, the distance between wave crests is increased, and we will perceive its spectrum as shifted to the red.*
Fig. 3.4b *The full spectrum of light covers a much wider range of wavelengths than those we are able to observe. They extend from the very short, such as gamma rays, to the very long, such as radio waves.*

Fig. 3.5

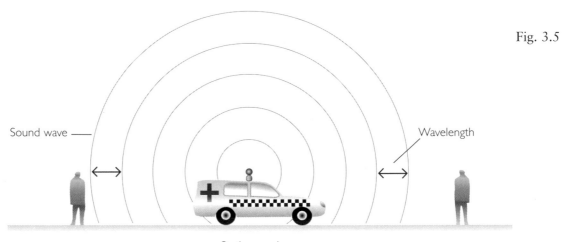

Sound wave ——

Wavelength

Stationary siren

Fig. 3.5 *The Doppler shift is a property of all types of waves, from sound to electromagnetic waves. When an emitter such as an ambulance siren travels towards an observer, the waves shift to a higher frequency. As it moves away from the receiver the waves shift to a lower frequency.*

radio waves is similar. Indeed, the police make use of the Doppler effect to measure the speed of cars by measuring the wavelength of pulses of radio waves reflected off them.

In the years following his proof of the existence of other galaxies, Hubble spent his time cataloging their distances and observing their spectra. At that time most people expected the galaxies to be moving around quite randomly, and so expected to find as many blue-shifted spectra as red-shifted ones. It was quite a surprise, therefore, to find that most galaxies

appeared red-shifted: nearly all were moving away from us! More surprising still was the finding that Hubble published in 1929: even the size of a galaxy's red shift is not random, but is directly proportional to the galaxy's distance from us. Or, in other words, the farther a galaxy is, the faster it is moving away! And that meant that the universe could not be static, as everyone previously had thought, but is in fact expanding; the distance between the different galaxies is growing all the time.

The discovery that the universe is expanding was one of the great intellectual revolutions of the twentieth century. With hindsight, it is easy to wonder why no one had thought of it before. Newton, and others, should have realized that a static universe would soon start to contract

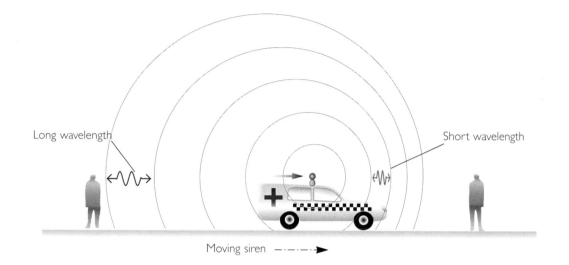

Long wavelength

Short wavelength

Moving siren ─ ·─ ·─ ·─ ▶

under the influence of gravity. But suppose instead that the universe is expanding. If it was expanding fairly slowly, the force of gravity would cause it eventually to stop expanding and then to start contracting. However, if it was expanding at more than a certain critical rate, gravity would never be strong enough to stop it, and the universe would continue to expand forever. This is a bit like what happens when one fires a rocket upward from the surface of the earth. If it has a fairly low speed, gravity will eventually stop the rocket and it will start falling back. On the other hand, if the rocket has more than a certain critical speed (about seven miles per second) gravity will not be strong enough to pull it back, so it will keep going away from the earth forever. This behavior of the universe could have been predicted from Newton's theo-

ry of gravity at any time in the nineteenth, the eighteenth, or even the late seventeenth centuries. Yet so strong was the belief in a static universe that it persisted into the early twentieth century. Even Einstein, when he formulated the general theory of relativity in 1915, was so sure that the universe had to be static that he modified his theory to make this possible, introducing a so-called cosmological constant into his equations. Einstein introduced a new "antigravity" force, which, unlike other forces, did not come from any particular source but was built into the very fabric of space-time. He claimed that space-time had an inbuilt tendency to expand, and this could be made to balance exactly the attraction of all the matter in the universe, so that a static universe would result. Only one man, it seems, was willing to take gen-

eral relativity at face value, and while Einstein and other physicists were looking for ways of avoiding general relativity's prediction of a non-static universe, the Russian physicist and mathematician Alexander Friedmann instead set about explaining it.

Friedmann made two very simple assumptions about the universe: that the universe looks identical in whichever direction we look, and

Arno Penzias (left) and Robert Wilson, in front of the Holmdel, N.J. horn antenna, with which they inadvertently discovered the cosmic microwave background.

that this would also be true if we were observing the universe from anywhere else. From these two ideas alone, Friedmann showed that we should not expect the universe to be static. In fact, in 1922, several years before Edwin

Hubble's discovery, Friedmann predicted exactly what Hubble found!

The assumption that the universe looks the same in every direction is clearly not true in reality. For example, as we have seen, the other stars in our galaxy form a distinct band of light across the night sky, called the Milky Way. But if we look at distant galaxies, there seems to be more or less the same number of them. So the universe does seem to be roughly the same in every direction, provided one views it on a large scale compared to the distance between galaxies, and ignores the differences on small scales. For a long time, this was sufficient justification for Friedmann's assumption — as a rough approximation to the real universe. But more recently a lucky accident uncovered the fact that Friedmann's assumption is in fact a remarkably accurate description of our universe.

In 1965 two American physicists at the Bell Telephone Laboratories in New Jersey, Arno Penzias and Robert Wilson, were testing a very sensitive microwave detector. (Microwaves are just like light waves, but with a wavelength of around a centimetre.) Penzias and Wilson were worried when they found that their detector was picking up more noise than it ought to. The noise did not appear to be coming from any particular direction. First they discovered bird droppings in their detector and checked for other possible malfunctions, but soon ruled these out. They knew that any noise from within the atmosphere would be stronger when the detector was not pointing straight up than when it was, because light rays travel through much more atmosphere when received from near the horizon than when received from directly overhead. The extra noise was the same whichever direction the detector was pointed, so it must come from *outside* the atmosphere. It was also the same day and night and throughout the year, even though the earth was rotating on its axis and orbiting around the sun. This showed that the radiation must come from beyond the Solar System, and even from beyond the galaxy, as otherwise it would vary as the movement of earth pointed the detector in different directions.

In fact, we know that the radiation must have traveled to us across most of the observable universe, and since it appears to be the same in different directions, the universe must also be the same in every direction, if only on a large scale. We now know that whichever direction we look, this noise never varies by more than a tiny fraction: so Penzias and Wilson had unwittingly stumbled across a remarkably accurate confirmation of Friedmann's first assumption. However, because

Fig. 3.6

Fig 3.6 The expanding universe is like a balloon being inflated. Points on the surface of the balloon move apart, but none of them is the center of expansion.

the universe is not exactly the same in every direction, but only on average on a large scale, the microwaves cannot be exactly the same in every direction either. There have to be slight variations between different directions. These were first detected in 1992 by the Cosmic Background Explorer satellite, or COBE, at a level of about one part in a hundred thousand. Small though these variations are, they are very important, as will be explained in Chapter 8.

At roughly the same time as Penzias and Wilson were investigating noise in their detector, two American physicists at nearby Princeton University, Bob Dicke and Jim Peebles, were also taking an interest in microwaves. They were working on a suggestion, made by George Gamow (once a student of Alexander Friedmann), that the early universe should have been very hot and dense, glowing white hot. Dicke and Peebles argued that we should still be able to see the glow of the early universe, because light from very distant parts of it would only just be reaching us now. However, the expansion of the universe meant that this light should be so greatly red-shifted that it would appear to us now as microwave radiation. Dicke and Peebles were preparing to look for this radiation when Penzias and Wilson heard about their work and realized that they had already found it. For this, Penzias and Wilson were awarded the Nobel prize in 1978 (which seems a bit hard on Dicke and Peebles, not to mention Gamow!).

Now at first sight, all this evidence that the universe looks the same whichever direction we look in might seem to suggest there is something special about our place in the universe. In particular, it might seem that if we observe all other galaxies to be moving away from us, then we must be at the center of the universe. There is, however, an alternate explanation: the universe might look the same in every direction as seen from any other galaxy, too. This, as we have seen, was Friedmann's second assumption. We

have no scientific evidence for, or against, this assumption. We believe it only on grounds of modesty: it would be most remarkable if the universe looked the same in every direction around us, but not around other points in the universe! In Friedmann's model, all the galaxies are moving directly away from each other. The situation is rather like a balloon with a number of spots painted on it being steadily blown up. As the balloon expands, the distance between any two spots increases, but there is no spot that can be said to be the center of the expansion (Fig. 3.6). Moreover, the farther apart the spots are, the faster they will be moving apart. Similarly, in Friedmann's model the speed at which any two galaxies are moving apart is proportional to the distance between them. So it predicted that the red shift of a galaxy should be directly proportional to its distance from us, exactly as Hubble found. Despite the success of his model and his prediction of Hubble's observations, Friedmann's work remained largely unknown in the West until similar models were discovered in 1935 by the American physicist Howard Robertson and the British mathematician Arthur Walker, in response to Hubble's discovery of the uniform expansion of the universe.

Although Friedmann found only one, there are in fact three different kinds of models that

Fig. 3.7

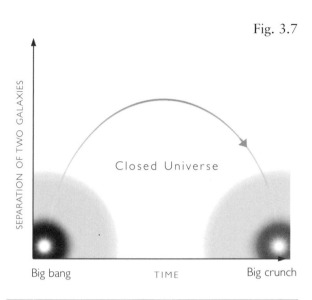

Fig. 3.7 *In Friedmann's model of the universe all the galaxies are initially moving away from each other. The universe expands until it reaches a maximum size and then contracts back to a point.*

obey Friedmann's two fundamental assumptions. In the first kind (which Friedmann found) the universe is expanding sufficiently slowly that the gravitational attraction between the different galaxies causes the expansion to slow down and eventually to stop. The galaxies then start to move toward each other and the universe contracts. Fig. 3.7 shows how the distance between two neighboring galaxies changes as time increases. It starts at zero, increases to a maximum, and then decreases to zero again. In the second kind of solution, the universe is expand-

Fig. 3.8

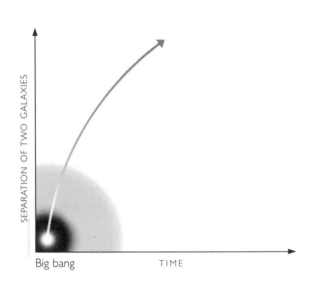

SEPARATION OF TWO GALAXIES

Big bang   TIME

Fig. 3.9

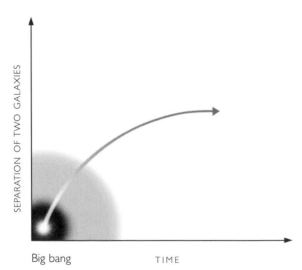

SEPARATION OF TWO GALAXIES

Big bang   TIME

ing so rapidly that the gravitational attraction can never stop it, though it does slow it down a bit. Fig. 3.8 shows the separation between neighboring galaxies in this model. It starts at zero and eventually the galaxies are moving apart at a steady speed. Finally, there is a third kind of solution, in which the universe is expanding only just fast enough to avoid recollapse. In this case the separation, shown in Fig. 3.9, also starts at zero and increases forever. However, the speed at which the galaxies are moving apart gets smaller and smaller, although it never quite reaches zero.

A remarkable feature of the first kind of Friedmann model is that in it the universe is not infinite in space, but neither does space have any boundary. Gravity is so strong that space is bent round onto itself, making it rather like the surface of the earth. If one keeps traveling in a certain direction on the surface of the earth, one never comes up against an impassable barrier or falls over the edge, but eventually comes back to

Fig. 3.8 *In the "open" model of the universe, gravity never overcomes the motion of the galaxies and the universe keeps expanding forever.*
Fig. 3.9 *In the "flat" model of the universe, the gravitational attraction exactly balances the motion of the galaxies. The universe avoids recollapse while the motion of the galaxies gets smaller and smaller, but never quite comes to rest.*

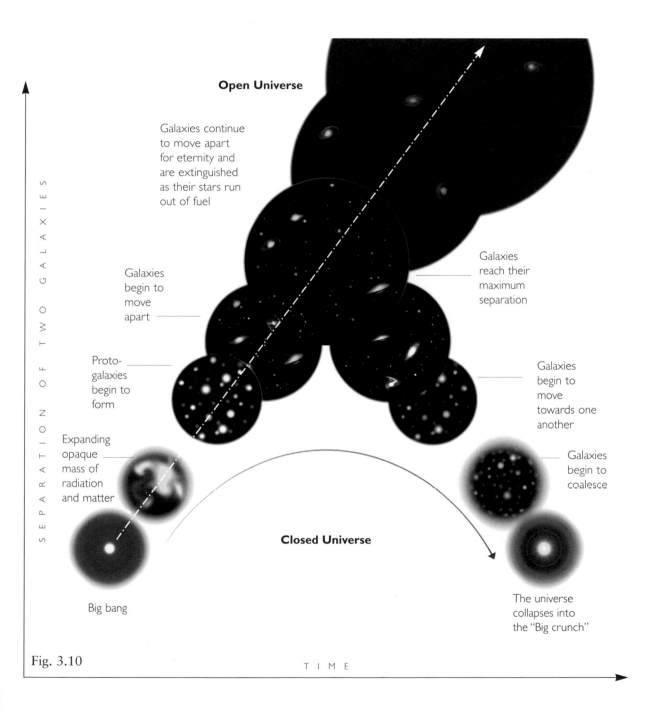

Open Universe

Galaxies continue
to move apart
for eternity and
are extinguished
as their stars run
out of fuel

Galaxies
begin to
move
apart

Proto-
galaxies
begin to
form

Expanding
opaque
mass of
radiation
and matter

Galaxies
reach their
maximum
separation

Galaxies
begin to
move
towards one
another

Galaxies
begin to
coalesce

Closed Universe

Big bang

The universe
collapses into
the "Big crunch"

SEPARATION OF TWO GALAXIES

TIME

Fig. 3.10

where one started. In the first Friedmann model, space is just like this, but with three dimensions instead of two for the earth's surface. The fourth dimension, time, is also finite in extent, but it is like a line with two ends or boundaries, a beginning and an end. We shall see later that when one combines general relativity with the uncertainty principle of quantum mechanics, it is possible for both space and time to be finite without any edges or boundaries.

The idea that one could go right round the universe and end up where one started makes good science fiction, but it doesn't have much practical significance, because it can be shown that the universe would recollapse to zero size before one could get round. You would need to travel faster than light in order to end up where you started before the universe came to an end — and that is not allowed!

In the first kind of Friedmann model, which expands and recollapses, space is bent in on itself, like the surface of the earth. It is therefore finite in extent. In the second kind of model, which expands forever, space is bent the other way, like the surface of a saddle. So in this case space is infinite. Finally, in the third kind of Friedmann model, with just the critical rate of expansion, space is flat (and therefore is also infinite).

But which Friedmann model describes our universe? Will the universe eventually stop expanding and start contracting, or will it expand forever? To answer this question we need to know the present rate of expansion of the universe and its present average density. If the density is less than a certain critical value, determined by the rate of expansion, the gravitational attraction will be too weak to halt the expansion. If the density is greater than the critical value, gravity will stop the expansion at some time in the future and cause the universe to recollapse.

We can determine the present rate of expansion by measuring the velocities at which other galaxies are moving away from us, using the Doppler effect. This can be done very accurately. However, the distances to the galaxies are not very well known because we can only measure them indirectly. So all we know is that the universe is expanding by between 5 percent and 10 percent every thousand million years. However, our uncertainty about the present average density of the universe is even greater. If we add up the masses of all the stars that we can see in our galaxy and other galaxies, the total is less than one hundredth of the amount required to halt the expansion of the universe, even for the low-

est estimate of the rate of expansion. Our galaxy and other galaxies, however, must contain a large amount of "dark matter" that we cannot see directly, but which we know must be there because of the influence of its gravitational attraction on the orbits of stars in the galaxies. Moreover, most galaxies are found in clusters, and we can similarly infer the presence of yet more dark matter in between the galaxies in these clusters by its effect on the motion of the galaxies. When we add up all this dark matter, we still get only about one tenth of the amount required to halt the expansion. However, we cannot exclude the possibility that there might be some other form of matter, distributed almost uniformly throughout the universe, that we have not yet detected and that might still raise the average density of the universe up to the critical value needed to halt the expansion. The present evidence therefore suggests that the universe will probably expand forever, but all we can really be sure of is that even if the universe is going to recollapse, it won't do so for at least another ten thousand million years, since it has already been expanding for at least that long. This should not unduly worry us: by that time, unless we have colonized beyond the Solar System, mankind will long since have died out, extinguished along with our sun!

All of the Friedmann solutions have the feature that at some time in the past (between ten and twenty thousand million years ago) the distance between neighboring galaxies must have been zero. At that time, which we call the big bang, the density of the universe and the curvature of space-time would have been infinite. Because mathematics cannot really handle infinite numbers, this means that the general theory of relativity (on which Friedmann's solutions are based) predicts that there is a point in the universe where the theory itself breaks down. Such a point is an example of what mathematicians call a singularity. In fact, all our theories of science are formulated on the assumption that space-time is smooth and nearly flat, so they break down at the big bang singularity,

From left to right:
Fred Hoyle, Thomas Gold,
and Hermann Bondi, the
developers of the steady
state theory. Subsequent
observations did not
support the theory,
although Hoyle believes
that these observations
were misinterpreted and
continues to uphold it.

where the curvature of space-time is infinite. This means that even if there were events before the big bang, one could not use them to determine what would happen afterward, because predictability would break down at the big bang.

Correspondingly, if, as is the case, we know only what has happened since the big bang, we could not determine what happened beforehand. As far as we are concerned, events before the big bang can have no consequences, so they should not form part of a scientific model of the universe. We should therefore cut them out of the model and say that time had a beginning at the big bang.

Many people do not like the idea that time has a beginning, probably because it smacks of divine intervention. (The Catholic Church, on the other hand, seized on the big bang model

and in 1951 officially pronounced it to be in accordance with the Bible.) There were therefore a number of attempts to avoid the conclusion that there had been a big bang. The proposal that gained widest support was called the steady state theory. It was suggested in 1948 by two refugees from Nazi-occupied Austria, Hermann Bondi and Thomas Gold, together with a Briton, Fred Hoyle, who had worked with them on the development of radar during the war. The idea was that as the galaxies moved away from each other, new galaxies were continually forming in the gaps in between, from new matter that was being continually created (Fig. 3.11). The universe would therefore look roughly the same at all times as well as at all points of space. The steady state theory required a modification of general relativity to allow for the continual creation of matter, but the rate

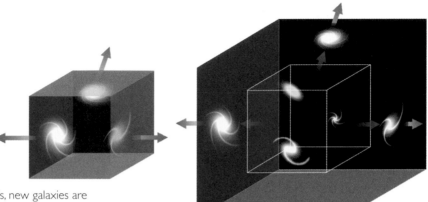

As the universe expands, new galaxies are continuously formed to maintain its density

Fig. 3.11

that was involved was so low (about one particle per cubic kilometer per year) that it was not in conflict with experiment. The theory was a good scientific theory, in the sense described in Chapter 1: it was simple and it made definite predictions that could be tested by observation. One of these predictions was that the number of galaxies or similar objects in any given volume of space should be the same wherever and whenever we look in the universe. In the late 1950s and early 1960s a survey of sources of radio waves from outer space was carried out at Cambridge by a group of astronomers led by Martin Ryle (who had also worked with Bondi, Gold, and Hoyle on radar during the war). The Cambridge group showed that most of these radio sources must lie outside our galaxy (indeed many of them could be identified with other galaxies) and also that there were many

more weak sources than strong ones. They interpreted the weak sources as being the more distant ones, and the stronger ones as being nearer. Then there appeared to be less common sources per unit volume of space for the nearby sources than for the distant ones. This could mean that we are at the center of a great region in the universe in which the sources are fewer than elsewhere. Alternatively, it could mean that the sources were more numerous in the past, at the time that the radio waves left on their journey to us, than they are now. Either explanation contradicted the predictions of the steady state theory. Moreover, the discovery of the microwave radiation by Penzias and Wilson in 1965 also indicated that the universe must have been much denser in the past. The steady state theory therefore had to be abandoned.

Another attempt to avoid the conclusion that

there must have been a big bang, and therefore a beginning of time, was made by two Russian scientists, Evgenii Lifshitz and Isaac Khalatnikov, in 1963. They suggested that the big bang might be a peculiarity of Friedmann's models alone, which after all were only approximations to the real universe. Perhaps, of all the models that were roughly like the real universe, only Friedmann's would contain a big bang singularity. In Friedmann's models, the galaxies are all moving directly away from each other — so it is not surprising that at some time in the past they were all at the same place. In the real universe, however, the galaxies are not just moving directly away from each other — they also have small sideways velocities. So in reality they need never have been all at exactly the same place, only very close together. Perhaps then the current expanding universe resulted not from a big bang singularity, but from an earlier contracting phase; as the universe had collapsed the particles in it might not have all collided, but had flown past and then away from each other, producing the present expansion of the universe. How then could we tell whether the real universe should have started out with a big bang? What Lifshitz and Khalatnikov did was to study models of the universe that were roughly like Friedmann's models but took account of the irregularities

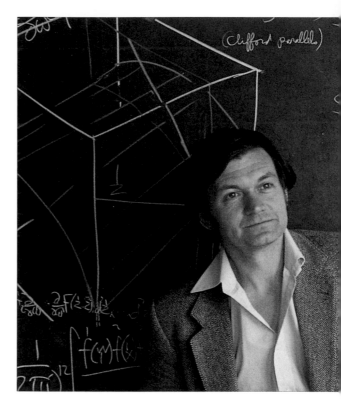

Theoretical mathematician Roger Penrose photographed at Oxford in 1980.

and random velocities of galaxies in the real universe. They showed that such models could start with a big bang, even though the galaxies were no longer always moving directly away from each other, but they claimed that this was still only possible in certain exceptional models in which the galaxies were all moving in just the right way. They argued that since there seemed

$$M^{13} = \frac{1}{2}(Z^0 \bar{Z}_1 + Z^1 \bar{Z}_0 + Z^2 \bar{Z}_3 + Z^3 \bar{Z}_2$$

$$M^{\cdots} = \cdots$$

could have had a singularity, a big bang, if the general theory of relativity was correct. However, it did not resolve the crucial question: Does general relativity predict that our universe *should* have had a big bang, a beginning of time? The answer to this came out of a completely different approach introduced by a British mathematician and physicist, Roger Penrose, in 1965. Using the way light cones behave in general relativity, together with the fact that gravity is always attractive, he showed that a star collapsing under its own gravity is trapped in a region whose surface eventually shrinks to zero size. And, since the surface of the region shrinks to zero, so too must its volume. All the matter in the star will be compressed into a region of zero volume, so the density of matter and the curvature of space-time become infinite. In other words, one has a singularity contained within a region of space-time known as a black hole (Fig. 3.12A).

At first sight, Penrose's result applied only to stars; it didn't have anything to say about the question of whether the entire universe had a big bang singularity in its past. However, at the time that Penrose produced his theorem, I was a research student desperately looking for a problem with which to complete my Ph.D. thesis. Two years before, I had been diagnosed as suffering

to be infinitely more Friedmann-like models without a big bang singularity than there were with one, we should conclude that there had not in reality been a big bang. They later realized, however, that there was a much more general class of Friedmann-like models that did have singularities, and in which the galaxies did not have to be moving any special way. They therefore withdrew their claim in 1970.

The work of Lifshitz and Khalatnikov was valuable because it showed that the universe

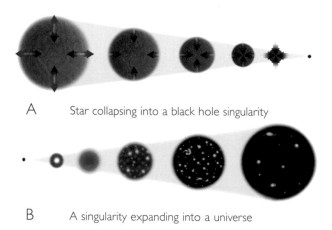

A   Star collapsing into a black hole singularity

B   A singularity expanding into a universe

Fig. 3.12 *The expansion of the universe from the big bang is like the time reverse of the collapse of a star to a singularity in a black hole.*

from ALS, commonly known as Lou Gehrig's disease, or motor neurone disease, and given to understand that I had only one or two more years to live. In these circumstances there had not seemed much point in working on my Ph.D. — I did not expect to survive that long. Yet two years had gone by and I was not that much worse. In fact, things were going rather well for me and I had gotten engaged to a very nice girl, Jane Wilde. But in order to get married, I needed a job, and in order to get a job, I needed a Ph.D.

In 1965 I read about Penrose's theorem that

any body undergoing gravitational collapse must eventually form a singularity. I soon realized that if one reversed the direction of time in Penrose's theorem, so that the collapse became an expansion, the conditions of his theorem would still hold, provided the universe were roughly like a Friedmann model on large scales at the present time. Penrose's theorem had shown that any collapsing star *must* end in a singularity; the time-reversed argument showed that any Friedmann-like expanding universe *must* have begun with a singularity. For technical reasons, Penrose's theorem required that the universe be infinite in space. So I could in fact use it to prove that there should be a singularity only if the universe was expanding fast enough to avoid collapsing again (since only those Friedmann models were infinite in space).

During the next few years I developed new mathematical techniques to remove this and other technical conditions from the theorems that proved that singularities must occur. The final result was a joint paper by Penrose and myself in 1970, which at last proved that there must have been a big bang singularity provided only that general relativity is correct and the universe contains as much matter as we observe. There was a lot of opposition to our work, partly from the Russians because of their Marxist belief in scientific determinism, and partly from people who felt that the whole idea of singularities was repugnant and spoiled the beauty of Einstein's theory. However, one cannot really argue with a mathematical theorem. So in the end our work became generally accepted and nowadays nearly everyone assumes that the universe started with a big bang singularity. It is perhaps ironic that, having changed my mind, I am now trying to convince other physicists that there was in fact no singularity at the beginning of the universe — as we shall see later, it can disappear once quantum effects are taken into account.

Stephen Hawking at his Oxford gradution in 1962.

We have seen in this chapter how, in less than half a century, man's view of the universe, formed over millennia, has been transformed. Hubble's discovery that the universe was expanding, and the realization of the insignificance of our own planet in the vastness of the universe, were just the starting point. As experimental and theoretical evidence mounted, it became more and more clear that the universe must have had a beginning in time, until in 1970 this was finally proved by Penrose and myself, on the basis of Einstein's general theory of relativity. That proof showed that general relativity is only an incomplete theory: it cannot tell us how the universe started off, because it predicts that all physical theories, including itself, break down at the beginning of the universe. However, general relativity claims to be only a partial theory, so what the singularity theorems really show is that there must have been a time in the very early universe when the universe was so small that one could no longer ignore the small-scale effects of the other great partial theory of the twentieth century, quantum mechanics. At the start of the 1970s, then, we were forced to turn our search for an understanding of the universe from our theory of the extraordinarily vast to our theory of the extraordinarily tiny. That theory, quantum mechanics, will be described next, before we turn to the efforts to combine the two partial theories into a single quantum theory of gravity.

4

The Uncertainty Principle

THE SUCCESS OF SCIENTIFIC THEORIES, particularly Newton's theory of gravity, led the French scientist the Marquis de Laplace at the beginning of the nineteenth century to argue that the universe was completely deterministic. Laplace suggested that there should be a set of scientific laws that would allow us to predict everything that would happen in the universe, if only we knew the complete state of the universe at one time. For example, if we knew the positions and speeds of the sun and the planets at one time, then we could use Newton's laws to calculate the state of the Solar System at any other time. Determinism seems fairly obvious in this case, but Laplace went further to assume that there were similar laws governing everything else, including human behavior.

The doctrine of scientific determinism was strongly resisted by many people, who felt that it infringed God's freedom to intervene in the world, but it remained the standard assumption of science until the early years of this century. One of the first indications that this belief would have to be abandoned came when calculations by the British scientists Lord Rayleigh and Sir James Jeans suggested that a hot object, or body, such as a star, must radiate energy at an infinite rate. According to the laws we believed at the time, a hot body ought to give off electromagnetic waves (such as radio waves, visible light, or X rays) equally at all frequencies. For example, a hot body should radiate the same amount of energy in waves with frequencies between one and two million million waves a second as in waves with frequencies between two and three million million waves a second. Now since the number of waves a second is unlimited, this would mean that the total energy radiated would be infinite.

In order to avoid this obviously ridiculous result, the German scientist Max Planck sug-

Fig. 4.1

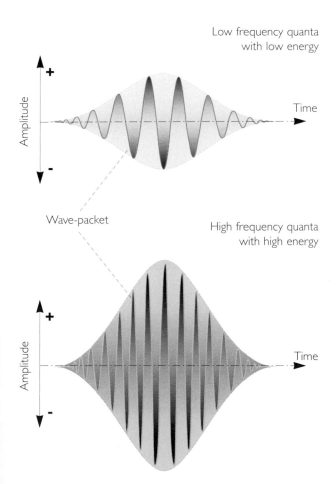

Low frequency quanta
with low energy

Amplitude

+

−

Time

Wave-packet

High frequency quanta
with high energy

Amplitude

+

−

Time

gested in 1900 that light, X rays, and other waves could not be emitted at an arbitrary rate, but only in certain packets that he called quanta. Moreover, each quantum had a certain amount of energy that was greater the higher the frequency of the waves, so at a high enough frequency the emission of a single quantum would require more energy than was available. Thus the radiation at high frequencies would be reduced, and so the rate at which the body lost energy would be finite.

The quantum hypothesis explained the observed rate of emission of radiation from hot bodies very well, but its implications for determinism were not realized until 1926, when another German scientist, Werner Heisenberg, formulated his famous uncertainty principle. In order to predict the future position and velocity of a particle, one has to be able to measure its

Opposite: *Pierre Simon Laplace (1749-1827).*
Fig. 4.1 *Max Planck suggested that light came only in packets or quanta which were wave trains with an energy proportional to their frequency.*

Fig. 4.2

Higher frequency wave-lengths of light disturb the velocity of the particle more than do lower frequencies

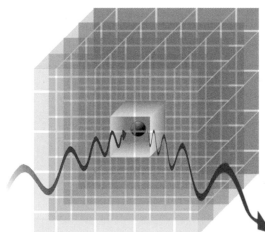

The longer the wavelength of light used to observe the particle the greater the uncertainty in its position but the greater the certainty of its velocity

The observer

The shorter the wavelength of light used to observe the particle, the greater the certainty of its position but the greater the uncertainty of its velocity

Fig. 4.3

The uncertainty
of the position
of the particle

The mass of
the particle

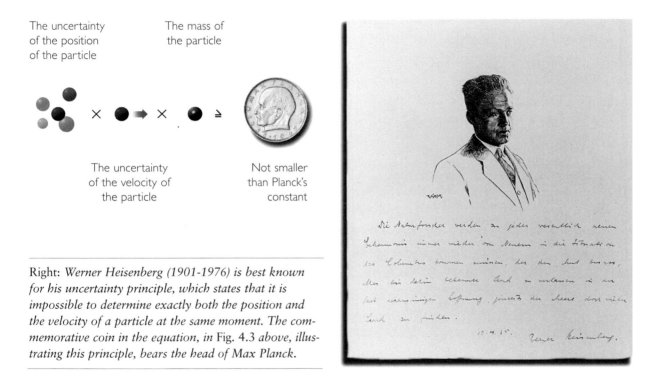

The uncertainty
of the velocity of
the particle

Not smaller
than Planck's
constant

Right: *Werner Heisenberg (1901-1976) is best known for his uncertainty principle, which states that it is impossible to determine exactly both the position and the velocity of a particle at the same moment. The commemorative coin in the equation, in* Fig. 4.3 *above, illustrating this principle, bears the head of Max Planck.*

present position and velocity accurately. The obvious way to do this is to shine light on the particle (Fig. 4.2). Some of the waves of light will be scattered by the particle and this will indicate its position. However, one will not be able to determine the position of the particle more accurately than the distance between the wave crests of light, so one needs to use light of a short wavelength in order to measure the position of the particle precisely. Now, by Planck's quantum hypothesis, one cannot use an arbitrarily small amount of light; one has to use at least one quantum. This quantum will disturb the particle and change its velocity in a way that cannot be predicted. Moreover, the more accurately one measures the position, the shorter the wavelength of the light that one needs and hence the higher the energy of a single quantum. So the velocity of the particle will be disturbed by a larger amount. In other words, the more accurately you try to measure the position of the particle, the less accurately you can measure its speed, and vice versa. Heisenberg showed that the uncertainty in the position of the particle times the uncertainty in its velocity times the mass of the particle can never be smaller than a certain quantity, which is known as Planck's constant (Fig. 4.3). Moreover, this limit does not depend on the way in which one tries to measure the position or velocity of the particle, or on the type of particle: Heisenberg's uncertainty principle is a fundamental, inescapable property of the world.

The uncertainty principle had profound implications for the way in which we view the world. Even after more than fifty years they have not been fully appreciated by many philosophers, and are still the subject of much controversy. The uncertainty principle signaled an end to Laplace's dream of a theory of science, a model of the universe that would be completely deterministic: one certainly cannot predict future events exactly if one cannot even measure the present state of the universe precisely! We could still imagine that there is a set of laws that determines events completely for some supernatural being, who could observe the present state of the universe without disturbing it. However, such models of the universe are not of much interest to us ordinary mortals. It seems better to employ the principle of economy known as Occam's razor and cut out all the features of the theory that cannot be observed. This approach led Heisenberg, Erwin Schrödinger, and Paul Dirac in the 1920s to reformulate mechanics into a new theory called quantum mechanics, based on the uncertainty principle.

Erwin Schrödinger (1887-1961)

In this theory particles no longer had separate, well-defined positions and velocities that could not be observed. Instead, they had a quantum state, which was a combination of position and velocity.

In general, quantum mechanics does not predict a single definite result for an observation. Instead, it predicts a number of different possible outcomes and tells us how likely each of these is. That is to say, if one made the same measurement on a large number of similar systems, each of which started off in the same way, one would find that the result of the measurement would be A in a certain number of cases, B in a different number, and so on. One could predict the approximate number of times that the result would be A or B, but one could not predict the specific result of an individual measurement. Quantum mechanics therefore introduces an unavoidable element of unpredictability or randomness into science. Einstein objected to this very strongly, despite the important role he had played in the development of these ideas. Einstein was awarded the Nobel prize for his contribution to quantum theory. Nevertheless, Einstein never accepted that the universe was governed by chance; his feelings were summed up in his famous statement "God does not play dice." Most other scientists, however, were willing to accept quantum mechanics because it agreed perfectly with experiment. Indeed, it has been an outstandingly successful theory and underlies nearly all of modern science and technology. It governs the behavior of transistors and integrated circuits, which are the essential components of electronic devices such as televisions and computers, and is also the basis of modern chemistry and biology. The only areas of physical science into which quantum mechanics has not yet been properly incorporated are gravity and the large-scale structure of the universe.

Although light is made up of waves, Planck's quantum hypothesis tells us that in some ways it behaves as if it were composed of particles: it can be emitted or absorbed only in packets, or quanta. Equally, Heisenberg's uncertainty principle implies that particles behave in some respects like waves: they do not have a definite position but are "smeared out" with a certain probability distribution. The theory of quantum mechanics is based on an entirely new type of mathematics that no longer describes the real world in terms of particles and waves; it is only

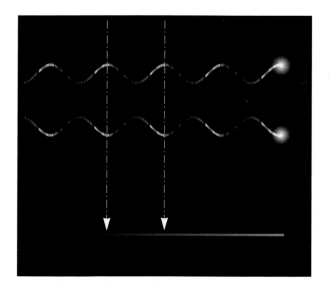

Fig. 4.4 *Wave crests and troughs cancel each other out when the waves are out of phase.*

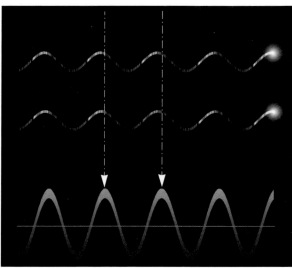

Fig. 4.5 *Wave crests and troughs coincide and reinforce each other when the waves are in phase.*

the observations of the world that may be described in those terms. There is thus a duality between waves and particles in quantum mechanics: for some purposes it is helpful to think of particles as waves and for other purposes it is better to think of waves as particles. An important consequence of this is that one

Left: *Soap Bubbles. The brilliant colors seen in bubbles are caused by the interference patterns due to the reflection of light from the two sides of the thin film of water.*

can observe what is called interference between two sets of waves or particles. That is to say, the crests of one set of waves may coincide with the troughs of the other set. The two sets of waves then cancel each other out (Fig. 4.4) rather than adding up to a stronger wave as one might expect (Fig. 4.5). A familiar example of interference in the case of light is the colors that are often seen in soap bubbles. These are caused by reflection of light from the two sides of the thin film of water forming the bubble. White light

Fig. 4.6 *Two slits produce a pattern of light and dark fringes. The reason is that waves from the two slits add up or cancel out at different parts of the screen. Similar fringe patterns are obtained with particles such as electrons, showing that they behave like waves.*

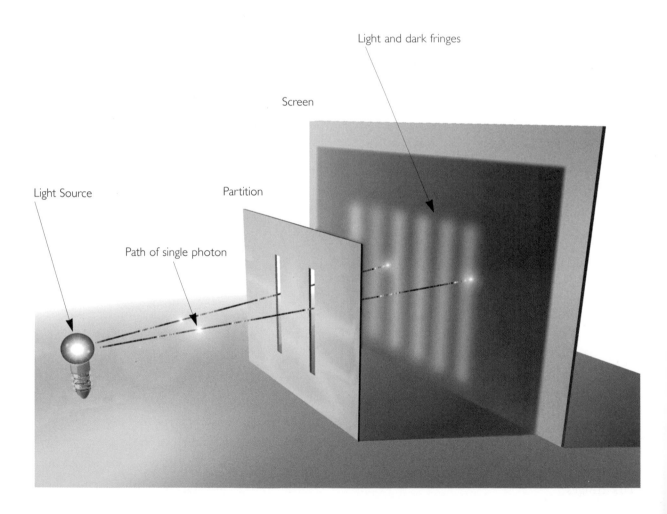

Light and dark fringes

Screen

Light Source

Partition

Path of single photon

consists of light waves of all different wavelengths, or colors. For certain wavelengths the crests of the waves reflected from one side of the soap film coincide with the troughs reflected from the other side. The colors corresponding to these wavelengths are absent from the reflected light, which therefore appears to be colored.

Interference can also occur for particles, because of the duality introduced by quantum mechanics. A famous example is the so-called two-slit experiment (Fig. 4.6). Consider a partition with two narrow parallel slits in it. On one side of the partition one places a source of light of a particular color (that is, of a particular wavelength). Most of the light will hit the partition, but a small amount will go through the slits. Now suppose one places a screen on the far side of the partition from the light. Any point on the screen will receive waves from the two slits. However, in general, the distance the light has to travel from the source to the screen via the two slits will be different. This will mean that the waves from the slits will not be in phase with each other when they arrive at the screen: in some places the waves will cancel each other out, and in others they will reinforce each other. The result is a characteristic pattern of light and dark fringes.

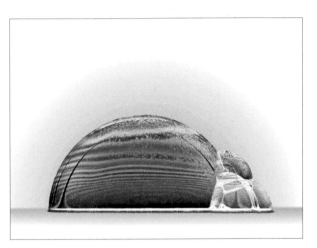

The remarkable thing is that one gets exactly the same kind of fringes if one replaces the source of light by a source of particles such as electrons with a definite speed (this means that the corresponding waves have a definite length). It seems the more peculiar because if one only has one slit, one does not get any fringes, just a uniform distribution of electrons across the screen. One might therefore think that opening another slit would just increase the number of electrons hitting each point of the screen, but, because of interference, it actually decreases it in some places. If electrons are sent through the slits one at a time, one would expect each to pass through one slit or the other, and so behave just as if the slit it passed through were the only one there — giving a uniform distribution on the screen. In reality, however, even when the electrons are sent one at a time, the fringes still appear. Each electron, therefore, must be passing through *both* slits at the same time!

The phenomenon of interference between particles has been crucial to our understanding of the structure of atoms, the basic units of chemistry and biology and the building blocks out of which we, and everything around us, are made. At the beginning of this century it was thought that atoms were rather like the planets orbiting the sun, with electrons (particles of negative electricity) orbiting around a central nucleus, which carried positive electricity. The attraction between the positive and negative electricity was supposed to keep the electrons in their orbits in the same way that the gravitational attraction between the sun and the planets keeps the planets in their orbits (Fig. 4.7-2). The trouble with this was that the laws of mechanics and electricity, before quantum mechanics, predicted that the electrons would lose energy and so spiral inward until they collided with the nucleus. This would mean that the atom, and indeed all matter, should rapidly collapse to a state of very high density. A partial solution to this problem was found by the Danish scientist Niels Bohr in 1913. He suggested that maybe the electrons were not able to orbit at just any distance from the central nucleus but only at certain specified distances. If one also supposed that only one or two electrons could orbit at any one of these distances, this would solve the problem of the collapse of the atom, because the electrons could not spiral in any farther than to fill up the orbits with the least distances and energies.

This model explained quite well the structure of the simplest atom, hydrogen, which has only one electron orbiting around the nucleus. But it was not clear how one ought to extend it to more complicated atoms. Moreover, the idea of a limited set of allowed orbits seemed very arbitrary. The new theory of quantum mechanics resolved this difficulty. It revealed that an electron orbiting around the nucleus could be thought of as a wave, with a wavelength that depended on its velocity. For certain orbits, the length of the orbit would correspond to a whole number (as opposed to a fractional number) of wavelengths of the electron. For these orbits the wave crest would be in the same position each time round, so the waves would add up: these orbits would correspond to Bohr's allowed orbits. However, for orbits whose lengths were

Right: *Portrait of Niels Bohr (1885-1962).*
Below: Fig. 4.7 *The evolution of the atom, from the grain-like atom (1) of the Greek philosopher Democritus (above), through Rutherford's model of electrons orbiting the nucleus (2) to Schrödinger's quantum mechanical model of the atom (3).*

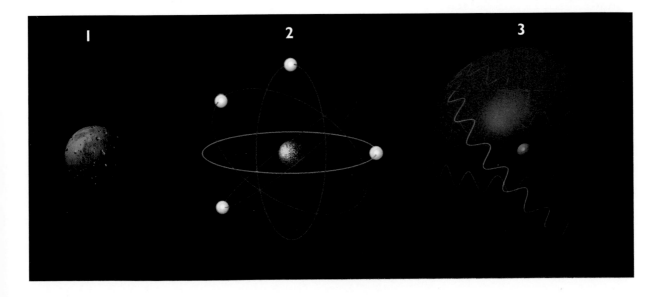

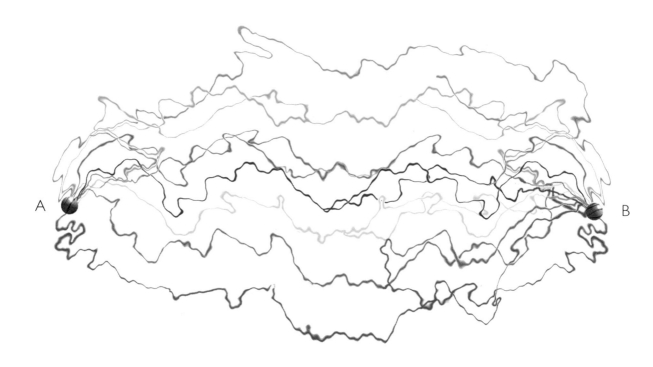

Fig. 4.8 *In Richard Feynman's theory of sum over histories, a particle in space-time would go from A to B by every possible path.*

not a whole number of wavelengths, each wave crest would eventually be canceled out by a trough as the electrons went round; these orbits would not be allowed.

A nice way of visualizing the wave/particle duality is the so-called sum over histories introduced by the American scientist Richard Feynman. In this approach the particle is not supposed to have a single history or path in space-time, as it would in a classical, nonquantum theory. Instead it is supposed to go from A to B by every possible path (Fig. 4.8). With each path there are associated a couple of numbers: one represents the size of a wave and the other represents the position in the cycle (i.e., whether it is at a crest or a trough). The probability of going from A to B is found by adding up the waves for all the paths. In general, if one compares a set of neighboring paths, the phases or positions in the cycle will differ greatly. This means that the waves associated with these paths will almost exactly cancel each other out. However, for some sets of neighboring paths the phase will not vary much between paths. The waves for these paths will not cancel out. Such paths correspond to Bohr's allowed orbits.

With these ideas, in concrete mathematical form, it was relatively straightforward to calculate the allowed orbits in more complicated atoms and even in molecules, which are made up of a number of atoms held together by electrons in orbits that go round more than one nucleus. Since the structure of molecules and their reactions with each other underlie all of chemistry and biology, quantum mechanics allows us in principle to predict nearly everything we see around us, within the limits set by the uncertainty principle. (In practice, however, the calculations required for systems containing more than a few electrons are so complicated that we cannot do them.)

Einstein's general theory of relativity seems to govern the large-scale structure of the universe. It is what is called a classical theory; that is, it does not take account of the uncertainty

principle of quantum mechanics, as it should for consistency with other theories. The reason that this does not lead to any discrepancy with observation is that all the gravitational fields that we normally experience are very weak. However, the singularity theorems discussed earlier indicate that the gravitational field should get very strong in at least two situations, black holes and the big bang. In such strong fields the effects of quantum mechanics should be important. Thus, in a sense, classical general relativity, by predicting points of infinite density, predicts its own downfall, just as classical (that is, nonquantum) mechanics predicted its downfall by suggesting that atoms should collapse to infinite density. We do not yet have a complete consistent theory that unifies general relativity and quantum mechanics, but we do know a number of the features it should have. The consequences that these would have for black holes and the big bang will be described in later chapters. For the moment, however, we shall turn to the recent attempts to bring together our understanding of the other forces of nature into a single, unified quantum theory.

5

Elementary Particles and the Forces of Nature

ARISTOTLE BELIEVED THAT all the matter in the universe was made up of four basic elements — earth, air, fire, and water. These elements were acted on by two forces: gravity, the tendency for earth and water to sink, and levity, the tendency for air and fire to rise. This division of the contents of the universe into matter and forces is still used today.

Aristotle believed that matter was continuous, that is, one could divide a piece of matter into smaller and smaller bits without any limit: one never came up against a grain of matter that could not be divided further. A few Greeks, however, such as Democritus, held that matter was inherently grainy and that everything was made up of large numbers of various different kinds of atoms. (The word *atom* means "indivisible" in

Greek.) For centuries the argument continued without any real evidence on either side, but in 1803 the British chemist and physicist John Dalton pointed out that the fact that chemical compounds always combined in certain proportions could be explained by the grouping together of atoms to form units called molecules. However, the argument between the two schools of thought was not finally settled in favor of the

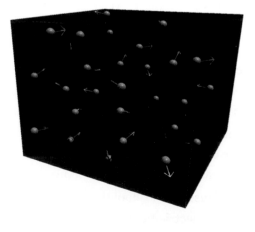

Fig 5.1 *Using a microscope, dust particles suspended in water can be seen to move in a very irregular, random way. Einstein used this "Brownian motion" to demonstrate that the water was composed of atoms.*

Far left: Joseph John Thomson (1856–1940). An English physicist, Thomson is credited with having discovered the electron.
Left: Ernest Rutherford (1871-1937), from a photograph taken while he was at McGill University.

atomists until the early years of this century. One of the important pieces of physical evidence was provided by Einstein. In a paper written in 1905, a few weeks before the famous paper on special relativity, Einstein pointed out that what was called Brownian motion — the irregular, random motion of small particles of dust suspended in a liquid — could be explained as the effect of atoms of the liquid colliding with the dust particles (Fig. 5.1).

By this time there were already suspicions that these atoms were not, after all, indivisible. Several years previously a fellow of Trinity College, Cambridge, J. J. Thomson, had demonstrated the existence of a particle of matter, called the electron, that had a mass less than one thousandth of that of the lightest atom. He used a set up rather like a modern TV picture tube: a red-hot metal filament gave off the electrons, and because these have a negative electric charge, an electric field could be used to acceler-

ate them toward a phosphor-coated screen. When they hit the screen, flashes of light were generated. Soon it was realized that these electrons must be coming from within the atoms themselves, and in 1911 the British physicist Ernest Rutherford finally showed that the atoms of matter do have internal structure: they are made up of an extremely tiny, positively charged nucleus, around which a number of electrons orbit. He deduced this by analyzing the way in which alpha-particles, which are positively charged particles given off by radioactive atoms, are deflected when they collide with atoms.

At first it was thought that the nucleus of the atom was made up of electrons and different numbers of a positively charged particle called the proton, from the Greek word meaning "first," because it was believed to be the fundamental unit from which matter was made. However, in 1932 a colleague of Rutherford's at Cambridge, James Chadwick, discovered that

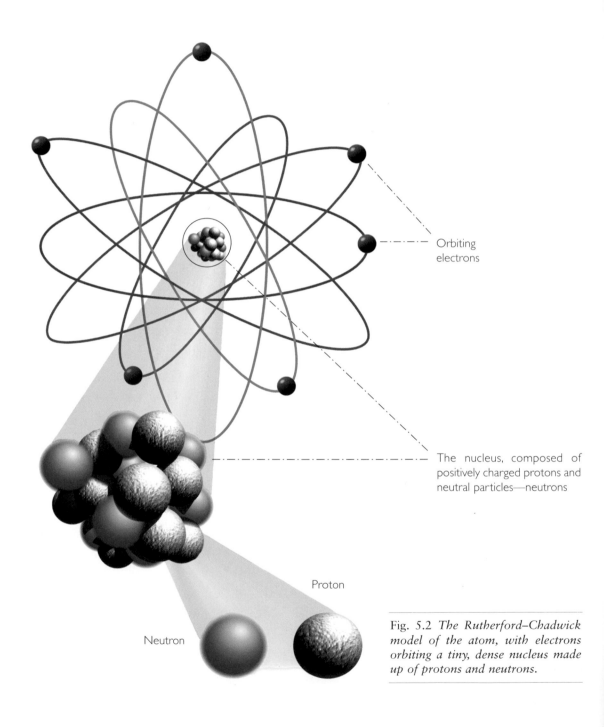

Orbiting
electrons

The nucleus, composed of
positively charged protons and
neutral particles—neutrons

Proton

Neutron

Fig. 5.2 *The Rutherford–Chadwick
model of the atom, with electrons
orbiting a tiny, dense nucleus made
up of protons and neutrons.*

the nucleus contained another particle, called the neutron, which had almost the same mass as a proton but no electrical charge. Chadwick received the Nobel prize for his discovery, and was elected Master of Gonville and Caius College, Cambridge (the college of which I am now a fellow). He later resigned as Master because of disagreements with the Fellows. There had been a bitter dispute in the college ever since a group of young Fellows returning after the war had voted many of the old Fellows out of the college offices they had held for a long time. This was before my time; I joined the college in 1965 at the tail end of the bitterness, when similar disagreements forced another Nobel-prize-winning Master, Sir Nevill Mott, to resign.

Up to about thirty years ago, it was thought that protons and neutrons were "elementary" particles, but experiments in which protons were collided with other protons or electrons at high speeds indicated that they were in fact made up of smaller particles. These particles were named quarks by the Caltech physicist Murray Gell-Mann, who won the Nobel prize in 1969 for his work on them. The origin of the name is an enigmatic quotation from James Joyce: "Three quarks for Muster Mark!" The word *quark* is supposed to be pronounced like

Sir James Chadwick (1891-1974). Head of the British atomic bomb project during the Second World War, Chadwick is best remembered for his discovery of the neutron, for which he received the Nobel prize in 1935.

quart, but with a *k* at the end instead of a *t*, but is usually pronounced to rhyme with *lark*.

There are a number of different varieties of quarks: there are six "flavors," which we call up, down, strange, charmed, bottom, and top. The first three flavors had been known since the 1960s but the charmed quark was discovered only in 1974, the bottom in 1977, and the top in 1995. Each flavor comes in three "colors," red, green, and blue. (It should be emphasized that these terms are just labels: quarks are much smaller than the wavelength of visible light and so do not have any color in the normal sense. It is just that modern physicists seem to have more imaginative ways of naming new particles and phenomena — they no longer restrict themselves to Greek!) A proton or neutron is made up of three quarks, one of each color. A proton con-

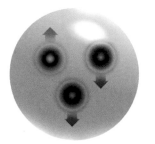 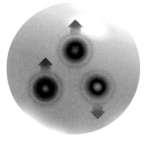

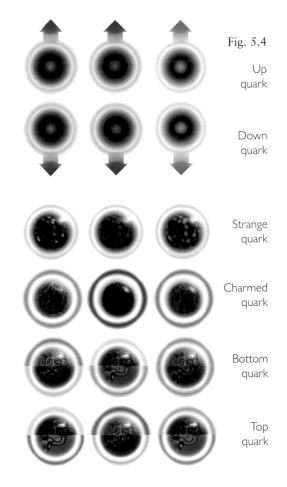

Fig. 5.4

Up quark

Down quark

Strange quark

Charmed quark

Bottom quark

Top quark

Fig. 5.3 The neutron consists of two down quarks with -1/3 charge and one up quark with +2/3 charge, giving a total electric charge of 0.

The proton consists of two up quarks, each with +2/3 electrical charge, and one down quark with -1/3 charge.

tains two up quarks and one down quark; a neutron contains two down and one up (Fig. 5.3). We can create particles made up of the other quarks (strange, charmed, bottom, and top), but these all have a much greater mass and decay very rapidly into protons and neutrons (Figs. 5.4 and 5.5).

We now know that neither the atoms nor the protons and neutrons within them are indivisible. So the question is: What are the truly elementary particles, the basic building blocks from which everything is made? Since the wavelength of light is much larger than the size of an atom, we cannot hope to "look" at the parts of an atom in the ordinary way. We need to use something with a much smaller wavelength. As we saw in the last chapter, quantum mechanics tells us that all particles are in fact waves, and

that the higher the energy of a particle, the smaller the wavelength of the corresponding wave. So the best answer we can give to our question depends on how high a particle energy we have at our disposal, because this determines on how small a length scale we can look. These particle energies are usually measured in units called electron volts. (In Thomson's experiments

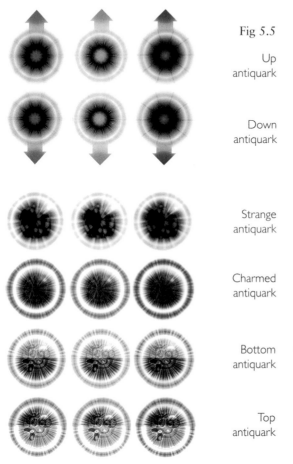

Fig 5.5

Up
antiquark

Down
antiquark

Strange
antiquark

Charmed
antiquark

Bottom
antiquark

Top
antiquark

Figs. 5.4 and 5.5 *There are six flavors of quark, each of which comes in three colors. As well as quarks there are six flavors of antiquarks, each of which comes in three anti–colors (see page 96).*

with electrons, we saw that he used an electric field to accelerate the electrons. The energy that an electron gains from an electric field of one volt is what is known as an electron volt.) In the nineteenth century, when the only particle energies that people knew how to use were the low energies of a few electron volts generated by chemical reactions such as burning, it was thought that atoms were the smallest unit. In Rutherford's experiment, the alpha-particles had energies of millions of electron volts. More recently, we have learned how to use electro-magnetic fields to give particles energies of at first millions and then thousands of millions of electron volts. And so we know that particles that were thought to be "elementary" thirty years ago are, in fact, made up of smaller particles. May these, as we go to still higher energies, in turn be found to be made from still smaller particles? This is certainly possible, but we do have some theoretical reasons for believing that we have, or are very near to, a knowledge of the ultimate building blocks of nature.

Using the wave/particle duality discussed in the last chapter, everything in the universe, including light and gravity, can be described in terms of particles. These particles have a property called spin. One way of thinking of spin is to imagine the particles as little tops spinning about an axis. However, this can be misleading, because quantum mechanics tells us that the particles do not have any well-defined axis. What the spin of a particle really tells us is what

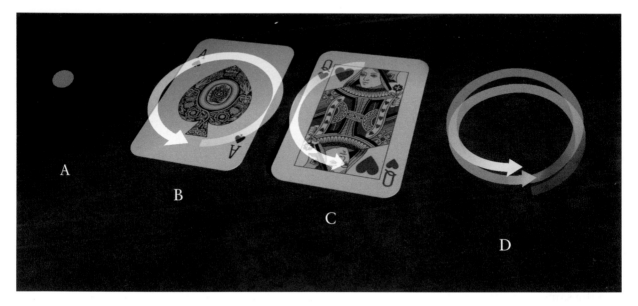

A

B

C

D

the particle looks like from different directions. A particle of spin 0 is like a dot: it looks the same from every direction (Fig. 5.6-A). On the other hand, a particle of spin 1 is like an arrow: it looks different from different directions (Fig. 5.6-B). Only if one turns it round a complete revolution (360 degrees) does the particle look the same. A particle of spin 2 is like a double-headed arrow (Fig. 5.6-C): it looks the same if one turns it round half a revolution (180 degrees). Similarly, higher spin particles look the same if one turns them through smaller fractions of a complete revolution. All this seems fairly straightforward, but the remarkable fact is that there are particles that do not look the same if one turns them through just one revolution: you

have to turn them through two complete revolutions! Such particles are said to have spin 1/2 (Fig. 5.6-D).

All the known particles in the universe can be divided into two groups: particles of spin 1/2, which make up the matter in the universe, and particles of spin 0, 1, and 2, which, as we shall see, give rise to forces between the matter particles. The matter particles obey what is called Pauli's exclusion principle. This was discovered in 1925 by an Austrian physicist, Wolfgang Pauli — for which he received the Nobel prize in 1945. He was the archetypal theoretical physicist: it was said of him that even his presence in the same town would make experiments go wrong! Pauli's exclusion principle says that two

Opposite: Fig. 5.6 *Elementary particles have a property called spin. A spin 0 particle looks the same from all directions (A). A spin 1 particle looks the same when it is rotated through a full 360° (B), and a spin 2 particle only needs 180° (C). However, spin 1/2 particles (D) must go through two complete rotations before they look the same.*
Right: *Paul Dirac (1902–1984), British physicist who proposed the existence of antimatter.*
Far right: *Wolfgang Pauli (1900–1958), who discovered the exclusion principle.*

similar particles cannot exist in the same state, that is, they cannot have both the same position and the same velocity, within the limits given by the uncertainty principle. The exclusion principle is crucial because it explains why matter particles do not collapse to a state of very high density under the influence of the forces produced by the particles of spin 0, 1, and 2: if the matter particles have very nearly the same positions, they must have different velocities, which means that they will not stay in the same position for long. If the world had been created without the exclusion principle, quarks would not form separate, well-defined protons and neutrons. Nor would these, together with electrons, form separate, well-defined atoms. They would all collapse to form a roughly uniform, dense "soup."

A proper understanding of the electron and other spin-1/2 particles did not come until 1928, when a theory was proposed by Paul Dirac, who later was elected to the Lucasian Professorship of Mathematics at Cambridge (the same professorship that Newton had once held and that I now hold). Dirac's theory was the first of its kind that was consistent with both quantum mechanics and the special theory of relativity. It explained mathematically why the electron had spin 1/2, that is, why it didn't look the same if you turned it through only one complete revolution, but did if you turned it through two revolutions. It also predicted that the electron should have a partner: an antielectron, or positron. The discovery of the positron in 1932 confirmed Dirac's theory and led to his being awarded the Nobel prize for physics in 1933. We now know that every particle has an antiparticle, with which it can annihilate. (In the case of the force-carrying particles, the antiparticles are the same

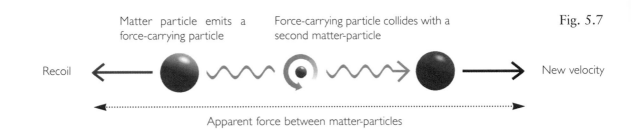

Matter particle emits a force-carrying particle

Force-carrying particle collides with a second matter-particle

Fig. 5.7

Recoil

New velocity

Apparent force between matter-particles

Fig. 5.7 *Interactions between particles of matter can be described as an exchange of force–carrying particles.*
Fig. 5.8 *If you should meet your antiself, prudence suggests not to shake hands!*

as the particles themselves.) There could be whole antiworlds and antipeople made out of antiparticles. However, if you meet your antiself (Fig. 5.8), don't shake hands! You would both vanish in a great flash of light. The question of why there seem to be so many more particles than antiparticles around us is extremely important, and I shall return to it later in the chapter.

In quantum mechanics, the forces or interactions between matter particles are all supposed to be carried by particles of integer spin — 0, 1, or 2. What happens is that a matter particle, such as an electron or a quark, emits a force-carrying particle. The recoil from this emission changes the velocity of the matter particle. The force-carrying particle then collides with another matter particle and is absorbed. This collision changes the velocity of the second particle, just

as if there had been a force between the two matter particles (Fig 5.7). It is an important property of the force-carrying particles that they do not obey the exclusion principle. This means that there is no limit to the number that can be exchanged, and so they can give rise to a strong force. However, if the force-carrying particles have a high mass, it will be difficult to produce and exchange them over a large distance. So the forces that they carry will have only a short range. On the other hand, if the force-carrying

Self   Antiself

Fig. 5.8

particles have no mass of their own, the forces will be long range. The force-carrying particles exchanged between matter particles are said to be virtual particles because, unlike "real" particles, they cannot be directly detected by a particle detector. We know they exist, however, because they do have a measurable effect: they give rise to forces between matter particles. Particles of spin 0, 1, or 2 do also exist in some circumstances as real particles, when they can be directly detected. They then appear to us as what a classical physicist would call waves, such as waves of light or gravitational waves. They may sometimes be emitted when matter particles interact with each other by exchanging virtual force-carrying particles. (For example, the electric repulsive force between two electrons is due to the exchange of virtual photons, which can never be directly detected; but if one electron moves past another, real photons may be given off, which we detect as light waves.)

Force-carrying particles can be grouped into four categories according to the strength of the force that they carry and the particles with which they interact. It should be emphasized that this division into four classes is man-made; it is convenient for the construction of partial theories, but it may not correspond to anything deeper. Ultimately, most physicists hope to find a unified theory that will explain all four forces as different aspects of a single force. Indeed, many would say this is the prime goal of physics today. Recently, successful attempts have been made to unify three of the four categories of force — and I shall describe these in this chapter. The question of the unification of the remaining category, gravity, we shall leave till later.

The first category is the gravitational force. This force is universal, that is, every particle feels the force of gravity, according to its mass or energy. Gravity is the weakest of the four forces by a long way; it is so weak that we would not notice it at all were it not for two special properties that it has: it can act over large distances, and it is always attractive. This means that the very weak gravitational forces between the individual particles in two large bodies, such as the earth and the sun, can all add up to produce a significant force. The other three forces are either short range, or are sometimes attractive and sometimes repulsive, so they tend to cancel out. In the quantum mechanical way of looking at the gravitational field, the force between two matter particles is pictured as being carried by a particle of spin 2 called the graviton. This has no mass of its own, so the force that it carries is long range. The gravita-

Fig. 5.9

Earth   Virtual graviton   Sun
(particle of spin 2)

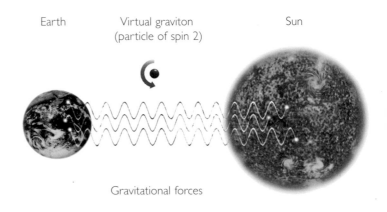

Gravitational forces

The gravitational force between the earth and sun is caused by the exchange of virtual gravitons. Because gravity is always attractive, the weak forces between individual particles in the earth and sun all add up to a significant force.

tional force between the sun and the earth is ascribed to the exchange of gravitons between the particles that make up these two bodies. Although the exchanged particles are virtual, they certainly do produce a measurable effect — they make the earth orbit the sun! Real gravitons make up what classical physicists would call gravitational waves, which are very weak — and so difficult to detect that they have not yet been observed.

The next category is the electromagnetic force, which interacts with electrically charged particles like electrons and quarks, but not with uncharged particles such as gravitons. It is much stronger than the gravitational force: the electromagnetic force between two electrons is about a million million million million million million million (1 with forty-two zeros after it) times bigger than the gravitational force. However, there are two kinds of electric charge,

positive and negative. The force between two positive charges is repulsive, as is the force between two negative charges, but the force is attractive between a positive and a negative charge. A large body, such as the earth or the sun, contains nearly equal numbers of positive and negative charges. Thus the attractive and repulsive forces between the individual particles nearly cancel each other out, and there is very little net electromagnetic force. However, on the small scales of atoms and molecules, electromagnetic forces dominate. The electromagnetic attraction between negatively charged electrons and positively charged protons in the nucleus causes the electrons to orbit the nucleus of the atom, just as gravitational attraction causes the earth to orbit the sun. The electromagnetic attraction is pictured as being caused by the exchange of large numbers of virtual massless particles of spin 1, called photons. Again, the

Earth   Virtual photon   Sun
(particle of spin 1)

Fig. 5.10

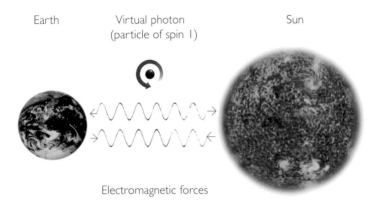

Electromagnetic forces

In the case of electromagnetic forces carried by virtual photons, the forces can be both attractive and repulsive, so the forces between the particles in the earth and sun largely cancel each other out.

photons that are exchanged are virtual particles. However, when an electron changes from one allowed orbit to another one nearer to the nucleus, energy is released and a real photon is emitted — which can be observed as visible light by the human eye, if it has the right wavelength, or by a photon detector such as photographic film. Equally, if a real photon collides with an atom, it may move an electron from an orbit nearer the nucleus to one farther away. This uses up the energy of the photon, so it is absorbed.

The third category is called the weak nuclear force, which is responsible for radioactivity and which acts on all matter particles of spin 1/2, but not on particles of spin 0, 1, or 2, such as photons and gravitons. The weak nuclear force was not well understood until 1967, when Abdus Salam at Imperial College, London, and Steven Weinberg at Harvard both proposed theories that unified this interaction with the elec-

tromagnetic force, just as Maxwell had unified electricity and magnetism about a hundred years earlier. They suggested that in addition to the photon, there were three other spin-1 particles, known collectively as massive vector bosons, that carried the weak force. These were called W^+ (pronounced W plus), W^- (pronounced W minus), and Z^0 (pronounced Z naught), and each had a mass of around 100 GeV (GeV stands for gigaelectron-volt, or one thousand million electron volts). The Weinberg–Salam theory exhibits a property known as spontaneous symmetry breaking. This means that what appear to be a number of completely different particles at low energies are in fact found to be all the same type of particle, only in different states. At high energies all these particles behave similarly. The effect is rather like the behavior of a roulette ball on a roulette wheel (see above). At high energies (when the wheel is spun quickly)

When a roulette wheel is spinning rapidly, the ball can move freely between all possible positions. However, when the wheel slows down the ball will settle into one of thirty-seven different positions.

the ball behaves in essentially only one way — it rolls round and round. But as the wheel slows, the energy of the ball decreases, and eventually the ball drops into one of the thirty-seven slots in the wheel. In other words, at low energies there are thirty-seven different states in which the ball can exist. If, for some reason, we could only observe the ball at low energies, we would then think that there were thirty-seven different types of ball!

In the Weinberg–Salam theory, at energies much greater than 100 GeV, the three new particles and the photon would all behave in a similar manner. But at the lower particle energies that occur in most normal situations, this symmetry between the particles would be broken. W^+, W^- and Z^0 would acquire large masses, making the forces they carry have a very short range. At the time that Salam and Weinberg proposed their theory, few people believed them, and particle accelerators were not powerful enough to reach the energies of 100 GeV required to produce real W^+, W^-, or Z^0 particles. However, over the next ten years or so, the other predictions of the theory at lower energies agreed so well with experiment that, in 1979, Salam and Weinberg were awarded the Nobel prize for physics, together with Sheldon Glashow, also at Harvard, who had suggested similar unified theories of the electromagnetic and weak nuclear forces. The Nobel committee was spared the embarrassment of having made a mistake by the discovery in 1983 at CERN (European Centre for Nuclear Research) of the three massive partners of the photon, with the correct predicted masses and other properties. Carlo Rubbia, who led the team of several hundred physicists that made the discovery, received the Nobel prize in 1984, along with Simon van der Meer, the CERN engineer who developed the antimatter storage system employed. (It is very difficult to make a mark in experimental physics these days unless you are already at the top!)

The fourth category is the strong nuclear force, which holds the quarks together in the proton and neutron, and holds the protons and neutrons together in the nucleus of an atom. It is believed that this force is carried by another spin-1 particle, called the gluon, which interacts only with itself and with the quarks. The strong nuclear force has a curious property called confinement: it always binds particles together into combinations that have no color. One cannot have a single quark on its own because it would have a color (red, green, or blue). Instead, a red quark has to be joined to a green and a blue quark by a "string" of gluons (red + green + blue = white). Such a triplet constitutes a proton or a neutron (Fig. 5.11). Another possibility is a

Left: *Steven Weinberg (1933–). Weinberg's most important work was on the unification of the electromagnetic and weak nuclear forces.*
Right: *Sheldon Glashow (1932–). Glashow produced one of the earliest models linking the electromagnetic and weak nuclear forces.*

pair consisting of a quark and an antiquark (red + antired, or green + antigreen, or blue + antiblue = white) (Fig. 5.12). Such combinations make up the particles known as mesons, which are unstable because the quark and antiquark can annihilate each other, producing electrons and other particles. Similarly, confinement prevents one having a single gluon on its own, because gluons also have color. Instead, one has to have a collection of gluons whose colors add

Quarks joined by
a string of gluons

Neutron

A pair consisting of a quark
and an antiquark

Meson

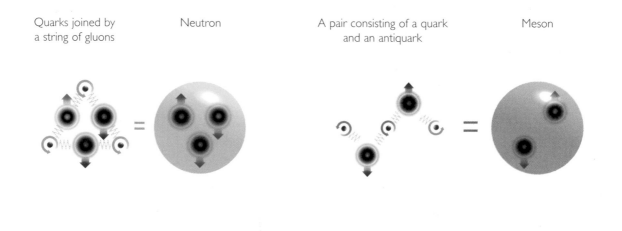

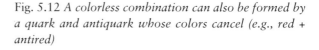

Fig. 5.11 *Quarks can only exist in combinations without color. Red, green, and blue quarks are bound by gluons to form a "white" neutron.*

Fig. 5.12 *A colorless combination can also be formed by a quark and antiquark whose colors cancel (e.g., red + antired)*

up to white. Such a collection forms an unstable particle called a glueball.

The fact that confinement prevents one from observing an isolated quark or gluon might seem to make the whole notion of quarks and gluons as particles somewhat metaphysical. However, there is another property of the strong nuclear force, called asymptotic freedom, that makes the concept of quarks and gluons well-defined. At normal energies, the strong nuclear force is indeed strong, and it binds the quarks tightly together. However, experiments with large particle accelerators indicate that at high energies the strong force becomes much weaker, and the quarks and gluons behave almost like free particles. Fig. 5.13 on page 98 shows a pho-

tograph of a collision between a high energy proton and antiproton. The success of the unification of the electromagnetic and weak nuclear forces led to a number of attempts to combine these two forces with the strong nuclear force into what is called a grand unified theory (or GUT). This title is rather an exaggeration: the resultant theories are not all that grand, nor are they fully unified, as they do not include gravity. Nor are they really complete theories, because they contain a number of parameters whose values cannot be predicted from the theory but have to be chosen to fit in with experiment. Nevertheless, they may be a step toward a complete, fully unified theory. The basic idea of GUTs is as follows: as was mentioned above, the strong nuclear force gets weaker at high energies. On the other hand, the electromagnetic and weak forces, which are not asymptotically free, get stronger at high energies. At some very high energy, called the grand unification energy, these three forces would all have the same strength and so could just be different aspects of a single force. The GUTs also predict that at this energy the different spin-1/2 matter particles, like quarks and electrons, would also all be essentially the same, thus achieving another unification.

The value of the grand unification energy is not very well known, but it would probably have to be at least a thousand million million GeV. The present generation of particle accelerators can collide particles at energies of about one hundred GeV, and machines are planned

Below: *One of the end caps of the ALEPH detector at CERN near Geneva, Switzerland. By creating high-energy particle collisions in such accelerators, researchers can create conditions similar to those that existed after the big bang.*

that would raise this to a few thousand GeV. But a machine that was powerful enough to accelerate particles to the grand unification energy would have to be as big as the Solar System — and would be unlikely to be funded in the present economic climate. Thus it is impossible to test grand unified theories directly in the laboratory. However, just as in the case of the electromagnetic and weak unified theory, there are low-energy consequences of the theory that can be tested.

The most interesting of these is the prediction that protons, which make up much of the mass of ordinary matter, can spontaneously decay into lighter particles such as antielectrons. The reason this is possible is that at the grand unification energy there is no essential difference between a quark and an antielectron. The three quarks inside a proton normally do not have enough energy to change into antielectrons, but very occasionally one of them may acquire sufficient energy to make the transition because the uncertainty principle means that the energy of the quarks inside the proton cannot be fixed exactly. The proton would then decay. The probability of a quark gaining sufficient energy is so low that one is likely to have to wait at least a million million million million million years (1 followed by thirty zeros). This is much

longer than the time since the big bang, which is a mere ten thousand million years or so (1 followed by ten zeros). Thus one might think that the possibility of spontaneous proton decay could not be tested experimentally. However, one can increase one's chances of detecting a decay by observing a large amount of matter containing a very large number of protons. (If, for example, one observed a number of protons equal to 1 followed by thirty-one zeros for a period of one year, one would expect, according

Above: Fig. 5.13 *False color image showing tracks made by accelerated particles inside a cloud chamber. The annihilation of an antiproton and a proton occurs at the central intersection.* Opposite: *The most recent research using the* ALEPH *detector at CERN produces computer-generated images showing the decay of a particle, via quark-antiquark pairs, into many particles.*

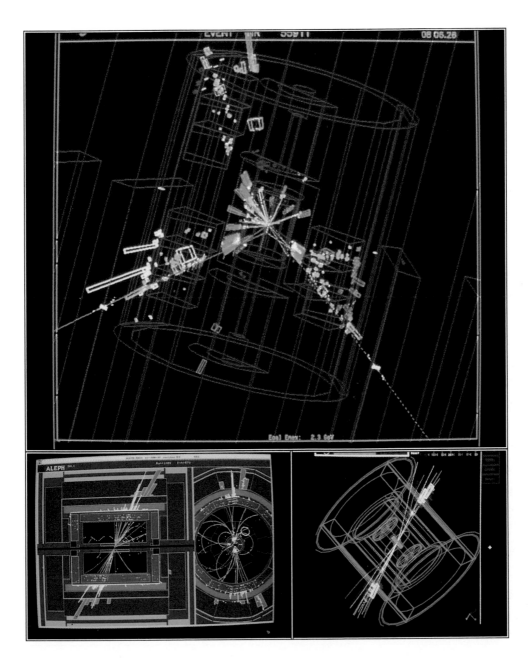

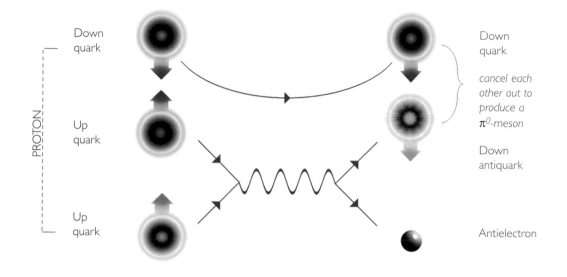

Fig. 5.14 *In grand unified theories the two up and one down quarks in a proton might change into a down/antidown π^0-meson and an antielectron.*

to the simplest GUT, to observe more than one proton decay.)

A number of such experiments have been carried out, but none have yielded definite evidence of proton or neutron decay. One experiment used eight thousand tons of water and was performed in the Morton Salt Mine in Ohio (to avoid other events taking place, caused by cosmic rays, that might be confused with proton decay). Since no spontaneous proton decay had been observed during the experiment, one can calculate that the probable life of the proton must be greater than ten million million million million million years (1 with thirty-one zeros). This is longer than the lifetime predicted by the simplest grand unified theory, but there are more elaborate theories in which the predicted lifetimes are longer. Still more sensitive experiments involving even larger quantities of matter will be needed to test them.

Even though it is very difficult to observe spontaneous proton decay, it may be that our very existence is a consequence of the reverse process, the production of protons, or more simply, of quarks, from an initial situation in which there were no more quarks than antiquarks, which is the most natural way to imagine the universe starting out. Matter on the earth is made up mainly of protons and neutrons, which in turn are made up of quarks. There are no antiprotons or antineutrons, made up from antiquarks, except for a few that physicists produce in large particle accelerators. We have evidence from cosmic rays that the same is true for all the matter in our galaxy: there are no antiprotons or antineutrons apart from a small number that are produced as particle/antiparticle pairs in high-energy collisions. If there were large regions of antimatter in our galaxy, we would expect to observe large quantities of radiation from the borders between the regions of matter and antimatter, where many particles would be colliding with their antiparticles, annihilating each other and giving off high energy radiation.

We have no direct evidence as to whether the matter in other galaxies is made up of protons and neutrons or antiprotons and antineutrons, but it must be one or the other: there cannot be a mixture in a single galaxy because in that case we would again observe a lot of radiation from annihilations. We therefore believe that all galaxies are composed of quarks rather than antiquarks; it seems implausible that some galaxies should be matter and some antimatter.

Why should there be so many more quarks than antiquarks? Why are there not equal numbers of each? It is certainly fortunate for us that

the numbers are unequal because, if they had been the same, nearly all the quarks and antiquarks would have annihilated each other in the early universe and left a universe filled with radiation but hardly any matter. There would then have been no galaxies, stars, or planets on which human life could have developed. Luckily, grand unified theories may provide an explanation of why the universe should now contain more quarks than antiquarks, even if it started out with equal numbers of each. As we have seen, GUTs allow quarks to change into antielectrons at high energy. They also allow the reverse processes, antiquarks turning into electrons, and electrons and antielectrons turning into antiquarks and quarks. There was a time in the very early universe when it was so hot that the particle energies would have been high enough for these transformations to take place. But why should that lead to more quarks than antiquarks? The reason is that the laws of physics are not quite the same for particles and antiparticles.

Up to 1956 it was believed that the laws of physics obeyed each of three separate symmetries called C, P, and T. The symmetry C means that the laws are the same for particles and antiparticles. The symmetry P means that the laws are the same for any situation and its mir-

ror image (the mirror image of a particle spinning in a right-handed direction is one spinning in a left-handed direction). The symmetry T means that if you reverse the direction of motion of all particles and antiparticles, the system should go back to what it was at earlier times; in other words, the laws are the same in the forward and backward directions of time. In 1956 two American physicists, Tsung-Dao Lee and Chen Ning Yang, suggested that the weak force does not in fact obey the symmetry P. In other words, the weak force would make the universe develop in a different way from the way in which the mirror image of the universe would develop. The same year, a colleague, Chien-Shiung Wu, proved their prediction correct. She did this by lining up the nuclei of radioactive atoms in a magnetic field, so that they were all spinning in the same direction, and showed that the electrons were given off more in one direction than another. The following year, Lee and Yang received the Nobel prize for their idea. It was also found that the weak force did not obey the symmetry C. That is, it would cause a universe composed of antiparticles to behave differently from our universe. Nevertheless, it seemed that the weak force did obey the combined symmetry CP. That is, the universe would develop in the same way as its mirror image if, in addition,

every particle was swapped with its antiparticle! However, in 1964 two more Americans, J. W. Cronin and Val Fitch, discovered that even the CP symmetry was not obeyed in the decay of certain particles called K-mesons. Cronin and Fitch eventually received the Nobel prize for their work in 1980. (A lot of prizes have been awarded for showing that the universe is not as simple as we might have thought!)

There is a mathematical theorem that says that any theory that obeys quantum mechanics and relativity must always obey the combined symmetry CPT. In other words, the universe would have to behave the same if one replaced particles by antiparticles, took the mirror image, and also reversed the direction of time. But Cronin and Fitch showed that if one replaces particles by antiparticles and takes the mirror image, but does not reverse the direction of time, then the universe does *not* behave the same. The laws of physics, therefore, must change if one reverses the direction of time — they do not obey the symmetry T.

Certainly the early universe does not obey the symmetry T: as time runs forward the universe expands — if it ran backward, the universe would be contracting. And since there are forces that do not obey the symmetry T, it follows that as the universe expands, these forces could cause

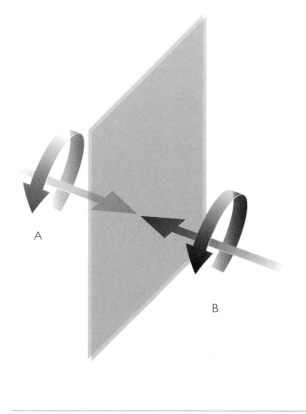

A

B

Fig. 5.15 *The mirror image of a particle with right hand spin is a particle with left hand spin. If symmetry P holds, the laws of physics are the same for both.*

more antielectrons to turn into quarks than electrons into antiquarks. Then, as the universe expanded and cooled, the antiquarks would annihilate with the quarks, but since there would be more quarks than antiquarks, a small excess of quarks would remain. It is these that make up the matter we see today and out of which we ourselves are made. Thus our very existence could be regarded as a confirmation of

grand unified theories, though a qualitative one only; the uncertainties are such that one cannot predict the numbers of quarks that will be left after the annihilation, or even whether it would be quarks or antiquarks that would remain. (Had it been an excess of antiquarks, however, we would simply have named antiquarks quarks, and quarks antiquarks.)

Grand unified theories do not include the force of gravity. This does not matter too much, because gravity is such a weak force that its effects can usually be neglected when we are dealing with elementary particles or atoms. However, the fact that it is both long range and always attractive means that its effects all add up. So for a sufficiently large number of matter particles, gravitational forces can dominate over all other forces. This is why it is gravity that determines the evolution of the universe. Even for objects the size of stars, the attractive force of gravity can win over all the other forces and cause the star to collapse. My work in the 1970s focused on the black holes that can result from such stellar collapse and the intense gravitational fields around them. It was this that led to the first hints of how the theories of quantum mechanics and general relativity might affect each other — a glimpse of the shape of a quantum theory of gravity yet to come.

6

Black Holes

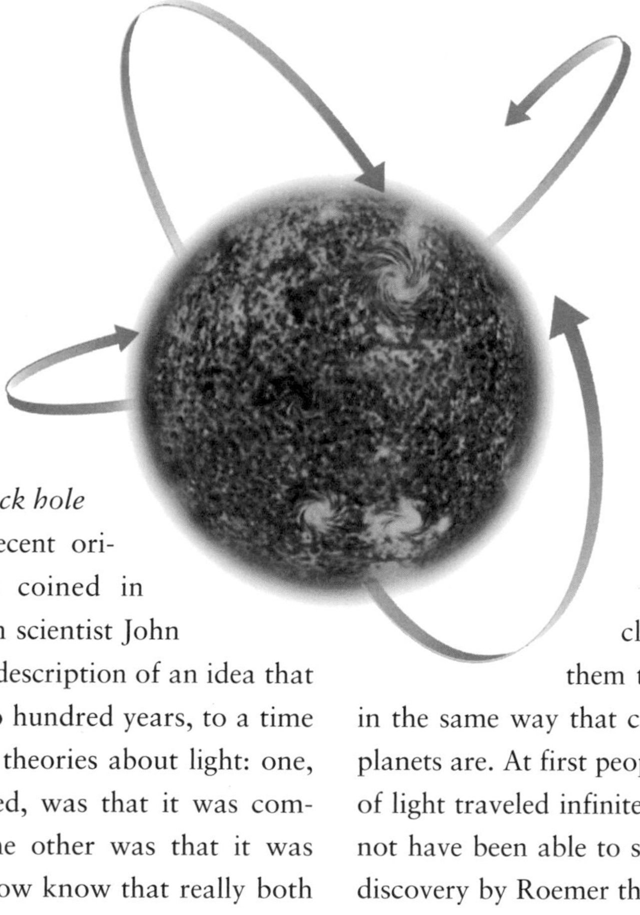

THE TERM *black hole* is of very recent origin. It was coined in 1969 by the American scientist John Wheeler as a graphic description of an idea that goes back at least two hundred years, to a time when there were two theories about light: one, which Newton favored, was that it was composed of particles; the other was that it was made of waves. We now know that really both theories are correct. By the wave/particle duality of quantum mechanics, light can be regarded as both a wave and a particle. Under the theory that light is made up of waves, it was not clear

Fig. 6.1

how it would respond to gravity. But if light is composed of particles, one might expect them to be affected by gravity in the same way that cannonballs, rockets, and planets are. At first people thought that particles of light traveled infinitely fast, so gravity would not have been able to slow them down, but the discovery by Roemer that light travels at a finite speed meant that gravity might have an important effect.

On this assumption, a Cambridge don, John Michell, wrote a paper in 1783 in the *Philoso-*

phical Transactions of the Royal Society of London in which he pointed out that a star that was sufficiently massive and compact would have such a strong gravitational field that light could not escape: any light emitted from the surface of the star would be dragged back by the star's gravitational attraction before it could get very far. Michell suggested that there might be a large number of stars like this. Although we would not be able to see them because the light from them would not reach us, we would still feel their gravitational attraction. Such objects are what we now call black holes, because that is what they are: black voids in space. A similar suggestion was made a few years later by the French scientist the Marquis de Laplace, apparently independently of Michell. Interestingly enough, Laplace included it in only the first and second editions of his book *The System of the World*, and left it out of later editions; perhaps he decided that it was a crazy idea. (Also, the particle theory of light went out of favor during the nineteenth century; it seemed that everything

could be explained by the wave theory, and according to the wave theory, it was not clear that light would be affected by gravity at all.)

In fact, it is not really consistent to treat light like cannonballs in Newton's theory of gravity because the speed of light is fixed. (A cannonball fired upward from the earth will be slowed down by gravity and will eventually stop and fall back; a photon, however, must continue upward at a constant speed. How then can Newtonian gravity affect light?) A consistent theory of how gravity affects light did not come along until Einstein proposed general relativity in 1915. And even then it was a long time before the implications of the theory for massive stars were understood.

To understand how a black hole might be formed, we first need an understanding of the life cycle of a star. A star is formed when a large amount of gas (mostly hydrogen) starts to collapse in on itself due to its gravitational attraction. As it contracts the atoms of the gas collide with each other more and more frequently and at greater and greater speeds — the gas heats up. Eventually, the gas will be so hot that when the hydrogen atoms collide they no longer bounce off each other, but instead coalesce to form helium. The heat released in this reaction, which is

Fig. 6.1 *John Michell's concept was of a star so massive, that light emitted from its surface would be pulled back by its vast gravitational field, making it invisible. These "dark stars" were the eighteenth century precursors of today's black holes.*

like a controlled hydrogen bomb explosion, is what makes the star shine. This additional heat also increases the pressure of the gas until it is sufficient to balance the gravitational attraction, and the gas stops contracting. It is a bit like a balloon — there is a balance between the pressure of the air inside, which is trying to make the balloon expand, and the tension in the rubber, which is trying to make the balloon smaller. Stars will remain stable like this for a long time, with heat from the nuclear reactions balancing the gravitational attraction (see "main-sequence stars" in Fig. 6.2). Eventually, however, the star will run out of its hydrogen and other nuclear fuels. Paradoxically, the more fuel a star starts off with, the sooner it runs out. This is because the more massive the star is, the hotter it needs to be to balance its gravitational attraction. And the hotter it is, the faster it will use up its fuel. Our sun has probably got enough fuel for another five thousand million years or so, but more massive stars can use up their fuel in as little as one hundred million years, much less than the age of the universe. When a star runs out of

Fig. 6.2 *The birth, evolution, and death of typical stars. If a star's mass is less than the Chandrasekhar limit it eventually becomes a brown or white dwarf. If it is above the limit, the supergiant's final gravitational collapse produces either a neutron star or a black hole.*

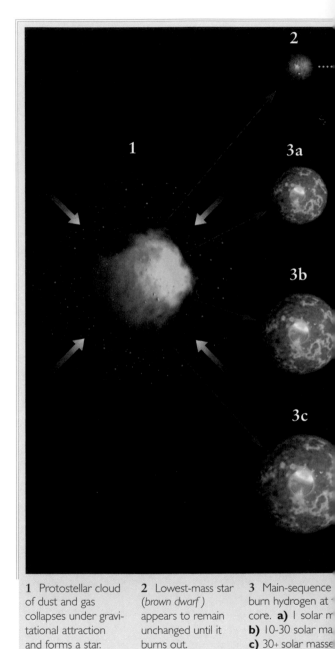

1 Protostellar cloud of dust and gas collapses under gravitational attraction and forms a star.

2 Lowest-mass star (*brown dwarf*) appears to remain unchanged until it burns out.

3 Main-sequence burn hydrogen at core. **a)** 1 solar m **b)** 10-30 solar ma **c)** 30+ solar masse

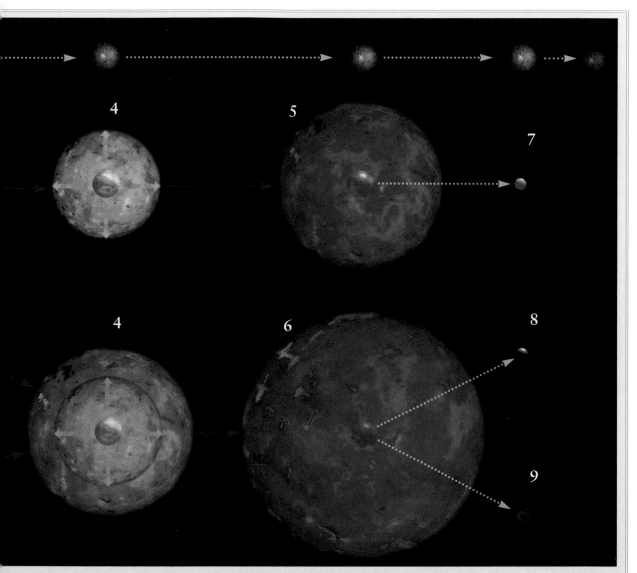

4

5

7

4

6

8

9

elium core as hydrogen exhausted. velope of gas s to expand.

5 *Red giant* of 1 solar mass has a carbon core surrounded by a hydrogen-burning shell and gaseous envelope.

6 *A supergiant.* Massive stars ranging from 10 to over 30 solar masses.

7 *A white dwarf* resulting from the collapse of a 1 solar-mass star.

8 *A neutron star* resulting from the gravitational collapse of a 10 solar-mass star.

9 *A black hole* resulting from the gravitational collapse of a 30 solar-mass star.

Arthur Stanley Eddington
(1882-1944)

Lev Davidovich Landau
(1908-1968)

Subrahmanyan Chandrasekhar
(1910-1995)

fuel, it starts to cool off and so to contract. What might happen to it then was first understood only at the end of the 1920s.

In 1928 an Indian graduate student, Subrahmanyan Chandrasekhar, set sail for England to study at Cambridge with the British astronomer Sir Arthur Eddington, an expert on general relativity. (According to some accounts, a journalist told Eddington in the early 1920s that he had heard there were only three people in the world who understood general relativity. Eddington paused, then replied, "I am trying to think who the third person is.") During his voyage from India, Chandrasekhar worked out how big a star could be and still support itself against its own gravity after it had used up all its fuel. The idea was this: when the star becomes small, the matter particles get very near each other, and so according to the Pauli exclusion principle, they must have very different velocities. This makes them move away from each other and so tends to make the star expand. A star can therefore maintain itself at a constant radius by a balance between the attraction of gravity and the repulsion that arises from the exclusion principle, just as earlier in its life gravity was balanced by the heat.

Chandrasekhar realized, however, that there is a limit to the repulsion that the exclusion principle can provide. The theory of relativity limits the maximum difference in the velocities of the matter particles in the star to the speed of light. This means that when the star got sufficiently dense, the repulsion caused by the exclusion principle would be less than the attraction of gravity. Chandrasekhar calculated that a cold star of more than about one and a half times the mass of the sun would not be able to support itself against its own gravity. (This mass is now known as the Chandrasekhar limit.) A similar discovery was made about the same time by the Russian scientist Lev Davidovich Landau.

This had serious implications for the ultimate fate of massive stars. If a star's mass is less than the Chandrasekhar limit, it can eventually stop contracting and settle down to a possible final state as a "white dwarf" with a radius of a few thousand miles and a density of hundreds of tons per cubic inch. A white dwarf is supported by the exclusion principle repulsion between the electrons in its matter. We observe a large number of these white dwarf stars. One of the first to be discovered is a star that is orbiting around Sirius, the brightest star in the night sky.

Landau pointed out that there was another possible final state for a star, also with a limiting mass of about one or two times the mass of the sun but much smaller even than a white dwarf. These stars would be supported by the exclusion principle repulsion between neutrons and protons, rather than between electrons. They were therefore called neutron stars. They would have a radius of only ten miles or so and a density of

hundreds of millions of tons per cubic inch. At the time they were first predicted, there was no way that neutron stars could be observed. They were not actually detected until much later.

Stars with masses above the Chandrasekhar limit, on the other hand, have a big problem when they come to the end of their fuel. In some cases they may explode or manage to throw off enough matter to reduce their mass below the limit and so avoid catastrophic gravitational collapse, but it was difficult to believe that this always happened, no matter how big the star. How would it know that it had to lose weight? And even if every star managed to lose enough mass to avoid collapse, what would happen if you added more mass to a white dwarf or neutron star to take it over the limit? Would it collapse to infinite density? Eddington was shocked by that implication, and he refused to believe Chandrasekhar's result. Eddington thought it was simply not possible that a star could collapse to a point. This was the view of most scientists: Einstein himself wrote a paper in which he claimed that stars would not shrink to zero size. The hostility of other scientists, particularly Eddington, his former teacher and the leading authority on the structure of stars, persuaded Chandrasekhar to abandon this line of work and turn instead to other problems in astronomy, such as the motion of star clusters. However, when he was awarded the Nobel prize in 1983, it was, at least in part, for his early work on the limiting mass of cold stars.

Chandrasekhar had shown that the exclusion principle could not halt the collapse of a star more massive than the Chandrasekhar limit, but the problem of understanding what would happen to such a star, according to general relativity, was first solved by a young American, Robert Oppenheimer, in 1939. His result, however, suggested that there would be no observational consequences that could be detected by the telescopes of the day. Then World War II intervened and Oppenheimer himself became closely involved in the atom bomb project. After the war the problem of gravitational collapse was largely forgotten as most scientists became caught up in what happens on the scale of the atom and its nucleus. In the 1960s, however, interest in the large-scale problems of astronomy and cosmology was revived by a great increase in the number and range of astronomical observations brought about by the application of modern technology. Oppenheimer's work was then rediscovered and extended by a number of people.

The picture that we now have from Oppenheimer's work is as follows. The gravita-

Robert Oppenheimer (1904-1967). From 1942 to 1945 he was the director of the laboratory at Los Alamos, New Mexico, that designed and built the first atomic bombs.

tional field of the star changes the paths of light rays in space-time from what they would have been had the star not been present. The light cones, which indicate the paths followed in space and time by flashes of light emitted from their tips, are bent slightly inward near the surface of the star. This can be seen in the bending of light from distant stars observed during an eclipse of the sun. As the star contracts, the gravitational field at its surface gets stronger and the light cones get bent inward more. This makes it more difficult for light from the star to escape, and the light appears dimmer and redder to an observer at a distance. Eventually, when the star has shrunk to a certain critical radius, the gravitational field at the surface becomes so strong that the light cones are bent inward so much that light can no longer escape (Fig. 6.3). According to the theory of relativity, nothing

can travel faster than light. Thus if light cannot escape, neither can anything else; everything is dragged back by the gravitational field. So one has a set of events, a region of space-time, from which it is not possible to escape to reach a distant observer. This region is what we now call a black hole. Its boundary is called the event horizon and it coincides with the paths of light rays that just fail to escape from the black hole

In order to understand what you would see if you were watching a star collapse to form a black hole, one has to remember that in the theory of relativity there is no absolute time. Each observer has his own measure of time. The time for someone on a star will be different from that for someone at a distance, because of the gravitational field of the star. Suppose an intrepid astronaut on the surface of the collapsing star, collapsing inward with it, sent a signal every second, according to his watch, to his spaceship orbiting about the star. At some time on his watch, say 11:00, the star would shrink below the

Fig. 6.3 *Space-time diagram of a massive star collapsing to form a black hole.*

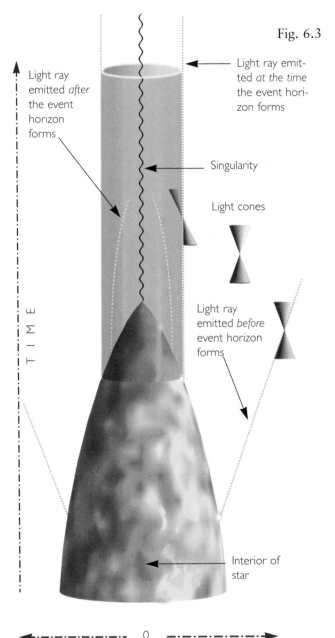

Fig. 6.3

Light ray emitted *after* the event horizon forms

Light ray emitted *at the time* the event horizon forms

Singularity

Light cones

Light ray emitted *before* event horizon forms

Interior of star

TIME

DISTANCE FROM CENTER OF STAR

0

Fig. 6.4

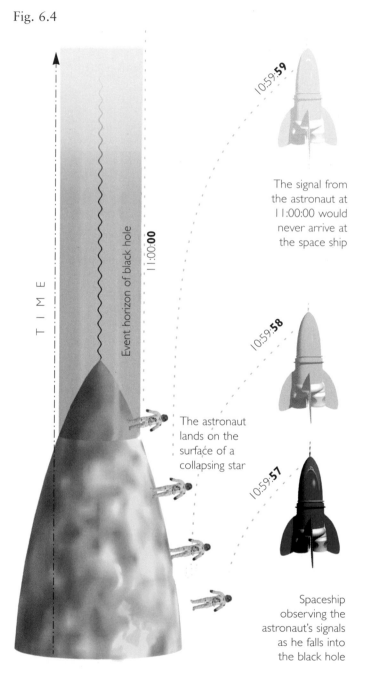

The signal from the astronaut at 11:00:00 would never arrive at the space ship

The astronaut lands on the surface of a collapsing star

Spaceship observing the astronaut's signals as he falls into the black hole

critical radius at which the gravitational field becomes so strong nothing can escape, and his signals would no longer reach the spaceship. As 11:00 approached, his companions watching from the spaceship would find the intervals between successive signals from the astronaut getting longer and longer, but this effect would be very small before 10:59:59. They would have to wait only very slightly more than a second between the astronaut's 10:59:58 signal and the one that he sent when his watch read 10:59:59, but they would have to wait forever for the 11:00 signal. The light waves emitted from the surface of the star between 10:59:59 and 11:00, by the astronaut's watch, would be spread out over an infinite period of time, as seen from the spaceship. The time interval between the arrival of successive waves at the spaceship would get longer and longer, so the light from the star would appear redder and redder and fainter and fainter. Eventually, the star would be so dim that it could no longer be seen from the spaceship: all that would be left would be a black hole in space. The

Fig. 6.5

An astronaut approaches a black hole. The gravitational forces tear him apart as he nears the event horizon

the universe, like the central regions of galaxies, that can also undergo gravitational collapse to produce black holes; an astronaut on one of these would not be torn apart before the black hole formed. He would not, in fact, feel anything special as he reached the critical

The astronaut's feet are subject to greater gravitational force than his head so stretch him apart

star would, however, continue to exert the same gravitational force on the spaceship, which would continue to orbit the black hole. This scenario is not entirely realistic, however, because of the following problem. Gravity gets weaker the farther you are from the star, so the gravitational force on our intrepid astronaut's feet would always be greater than the force on his head. This difference in the forces would stretch our astronaut out like spaghetti or tear him apart before the star had contracted to the critical radius at which the event horizon formed! (See Fig. 6.5) However, we believe that there are much larger objects in

A massive star begins to collapse under its
own gravitational pressure

As the star implodes it falls deeper into
its own gravity well

Fig. 6.6

radius, and could pass the point of no return without noticing it. However, within just a few hours, as the region continued to collapse, the difference in the gravitational forces on his head and his feet would become so strong that again it would tear him apart.

The work that Roger Penrose and I did between 1965 and 1970 showed that, according to general relativity, there must be a singularity of infinite density and space-time curvature within a black hole. This is rather like the big bang at the beginning of time, only it would be an end of time for the collapsing body and the astronaut. At this singularity the laws of science and our ability to predict the future would break

Fig. 6.6 *The effect of the increasing gravitational field of a contracting star on the surrounding space can be visualized by imagining space to be a sensitive elastic sheet. The heavier the mass, the deeper the indentation. The final gravitational implosion seen here represents the singularity of a black hole.*

down. However, any observer who remained outside the black hole would not be affected by this failure of predictability, because neither light nor any other signal could reach him from the singularity. This remarkable fact led Roger Penrose to propose the cosmic censorship hypothesis, which might be paraphrased as "God abhors a naked singularity." In other words, the singularities produced by gravita-

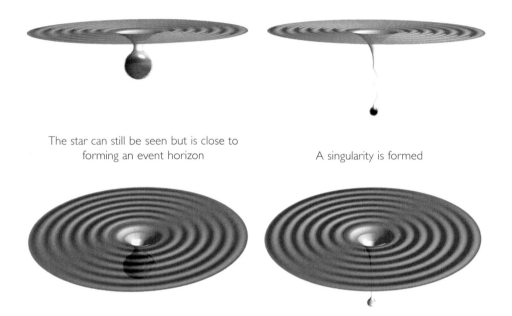

The star can still be seen but is close to forming an event horizon

A singularity is formed

tional collapse occur only in places, like black holes, where they are decently hidden from outside view by an event horizon. Strictly, this is what is known as the weak cosmic censorship hypothesis: it protects observers who remain outside the black hole from the consequences of the breakdown of predictability that occurs at the singularity, but it does nothing at all for the poor unfortunate astronaut who falls into the hole.

There are some solutions of the equations of general relativity in which it is possible for our astronaut to see a naked singularity: he may be able to avoid hitting the singularity and instead fall through a "wormhole" and come out in another region of the universe. This would offer great possibilities for travel in space and time, but unfortunately it seems that these solutions may all be highly unstable; the least disturbance, such as the presence of an astronaut, may change them so that the astronaut could not see the singularity until he hit it and his time came to an end. In other words, the singularity would always lie in his future and never in his past. The strong version of the cosmic censorship hypothesis states that in a realistic solution, the singularities would always lie either entirely in the future (like the singularities of gravitational collapse) or entirely in the past (like the big bang). I strongly believe in cosmic censorship so I bet

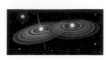

Fig. 6.7 *Powerful gravitational waves can be generated by two stars or even two black holes orbiting each other as above. Observations in the region of PSR 1913 + 16 clearly show two neutron stars spiraling in towards each other because they are losing energy by emitting gravitational waves.*

Kip Thorne and John Preskill of Cal Tech that it would always hold. I lost the bet on a technicality because examples were produced of solutions with a singularity that was visible from a long way away. So I had to pay up, which according to the terms of the bet meant I had to clothe their nakedness. But I can claim a moral victory. The naked singularities were unstable:

the least disturbance would cause them either to disappear or to be hidden behind an event horizon. So they would not occur in realistic situations.

The event horizon, the boundary of the region of space-time from which it is not possible to escape, acts rather like a one-way membrane around the black hole: objects, such as unwary astronauts, can fall through the event horizon into the black hole, but nothing can ever get out of the black hole through the event horizon. (Remember that the event horizon is the path in space-time of light that is trying to escape from the black hole, and nothing can

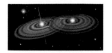

travel faster than light.) One could well say of the event horizon what the poet Dante said of the entrance to Hell: "All hope abandon, ye who enter here." Anything or anyone who falls through the event horizon will soon reach the region of infinite density and the end of time.

General relativity predicts that heavy objects that are moving will cause the emission of gravitational waves, ripples in the curvature of space that travel at the speed of light. These are similar to light waves, which are ripples of the electromagnetic field, but they are much harder to detect. They can be observed by the very slight change in separation they produce between neighboring freely moving objects. A number of detectors are being built in the U.S., Europe, and Japan that will measure displacements of one part in a thousand million million million (1 with twenty-one zeros after it), or less than the nucleus of an atom over a distance of ten miles.

Like light, gravitational waves carry energy away from the objects that emit them. One would therefore expect a system of massive objects to settle down eventually to a stationary state, because the energy in any movement would be carried away by the emission of gravitational waves. (It is rather like dropping a cork into water: at first it bobs up and down a great deal, but as the ripples carry away its energy, it

eventually settles down to a stationary state.) For example, the movement of the earth in its orbit round the sun produces gravitational waves. The effect of the energy loss will be to change the orbit of the earth so that gradually it gets nearer and nearer to the sun, eventually collides with it, and settles down to a stationary state. The rate of energy loss in the case of the earth and the sun is very low — about enough to run a small electric heater. This means it will take about a thousand million million million million years for the earth to run into the sun, so there's no immediate cause for worry! The change in the orbit of the earth is too slow to be observed, but this same effect has been observed over the past few years occurring in the system called PSR 1913 + 16 (*PSR* stands for "pulsar," a special type of neutron star that emits regular pulses of radio waves). This system contains two neutron stars orbiting each other (Fig. 6.7), and the energy they are losing by the emission of gravitational waves is causing them to spiral in toward each other. This confirmation of general relativity won J. H. Taylor and R. A. Hulse the Nobel prize in 1993. It will take about three-hundred million years for them to collide. Just before they do, they will be orbiting so fast that they will emit enough gravitational waves for detectors like LIGO to pick up.

Fig. 6.8 *A rotating "Kerr" black hole bulges around its equator as its rate of rotation increases. A rotation of zero produces a perfectly round spheroid.*

During the gravitational collapse of a star to form a black hole, the movements would be much more rapid, so the rate at which energy is carried away would be much higher. It would therefore not be too long before it settled down to a stationary state. What would this final stage look like? One might suppose that it would depend on all the complex features of the star from which it had formed — not only its mass and rate of rotation, but also the different densities of various parts of the star, and the complicated movements of the gases within the star. And if black holes were as varied as the objects that collapsed to form them, it might be very difficult to make any predictions about black holes in general.

In 1967, however, the study of black holes was revolutionized by Werner Israel, a Canadian scientist (who was born in Berlin, brought up in South Africa, and took his doctoral degree in Ireland). Israel showed that, according to general relativity, non-rotating black holes must be very simple; they were perfectly spherical, their size depended only on their mass, and any two such black holes with the same mass were identical. They could, in fact, be described by a particular solution of Einstein's equations that had been known since 1917, found by Karl Schwarzschild shortly after the discovery of general relativity. At first many people, including Israel himself, argued that since black holes had to be perfectly spherical, a black hole could only form from the collapse of a perfectly spherical object. Any real star — which would never be perfectly spherical — could therefore only collapse to form a naked singularity.

There was, however, a different interpretation of Israel's result, which was advocated by Roger Penrose and John Wheeler in particular. They argued that the rapid movements involved in a star's collapse would mean that the gravitational waves it gave off would make it ever more spherical, and by the time it had settled down to a stationary state, it would be precisely spherical.

Spheroidal body   Cuboid body   Conical body   Body with mountain

Fig. 6.9

The final state of the black hole depends on its mass and rate of rotation. A large amount of information about the body that collapses gets lost.

A black hole has no hair

According to this view, any non-rotating star, however complicated its shape and internal structure, would end up after gravitational collapse as a perfectly spherical black hole, whose size would depend only on its mass. Further calculations supported this view, and it soon came to be adopted generally.

Israel's result dealt with the case of black holes formed from non-rotating bodies only. In 1963, Roy Kerr, a New Zealander, found a set of solutions of the equations of general relativity that described rotating black holes. These "Kerr" black holes rotate at a constant rate, their size and shape depending only on their mass and rate of rotation. If the rotation is zero, the black hole is perfectly round and the solution is identical to the Schwarzschild solution. If the rotation is non-zero, the black hole bulges outward near its equator (just as the earth or the sun bulge due to their rotation), and the faster it rotates, the more it bulges (Fig. 6.8). So, to extend Israel's result to include rotating bodies, it was conjectured that any rotating body that collapsed to form a black hole would eventually settle down to a stationary state described by the Kerr solution.

In 1970 a colleague and fellow research student of mine at Cambridge, Brandon Carter, took the first step toward proving this conjecture. He showed that, provided a stationary rotating black hole had an axis of symmetry, like a spinning top, its size and shape would depend only on its mass and rate of rotation. Then, in 1971, I proved that any stationary rotating black hole would indeed have such an axis of symmetry. Finally, in 1973, David Robinson at Kings College, London, used Carter's and my results to show that the conjecture had been correct: such a black hole had indeed to be the Kerr solution. So after gravitational collapse a black hole must settle down into a state in which it could be rotating, but not pulsating. Moreover, its size and shape would depend only on its mass and rate of rotation, and not on the nature of the body that had collapsed to form it. This result became known by the maxim: "A black hole has no hair." The "no hair" theorem is of great practical importance, because it so greatly restricts the possible types of black holes. One can therefore make detailed models of objects that might contain black holes and compare the predictions of the models with observations. It also means that a very large amount of information about the body that has collapsed must be lost when a black hole is formed, because afterward all we can possibly measure about the body is its mass and rate of rotation (Fig. 6.9). The significance of this will be seen in the next chapter.

Black holes are one of only a fairly small number of cases in the history of science in which a theory was developed in great detail as a mathematical model before there was any evidence from observations that it was correct. Indeed, this used to be the main argument of opponents of black holes: how could one believe in objects for which the only evidence was calculations based on the dubious theory of general relativity? In 1963, however, Maarten Schmidt, an astronomer at the Palomar Observatory in California, measured the red

shift of a faint starlike object in the direction of the source of radio waves called 3C273 (that is, source number 273 in the third Cambridge catalogue of radio sources). He found it was too large to be caused by a gravitational field: if it had been a gravitational red shift, the object would have to be so massive and so near to us that it would disturb the orbits of planets in the Solar System. This suggested that the red shift was instead caused by the expansion of the universe, which, in turn, meant that the object was a very long distance away. And to be visible at such a great distance, the object must be very bright, must, in other words, be emitting a huge amount of energy. The only mechanism that people could think of that would produce such large quantities of energy seemed to be the gravitational collapse not just of a star but of a whole central region of a galaxy. A number of other similar "quasi-stellar objects," or quasars, have been discovered, all with large red shifts. But they are all too far away and therefore too difficult to observe to provide conclusive evidence of black holes.

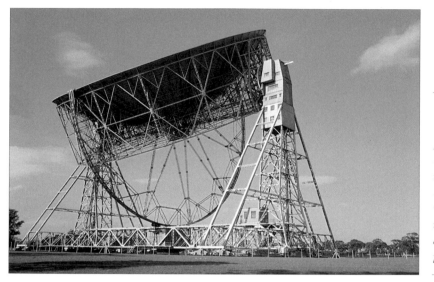

Left: *Radio telescope at Jodrell Bank, U.K. Pulsars, being powerful sources of radio waves, are identified by the antennae of such massive telescopes more easily than by visual searches.*
Opposite: *Jocelyn Bell-Burnell, a member of Antony Hewish's team at Cambridge, discovered the first pulsar in 1967.*

Further encouragement for the existence of black holes came in 1967 with the discovery by a research student at Cambridge, Jocelyn Bell-Burnell, of objects in the sky that were emitting regular pulses of radio waves. At first Bell and her supervisor, Antony Hewish, thought they might have made contact with an alien civilization in the galaxy! Indeed, at the seminar at which they announced their discovery, I remember that they called the first four sources to be found *LGM* 1–4, *LGM* standing for "Little Green Men." In the end, however, they and everyone else came to the less romantic conclusion that these objects, which were given the name pulsars, were in fact rotating neutron stars that were emitting pulses of radio waves because of a complicated interaction between their magnetic fields and surrounding matter. This was bad news for writers of space westerns, but very hopeful for the small number of us who believed in black holes at that time: it was the first positive evidence that neutron stars existed. A neutron star has a radius of about ten miles, only a few times the critical radius at which a star becomes a black hole. If a star could collapse to such a small size, it is not unreasonable to expect that other stars could collapse to even smaller size and become black holes.

How could we hope to detect a black hole, as by its very definition it does not emit any light? It might seem a bit like looking for a black cat in a coal cellar. Fortunately, there is a way. As

Fig. 6.10 *The intense gravitational field of an orbiting black hole rips matter from the companion star, creating an accretion disc which spirals in towards the event horizon. The incredible energies released, in the form of X rays, are one of the signatures of a black hole.*

Fig. 6.11 *The brighter of the two stars near the center of the photograph is Cygnus X-1, which is thought to consist of a black hole and a normal star, orbiting around each other as depicted in Fig. 6.10.*

Fig. 6.12

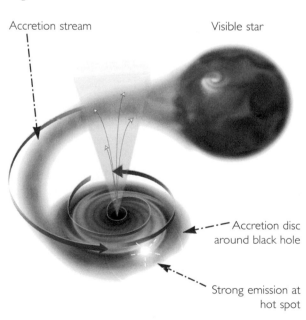

Accretion stream

Visible star

Accretion disc around black hole

Strong emission at hot spot

John Michell pointed out in his pioneering paper in 1783, a black hole still exerts a gravitational force on nearby objects. Astronomers have observed many systems in which two stars orbit around each other, attracted toward each other by gravity. They also observe systems in which there is only one visible star that is orbiting around some unseen companion. One cannot, of course, immediately conclude that the companion is a black hole: it might merely be a star that is too faint to be seen. However, some of these systems, like the one called Cygnus X-1 (Fig. 6.11), are also strong sources of X rays. The best explanation for this phenomenon is that matter has been blown off the surface of the visible star. As it falls toward the unseen companion, it develops a spiral motion (rather like water running out of a bath), and it gets very hot, emitting X rays (Fig 6.12). For this mechanism to work, the unseen object has to be very small, like a white dwarf, neutron star, or black hole. From the observed orbit of the visible star, one can determine the lowest possible mass of the unseen object. In the case of Cygnus X-1, this is about six times the mass of the sun, which, according to Chandrasekhar's result, is too great for the unseen object to be a white dwarf. It is also too large a mass to be a neutron star. It seems, therefore, that it must be a black hole.

There are other models to explain Cygnus X-1 that do not include a black hole, but they are all rather far-fetched. A black hole seems to be the only really natural explanation of the observations. Despite this, I had a bet with Kip Thorne of the California Institute of Technology that in fact Cygnus X-1 does not contain a black hole! This was a form of insurance policy for me. I have done a lot of work on black holes, and it would all be wasted if it turned out that black holes do not exist. But in that case, I would have the consolation of winning my bet, which would bring me four years of the magazine *Private Eye*. In fact, although the situation with Cygnus X-1 has not changed much since we made the bet in 1975, there is now so much other observational evidence in favor of black holes that I have conceded the bet. I paid the specified penalty, which was a one-year subscription to *Penthouse*, to the outrage of Kip's liberated wife.

We also now have evidence for several other black holes in systems like Cygnus X-1 in our galaxy and in two neighboring galaxies called the Magellanic Clouds. The number of black holes, however, is almost certainly very much higher; in the long history of the universe, many stars must have burned all their nuclear fuel and have had to collapse. The number of black holes may well be greater even than the number of visible stars, which totals about a hundred thousand million in our galaxy alone. The extra gravitational attraction of such a large number of black holes could explain why our galaxy rotates at the rate it does: the mass of the visible stars is insufficient to account for this. We also have some evidence that there is a much larger black hole, with a mass of about a hundred thousand times that of the sun, at the center of our galaxy. Stars in the galaxy that come too near this black hole will be torn apart by the difference in the gravitational forces on their near and far sides. Their remains, and gas that is thrown off other stars, will fall toward the black hole. As in the case of Cygnus X-1, the gas will spiral inward and will heat up, though not as much as in that case. It will not get hot enough to emit X rays, but it could account for the very compact source of radio waves and infrared rays that is observed at the galactic center.

Whereas Stephen Hawking has such a large investment in General Relativity and Black Holes and desires an insurance policy, and whereas Kip Thorne likes to live dangerously without an insurance policy,

Therefore be it resolved that Stephen Hawking bets 1 year's subscription to "Penthouse" as against Kip Thorne's wager of a 4-year subscription to "Private Eye", that Cygnus X 1 does not contain a black hole of mass above the Chandrasekhar limit.

Kip S. Thorne

Stephen Hawking

Witnessed this tenth day ? December 1974

Fig. 6.13 *The supermassive black hole at the center of a galaxy would rotate with the spiraling matter it attracts, creating a vast magnetic field. This focuses very high energy particles into jets along the black hole's axis of rotation.*

It is thought that similar but even larger black holes, with masses of about a hundred million times the mass of the sun, occur at the centers of quasars. For example, observations with the Hubble telescope of the galaxy known as M87 reveal that it contains a disk of gas 130 light-years across rotating about a central object two thousand million times the mass of the Sun.

This can only be a black hole. Matter falling into such a supermassive black hole would provide the only source of power great enough to explain the enormous amounts of energy that these objects are emitting. As the matter spirals into the black hole, it would make the black hole rotate in the same direction, causing it to develop a magnetic field rather like that of the earth. Very high energy particles would be generated near the black hole by the in-falling matter. The magnetic field would be so strong that it could focus these particles into jets ejected outward along the axis of rotation of the black

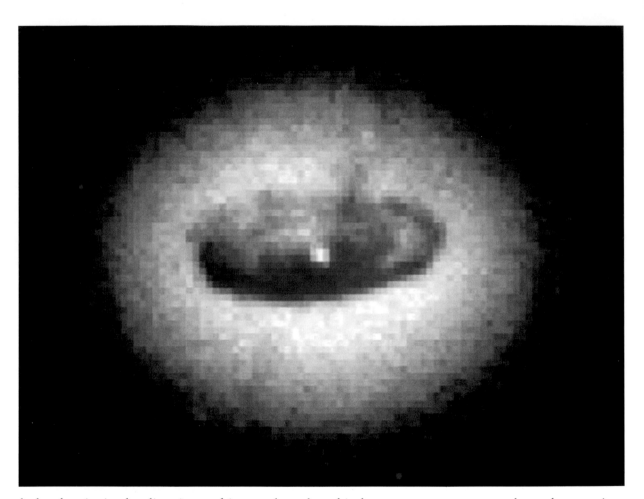

hole, that is, in the directions of its north and south poles. Such jets are indeed observed in a number of galaxies and quasars. One can also consider the possibility that there might be black holes with masses much less than that of the sun. Such black holes could not be formed by gravitational collapse, because their masses are below the Chandrasekhar mass limit: stars of this low mass can support themselves against the force of gravity even when they have exhausted their nuclear fuel. Low-mass black holes could form only if matter was compressed to enormous densities by very large external pressures. Such conditions could occur in a very big hydrogen bomb: the physicist John Wheeler once calculated that if one took all the heavy

water in all the oceans of the world, one could build a hydrogen bomb that would compress matter at the center so much that a black hole would be created. (Of course, there would be no one left to observe it!) A more practical possibility is that such low-mass black holes might have been formed in the high temperatures and pressures of the very early universe. Black holes would have been formed only if the early universe had not been perfectly smooth and uniform, because only a small region that was denser than average could be compressed in this way to form a black hole. But we know that there must have been some irregularities, because otherwise the matter in the universe would still be perfectly uniformly distributed at the present epoch, instead of being clumped together in stars and galaxies.

Whether the irregularities required to account for stars and galaxies would have led to the formation of a significant number of "primordial" black holes clearly depends on the details of the conditions in the early universe. So if we could determine how many primordial black holes there are now, we would learn a lot about the very early stages of the universe. Primordial black holes with masses more than a thousand million tons (the mass of a large mountain) could be detected only by their gravitational influence on other, visible matter or on

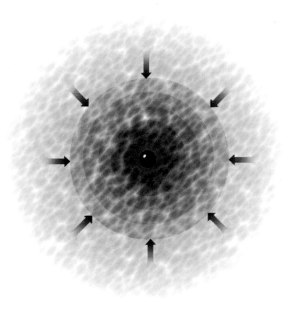

Fig 6.14 *A primordial black hole created by external, rather than internal, pressures.*
Opposite: *This Hubble Space Telescope picture of a galaxy called NGC 4261, in the Virgo cluster, appears to show a disc of dust and gas spiraling in to a massive black hole. Calculations based on the speed of the rotating gas suggest that the central object is 1.2 billion times the mass of the sun, yet is not much larger than our Solar System. The picture was taken in January 1996.*

the expansion of the universe. However, as we shall learn in the next chapter, black holes are not really black after all: they glow like a hot body, and the smaller they are, the more they glow. So, paradoxically, smaller black holes might actually turn out to be easier to detect than large ones!

127

7

Black Holes Ain't So Black

BEFORE 1970, MY RESEARCH ON GENERAL relativity had concentrated mainly on the question of whether or not there had been a big bang singularity. However, one evening in November that year, shortly after the birth of my daughter, Lucy, I started to think about black holes as I was getting into bed. My disability makes this rather a slow process, so I had plenty of time. At that date there was no precise definition of which points in space-time lay inside a black hole and which lay outside. I had already discussed with Roger Penrose the idea of defining a black hole as the set of events from which it was not possible to escape to a large distance, which is now the generally accepted definition. It means that the boundary of the black hole, the event horizon, is formed by the light rays that just fail to escape from the

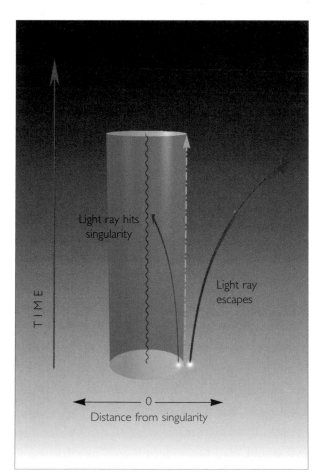

Fig. 7.1 *The event horizon, or boundary, of a black hole is formed by the light rays that just fail to escape from the black hole.*

black hole, hovering forever just on the edge (Fig. 7.1). It is a bit like running away from the police and just managing to keep one step ahead but not being able to get clear away!

Suddenly I realized that the paths of these light rays could never approach one another. If they did, they must eventually run into one another. It would be like meeting someone else running away from the police in the opposite direction — you would both be caught! (Or, in this case, fall into a black hole.) But if these light rays were swallowed up by the black hole, then they could not have been on the boundary of the black hole. So the paths of light rays in the event horizon had always to be moving parallel to, or away from, each other. Another way of seeing this is that the event horizon, the boundary of the black hole, is like the edge of a shadow — the shadow of impending doom. If you look at the shadow cast by a source at a great distance, such as the sun, you will see that the rays of light in the edge are not approaching each other.

If the rays of light that form the event horizon, the boundary of the black hole, can never approach each other, the area of the event horizon might stay the same or increase with time but it could never decrease because that would

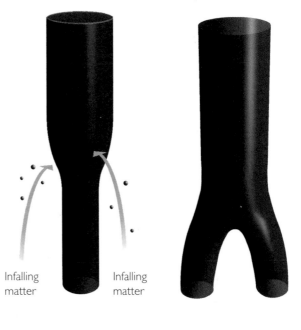

Infalling matter   Infalling matter

Fig. 7.2   Fig. 7.3

Figs. 7.2 and 7.3 *The area of the event horizon becomes larger as matter falls into a black hole. In Fig. 7.3 two black holes collide to create an event horizon greater than the sum of the areas of the originals.*

mean that at least some of the rays of light in the boundary would have to be approaching each other. In fact, the area would increase whenever matter or radiation fell into the black hole (Fig. 7.2). Or if two black holes collided and merged together to form a single black hole, the area of the event horizon of the final black hole would be greater than or equal to the sum of the areas

129

of the event horizons of the original black holes (Fig. 7.3). This nondecreasing property of the event horizon's area placed an important restriction on the possible behavior of black holes. I was so excited with my discovery that I did not get much sleep that night. The next day I rang up Roger Penrose. He agreed with me. I think, in fact, that he had been aware of this property of the area. However, he had been using a slightly different definition of a black hole. He had not realized that the boundaries of the black hole according to the two definitions would be the same, and hence so would their areas, provided the black hole had settled down to a state in which it was not changing with time.

The nondecreasing behavior of a black hole's area was very reminiscent of the behavior of a physical quantity called entropy, which measures the degree of disorder of a system. It is a matter of common experience that disorder will tend to increase if things are left to themselves. (One has only to stop making repairs around the house to see that!) One can create order out of disorder (for example, one can paint the house), but that requires expenditure of effort or energy and so decreases the amount of ordered energy available.

A precise statement of this idea is known as the second law of thermodynamics. It states that the entropy of an isolated system always increases, and that when two systems are joined together, the entropy of the combined system is greater than the sum of the entropies of the individual systems. For example, consider a system of gas molecules in a box. The molecules can be thought of as little billiard balls continually colliding with each other and bouncing off the walls of the box. The higher the temperature of the gas, the faster the molecules move, and so the more frequently and harder they collide with the walls of the box and the greater the outward

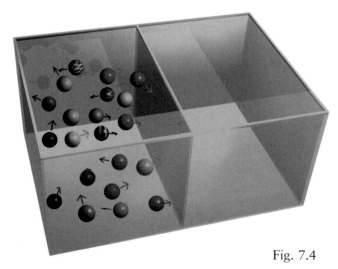

Fig. 7.4

Fig. 7.4 *A box full of gas molecules, all confined to the left-hand side of the box by a partition.*

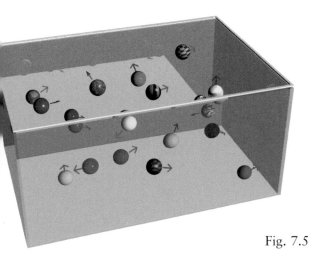

Fig. 7.5

pressure they exert on the walls. Suppose that initially the molecules are all confined to the left-hand side of the box by a partition (Fig. 7.4). If the partition is then removed, the molecules will tend to spread out and occupy both halves of the box (Fig. 7.5). At some later time they could, by chance, all be in the right half or back in the left half, but it is overwhelmingly more probable that there will be roughly equal numbers in the two halves. Such a state is less

Fig. 7.5 *With the wall removed, the molecules spread out to a less ordered state occupying the whole box.*
Fig. 7.6 *A box containing a gas falls into a black hole. The total entropy outside the black hole goes down as the box enters the black hole, though the total entropy in the universe (including the black hole) might well stay constant.*

ordered, or more disordered, than the original state in which all the molecules were in one half. One therefore says that the entropy of the gas has gone up. Similarly, suppose one starts with two boxes, one containing oxygen molecules and the other containing nitrogen molecules. If one joins the boxes together and removes the intervening wall, the oxygen and the nitrogen molecules will start to mix. At a later time the most probable state would be a fairly uniform mixture of oxygen and nitrogen molecules throughout the two boxes. This state would be less ordered, and hence have more entropy, than the initial state of two separate boxes.

The second law of thermodynamics has a rather different status than that of other laws of science, such as Newton's law of gravity, for example, because it does not hold always, just in the vast majority of cases. The probability of all the gas molecules in our first box being found in one half of

Fig. 7.6

the box at a later time is many millions of millions to one, but it can happen. However, if one has a black hole around, there seems to be a rather easier way of violating the second law: just throw some matter with a lot of entropy, such as a box of gas, down the black hole. The total entropy of matter outside the black hole would go down (see Fig. 7.6). One could, of course, still say that the total entropy, including the entropy inside the black hole, has not gone down — but since there is no way to look inside the black hole, we cannot see how much entropy the matter inside it has. It would be nice, then, if there was some feature of the black hole by which observers outside the black hole could tell its entropy, and which would increase whenever matter carrying entropy fell into the black hole. Following the discovery, described above, that the area of the event horizon increased whenever matter fell into a black hole, a research student at Princeton named Jacob Bekenstein suggested that the area of the event horizon was a measure of the entropy of the black hole. As matter carrying entropy fell into a black hole, the area of its event horizon would go up, so that the sum of the entropy of matter outside black holes and the area of the horizons would never go down.

This suggestion seemed to prevent the second

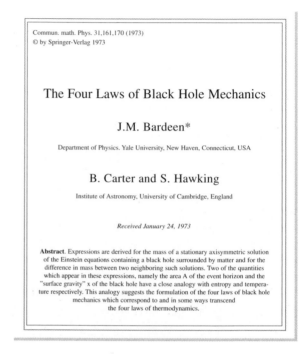

Commun. math. Phys. 31,161,170 (1973)
© by Springer-Verlag 1973

The Four Laws of Black Hole Mechanics

J.M. Bardeen*

Department of Physics. Yale University, New Haven, Connecticut, USA

B. Carter and S. Hawking

Institute of Astronomy, University of Cambridge, England

Received January 24, 1973

Abstract. Expressions are derived for the mass of a stationary axisymmetric solution of the Einstein equations containing a black hole surrounded by matter and for the difference in mass between two neighboring such solutions. Two of the quantities which appear in these expressions, namely the area A of the event horizon and the "surface gravity" x of the black hole have a close analogy with entropy and temperature respectively. This analogy suggests the formulation of the four laws of black hole mechanics which correspond to and in some ways transcend the four laws of thermodynamics.

The title page of "The Four Laws of Black Hole Mechanics," written in 1972.

law of thermodynamics from being violated in most situations. However, there was one fatal flaw. If a black hole has entropy, then it ought also to have a temperature. But a body with a particular temperature must emit radiation at a certain rate. It is a matter of common experience that if one heats up a poker in a fire it glows red hot and emits radiation, but bodies at lower temperatures emit radiation too; one just does not normally notice it because the amount is fairly small. This radiation is required in order to prevent violation of the second law. So black holes ought to emit radiation. But by their very definition, black holes are objects that are not supposed to emit anything. It therefore seemed that the area of the event horizon of a black hole could not be regarded as its entropy. In 1972 I wrote a paper with Brandon Carter and an American colleague, Jim Bardeen, in which we pointed out that although there were many similarities between entropy and the area of the event horizon, there was this apparently fatal difficulty. I must admit that in writing this paper I was motivated partly by irritation with Bekenstein, who, I felt, had misused my discovery of the increase of the area of the event horizon. However, it turned out in the end that he was basically correct, though in a manner he had certainly not expected.

In September 1973, while I was visiting Moscow, I discussed black holes with two leading Soviet experts, Yakov Zeldovich and Alexander Starobinsky. They convinced me that, according to the quantum mechanical uncertainty principle, rotating black holes should create and emit particles. I believed their arguments on physical grounds, but I did not like the mathematical way in which they calculated the emission. I therefore set about devising a better

mathematical treatment, which I described at an informal seminar in Oxford at the end of November 1973. At that time I had not done the calculations to find out how much would actually be emitted. I was expecting to discover just the radiation that Zeldovich and Starobinsky had predicted from rotating black holes. However, when I did the calculation, I found, to my surprise and annoyance, that even nonrotating black holes should apparently create and emit particles at a steady rate. At first I thought that this emission indicated that one of the approximations I had used was not valid. I was afraid that if Bekenstein found out about it, he would use it as a further argument to support his ideas about the entropy of black holes, which I still did not like. However, the more I thought about it, the more it seemed that the approximations really ought to hold. But what finally convinced me that the emission was real was that the spectrum of the emitted particles was exactly that which would be emitted by a hot body, and that the black hole was emitting particles at exactly the correct rate to prevent violations of the second law. Since then the calculations have been repeated in a number of different forms by other people. They all confirm that a black hole ought to emit particles and radiation as if it were a hot body with a temper-

ature that depends only on the black hole's mass: the higher the mass, the lower the temperature.

How is it possible that a black hole appears to emit particles when we know that nothing can escape from within its event horizon? The answer, quantum theory tells us, is that the particles do not come from within the black hole, but from the "empty" space just outside the black hole's event horizon! We can understand this in the following way: what we think of as "empty" space cannot be completely empty because that would mean that all the fields, such as the gravitational and electromagnetic fields, would have to be exactly zero. However, the value of a field and its rate of change with time are like the position and velocity of a particle: the uncertainty principle implies that the more accurately one knows one of these quantities, the less accurately one can know the other. So in empty space the field cannot be fixed at exactly zero, because then it would have both a precise value (zero) and a precise rate of change (also zero). There must be a certain minimum amount of uncertainty, or quantum fluctuations, in the value of the field. One can think of these fluctuations as pairs of particles of light or gravity that appear together at some time, move apart,

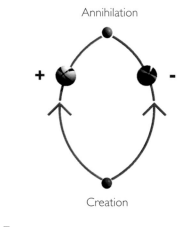

Annihilation

Creation

Fig. 7.7

Fig. 7.7 *"Empty" space is filled with pairs of virtual particles and antiparticles. They are created together, move apart, and come back together and annihilate.*

Fig. 7.8 *If a black hole is present, one member of a virtual pair may fall in and become a real particle. The other can escape from the vicinity of the black hole.*

---

and then come together again and annihilate each other (Fig. 7.7). These particles are virtual particles like the particles that carry the gravitational force of the sun: unlike real particles, they cannot be observed directly with a particle detector. However, their indirect effects, such as small changes in the energy of electron orbits in atoms, can be measured and agree with the theoretical predictions to a remarkable degree of accuracy. The uncertainty principle also predicts that there will be similar virtual pairs of matter

Fig. 7.8

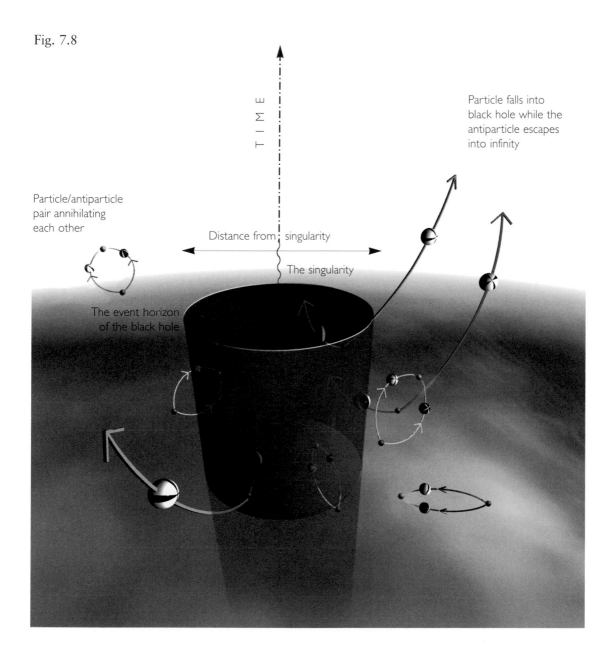

Particle falls into
black hole while the
antiparticle escapes
into infinity

TIME

Distance from singularity

The singularity

Particle/antiparticle
pair annihilating
each other

The event horizon
of the black hole

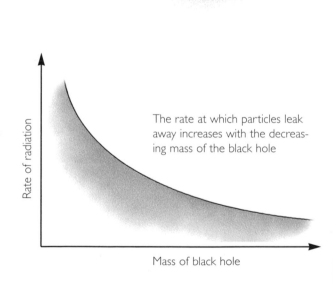

Fig. 7.9

particles, such as electrons or quarks. In this case, however, one member of the pair will be a particle and the other an antiparticle (the antiparticles of light and gravity are the same as the particles).

Because energy cannot be created out of nothing, one of the partners in a particle/anti-particle pair will have positive energy, and the other partner negative energy. The one with negative energy is condemned to be a short-lived virtual particle because real particles always have positive energy in normal situations. It must therefore seek out its partner and annihilate with it. However, a real particle close to a massive body has less energy than if it were far away, because it would take energy to lift it far away against the gravitational attraction of the

The rate at which particles leak away increases with the decreasing mass of the black hole

Rate of radiation

Mass of black hole

Fig. 7.9 *Black holes emit radiation and so lose energy and mass at a rate that increases the smaller the black hole becomes. It is thought that eventually the black hole will disappear completely in a tremendous explosion.*

body. Normally, the energy of the particle is still positive, but the gravitational field inside a black hole is so strong that even a real particle can have negative energy there. It is therefore possible, if a black hole is present, for the virtual particle with negative energy to fall into the black hole and become a real particle or antiparticle. In this case it no longer has to annihilate with its partner. Its forsaken partner may fall into the black hole as well. Or, having positive energy, it might also escape from the vicinity of the black hole as a real particle or antiparticle (Fig. 7.8). To an observer at a distance, it will appear to have been emitted from the black hole. The smaller the black hole, the shorter the distance the particle with negative energy will have to go before it becomes a real particle, and thus the greater the rate of emission, and the apparent temperature, of the black hole.

The positive energy of the outgoing radiation would be balanced by a flow of negative energy particles into the black hole. By Einstein's equation $E = mc^2$ (where E is energy, m is mass, and c is the speed of light), energy is proportional to mass. A flow of negative energy into the black hole therefore reduces its mass. As the black hole loses mass, the area of its event horizon gets smaller, but this decrease in the entropy of the black hole is more than compensated for by the entropy of the emitted radiation, so the second law is never violated.

Moreover, the lower the mass of the black hole, the higher its temperature. So as the black hole loses mass, its temperature and rate of emission increase, so it loses mass more quickly (Fig. 7.9). What happens when the mass of the black hole eventually becomes extremely small is not quite clear, but the most reasonable guess is that it would disappear completely in a tremendous final burst of emission, equivalent to the explosion of millions of H-bombs.

A black hole with a mass a few times that of the sun would have a temperature of only one ten millionth of a degree above absolute zero. This is much less than the temperature of the microwave radiation that fills the universe (about 2.7° above absolute zero), so such black holes would emit even less than they absorb. If the universe is destined to go on expanding forever, the temperature of the microwave radiation will eventually decrease to less than that of such a black hole, which will then begin to lose mass. But, even then, its temperature would be so low that it would take about a million million million million million million million million million years (1 with sixty-six

137

Fig. 7.10

zeros after it) to evaporate completely. This is much longer than the age of the universe, which is only about ten or twenty thousand million years (1 or 2 with ten zeros after it). On the other hand, as mentioned in Chapter 6, there might be primordial black holes with a very much smaller mass that were made by the collapse of irregularities in the very early stages of the universe. Such black holes would have a much higher temperature and would be emitting radiation at a much greater rate. A primordial black hole with an initial mass of a thousand million tons would have a lifetime roughly equal to the age of the universe. Primordial black holes with initial masses less than this figure would already have completely evaporated, but

those with slightly greater masses would still be emitting radiation in the form of X rays and gamma rays. These X rays and gamma rays are like waves of light, but with a much shorter wavelength. Such holes hardly deserve the epithet black: they really are white hot and are emitting energy at a rate of about ten thousand megawatts.

One such black hole could run ten large power stations, if only we could harness its power. This would be rather difficult, however: the black hole would have the mass of a mountain compressed into less than a million millionth of an inch, the size of the nucleus of an atom! If you had one of these black holes on the surface of the earth, there would be no way to stop it from falling through the floor to the center of the earth. It would oscillate through the earth and back, until eventually it settled down at the center. So the only place to put such a black hole, in which one might use the energy that it emitted, would be in orbit around the earth — and the only way that one could get it to orbit the earth would be to attract it there by towing a large mass in front of it, rather like a carrot in front of a donkey (Fig. 7.10). This does not sound like a very practical proposition, at least not in the immediate future.

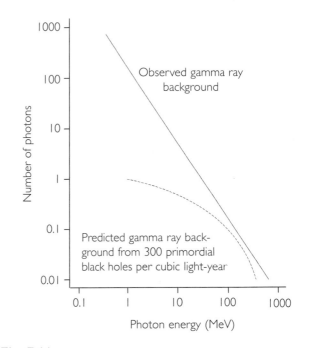

Fig. 7.11

But even if we cannot harness the emission from these primordial black holes, what are our chances of observing them? We could look for the gamma rays that the primordial black holes emit during most of their lifetime. Although the radiation from most would be very weak because they are far away, the total from all of them might be detectable. We do observe such a background of gamma rays: Fig. 7.11 shows how the observed intensity differs at different frequencies (the number of waves per second).

However, this background could have been, and probably was, generated by processes other than primordial black holes. The dotted line in Fig. 7.11 shows how the intensity should vary with frequency for gamma rays given off by primordial black holes, if there were on average 300 per cubic light-year. One can therefore say that the observations of the gamma ray background do not provide any positive evidence for primordial black holes, but they do tell us that on average there cannot be more than 300 in every cubic light-year in the universe. This limit means that primordial black holes could make up at most one millionth of the matter in the universe.

With primordial black holes being so scarce, it might seem unlikely that there would be one near enough for us to observe as an individual source of gamma rays. But since gravity would draw primordial black holes toward any matter, they should be much more common in and around galaxies. So although the gamma ray background tells us that there can be no more than 300 primordial black holes per cubic light-year on average, it tells us nothing about how common they might be in our own galaxy. If they were, say, a million times more common than this, then the nearest black hole to us would probably be at a distance of about a thousand million kilometers, or about as far away as Pluto, the farthest known planet. At this distance it would still be very difficult to detect the steady emission of a black hole, even if it was ten thousand megawatts. In order to observe a primordial black hole one would have to detect several gamma ray quanta coming from the same direction within a reasonable space of time, such as a week. Otherwise, they might simply be part of the background. But Planck's quantum principle tells us that each gamma ray quantum has a very high energy, because gamma rays have a very high frequency, so it would not take many quanta to radiate even ten thousand megawatts. And to observe these few coming from the distance of Pluto would require a larger gamma ray detector than any that have been constructed so far. Moreover, the detector would have to be in space, because gamma rays cannot penetrate the atmosphere.

Of course, if a black hole as close as Pluto were to reach the end of its life and blow up it would be easy to detect the final burst of emission. But if the black hole has been emitting for the last ten or twenty thousand million years, the chance of it reaching the end of its life within the next few years, rather than several million years in the past or future, is really rather small!

Professor Stephen Hawking at Cambridge, when he was writing the first edition of "A Brief History of Time."

So in order to have a reasonable chance of seeing an explosion before your research grant ran out, you would have to find a way to detect any explosions within a distance of about one light-year. In fact bursts of gamma rays from space have been detected by satellites originally constructed to look for violations of the Test Ban Treaty. These seem to occur about sixteen times a month and to be roughly uniformly distributed in direction across the sky. This indicates that they come from outside the solar system since otherwise we would expect them to be concentrated towards the plane of the orbits of the planets. The uniform distribution also indicates that the sources are either fairly near to us in our galaxy or right outside it at cosmological distances because otherwise, again, they would be concentrated towards the plane of the galaxy. In the latter case, the energy required to account for the bursts would be far too high to have been produced by tiny black holes, but if the sources were close in galactic terms, it might be possible that they were exploding black holes. I would very much like this to be the case but I have to recognize that there are other possible explanations for the gamma ray bursts, such as colliding neutron stars. New observations in the next few years, particularly by gravitational wave detectors like LIGO, should enable us to discover the origin of the gamma ray bursts.

Even if the search for primordial black holes proves negative, as it seems it may, it will still give us important information about the very early stages of the universe. If the early universe

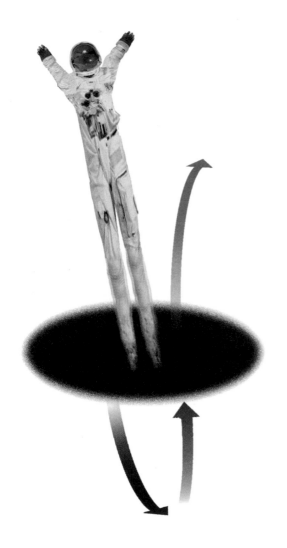

Fig. 7.12

An astronaut falling into a black hole will eventually be recycled in the form of particles and radiation emitted as the black hole evaporates

had been chaotic or irregular, or if the pressure of matter had been low, one would have expected it to produce many more primordial black holes than the limit already set by our observations of the gamma ray background. Only if the early universe was very smooth and uniform, with a high pressure, can one explain the absence of observable numbers of primordial black holes.

The idea of radiation from black holes was the first example of a prediction that depended in an essential way on both the great theories of this century, general relativity and quantum mechanics. It aroused a lot of opposition initially because it upset the existing viewpoint: "How can a black hole emit anything?" When I first announced the results of my calculations at a conference at the Rutherford-Appleton Laboratory near Oxford, I was greeted with general incredulity. At the end of my talk the chairman of the session, John G. Taylor from Kings College, London, claimed it was all nonsense. He even wrote a paper to that effect.

However, in the end most people, including John Taylor, have come to the conclusion that black holes must radiate like hot bodies if our other ideas about general relativity and quantum mechanics are correct. Thus, even though we have not yet managed to find a primordial black hole, there is fairly general agreement that if we did, it would have to be emitting a lot of gamma rays and X rays.

The existence of radiation from black holes seems to imply that gravitational collapse is not as final and irreversible as we once thought. If an astronaut falls into a black hole, its mass will increase, but eventually the energy equivalent of that extra mass will be returned to the universe in the form of radiation (Fig. 7.12). Thus, in a sense, the astronaut will be "recycled." It would be a poor sort of immortality, however, because any personal concept of time for the astronaut would almost certainly come to an end as he was torn apart inside the black hole! Even the types of particles that were eventually emitted by the black hole would in general be different from those that made up the astronaut: the only feature of the astronaut that would survive would be his mass or energy.

The approximations I used to derive the emission from black holes should work well when the black hole has a mass greater than a fraction of a gram. However, they will break down at the end of the black hole's life when its mass gets very small. The most likely outcome seems to be that the black hole will just disappear, at least from our region of the universe, taking with it the astronaut and any singularity there might be inside it, if indeed there is one. This was the first indication that quantum mechanics might remove the singularities that were predicted by general relativity. However, the methods that I and other people were using in 1974 were not able to answer questions such as whether singularities would occur in quantum gravity. From 1975 onward I therefore started to develop a more powerful approach to quantum gravity based on Richard Feynman's idea of a sum over histories. The answers that this approach suggests for the origin and fate of the universe and its contents, such as astronauts, will be described in the next two chapters. We shall see that although the uncertainty principle places limitations on the accuracy of all our predictions, it may at the same time remove the fundamental unpredictability that occurs at a space-time singularity.

8

The Origin and Fate of the Universe

EINSTEIN'S GENERAL THEORY of relativity, on its own, predicted that space-time began at the big bang singularity and would come to an end either at the big crunch singularity (if the whole universe recollapsed), or at a singularity inside a black hole (if a local region, such as a star, were to collapse). Any matter that fell into the hole would be destroyed at the singularity, and only the gravitational effect of its mass would continue to be felt outside. On the other hand, when quantum effects were taken into account, it seemed that the mass or energy of the matter would eventually be returned to the rest of the universe, and that the black hole, along with any singularity inside it, would evaporate away and finally disappear. Could quantum mechanics have an equally dramatic effect on the big bang and big crunch singularities? What really happens during the very early or late stages of the universe, when gravitational fields are so strong that quantum effects

cannot be ignored? Does the universe in fact have a beginning or an end? And if so, what are they like?

Throughout the 1970s I had been mainly studying black holes, but in 1981 my interest in

The author meeting with Pope Paul in 1981.

questions about the origin and fate of the universe was reawakened when I attended a conference on cosmology organized by the Jesuits in the Vatican. The Catholic Church had made a bad mistake with Galileo when it tried to lay down the law on a question of science, declaring that the sun went round the earth. Now, centuries later, it had decided to invite a number of experts to advise it on cosmology. At the end of the conference the participants were granted an audience with the Pope. He told us that it was all right to study the evolution of the universe after the big bang, but we should not inquire into the big bang itself because that was the moment of Creation and therefore the work of God. I was glad then that he did not know the subject of the talk I had just given at the conference — the possibility that space-time was finite but had no boundary, which means that it had no beginning, no moment of Creation. I had no desire to share the fate of Galileo, with whom I feel a strong sense of identity, partly because of the coincidence of having been born exactly 300 years after his death!

In order to explain the ideas that I and other people have had about how quantum mechanics may affect the origin and fate of the universe, it

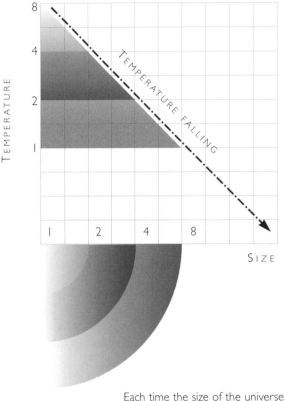

Fig. 8.1   Each time the size of the universe doubles, its temperature falls by half

is necessary first to understand the generally accepted history of the universe, according to what is known as the "hot big bang model." (See Fig. 8.2 on page 148.) This assumes that the universe is described by a Friedmann model, right back to the big bang. In such models one

Nuclear bomb test at Bikini Atoll, 1954. At the heart of an atom bomb explosion, man can create temperatures of some ten thousand million degrees. This is comparable to the temperature of the universe one second after the big bang.

finds that as the universe expands, any matter or radiation in it gets cooler. (When the universe doubles in size, its temperature falls by half. See Fig. 8.1.) Since temperature is simply a measure of the average energy — or speed — of the particles, this cooling of the universe would have a major effect on the matter in it. At very high temperatures, particles would be moving around so fast that they could escape any attraction toward each other due to nuclear or electromagnetic forces, but as they cooled off one would expect particles that attract each other to start to clump together. Moreover, even the types of particles that exist in the universe would depend on the temperature. At high enough temperatures, particles have so much energy that whenever they collide many different particle/antiparticle pairs would be produced — and although some of these particles would annihilate on hitting antiparticles, they would be produced more rapidly than they could annihilate. At lower temperatures, however, when colliding particles have less energy, particle/antiparticle pairs would be produced less quickly — and annihilation would become faster than production.

At the big bang itself the universe is thought to have had zero size, and so to have been infinitely hot. But as the universe expanded, the temperature of the radiation decreased. One second after the big bang, it would have fallen to about ten thousand million degrees. This is about a thousand times the temperature at the center of the sun, but temperatures as high as this are reached in H-bomb explosions. At this time the universe would have contained mostly photons, electrons, and neutrinos (extremely light particles that are affected only by the weak force and gravity) and their antiparticles, together with some protons and neutrons. As the universe continued to expand and the temperature to drop, the rate at which electron/antielectron pairs were being produced in collisions would have fallen below the rate at which they were being destroyed by annihilation. So most of the electrons and antielectrons would have

George Gamow emerges in this collage as the genie of a bottle of "Ylem," the hypothetical primordial material of the big bang. It was Gamow and Ralph Alpher, who also appears in this picture, who first proposed that the universe had a very hot early stage.

annihilated with each other to produce more photons, leaving only a few electrons left over. The neutrinos and antineutrinos, however, would not have annihilated with each other, because these particles interact with themselves and with other particles only very weakly. So they should still be around today. If we could observe them, it would provide a good test of this picture of a very hot early stage of the universe. Unfortunately, their energies nowadays would be too low for us to observe them direct-

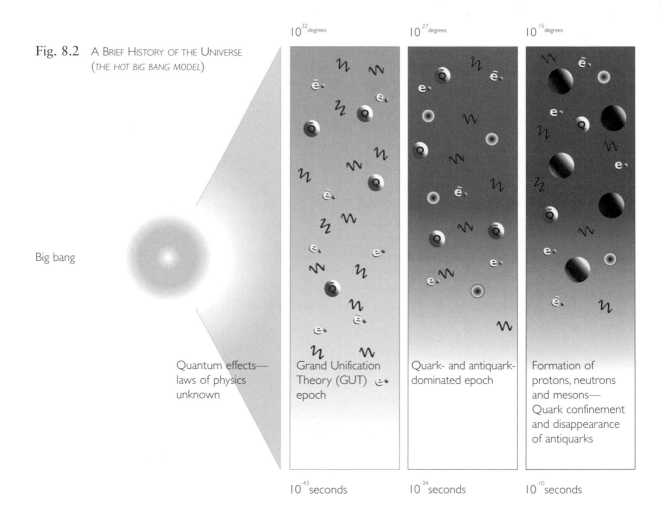

Fig. 8.2   A Brief History of the Universe
(*THE HOT BIG BANG MODEL*)

10^{32} degrees 10^{27} degrees 10^{15} degrees

Big bang

Quantum effects—
laws of physics
unknown

Grand Unification
Theory (GUT)
epoch

Quark- and antiquark-
dominated epoch

Formation of
protons, neutrons
and mesons—
Quark confinement
and disappearance
of antiquarks

10^{-43} seconds 10^{-34} seconds 10^{-10} seconds

ly. However, if neutrinos are not massless, but have a small mass of their own, as suggested by some recent experiments, we might be able to detect them indirectly: they could be a form of "dark matter," like that mentioned earlier, with sufficient gravitational attraction to stop the expansion of the universe and cause it to collapse again.

About one hundred seconds after the big bang, the temperature would have fallen to one thousand million degrees, the temperature inside the hottest stars. At this temperature protons

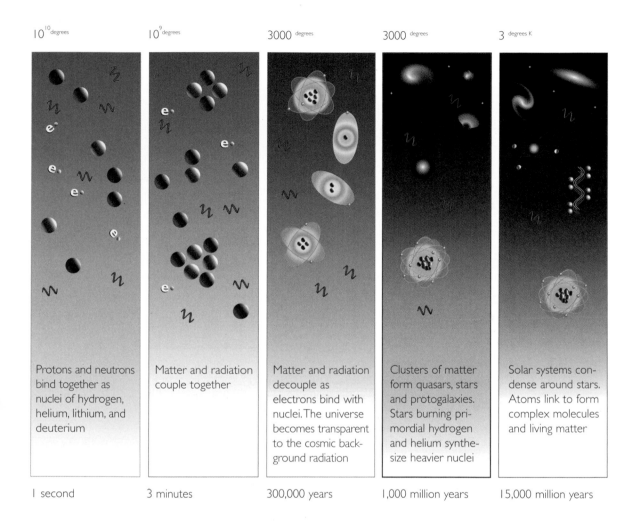

10^{10} degrees	10^9 degrees	3000 degrees	3000 degrees	3 degrees K
Protons and neutrons bind together as nuclei of hydrogen, helium, lithium, and deuterium	Matter and radiation couple together	Matter and radiation decouple as electrons bind with nuclei. The universe becomes transparent to the cosmic background radiation	Clusters of matter form quasars, stars and protogalaxies. Stars burning primordial hydrogen and helium synthesize heavier nuclei	Solar systems condense around stars. Atoms link to form complex molecules and living matter
1 second	3 minutes	300,000 years	1,000 million years	15,000 million years

and neutrons would no longer have sufficient energy to escape the attraction of the strong nuclear force, and would have started to combine together to produce the nuclei of atoms of deuterium (heavy hydrogen), which contain one proton and one neutron. The deuterium nuclei would then have combined with more protons and neutrons to make helium nuclei, which contain two protons and two neutrons, and also small amounts of a couple of heavier elements, lithium and beryllium. One can calculate that in the hot big bang model about a quarter of the protons and neutrons would have been converted into helium nuclei, along with a small amount of heavy hydrogen and other elements. The remaining neutrons would have decayed into protons, which are the nuclei of ordinary hydrogen atoms.

This picture of a hot early stage of the universe was first put forward by the scientist George Gamow in a famous paper written in 1948 with a student of his, Ralph Alpher. Gamow had quite a sense of humor — he persuaded the nuclear scientist Hans Bethe to add his name to the paper to make the list of authors "Alpher, Bethe, Gamow," like the first three letters of the Greek alphabet, alpha, beta, gamma: particularly appropriate for a paper on the beginning of the universe! In this paper they made the remarkable prediction that radiation (in the form of photons) from the very hot early

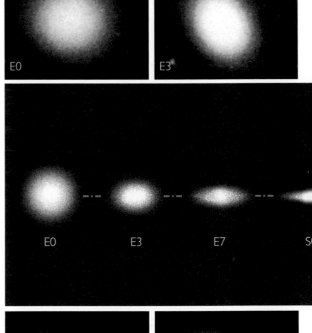

Fig. 8.3 *A revised version of the galactic classification system proposed by Edwin Hubble and Milton Humason in 1936. On the left are the four featureless elliptical, non-rotating systems, E0, E3, E7, and S0. The upper group on the right shows the spiral galaxies, Sa, Sb, and Sc, while those below are the barred spirals, SBa, SBb, SBc. The three categories a, b, and c in each group denote the central nuclear regions becoming smaller while the galactic arms become wider and more open.*

stages of the universe should still be around today, but with its temperature reduced to only a few degrees above absolute zero (-273°C). It was this radiation that Penzias and Wilson found in 1965. At the time that Alpher, Bethe, and Gamow wrote their paper, not much was

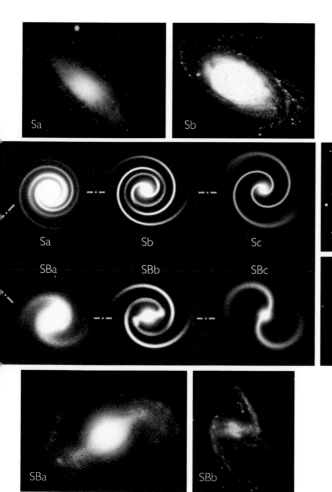

what we observe. It is, moreover, very difficult to explain in any other way why there should be so much helium in the universe. We are therefore fairly confident that we have the right picture, at least back to about one second after the big bang.

Within only a few hours of the big bang, the production of helium and other elements would have stopped. And after that, for the next million years or so, the universe would have just continued expanding, without anything much happening. Eventually, once the temperature had dropped to a few thousand degrees, and electrons and nuclei no longer had enough energy to overcome the electromagnetic attraction between them, they would have started combining to form atoms. The universe as a whole would have continued expanding and cooling, but in regions that were slightly denser than average, the expansion would have been slowed down by the extra gravitational attraction. This would eventually stop expansion in some regions and cause them to start to recollapse. As they were collapsing,

known about the nuclear reactions of protons and neutrons. Predictions made for the proportions of various elements in the early universe were therefore rather inaccurate, but these calculations have been repeated in the light of better knowledge and now agree very well with

the gravitational pull of matter outside these regions might start them rotating slightly. As the collapsing region got smaller, it would spin faster — just as skaters spinning on ice spin faster as they draw in their arms. Eventually, when the region got small enough, it would be spinning fast enough to balance the attraction of gravity, and in this way disklike rotating galaxies were born (Fig. 8.3). Other regions, which did not happen to pick up a rotation, would become oval-shaped objects called elliptical galaxies. In these, the region would stop collapsing because individual parts of the galaxy would be orbiting stably round its center, but the galaxy would have no overall rotation.

As time went on, the hydrogen and helium gas in the galaxies would break up into smaller clouds that would collapse under their own gravity. As these contracted, and the atoms within them collided with one another, the temperature of the gas would increase, until eventually it became hot enough to start nuclear fusion reactions. These would convert the hydrogen into more helium, and the heat given off would raise the pressure, and so stop the clouds from contracting any further. They would remain stable in this state for a long time as stars like our sun, burning hydrogen into helium and radiating the resulting energy as heat and light. More massive stars would need to be hotter to balance

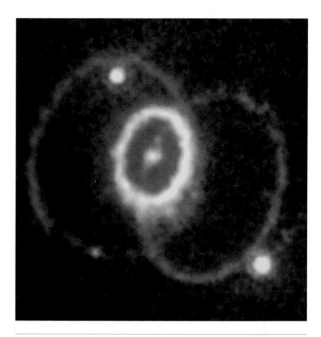

Above: *The aftermath of supernova 1987a. The central ring is an expanding doughnut of material blown off by the explosion. The central spot is a new neutron star.*
Opposite: *New stars being born inside clouds of dust and gas in the Eagle Cluster. Both of these photos were taken by the Hubble Space Telescope, seen being repaired in orbit (inset).*

their stronger gravitational attraction, making the nuclear fusion reactions proceed so much more rapidly that they would use up their hydrogen in as little as a hundred million years. They would then contract slightly, and as they heated up further, would start to convert helium into heavier elements like carbon or oxygen. This, however, would not release much more energy, so a crisis would occur, as was described in the chapter on black holes. What happens next is not completely clear, but it seems likely that the central regions of the star would collapse to a very dense state, such as a neutron star or black hole. The outer regions of the star may sometimes get blown off in a tremendous explosion called a supernova, which would outshine all the other stars in its galaxy. Some of the heavier elements produced near the end of the star's life would be flung back into the gas in the galaxy, and would provide some of the raw material for the next generation of stars. Our own sun contains about 2 percent of these heavier elements because it is a second- or third-generation star, formed some five thousand million years ago out of a cloud of rotating gas containing the debris of earlier supernovas. Most of the gas in that cloud went to form the sun or got blown away, but a small amount of the heavier elements collected together to form the bodies that now orbit the sun as planets like the earth.

The earth was initially very hot and without an atmosphere. In the course of time it cooled and acquired an atmosphere from the emission of gases from the rocks. This early atmosphere was not one in which we could have survived. It contained no oxygen, but a lot of other gases that are poisonous to us, such as hydrogen sulfide (the gas that gives rotten eggs their smell).

There are, however, other primitive forms of life that can flourish under such conditions. It is thought that they developed in the oceans, possibly as a result of chance combinations of atoms into large structures, called macromolecules, which were capable of assembling other atoms in the ocean into similar structures. They would thus have reproduced themselves and multiplied. In some cases there would be errors in the reproduction. Mostly these errors would have been such that the new macromolecule could not reproduce itself and eventually would have been destroyed. However, a few of the errors would have produced new macromolecules that were even better at reproducing themselves. They would have therefore had an advantage and would have tended to replace the original macromolecules. In this way a process of evolution was started that led to the development of more and more complicated, self-reproducing organisms. The first primitive forms of life consumed various materials, including hydrogen sulfide, and released oxygen. This gradually changed the atmosphere to the composition that it has today, and allowed the development of higher forms of life such as fish, reptiles, mammals, and ultimately the human race.

This picture of a universe that started off very hot and cooled as it expanded is in agree-

Fig. 8.4

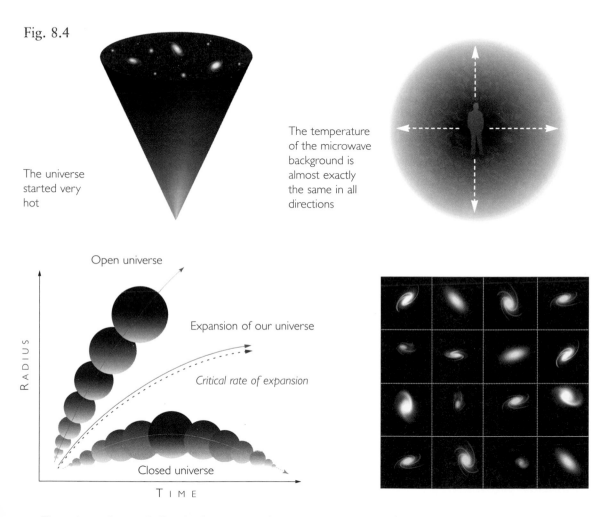

The universe started very hot

The temperature of the microwave background is almost exactly the same in all directions

The universe is on a knife edge between continuous expansion and recollapse

Small fluctuations in the density of the universe give rise to galaxies and stars

ment with all the observational evidence that we have today. Nevertheless, it leaves a number of important questions unanswered (Fig. 8.4):

(1) Why was the early universe so hot?

(2) Why is the universe so uniform on a large scale? Why does it look the same at all points of space and in all directions? In particular, why is the temperature of the microwave background

155

"The Ancient of Days" by William Blake (1757–1827).

have been time since the big bang for light to get from one distant region to another, even though the regions were close together in the early universe. According to the theory of relativity, if light cannot get from one region to another, no other information can. So there would be no way in which different regions in the early universe could have come to have had the same temperature as each other, unless for some unexplained reason they happened to start out with the same temperature.

(3) Why did the universe start out with so nearly the critical rate of expansion that separates models that recollapse from those that go on expanding forever, that even now, ten thousand million years later, it is still expanding at nearly the critical rate? If the rate of expansion one second after the big bang had been smaller by even one part in a hundred thousand million million, the universe would have recollapsed before it ever reached its present size.

(4) Despite the fact that the universe is so uniform and homogeneous on a large scale, it contains local irregularities, such as stars and galaxies. These are thought to have developed from small differences in the density of the early universe from one region to another. What was the origin of these density fluctuations?

radiation so nearly the same when we look in different directions? It is a bit like asking a number of students an exam question. If they all give exactly the same answer, you can be pretty sure they have communicated with each other. Yet, in the model described above, there would not

The general theory of relativity, on its own, cannot explain these features or answer these questions because of its prediction that the universe started off with infinite density at the big bang singularity. At the singularity, general relativity and all other physical laws would break down: one couldn't predict what would come out of the singularity. As explained before, this means that one might as well cut the big bang, and any events before it, out of the theory, because they can have no effect on what we observe. Space-time *would* have a boundary — a beginning at the big bang.

Science seems to have uncovered a set of laws that, within the limits set by the uncertainty principle, tell us how the universe will develop with time, if we know its state at any one time. These laws may have originally been decreed by God, but it appears that he has since left the universe to evolve according to them and does not now intervene in it. But how did he choose the initial state or configuration of the universe? What were the "boundary conditions" at the beginning of time?

One possible answer is to say that God chose the initial configuration of the universe for reasons that we cannot hope to understand. This would certainly have been within the power of an omnipotent being, but if he had started it off in such an incomprehensible way, why did he choose to let it evolve according to laws that we could understand? The whole history of science has been the gradual realization that events do not happen in an arbitrary manner, but that they reflect a certain underlying order, which may or may not be divinely inspired. It would be only natural to suppose that this order should apply not only to the laws, but also to the conditions at the boundary of space-time that specify the initial state of the universe. There may be a large number of models of the universe with different initial conditions that all obey the laws. There ought to be some principle that picks out one initial state, and hence one model, to represent our universe.

One such possibility is what are called chaotic boundary conditions. These implicitly assume either that the universe is spatially infinite or that there are infinitely many universes. Under chaotic boundary conditions, the probability of finding any particular region of space in any given configuration just after the big bang is the same, in some sense, as the probability of finding it in any other configuration: the initial state of the universe is chosen purely randomly. This would mean that the early universe would have

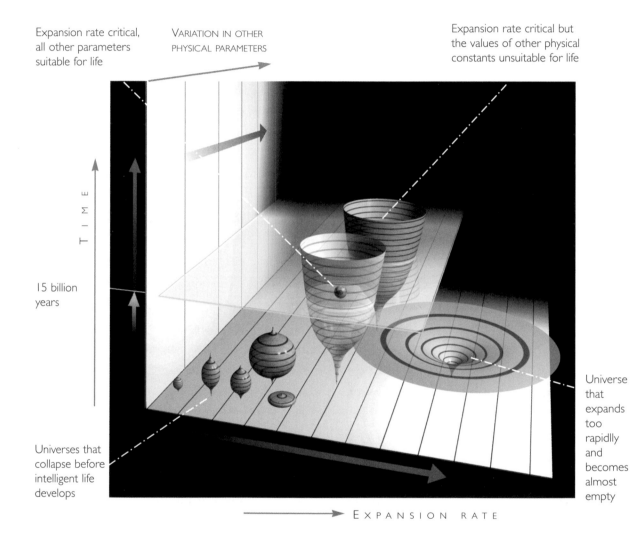

Expansion rate critical, all other parameters suitable for life

VARIATION IN OTHER PHYSICAL PARAMETERS

Expansion rate critical but the values of other physical constants unsuitable for life

TIME

15 billion years

Universes that collapse before intelligent life develops

Universe that expands too rapidlly and becomes almost empty

EXPANSION RATE

probably been very chaotic and irregular because there are many more chaotic and disordered configurations for the universe than there are smooth and ordered ones. (If each configu-

Fig. 8.5 *The strong anthropic principle supposes that there are many different universes with different initial expansion rates and other fundamental physical attributes. Only a few are suitable for life.*

158

ration is equally probable, it is likely that the universe started out in a chaotic and disordered state, simply because there are so many more of them.) It is difficult to see how such chaotic initial conditions could have given rise to a universe that is so smooth and regular on a large scale as ours is today. One would also have expected the density fluctuations in such a model to have led to the formation of many more primordial black holes than the upper limit that has been set by observations of the gamma ray background.

If the universe is indeed spatially infinite, or if there are infinitely many universes, there would probably be some large regions somewhere that started out in a smooth and uniform manner. It is a bit like the well-known horde of monkeys hammering away on typewriters — most of what they write will be garbage, but very occasionally by pure chance they will type out one of Shakespeare's sonnets. Similarly, in the case of the universe, could it be that we are living in a region that just happens by chance to be smooth and uniform? At first sight this might seem very improbable, because such smooth regions would be heavily outnumbered by chaotic and irregular regions. However, suppose that only in the smooth regions were galaxies and stars formed and were conditions right for

the development of complicated self-replicating organisms like ourselves who were capable of asking the question: why is the universe so smooth? This is an example of the application of what is known as the anthropic principle, which can be paraphrased as "We see the universe the way it is because we exist."

There are two versions of the anthropic principle, the weak and the strong. The weak anthropic principle states that in a universe that is large or infinite in space and/or time, the conditions necessary for the development of intelligent life will be met only in certain regions that are limited in space and time. The intelligent beings in these regions should therefore not be surprised if they observe that their locality in the universe satisfies the conditions that are necessary for their existence. It is a bit like a rich person living in a wealthy neighborhood not seeing any poverty.

One example of the use of the weak anthropic principle is to "explain" why the big bang occurred about ten thousand million years ago — it takes about that long for intelligent beings to evolve. As explained above, an early generation of stars first had to form. These stars converted some of the original hydrogen and helium into elements like carbon and oxygen, out of which we are made. The stars then exploded as

supernovas, and their debris went to form other stars and planets, among them those of our Solar System, which is about five thousand million years old. The first one or two thousand million years of the earth's existence were too hot for the development of anything complicated. The remaining three thousand million years or so have been taken up by the slow process of biological evolution, which has led from the simplest organisms to beings who are capable of measuring time back to the big bang.

Few people would quarrel with the validity or utility of the weak anthropic principle. Some, however, go much further and propose a strong version of the principle (Fig. 8.5). According to this theory, there are either many different universes or many different regions of a single universe, each with its own initial configuration and, perhaps, with its own set of laws of science. In most of these universes the conditions would not be right for the development of complicated organisms; only in the few universes that are like ours would intelligent beings develop and ask the question, "Why is the universe the way we see it?" The answer is then simple: if it had been different, we would not be here!

The laws of science, as we know them at present, contain many fundamental numbers, like the size of the electric charge of the electron and the ratio of the masses of the proton and the electron. We cannot, at the moment at least, predict the values of these numbers from theory — we have to find them by observation. It may be that one day we shall discover a complete unified theory that predicts them all, but it is also possible that some or all of them vary from universe to universe or within a single universe. The remarkable fact is that the values of these numbers seem to have been very finely adjusted to make possible the development of life. For example, if the electric charge of the electron had been only slightly different, stars either would have been unable to burn hydrogen and helium, or else they would not have exploded. Of course, there might be other forms of intelligent life, not dreamed of even by writers of science fiction, that did not require the light of a star like the sun or the heavier chemical elements that are made in stars and are flung back into space when the stars explode. Nevertheless, it seems clear that there are relatively few ranges of values for the numbers that would allow the development of any form of intelligent life. Most sets of values would give rise to universes that, although they might be very beautiful, would contain no one able to wonder at that beauty. One can take this either as evidence of a divine purpose in Creation and the choice of the

Fig. 8.6

Geocentric
cosmology of
Ptolemy, with
Earth at the
center of the
universe

Heliocentric
cosmology of
Copernicus
showing the Earth
within a solar
system and the
stars orbiting on
the outer sphere

Galactic
cosmology in
which Earth
orbits an average
star in the outer
reaches of a
spiral of the
Milky Way

Our present
picture is of the
Milky Way as just
one amongst one
million million
observable galaxies
in our particular
region of the
universe

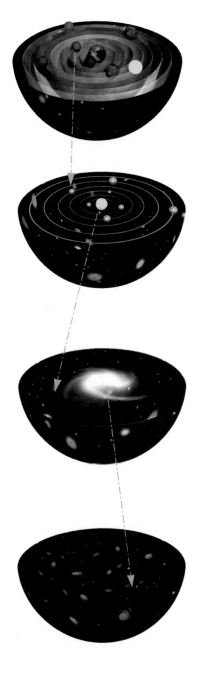

laws of science or as support for the strong anthropic principle.

There are a number of objections that one can raise to the strong anthropic principle as an explanation of the observed state of the universe. First, in what sense can all these different universes be said to exist? If they are really separate from each other, what happens in another universe can have no observable consequences in our own universe. We should therefore use the principle of economy and cut them out of the theory. If, on the other hand, they are just different regions of a single universe, the laws of science would have to be the same in each region, because otherwise one could not move continuously from one region to another. In this case the only difference between the regions would be their initial configurations and so the strong anthropic principle would reduce to the weak one.

A second objection to the strong anthropic principle is that it runs against the tide of the whole history of science. We have developed from the geocentric cosmologies of Ptolemy and his forebears, through the heliocentric cosmology of Copernicus and Galileo, to the modern

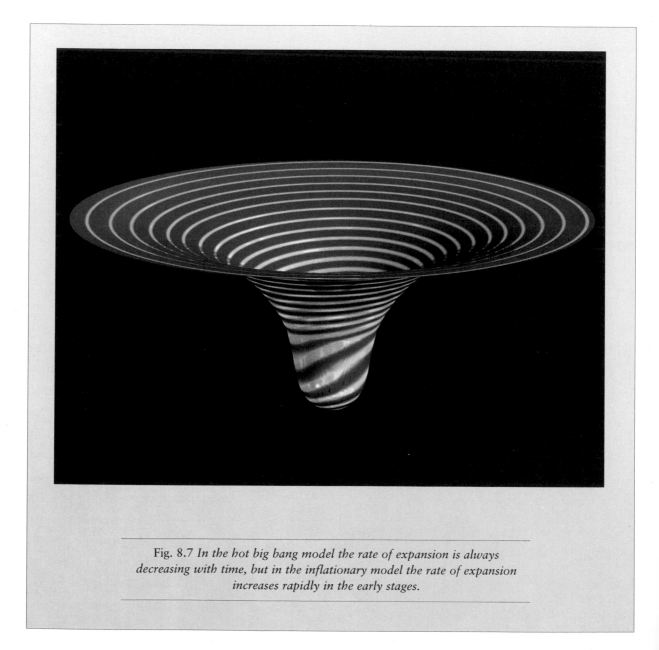

Fig. 8.7 *In the hot big bang model the rate of expansion is always decreasing with time, but in the inflationary model the rate of expansion increases rapidly in the early stages.*

picture in which the earth is a medium-sized planet orbiting around an average star in the outer suburbs of an ordinary spiral galaxy, which is itself only one of about a million million galaxies in the observable universe (Fig. 8.6). Yet the strong anthropic principle would claim that this whole vast construction exists simply for our sake. This is very hard to believe. Our Solar System is certainly a prerequisite for our existence, and one might extend this to the whole of our galaxy to allow for an earlier generation of stars that created the heavier elements. But there does not seem to be any need for all those other galaxies, nor for the universe to be so uniform and similar in every direction on the large scale.

One would feel happier about the anthropic principle, at least in its weak version, if one could show that quite a number of different initial configurations for the universe would have evolved to produce a universe like the one we observe. If this is the case, a universe that developed from some sort of random initial conditions should contain a number of regions that are smooth and uniform and are suitable for the evolution of intelligent life. On the other hand, if the initial state of the universe had to be chosen extremely carefully to lead to something like what we see around us, the universe would be unlikely to contain any region in which life would appear. In the hot big bang model described above, there was not enough time in the early universe for heat to have flowed from one region to another. This means that the initial state of the universe would have to have had exactly the same temperature everywhere in order to account for the fact that the microwave background has the same temperature in every direction we look. The initial rate of expansion also would have had to be chosen very precisely for the rate of expansion still to be so close to the critical rate needed to avoid recollapse. This means that the initial state of the universe must have been very carefully chosen indeed if the hot big bang model was correct right back to the beginning of time. It would be very difficult to explain why the universe should have begun in just this way, except as the act of a God who intended to create beings like us.

In an attempt to find a model of the universe in which many different initial configurations could have evolved to something like the present universe, a scientist at the Massachusetts Institute of Technology, Alan Guth, suggested that the early universe might have gone through a period of very rapid expansion. This expansion is said to be "inflationary," meaning that the universe at one time expanded at an increas-

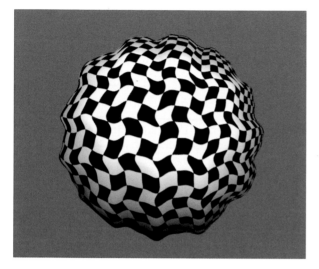

Fig. 8.8 *The rapid expansion of the universe in the first fraction of a second would flatten the universe and make the expansion almost the critical value.*

ing rate rather than the decreasing rate that it does today (Fig. 8.7). According to Guth, the radius of the universe increased by a million million million million million (1 with thirty zeros after it) times in only a tiny fraction of a second.

Guth suggested that the universe started out from the big bang in a very hot, but rather chaotic, state. These high temperatures would have meant that the particles in the universe would be moving very fast and would have high energies. As we discussed earlier, one would expect that at such high temperatures the strong and weak nuclear forces and the electromagnetic force would all be unified into a single force. As the universe expanded, it would cool, and particle energies would go down. Eventually there would be what is called a phase transition and the symmetry between the forces would be broken: the strong force would become different from the weak and electromagnetic forces. One common example of a phase transition is the freezing of water when you cool it down. Liquid water is symmetrical, the same at every point and in every direction. However, when ice crystals form, they will have definite positions and will be lined up in some direction. This breaks water's symmetry.

In the case of water, if one is careful, one can

"supercool" it: that is, one can reduce the temperature below the freezing point (0°C) without ice forming. Guth suggested that the universe might behave in a similar way: the temperature might drop below the critical value without the symmetry between the forces being broken. If this happened, the universe would be in an unstable state, with more energy than if the symmetry had been broken. This special extra energy can be shown to have an antigravitational effect: it would have acted just like the cosmological constant that Einstein introduced into general relativity when he was trying to construct a static model of the universe. Since the universe would already be expanding just as in the hot big bang model, the repulsive effect of

this cosmological constant would therefore have made the universe expand at an ever-increasing rate. Even in regions where there were more matter particles than average, the gravitational attraction of the matter would have been outweighed by the repulsion of the effective cosmological constant. Thus these regions would also expand in an accelerating inflationary manner. As they expanded and the matter particles got farther apart, one would be left with an expanding universe that contained hardly any particles and was still in the supercooled state. Any irregularities in the universe would simply have been smoothed out by the expansion, as the wrinkles in a balloon are smoothed away when you blow it up (Fig. 8.8). Thus the present smooth and uniform state of the universe could have evolved from many different non-uniform initial states.

In such a universe, in which the expansion was accelerated by a cosmological constant rather than slowed down by the gravitational attraction of matter, there would be enough time for light to travel from one region to another in the early universe. This could provide a solution to the problem, raised earlier, of why different regions in the early universe have the same properties. Moreover, the rate of expansion of the universe would automatically become very close to the critical rate determined by the energy density of the universe. This could then explain why the rate of expansion is still so close to the critical rate, without having to assume that the initial rate of expansion of the universe was very carefully chosen.

The idea of inflation could also explain why there is so much matter in the universe. There are something like ten million million million million million million million million million million million million million (1 with eighty zeros after it) particles in the region of the universe that we can observe. Where did they all come from? The answer is that, in quantum theory, particles can be created out of energy in the form of particle/antiparticle pairs. But that just raises the question of where the energy came from. The answer is that the total energy of the universe is exactly zero. The matter in the universe is made out of positive energy. However, the matter is all attracting itself by gravity. Two pieces of matter that are close to each other have less energy than the same two pieces a long way apart, because you have to expend energy to separate them against the gravitational force that is pulling them together. Thus, in a sense, the gravitational field has negative energy. In the case of a universe that is approximately uniform in space, one can show that this negative gravitational energy exactly cancels the positive energy represented by the matter. So the total energy of the universe is zero.

Now twice zero is also zero. Thus the universe can double the amount of positive matter energy and also double the negative gravitational energy without violation of the conservation of energy. This does not happen in the normal expansion of the universe in which the matter energy density goes down as the universe gets bigger. It does happen, however, in the inflationary expansion because the energy density of the supercooled state remains constant while the

STATUS OF THE INFLATIONARY UNIVERSE SCENARIO SOME YEARS AGO (CAMBRIDGE 1982)

Cartoon drawn by Andrei Linde showing the state of the inflationary model in the early 1980's.

available to make particles becomes very large. As Guth has remarked, "It is said that there's no such thing as a free lunch. But the universe is the ultimate free lunch."

The universe is not expanding in an inflationary way today. Thus there has to be some mechanism that would eliminate the very large effective cosmological constant and so change the rate of expansion from an accelerated one to one that is slowed down by gravity, as we have today. In the inflationary expansion one might expect that eventually the symmetry between the forces would be broken, just as supercooled water always freezes in the end. The extra energy of the unbroken symmetry state would then be released and would reheat the universe to a temperature just below the critical temperature for symmetry between the forces. The universe would then go on to expand and cool just like the hot big bang model, but there would now be an explanation of why the universe was expanding at exactly the critical rate and why different regions had the same temperature.

In Guth's original proposal the phase transition was supposed to occur suddenly, rather like the appearance of ice crystals in very cold water. The idea was that "bubbles" of the new phase

universe expands: when the universe doubles in size, the positive matter energy and the negative gravitational energy both double, so the total energy remains zero. During the inflationary phase, the universe increases its size by a very large amount. Thus the total amount of energy

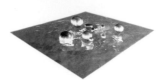

of broken symmetry would have formed in the old phase, like bubbles of steam surrounded by boiling water. The bubbles were supposed to expand and meet up with each other until the whole universe was in the new phase. The trouble was, as I and several other people pointed out, that the universe was expanding so fast that even if the bubbles grew at the speed of light, they would be moving away from each other and so could not join up. The universe would be left in a very non-uniform state, with some regions still having symmetry between the different forces. Such a model of the universe would not correspond to what we see.

In October 1981, I went to Moscow for a conference on quantum gravity. After the conference I gave a seminar on the inflationary model and its problems at the Sternberg Astronomical Institute. Before this, I had got someone else to give my lectures for me, because most people could not understand my voice. But there was not time to prepare this seminar, so I gave it myself, with one of my graduate students repeating my words. It worked well, and gave me much more contact with my audience. In the audience was a young Russian, Andrei Linde, from the Lebedev Institute in Moscow. He said

that the difficulty with the bubbles not joining up could be avoided if the bubbles were so big that our region of the universe is all contained inside a single bubble. In order for this to work, the change from symmetry to broken symmetry must have taken place very slowly inside the bubble, but this is quite possible according to grand unified theories. Linde's idea of a slow breaking of symmetry was very good, but I later realized that his bubbles would have to have been bigger than the size of the universe at the time! I showed that instead the symmetry would have broken everywhere at the same time, rather than just inside bubbles. This would lead to a uniform universe, as we observe. I was very excited by this idea and discussed it with one of my students, Ian Moss. As a friend of Linde's, I was rather embarrassed, however, when I was later sent his paper by a scientific journal and asked whether it was suitable for publication. I replied that there was this flaw about the bubbles being bigger than the universe, but that the basic idea of a slow breaking of symmetry was very good. I recommended that the paper be published as it was because it would take Linde several months to correct it, since anything he sent to the West would have to be passed by

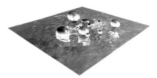

Soviet censorship, which was neither very skillful nor very quick with scientific papers. Instead, I wrote a short paper with Ian Moss in the same journal in which we pointed out this problem with the bubble and showed how it could be resolved.

The day after I got back from Moscow I set out for Philadelphia, where I was due to receive a medal from the Franklin Institute. My secretary, Judy Fella, had used her not inconsiderable charm to persuade British Airways to give herself and me free seats on a Concorde as a publicity venture. However, I was held up on my way to the airport by heavy rain and I missed the plane. Nevertheless, I got to Philadelphia in the end and received my medal. I was then asked to give a seminar on the inflationary universe at Drexel University in Philadelphia. I gave the same seminar about the problems of the inflationary universe, just as in Moscow.

A very similar idea to Linde's was put forth independently a few months later by Paul Steinhardt and Andreas Albrecht of the University of Pennsylvania. They are now given joint credit with Linde for what is called "the new inflationary model," based on the idea of a slow breaking of symmetry. (The old inflationary model was Guth's original suggestion of fast symmetry breaking with the formation of bubbles.)

The new inflationary model was a good attempt to explain why the universe is the way it is. However, I and several other people showed that, at least in its original form, it predicted much greater variations in the temperature of the microwave background radiation than are observed. Later work has also cast doubt on whether there could be a phase transition in the very early universe of the kind required. In my personal opinion, the new inflationary model is now dead as a scientific theory, although a lot of people do not seem to have heard of its demise and are still writing papers as if it were viable. A better model, called the chaotic inflationary model, was put forward by Linde in 1983. In this there is no phase transition or supercooling. Instead, there is a spin 0 field, which, because of quantum fluctuations, would have large values in some regions of the early universe. The energy of the field in those regions would behave like a cosmological constant. It would have a repulsive gravitational effect, and thus make those regions expand in an inflationary manner. As they expanded, the energy of the field in them would slowly

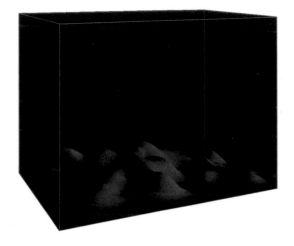

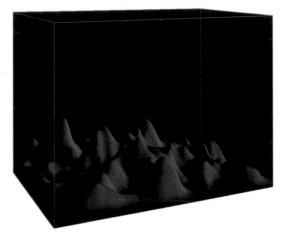

Fig. 8.9 *One inflationary model suggested by Andrei Linde is of a field in which quantum fluctuations occur, causing certain parts to expand rapidly as peaks while other domains such as our own, represented by the valleys, are no longer inflating.*

decrease until the inflationary expansion changed to an expansion like that in the hot big bang model. One of these regions would become what we now see as the observable universe. This model has all the advantages of the earlier inflationary models, but it does not depend on a dubious phase transition, and it can moreover give a reasonable size for the fluctuations in the temperature of the microwave background that agrees with observation.

This work on inflationary models showed that the present state of the universe could have arisen from quite a large number of different initial configurations. This is important, because it shows that the initial state of the part of the universe that we inhabit did not have to be chosen with great care. So we may, if we wish, use the weak anthropic principle to explain why the universe looks the way it does now. It cannot be the case, however, that every initial configuration would have led to a universe like the one we observe. One can show this by considering a very different state for the universe at the present time, say, a very lumpy and irregular one. One could use the laws of science to evolve the universe back in time to determine its configuration at earlier times. According to the singularity theorems of classical general relativity, there would still have been a big bang singular-

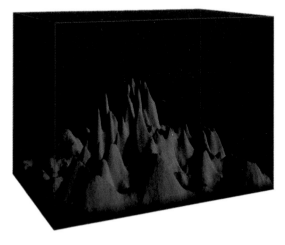 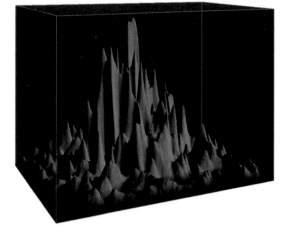

ity. If you evolve such a universe forward in time according to the laws of science, you will end up with the lumpy and irregular state you started with. Thus there must have been initial configurations that would not have given rise to a universe like the one we see today. So even the inflationary model does not tell us why the initial configuration was not such as to produce something very different from what we observe. Must we turn to the anthropic principle for an explanation? Was it all just a lucky chance? That would seem a counsel of despair, a negation of all our hopes of understanding the underlying order of the universe.

In order to predict how the universe should have started off, one needs laws that hold at the beginning of time. If the classical theory of gen-

eral relativity was correct, the singularity theorems that Roger Penrose and I proved show that the beginning of time would have been a point of infinite density and infinite curvature of space-time. All the known laws of science would break down at such a point. One might suppose that there were new laws that held at singularities, but it would be very difficult even to formulate such laws at such badly behaved points, and we would have no guide from observations as to what those laws might be. However, what the singularity theorems really indicate is that the gravitational field becomes so strong that quantum gravitational effects become important: classical theory is no longer a good description of the universe. So one has to use a quantum theory of gravity to discuss the very early

stages of the universe. As we shall see, it is possible in the quantum theory for the ordinary laws of science to hold everywhere, including at the beginning of time: it is not necessary to postulate new laws for singularities, because there need not be any singularities in the quantum theory.

We don't yet have a complete and consistent theory that combines quantum mechanics and gravity. However, we are fairly certain of some features that such a unified theory should have. One is that it should incorporate Feynman's proposal to formulate quantum theory in terms of a sum over histories. In this approach, a particle does not have just a single history, as it would in a classical theory. Instead, it is supposed to follow every possible path in space-time, and with each of these histories there are associated a couple of numbers, one representing the size of a wave and the other representing its position in the cycle (its phase). The probability that the particle, say, passes through some particular point is found by adding up the waves associated with every possible history that passes through that point. When one actually tries to perform these sums, however, one runs into severe technical problems. The only way around

these is the following peculiar prescription: one must add up the waves for particle histories that are not in the "real" time that you and I experience but take place in what is called imaginary time. Imaginary time may sound like science fiction but it is in fact a well-defined mathematical concept. If we take any ordinary (or "real") number and multiply it by itself, the result is a positive number. (For example, 2 times 2 is 4, but so is -2 times -2.) There are, however, special numbers (called imaginary numbers) that give negative numbers when multiplied by themselves. (The one called i, when multiplied by itself, gives -1, 2i multiplied by itself gives -4, and so on.)

One can picture real and imaginary numbers in the following way (Fig. 8.10). The real numbers can be represented by a line going from left to right, with zero in the middle, negative numbers like -1, -2, etc. on the left, and positive numbers, 1, 2, etc. on the right. Then imaginary numbers are represented by a line going up and down the page, with i, 2i, etc. above the middle, and -i, -2i, etc. below. Thus imaginary numbers are in a sense numbers at right angles to ordinary real numbers.

To avoid the technical difficulties with

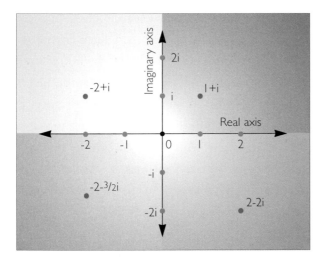

Fig. 8.10 *Real numbers can be represented by a horizontal line running left to right. Imaginary numbers can be represented by a vertical line.*

Feynman's sum over histories, one must use imaginary time. That is to say, for the purposes of the calculation one must measure time using imaginary numbers, rather than real ones. This has an interesting effect on space-time: the distinction between time and space disappears completely. A space-time in which events have imaginary values of the time coordinate is said to be Euclidean, after the ancient Greek Euclid, who founded the study of the geometry of two-dimensional surfaces. What we now call

Euclidean space-time is very similar except that it has four dimensions instead of two. In Euclidean space-time there is no difference between the time direction and directions in space. On the other hand, in real space-time, in which events are labeled by ordinary, real values of the time coordinate, it is easy to tell the difference — the time direction at all points lies within the light cone, and space directions lie outside. In any case, as far as everyday quantum mechanics is concerned, we may regard our use of imaginary time and Euclidean space-time as merely a mathematical device (or trick) to calculate answers about real space-time.

A second feature that we believe must be part of any ultimate theory is Einstein's idea that the gravitational field is represented by curved space-time: particles try to follow the nearest thing to a straight path in a curved space, but because space-time is not flat their paths appear to be bent, as if by a gravitational field. When we apply Feynman's sum over histories to Einstein's view of gravity, the analogue of the history of a particle is now a complete curved space-time that represents the history of the whole universe. To avoid the technical difficulties in actually performing the sum over histories, these

173

See the Bold-Shaddow of Vrania's Glory,
Immortall in His Race, no lesse in Story:
An Artist without Error, from whose Lyne,
Both Earth and Heav'ns, in sweet Proportions twine:
Behold Great EUCLID.'But, behold Him well!
For 'tis in Him. Divinity doth dwell./

G. Wharton.

Euclid, 295 BC.

curved space-times must be taken to be Euclidean. That is, time is imaginary and is indistinguishable from directions in space. To calculate the probability of finding a real space-time with some certain property, such as looking the same at every point and in every direction, one adds up the waves associated with all the histories that have that property.

In the classical theory of general relativity, there are many different possible curved space-times, each corresponding to a different initial state of the universe. If we knew the initial state of our universe, we would know its entire history. Similarly, in the quantum theory of gravity, there are many different possible quantum states for the universe. Again, if we knew how the Euclidean curved space-times in the sum over histories behaved at early times, we would know the quantum state of the universe.

In the classical theory of gravity, which is based on real space-time, there are only two possible ways the universe can behave: either it has existed for an infinite time, or else it had a beginning at a singularity at some finite time in the past. In the quantum theory of gravity, on the other hand, a third possibility arises. Because one is using Euclidean space-times, in which the time direction is on the same footing as directions in space, it is possible for space-time to be finite in extent and yet to have no singularities that formed a boundary or edge. Space-time would be like the surface of the earth, only with two more dimensions. The surface of the earth is finite in extent but it doesn't have a boundary or edge: if you sail off into the sunset, you don't fall off the edge or run into a singularity. (I know, because I have been round the world!)

If Euclidean space-time stretches back to infinite imaginary time, or else starts at a singularity in imaginary time, we have the same problem as in the classical theory of specifying the initial state of the universe: God may know how the universe began, but we cannot give any particular reason for thinking it began one way rather than another. On the other hand, the quantum theory of gravity has opened up a new possibility, in which there would be no boundary to space-time and so there would be no need to specify the behavior at the boundary. There would be no singularities at which the laws of science broke down, and no edge of space-time at which one would have to appeal to God or some new law to set the boundary conditions for space-time. One could say: "The boundary condition of the universe is that it has no boundary." The universe would be completely self-contained and not affected by anything outside itself. It would neither be created nor destroyed. It would just BE.

It was at the conference in the Vatican mentioned earlier that I first put forward the suggestion that maybe time and space together formed a surface that was finite in size but did not have any boundary or edge. My paper was rather mathematical, however, so its implications for the role of God in the creation of the universe were not generally recognized at the time (just as well for me). At the time of the Vatican conference, I did not know how to use the "no boundary" idea to make predictions about the universe. However I spent the following summer at the University of California, Santa Barbara. There a friend and colleague of mine, Jim Hartle, worked out with me what conditions the universe must satisfy if space-time had no boundary. When I returned to Cambridge, I continued this work with two of my research students, Julian Luttrel and Jonathan Halliwell.

I'd like to emphasize that this idea that time and space should be finite "without boundary" is just a *proposal*: it cannot be deduced from some other principle. Like any other scientific theory, it may initially be put forward for aesthetic or metaphysical reasons, but the real test is whether it makes predictions that agree with observation. This, however, is difficult to determine in the case of quantum gravity, for two reasons. First, as will be explained in chapter 11, we are not yet sure exactly which theory successfully combines general relativity and quantum mechanics, though we know quite a lot

Fig. 8.11

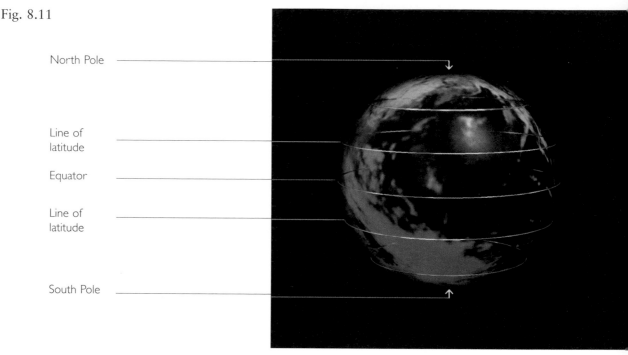

North Pole

Line of
latitude

Equator

Line of
latitude

South Pole

THE EARTH

about the form such a theory must have. Second, any model that described the whole universe in detail would be much too complicated mathematically for us to be able to calculate exact predictions. One therefore has to make simplifying assumptions and approximations — and even then, the problem of extracting predictions remains a formidable one.

Each history in the sum over histories will describe not only the space-time but everything in it as well, including any complicated organ-

Fig. 8.11 *In the "no boundary" proposal, the history of the universe in imaginary time is like the surface of the earth: it is finite in size but doesn't have a boundary.*

isms like human beings who can observe the history of the universe. This may provide another justification for the anthropic principle, for if all the histories are possible, then so long as we exist in one of the histories, we may use the anthropic principle to explain why the universe is found to be the way it is. Exactly what mean-

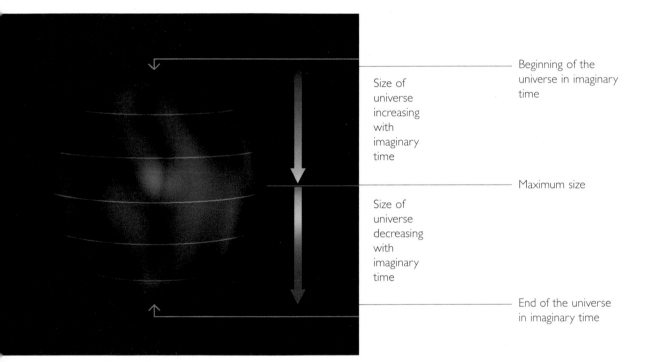

Beginning of the universe in imaginary time

Size of universe increasing with imaginary time

Maximum size

Size of universe decreasing with imaginary time

End of the universe in imaginary time

THE UNIVERSE

ing can be attached to the other histories, in which we do not exist, is not clear. This view of a quantum theory of gravity would be much more satisfactory, however, if one could show that, using the sum over histories, our universe is not just one of the possible histories but one of the most probable ones. To do this, we must perform the sum over histories for all possible Euclidean space-times that have no boundary.

Under the "no boundary" proposal one learns that the chance of the universe being found to be following most of the possible histories is negligible, but there is a particular family of histories that are much more probable than the others. These histories may be pictured as being like the surface of the earth, with the distance from the North Pole representing imaginary time and the size of a circle of constant distance from the North Pole representing the spatial size of the universe. The universe starts at the North Pole as a single point. As one moves south, the circles of latitude at constant distance

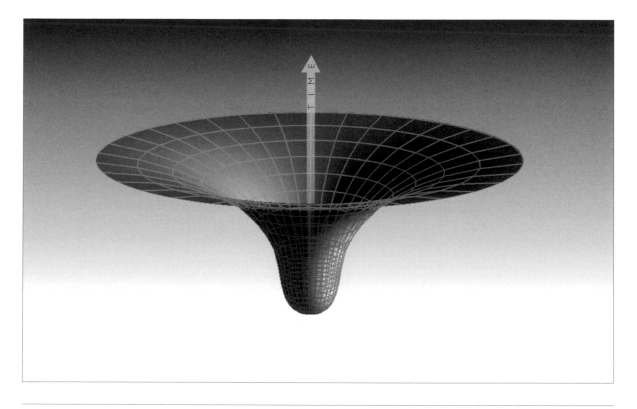

Fig. 8.12 *The universe expands in imaginary time like the surface of the earth from the North Pole to the equator, and then expands in real time at an increasing inflationary rate.*

from the North Pole get bigger, corresponding to the universe expanding with imaginary time (Fig. 8.11). The universe would reach a maximum size at the equator and would contract with increasing imaginary time to a single point at the South Pole. Even though the universe would have zero size at the North and South Poles, these points would not be singularities, any more than the North and South Poles on the earth are singular. The laws of science will hold at them, just as they do at the North and South Poles on the earth.

The history of the universe in real time, however, would look very different. At about ten or

twenty thousand million years ago, it would have a minimum size, which was equal to the maximum radius of the history in imaginary time. At later real times, the universe would expand like the chaotic inflationary model proposed by Linde (but one would not now have to assume that the universe was created somehow in the right sort of state). The universe would expand to a very large size (Fig. 8.12) and eventually it would collapse again into what looks like a singularity in real time. Thus, in a sense, we are still all doomed, even if we keep away from black holes. Only if we could picture the universe in terms of imaginary time would there be no singularities.

If the universe really is in such a quantum state, there would be no singularities in the history of the universe in imaginary time. It might seem therefore that my more recent work had completely undone the results of my earlier work on singularities. But, as indicated above, the real importance of the singularity theorems was that they showed that the gravitational field must become so strong that quantum gravitational effects could not be ignored. This in turn led to the idea that the universe could be finite in imaginary time but without boundaries or singularities. When one goes back to the real

time in which we live, however, there will still appear to be singularities. The poor astronaut who falls into a black hole will still come to a sticky end; only if he lived in imaginary time would he encounter no singularities.

This might suggest that the so-called imaginary time is really the real time, and that what we call real time is just a figment of our imaginations. In real time, the universe has a beginning and an end at singularities that form a boundary to space-time and at which the laws of science break down. But in imaginary time, there are no singularities or boundaries. So maybe what we call imaginary time is really more basic, and what we call real is just an idea that we invent to help us describe what we think the universe is like. But according to the approach I described in Chapter 1, a scientific theory is just a mathematical model we make to describe our observations: it exists only in our minds. So it is meaningless to ask: which is real, "real" or "imaginary" time? It is simply a matter of which is the more useful description.

One can also use the sum over histories, along with the no boundary proposal, to find which properties of the universe are likely to occur together. For example, one can calculate the probability that the universe is expanding at

nearly the same rate in all different directions at a time when the density of the universe has its present value. In the simplified models that have been examined so far, this probability turns out to be high; that is, the proposed no boundary condition leads to the prediction that it is extremely probable that the present rate of expansion of the universe is almost the same in each direction. This is consistent with the observations of the microwave background radiation, which show that it has almost exactly the same intensity in any direction. If the universe were expanding faster in some directions than in others, the intensity of the radiation in those directions would be reduced by an additional red shift.

Further predictions of the no boundary condition are currently being worked out. A particularly interesting problem is the size of the small departures from uniform density in the early universe that caused the formation first of the galaxies, then of stars, and finally of us. The uncertainty principle implies that the early universe cannot have been completely uniform because there must have been some uncertainties or fluctuations in the positions and velocities of the particles. Using the no boundary condition, we find that the universe must in fact have started off with just the minimum possible non-uniformity allowed by the uncertainty principle. The universe would have then undergone a period of rapid expansion, as in the inflationary models. During this period, the initial non-uniformities would have been amplified until they were big enough to explain the origin of the structures we observe around us. In 1992 the Cosmic Background Explorer satellite (COBE) first detected very slight variations in the intensity of the microwave background with direction. The way these non-uniformities depend on direction seems to agree with the predictions of the inflationary model and the no boundary proposal. Thus the no boundary proposal is a good scientific theory in the sense of Karl Popper: it could have been falsified by observations but instead its predictions have been confirmed. In an expanding universe in which the density of matter varied slightly from place to place, gravity would have caused the denser regions to slow down their expansion and start contracting. This would lead to the formation of galaxies, stars, and eventually even insignificant creatures like ourselves. Thus all the complicated structures that we see in the universe might be explained by the no boundary condition for the universe together with the uncertainty principle of quantum mechanics.

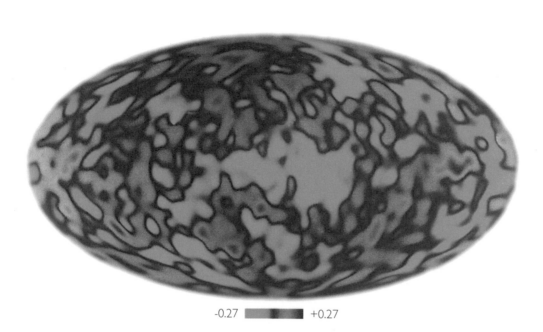

-0.27 +0.27

The idea that space and time may form a closed surface without boundary also has profound implications for the role of God in the affairs of the universe. With the success of scientific theories in describing events, most people have come to believe that God allows the universe to evolve according to a set of laws and does not intervene in the universe to break these laws. However, the laws do not tell us what the universe should have looked like when it started — it would still be up to God to wind up the clockwork and choose how to start it off. So

Above: A map of the tiny temperature variations in the microwave background observed by the COBE satellite. The hot spots correspond to slightly more dense regions that later developed into clusters of galaxies.

long as the universe had a beginning, we could suppose it had a creator. But if the universe is really completely self-contained, having no boundary or edge, it would have neither beginning nor end: it would simply be. What place, then, for a creator?

9

The Arrow of Time

IN PREVIOUS CHAPTERS WE have seen how our views of the nature of time have changed over the years. Up to the beginning of this century people believed in an absolute time. That is, each event could be labeled by a number called "time" in a unique way, and all good clocks would agree on the time interval between two events. However, the discovery that the speed of light appeared the same to every observer, no matter how he was moving, led to the theory of relativity — and in that one had to abandon the idea that there was a unique absolute time. Instead, each observer would have his own measure of time as recorded by a clock that he carried: clocks carried by different observers would not necessarily agree. Thus time became a more personal concept, relative to the observer who measured it.

When one tried to unify gravity with quantum mechanics, one had to introduce the idea of "imaginary" time. Imaginary time is indistinguishable from directions in space. If one can go north, one can turn around and head south; equally, if one can go forward in imaginary time, one ought to be able to turn round and go backward. This means that there can be no important difference between the forward and backward directions of imaginary time. On the other hand, when one looks at "real" time, there's a very big difference between the forward and backward directions, as we all know. Where does this difference between the past and the future come from? Why do we remember the past but not the future?

The laws of science do not distinguish between the past and the future. More precisely,

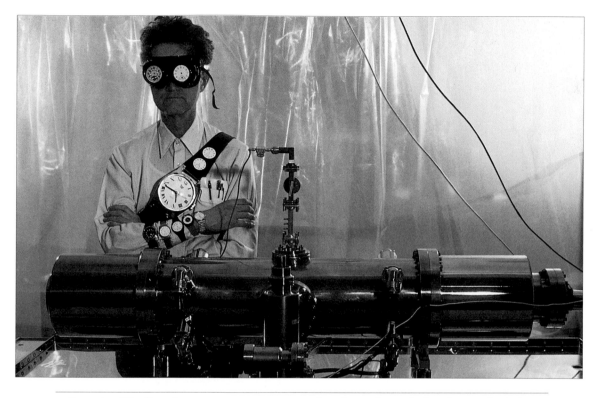

Opposite: *The first chronometer accurate enough to be used to calculate longitude, 1735.*
Above: *Keeper of the U.S. cesium clock. The standard second is based on the count of the number of oscillations of atoms of vaporized cesium 133 between two magnets.*

as explained earlier, the laws of science are unchanged under the combination of operations (or symmetries) known as C, P, and T. (C means changing particles for antiparticles. P means taking the mirror image, so left and right are interchanged. And T means reversing the direction of motion of all particles: in effect, running the motion backward.) The laws of science that govern the behavior of matter under all normal situations are unchanged under the combination of the two operations C and P on their own. In other words, life would be just the same for the inhabitants of another planet who were both mirror images of us and who were made of antimatter, rather than matter.

If the laws of science are unchanged by the combination of operations C and P, and also by the combination C, P, and T, they must also be unchanged under the operation T alone. Yet there is a big difference between the forward and backward directions of real time in ordinary life. Imagine a cup of water falling off a table and breaking into pieces on the floor (Fig. 9.1). If you take a film of this, you can easily tell whether it is being run forward or backward. If you run it backward you will see the pieces suddenly gather themselves together off the floor and jump back to form a whole cup on the table. You can tell that the film is being run backward because this kind of behavior is never observed in ordinary life. If it were, crockery manufacturers would go out of business.

The explanation that is usually given as to why we don't see broken cups gathering themselves together off the floor and jumping back onto the table is that it is forbidden by the second law of thermodynamics. This says that in any closed system disorder, or entropy, always increases with time. In other words, it is a form of Murphy's law: things always tend to go wrong! An intact cup on the table is a state of high order, but a broken cup on the floor is a disordered state. One can go readily from the cup on the table in the past to the broken cup on the floor in the future, but not the other way round.

The increase of disorder or entropy with time

is one example of what is called an arrow of time, something that distinguishes the past from the future, giving a direction to time. There are at least three different arrows of time. First, there is the thermodynamic arrow of time, the direction of time in which disorder or entropy increases. Then, there is the psychological arrow of time. This is the direction in which we feel time passes, the direction in which we remember the past but not the future. Finally, there is the

cosmological arrow of time. This is the direction of time in which the universe is expanding rather than contracting. (See Fig. 9.3.)

In this chapter I shall argue that the no boundary condition for the universe, together with the weak anthropic principle, can explain why all three arrows point in the same direction — and moreover, why a well-defined arrow of time should exist at all. I shall argue that the psychological arrow is determined by the thermody-

namic arrow, and that these two arrows necessarily always point in the same direction. If one assumes the no boundary condition for the universe, we shall see that there must be well-defined thermodynamic and cosmological arrows of

Fig. 9.1. *Watching a film of a cup breaking on the floor, it is easy for us to tell if the film is being run forward or backward. However, the laws of science are the same whether time runs forward or backward.*

Fig.9.2. *A game like pool is a closed system. Initially the balls are arranged in a highly ordered state, but once the game begins, the balls become disordered. It is very unlikely that one could play a shot that would return all the balls to their starting positions.*

time, but they will not point in the same direction for the whole history of the universe. However, I shall argue that it is only when they do point in the same direction that conditions are suitable for the development of intelligent

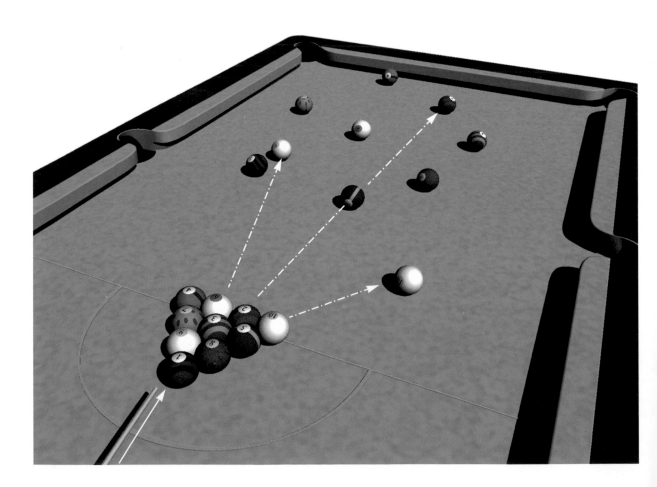

beings who can ask the question: why does disorder increase in the same direction of time as that in which the universe expands?

I shall discuss first the thermodynamic arrow of time. The second law of thermodynamics results from the fact that there are always many more disordered states than there are ordered ones. For example, consider the pieces of a jigsaw in a box. There is one, and only one, arrangement in which the pieces make a complete picture. On the other hand, there are a very large number of arrangements in which the pieces are disordered and don't make a picture.

Suppose a system starts out in one of the small number of ordered states. As time goes by, the system will evolve according to the laws of science and its state will change. At a later time, it is more probable that the system will be in a disordered state than in an ordered one because there are more disordered states. Thus disorder will tend to increase with time if the system obeys an initial condition of high order.

Suppose the pieces of the jigsaw start off in a box in the ordered arrangement in which they form a picture. If you shake the box, the pieces will take up another arrangement. This will probably be a disordered arrangement in which the pieces don't form a proper picture, simply because there are so many more disordered

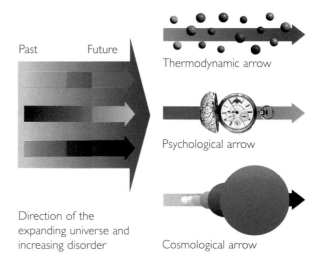

Fig. 9.3. *There are at least three arrows of time: the direction in which disorder increases, the direction in which we perceive time passes, and the direction in which the universe increases in size.*

arrangements. Some groups of pieces may still form parts of the picture, but the more you shake the box, the more likely it is that these groups will get broken up and the pieces will be in a completely jumbled state in which they don't form any sort of picture. So the disorder of the pieces will probably increase with time if the pieces obey the initial condition that they start off in a condition of high order.

Suppose, however, that God decided that the universe should finish up in a state of high order but that it didn't matter what state it started in.

At early times the universe would probably be in a disordered state. This would mean that disorder would *decrease* with time. You would see broken cups gathering themselves together and jumping back onto the table. However, any human beings who were observing the cups would be living in a universe in which disorder decreased with time. I shall argue that such beings would have a psychological arrow of time that was backward. That is, they would remember events in the future, and not remember events in their past. When the cup was broken, they would remember it being on the table, but when it was on the table, they would not remember it being on the floor.

It is rather difficult to talk about human memory because we don't know how the brain works in detail. We do, however, know all about how computer memories work. I shall therefore discuss the psychological arrow of time for computers. I think it is reasonable to assume that the arrow for computers is the same as that for humans. If it were not, one could make a killing on the stock exchange by having a computer that would remember tomorrow's prices! A computer memory is basically a device containing elements that can exist in either of two

Fig. 9.4. *An abacus works in a similar way to a computer memory. Each bead can be in one of two positions. To change the position of a bead, a certain amount of energy is required.*

states. A simple example is an abacus. In its simplest form, this consists of a number of wires; on each wire there are a number of beads which can be put in one of two positions. Before an item is recorded in a computer's memory, the memory is in a disordered state, with equal probabilities for the two possible states. (The abacus beads are scattered randomly on the wires of the abacus.) After the memory interacts with the system to be remembered, it will definitely be in one state or the other, according to the state of the system. (Each abacus bead will be at either the left or the right of the abacus wire.) So the memory has passed from a disordered state to an ordered one. However, in order to make sure that the memory is in the right state, it is necessary to use a certain amount of energy (to move the bead or to power the computer, for example). This energy is dissipated as heat, and increases the amount of disorder in the universe. One can show that this increase in disorder is always greater than the increase in the order of the memory itself. Thus the heat expelled by the computer's cooling fan means that when a computer records an item in memory, the total amount of disorder in the universe still goes up. The direction of time in which a computer remembers the past is the same as that in which disorder increases.

Our subjective sense of the direction of time, the psychological arrow of time, is therefore determined within our brain by the thermodynamic arrow of time. Just like a computer, we must remember things in the order in which entropy increases. This makes the second law of thermodynamics almost trivial. Disorder increases with time because we measure time in the direction in which disorder increases. You can't have a safer bet than that!

But why should the thermodynamic arrow of time exist at all? Or, in other words, why should the universe be in a state of high order at one end of time, the end that we call the past? Why is it not in a state of complete disorder at all times? After all, this might seem more probable. And why is the direction of time in which disorder increases the same as that in which the universe expands?

In the classical theory of general relativity one cannot predict how the universe would have begun because all the known laws of science would have broken down at the big bang singularity. The universe could have started out in a very smooth and ordered state. This would have led to well-defined thermodynamic and cosmological arrows of time, as we observe. But it could equally well have started out in a very lumpy and disordered state. In that case, the universe would already be in a state of complete disorder, so disorder could not increase with time. It would either stay constant, in which case there would be no well-defined thermodynamic arrow of time, or it would decrease, in which case the thermodynamic arrow of time would point in the opposite direction to the cosmological arrow. Neither of these possibilities agrees with what we observe. However, as we have seen, classical general relativity predicts its own downfall. When the curvature of spacetime becomes large, quantum gravitational

effects will become important and the classical theory will cease to be a good description of the universe. One has to use a quantum theory of gravity to understand how the universe began.

In a quantum theory of gravity, as we saw in the last chapter, in order to specify the state of the universe one would still have to say how the possible histories of the universe would behave at the boundary of space-time in the past. One could avoid this difficulty of having to describe what we do not and cannot know only if the histories satisfy the no boundary condition: they are finite in extent but have no boundaries, edges, or singularities. In that case, the beginning of time would be a regular, smooth point of space-time and the universe would have begun its expansion in a very smooth and ordered state. It could not have been completely uniform, because that would violate the uncertainty principle of quantum theory. There had to be small fluctuations in the density and velocities of particles. The no boundary condition, however, implied that these fluctuations were as small as they could be, consistent with the uncertainty principle.

The universe would have started off with a period of exponential or "inflationary" expansion in which it would have increased its size by a very large factor. During this expansion, the density fluctuations would have remained small at first, but later would have started to grow. Regions in which the density was slightly higher than average would have had their expansion slowed down by the gravitational attraction of the extra mass. Eventually, such regions would stop expanding and collapse to form galaxies, stars, and beings like us. The universe would have started in a smooth and ordered state, and would become lumpy and disordered as time went on. This would explain the existence of the thermodynamic arrow of time.

But what would happen if and when the universe stopped expanding and began to contract? Would the thermodynamic arrow reverse and disorder begin to decrease with time? This would lead to all sorts of science-fiction-like possibilities for people who survived from the expanding to the contracting phase. Would they see broken cups gathering themselves together off the floor and jumping back onto the table? Would they be able to remember tomorrow's prices and make a fortune on the stock market? It might seem a bit academic to worry about what will happen when the universe collapses

Opposite: The sands of time appear to be moving in only one direction, but does this change when the universe's hourglass is upended?

again, as it will not start to contract for at least another ten thousand million years. But there is a quicker way to find out what will happen: jump into a black hole. The collapse of a star to form a black hole is rather like the later stages of the collapse of the whole universe. So if disorder were to decrease in the contracting phase of the universe, one might also expect it to decrease inside a black hole. So perhaps an astronaut who fell into a black hole would be able to make money at roulette by remembering where the ball went before he placed his bet. (Unfortunately, however, he would not have long to play before he was turned to spaghetti. Nor would he be able to let us know about the reversal of the thermodynamic arrow, or even bank his winnings, because he would be trapped behind the event horizon of the black hole.)

At first, I believed that disorder would decrease when the universe recollapsed. This was because I thought that the universe had to return to a smooth and ordered state when it became small again. This would mean that the contracting phase would be like the time reverse of the expanding phase. People in the contracting phase would live their lives backward: they would die before they were born and get younger as the universe contracted.

This idea is attractive because it would mean

a nice symmetry between the expanding and contracting phases. However, one cannot adopt it on its own, independent of other ideas about the universe. The question is: is it implied by the no boundary condition, or is it inconsistent with that condition? As I said, I thought at first that the no boundary condition did indeed imply that disorder would decrease in the contracting phase. I was misled partly by the analogy with the surface of the earth. If one took the beginning of the universe to correspond to the North Pole, then the end of the universe should be similar to the beginning, just as the South Pole is similar to the North. However, the North and South Poles correspond to the beginning and

TIME →

If the thermodynamic arrow reversed in a contracting universe, then demolished buildings would rise from the rubble and people would be born old and "die" young.

dents, Raymond Laflamme, found that in a slightly more complicated model, the collapse of the universe was very different from the expansion. I realized that I had made a mistake: the no boundary condition implied that disorder would in fact continue to increase during the contraction. The thermodynamic and psychological arrows of time would not reverse when the universe begins to recontract or inside black holes.

What should you do when you find you have made a mistake like that? Some people never admit that they are wrong and continue to find new, and often mutually inconsistent, arguments to support their case — as Eddington did in opposing black hole theory. Others claim to have never really supported the incorrect view in the first place or, if they did, it was only to show that it was inconsistent. It seems to me much better and less confusing if you admit in print that you were wrong. A good example of this was Einstein, who called the cosmological constant, which he introduced when he was trying to make a static model of the universe, the biggest mistake of his life.

To return to the arrow of time, there remains the question: why do we observe that the thermodynamic and cosmological arrows point in the same direction? Or in other words, why does disorder increase in the same direction of time as

end of the universe in imaginary time. The beginning and end in real time can be very different from each other. I was also misled by work I had done on a simple model of the universe in which the collapsing phase looked like the time reverse of the expanding phase. However, a colleague of mine, Don Page, of Penn State University, pointed out that the no boundary condition did not require the contracting phase necessarily to be the time reverse of the expanding phase. Further, one of my stu-

that in which the universe expands? If one believes that the universe will expand and then contract again, as the no boundary proposal seems to imply, this becomes a question of why we should be in the expanding phase rather than the contracting phase.

One can answer this on the basis of the weak anthropic principle. Conditions in the contracting phase would not be suitable for the existence of intelligent beings who could ask the question: why is disorder increasing in the same direction of time as that in which the universe is expanding? The inflation in the early stages of the universe, which the no boundary proposal predicts, means that the universe must be expanding at very close to the critical rate at which it would just avoid recollapse, and so will not recollapse for a very long time. By then all the stars will have burned out and the protons and neutrons in them will probably have decayed into light particles and radiation. The universe would be in a state of almost complete disorder. There would be no strong thermodynamic arrow of time. Disorder couldn't increase much because the universe would be in a state of almost complete disorder already. However, a strong thermodynamic arrow is necessary for intelligent life to operate. In order to survive, human beings have to consume food, which is an ordered form of energy, and convert it into heat, which is a disordered form of energy. Thus intelligent life could not exist in the contracting phase of the universe. This is the explanation of why we observe that the thermodynamic and cosmological arrows of time point in the same direction. It is not that the expansion of the universe causes disorder to increase. Rather, it is that the no boundary condition causes disorder to increase and the conditions to be suitable for intelligent life only in the expanding phase.

To summarize, the laws of science do not distinguish between the forward and backward directions of time. However, there are at least three arrows of time that do distinguish the past from the future. They are the thermodynamic arrow, the direction of time in which disorder increases; the psychological arrow, the direction of time in which we remember the past and not the future; and the cosmological arrow, the direction of time in which the universe expands rather than contracts. I have shown that the psychological arrow is essentially the same as the thermodynamic arrow, so that the two would always point in the same direction. The no boundary proposal for the universe predicts the existence of a well-defined thermodynamic

Fig. 9.5

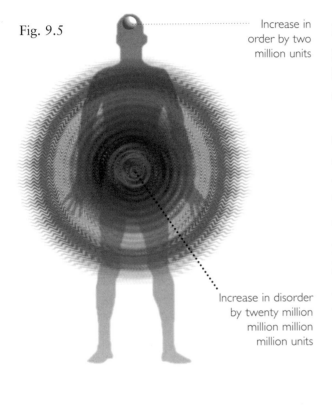

Increase in
order by two
million units

Increase in disorder
by twenty million
million million
million units

Fig. 9.5. *Reading this book will have increased the amount of ordered information in your brain. However, during the same time, the heat released by your body will have had a much greater effect increasing the disorder in the rest of the universe. I suggest you stop reading now.*

arrow of time because the universe must start off in a smooth and ordered state. And the reason we observe this thermodynamic arrow to agree with the cosmological arrow is that intel-

ligent beings can exist only in the expanding phase. The contracting phase will be unsuitable because it has no strong thermodynamic arrow of time.

The progress of the human race in understanding the universe has established a small corner of order in an increasingly disordered universe. If you remember every word in this book, your memory will have recorded about two million pieces of information: the order in your brain will have increased by about two million units. However, while you have been reading the book, you will have converted at least a thousand calories of ordered energy, in the form of food, into disordered energy, in the form of heat that you lose to the air around you by convection and sweat (Fig 9.5). This will increase the disorder of the universe by about twenty million million million million units — or about ten million million million times the increase in order in your brain — and that's if you remember *everything* in this book. In the next chapter but one I will try to increase the order in our neck of the woods a little further by explaining how people are trying to fit together the partial theories I have described to form a complete unified theory that would cover everything in the universe.

10

Wormholes and Time Travel

THE LAST CHAPTER discussed why we see time go forward: why disorder increases and why we remember the past but not the future. Time was treated as if it were a straight railway line on which one could only go one way or the other.

But what if the railway line had loops and branches so that a train could keep going forward but come back to a station it had already passed? (Fig. 10.1) In other words, might it be possible for someone to travel into the future or the past?

H. G. Wells in *The Time Machine* explored these possibilities as have countless other writers of science fiction. Yet many of the ideas of science fiction, like submarines and travel to the moon, have become matters of science fact. So what are the prospects for time travel?

The first indication that the laws of physics might really allow people to travel in time came in 1949 when Kurt Gödel discovered a new space-time allowed by general relativity. Gödel was a mathematician who was famous for proving that it is impossible to prove all true statements, even if you limit yourself to trying to prove all the true statements in a subject as apparently cut and dried as arithmetic. Like the uncertainty principle, Gödel's incompleteness theorem may be a fundamental limitation on our ability to understand and predict the universe, but so far at least it hasn't seemed to be an obstacle in our search for a complete unified theory.

Gödel got to know about general relativity

Above: *"The Time Machine" by the English writer H.G. Wells was the first popular work of fiction to explore the idea of travel through time.*

Fig. 10.1

"The train now arriving at platform one already arrived half an hour ago."

Time may not be like a single railway line but may loop back on itself.

TIME

when he and Einstein spent their later years at the Institute for Advanced Study in Princeton, U.S.A. His space-time had the curious property that the whole universe was rotating. One might ask: "Rotating with respect to what?" The answer is that distant matter would be rotating with respect to directions that little tops or gyroscopes point in.

This had the side effect that it would be possible for someone to go off in a rocket ship and return to earth before he set out. This property really upset Einstein, who had thought that general relativity wouldn't allow time travel. However, given Einstein's record of ill-founded opposition to gravitational collapse and the uncertainty principle, maybe this was an encouraging sign. The solution Gödel found doesn't correspond to the universe we live in because we can show that the universe is not rotating. It also had a non-zero value of the cosmological constant that Einstein introduced when he thought the universe was unchanging. After Hubble discovered the expansion of the universe, there was no need for a cosmological constant and it is now generally believed to be zero. However, other more reasonable space-times that are allowed by general relativity and which permit travel into the past have since been found. One is in the interior of a rotating black hole. Another is a space-time that contains two cosmic strings moving past each other at high speed. As their name suggests, cosmic strings are objects that are like string in that they have length but a tiny cross section. Actually, they are more like rubber bands because they are under enormous tension, something like a million million million million tons. A cosmic string attached to the earth could accelerate it from 0 to 60 mph in 1/30th of a second. Cosmic strings may sound like pure science fiction but there are reasons to believe they could have formed in the early universe as a result of symmetry-breaking of the kind discussed in Chapter 5. Because they would be under enormous tension and could start in any configuration, they might accelerate to very high speeds when they straighten out.

The Gödel solution and the cosmic string space-time start out so distorted that travel into the past was always possible. God might have created such a warped universe but we have no reason to believe he did. Observations of the microwave background and of the abundances of the light elements indicate that the early universe did not have the kind of curvature required to allow time travel. The same conclusion follows on theoretical grounds if the no boundary proposal is correct. So the question is: if the universe starts out without the kind of curvature required for time travel, can we subsequently warp local regions of space-time sufficiently to allow it?

A closely related problem that is also of concern to writers of science fiction is rapid interstellar or intergalactic travel. According to relativity, nothing can travel faster than light. If we therefore sent a spaceship to our nearest neighboring star, Alpha Centauri, which is about four light years away, it would take at least eight years before we could expect the travelers to return and tell us what they had found . If the expedition were to the center of our galaxy, it would be at least a hundred thousand years before it came back. The theory of relativity does allow one consolation. This is the so-called twins paradox mentioned in Chapter 2.

Because there is no unique standard of time, but rather observers each have their own time as measured by clocks that they carry with them, it is possible for the journey to seem to be much shorter for the space travelers than for those who remain on earth. But there would not be much joy in returning from a space voyage a few years older to find that everyone you had left behind was dead and gone thousands of years ago. So in order to have any human interest in their stories, science fiction writers had to suppose that we would one day discover how to travel faster than light. What most of these authors don't seem to have realized is that if you can travel faster than light, the theory of relativity implies you can also travel back in time, as the following limerick says:

There was a young lady of Wight
Who travelled much faster than light.
She departed one day,
In a relative way,
And arrived on the previous night.

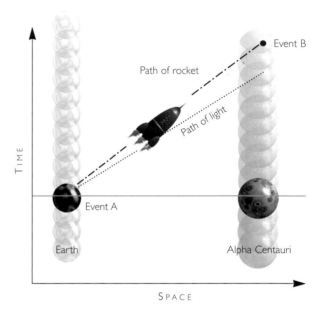

Fig. 10.2 *If a rocket can travel from event A on earth to event B on Alpha Centauri at a speed slower than the speed of light, then all observers will agree that event A occurs before event B.*

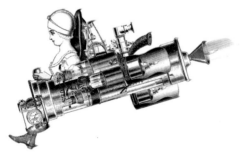

The point is that the theory of relativity says that there is no unique measure of time that all observers will agree on. Rather, each observer has his or her own measure of time. If it is possible for a rocket traveling below the speed of light to get from event A (say, the final of the 100-meter race of the Olympic Games in 2012) to event B (say, the opening of 100,004th meeting of the Congress of Alpha Centauri), then all observers will agree that event A happened before event B according to their times (Fig. 10.2). Suppose, however, that the spaceship would have to travel faster than light to carry the news of the race to the Congress. Then

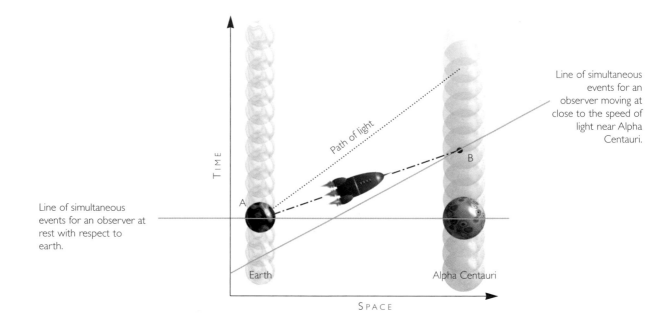

Line of simultaneous events for an observer moving at close to the speed of light near Alpha Centauri.

Line of simultaneous events for an observer at rest with respect to earth.

TIME

Path of light

B

A

Earth

Alpha Centauri

SPACE

Above: Fig. 10.3 *If it is not possible for a rocket to get from A to B at below the speed of light, observers moving at different speeds may not agree on which event occurs first.*
Opposite: Fig. 10.4 *Wormholes might be able to provide a shortcut for jumping between two distant regions of nearly flat space-time.*

---

observers moving at different speeds can disagree about whether event A occurred before B or vice versa. According to the time of an observer who is at rest with respect to the earth, it may be that the Congress opened after the race. Thus this observer would think that a spaceship could get from A to B in time if only it could ignore the speed-of-light speed limit.

However, to an observer at Alpha Centauri moving away from the earth at nearly the speed of light, it would appear that event B, the opening of the Congress, would occur before event A, the 100-meter race (Fig. 10.3). The theory of relativity says that the laws of physics appear the same to observers moving at different speeds.

This has been well tested by experiment and is likely to remain a feature even if we find a more advanced theory to replace relativity. Thus the moving observer would say that if faster-than-light travel is possible, it should be possible to get from event B, the opening of the Congress, to event A, the 100-meter race. If one went slightly faster, one could even get back before the race and place a bet on it in the sure knowledge that one would win.

There is a problem with breaking the speed-of-light barrier. The theory of relativity says that the rocket power needed to accelerate a spaceship gets greater and greater the nearer it gets to the speed of light. We have experimental evidence for this, not with spaceships but with elementary particles in particle accelerators like those at Fermilab or CERN (European Centre for Nuclear Research). We can accelerate particles to 99.99 percent of the speed of light, but however much power we feed in, we can't get them beyond the speed-of-light-barrier. Similarly with spaceships: no matter how much rocket power they have, they can't accelerate beyond the speed of light.

That might seem to rule out both rapid space travel and travel back in time. However, there is a possible way out. It might be that one could warp space-time so that there was a shortcut between A and B. One way of doing this would be to create a wormhole between A and B. As its name suggests, a wormhole is a thin tube of space-time which can connect two nearly flat regions far apart (Fig. 10.4).

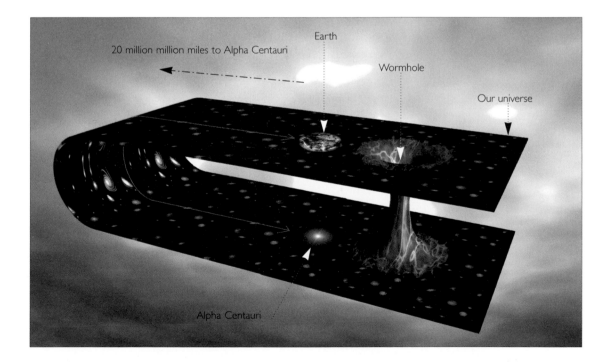

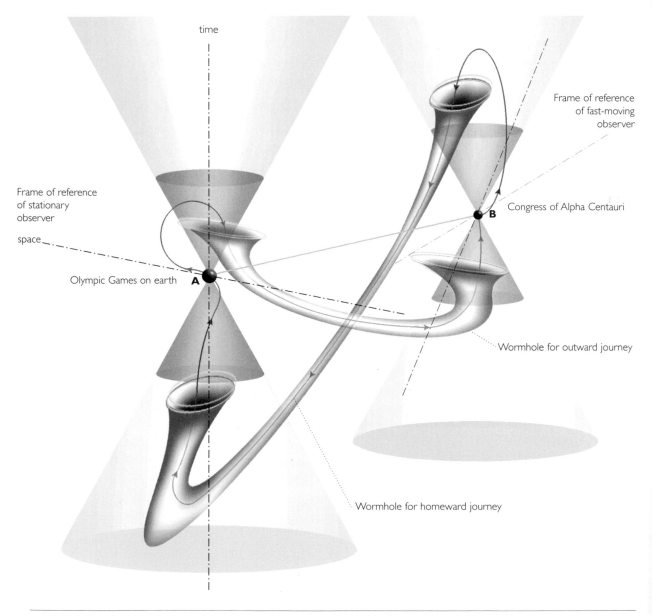

Fig. 10.5 *A space traveler could use a wormhole, which is stationary with respect to earth, as a shortcut to get from event A to B and then come back through a moving wormhole and return to earth before he set out.*

There need be no relation between the distance through the wormhole and the separation of its ends in the nearly flat background. Thus one could imagine that one could create or find a wormhole that would lead from the vicinity of the solar system to Alpha Centauri. The distance through the wormhole might be only a few million miles even though earth and Alpha Centauri are twenty million million miles apart in ordinary space. This would allow news of the 100-meter race to reach the opening of the Congress. But then an observer moving toward the earth should also be able to find another wormhole that would enable him to get from the opening of the Congress on Alpha Centauri back to earth before the start of the race (Fig. 10.5). So wormholes, like any other possible form of travel faster than light, would allow one to travel into the past.

The idea of wormholes between different regions of space-time was not an invention of science fiction writers but came from a very respectable source.

In 1935, Einstein and Nathan Rosen wrote a paper in which they showed that general relativity allowed what they called "bridges," but which are now known as wormholes. The Einstein-Rosen bridges didn't last long enough for a spaceship to get through: the ship would run into a singularity as the wormhole pinched

Fig. 10.6 *Ordinary matter gives space-time a positive curvature, like the surface of a sphere. To allow travel into the past, space-time must have negative curvature, like the surface of a saddle.*

off (see Fig. 10.7). However, it has been suggested that it might be possible for an advanced civilization to keep a wormhole open. To do this, or to warp space-time in any other way so as to permit time travel, one can show that one needs a region of space-time with negative curvature, like the surface of a saddle (Fig. 10.6). Ordinary matter, which has a positive energy density, gives space-time a positive curvature, like the surface

An Einstein-Rosen bridge is a wormhole connecting two distant regions.

The wormhole pinches off, to form two separate singularities, before a spaceship can get through.

of a sphere. So what one needs, in order to warp space-time in a way that will allow travel into the past, is matter with negative energy density.

Energy is a bit like money: if you have a positive balance, you can distribute it in various ways, but according to the classical laws that were believed at the beginning of the century, you weren't allowed to be overdrawn. So these classical laws would have ruled out any possibility of time travel. However, as has been described in earlier chapters, the classical laws

Fig. 10.7 *Einstein–Rosen bridges are wormholes that can connect distant regions, but they don't stay open long enough for anything to get through.*

were superseded by quantum laws based on the uncertainty principle. The quantum laws are more liberal and allow you to be overdrawn on one or two accounts provided the total balance is positive. In other words, quantum theory allows the energy density to be negative in some places, provided that this is made up for by positive energy densities in other places, so that the total energy remains positive. An example of how quantum theory can allow negative energy densities is provided by what is called the Casimir effect (Fig. 10.8). As we saw in Chapter 7, even what we think of as "empty" space is filled with pairs of virtual particles and antiparticles that appear together, move apart, and come back together and annihilate each other. Now, suppose one has two parallel metal plates a short distance apart. The plates will act like mirrors for the virtual photons or particles of light. In fact they will form a cavity between them, a bit like an organ pipe that will resonate only at certain notes. This means that virtual photons can occur in the space between the plates only if their wavelengths (the distance between the crest of one wave and the next) fit a whole number of times into the gap between the plates. If the width of a cavity is a whole number of wavelengths plus a fraction of a wavelength, then after some reflections backward and forward between the plates, the crests of one wave will coincide with the troughs of another and the waves will cancel out.

Because the virtual photons between the plates can have only the resonant wavelengths, there will be slightly fewer of them than in the region outside the plates where virtual photons can have any wavelength. Thus there will be

Fig. 10.8 *Empty space is "filled" with pairs of virtual particles and antiparticles. A pair of metal plates will act as mirrors for these particles, and allow only virtual pairs of certain resonant wavelengths to exist between them. This is known as the Casimir effect.*

slightly fewer virtual photons hitting the inside surfaces of the plates than the outside surfaces. One would therefore expect a force on the plates, pushing them toward each other. This force has actually been detected and has the predicted value. Thus we have experimental evidence that virtual particles exist and have real effects.

The fact that there are fewer virtual photons between the plates means that their energy density will be less than elsewhere. But the total energy density in "empty" space far away from the plates must be zero, because otherwise the energy density would warp the space and it would not be almost flat. So, if the energy density between the plates is less than the energy density far away, it must be negative.

We thus have experimental evidence both that space-time can be warped (from the bending of light during eclipses) and that it can be curved in the way necessary to allow time travel (from the Casimir effect). One might hope therefore that as we advance in science and technology, we would eventually manage to build a time machine. But if so, why hasn't anyone come back from the future and told us how to do it? There might be good reasons why it would be unwise to give us the secret of time travel at our present primitive state of development, but unless human nature changes radically, it is difficult to believe that some visitor from the future wouldn't spill the beans. Of course, some people would claim that sightings of UFOs are evidence that we are being visited either by aliens or by people from the future. (If the aliens were to get here in reasonable time, they would need faster-than-light travel, so the two possibilities may be equivalent.)

However, I think that any visit by aliens or people from the future would be much more obvious and, probably, much more unpleasant. If they are going to reveal themselves at all, why do so only to those who are not regarded as reli-

able witnesses? If they are trying to warn us of some great danger, they are not being very effective.

A possible way to explain the absence of visitors from the future would be to say that the past is fixed because we have observed it and seen that it does not have the kind of warping needed to allow travel back from the future. On the other hand, the future is unknown and open, so it might well have the curvature required. This would mean that any time travel would be confined to the future. There would be no chance of Captain Kirk and the Starship *Enterprise* turning up at the present time.

This might explain why we have not yet been overrun by tourists from the future, but it would

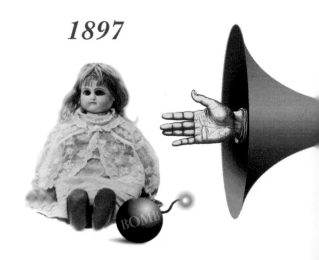

1897

not avoid the problems that would arise if one were able to go back and change history. Suppose, for example, you went back and killed your great great grandfather while he was still a child. There are many versions of this paradox but they are essentially equivalent: one would get contradictions if one were free to change the past.

There seem to be two possible resolutions to the paradoxes posed by time travel. One I shall call the consistent histories approach. It says that even if space-time is warped so that it would be possible to travel into the past, what happens in space-time must be a consistent solution of the laws of physics. According to this viewpoint, you could not go back in time unless history showed that you had already arrived in the past and, while there, had not killed your great great grandfather or committed any other acts that would conflict with your current situation in the present. Moreover, when you did go back, you wouldn't be able to change recorded history. That means you wouldn't have free will to do what you wanted. Of course, one could say that free will is an illusion anyway. If there really is a complete unified theory that governs everything, it presumably also determines your actions. But it does so in a way that is impossible to calculate for an organism that is as complicated as a human being. The reason we say that humans have free will is because we can't predict what they will do. However, if the human then goes off in a rocket ship and comes back before he or she set off, we *will* be able to predict what he or she will do because it will be part of recorded history. Thus, in that situation, the time traveler would have no free will.

The other possible way to resolve the paradoxes of time travel might be called the alternative histories hypothesis. The idea here is that when time travelers go back to the past, they enter alternative histories which differ from recorded history (Fig. 10.9). Thus they can act freely, without the constraint of consistency with their previous history. Steven Spielberg had

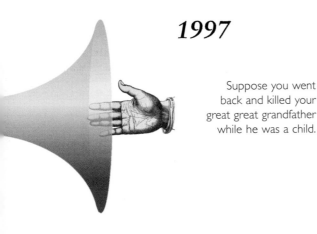

1997

Suppose you went back and killed your great great grandfather while he was a child.

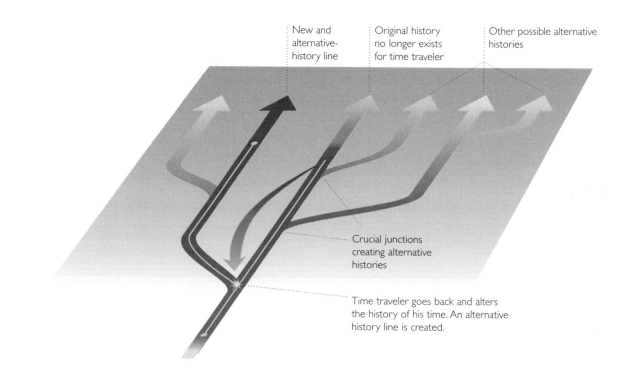

New and
alternative-
history line

Original history
no longer exists
for time traveler

Other possible alternative
histories

Crucial junctions
creating alternative
histories

Time traveler goes back and alters
the history of his time. An alternative
history line is created.

Fig. 10.9 *One solution to time travel paradoxes would be to assume there are a whole series of alternative histories which branch off from each other at certain crucial events.*

fun with this notion in the *Back to the Future* films: Marty McFly was able to go back and change his parent's courtship to a more satisfactory history.

The alternative histories hypothesis sounds rather like Richard Feynman's way of expressing quantum theory as a sum over histories, which was described in Chapters 4 and 8. This said that the universe didn't just have a single history: rather it had every possible history, each with its own probability. However, there seems to be an important difference between Feynman's proposal and alternative histories. In Feynman's sum, each history comprises a complete space-time and everything in it. The space-time may be so warped that it is possible to travel in a rocket into the past. But the rocket would remain in the same space-time and therefore the same history, which would have to be consistent. Thus Feynman's sum over histories proposal seems to support the consistent histories hypothesis rather than the alternative histories.

The Feynman sum over histories *does* allow travel into the past on a microscopic scale. In Chapter 9 we saw that the laws of science are unchanged by combinations of the operations C, P, and T. This means that an antiparticle spinning in the anticlockwise direction and moving from A to B can also be viewed as an ordinary particle spinning clockwise and moving backward in time from B to A. Similarly, an ordinary particle moving forward in time is equivalent to an antiparticle moving backward in time. As has been discussed in this chapter and Chapter 7, "empty" space is filled with pairs of virtual particles and antiparticles that appear together, move apart, and then come back together and annihilate each other.

So, one can regard the pair of particles as a single particle moving on a closed loop in space-time (Fig. 10.10). When the pair is moving forward in time (from the event at which it appears to that at which it annihilates), it is called a particle. But when the particle is traveling back in time (from the event at which the pair annihilates to that at which it appears), it is said to be an antiparticle traveling forward in time.

The explanation of how black holes can emit particles and radiation (given in Chapter 7) was

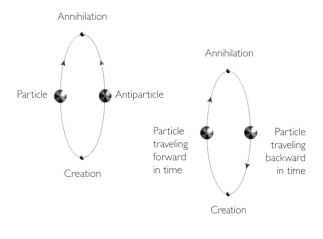

Fig. 10.10 *An antiparticle can be regarded as a particle moving backward in time. A virtual particle/ antiparticle pair can therefore be regarded as a particle moving on a closed loop in space-time.*

that one member of a virtual particle/antiparticle pair (say, the antiparticle) might fall into the black hole, leaving the other member without a partner with which to annihilate. The forsaken particle might fall into the hole as well, but it might also escape from the vicinity of the black hole. If so, to an observer at a distance it would appear to be a particle emitted by the black hole.

One can, however, have a different but equivalent intuitive picture of the mechanism for emission from black holes. One can regard the member of the virtual pair that fell into the black hole (say, the antiparticle) as a particle

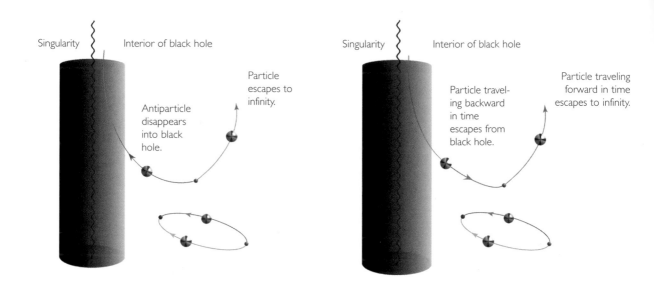

Fig. 10.11 *Two equivalent pictures of black hole radiation. On the left the antiparticle in a virtual pair falls into the hole, leaving the particle free to escape. On the right an antiparticle falling into the hole is regarded as a particle traveling backward in time and coming out of the hole.*

traveling backward in time out of the hole. When it gets to the point at which the virtual particle/antiparticle pair appeared together, it is scattered by the gravitational field into a particle traveling forward in time and escaping from the black hole (Fig. 10.11). If, instead, it were the particle member of the virtual pair that fell into the hole, one could regard it as an antiparticle traveling back in time and coming out of the black hole. Thus the radiation by black holes shows that quantum theory allows travel back in time on a microscopic scale and that such time travel can produce observable effects.

One can therefore ask: does quantum theory allow time travel on a macroscopic scale, which people could use? At first sight, it seems it should. The Feynman sum over histories proposal is supposed to be over *all* histories. Thus it should include histories in which space-time is so warped that it is possible to travel into the past. Why then aren't we in trouble with history? Suppose, for example, someone had gone back and given the Nazis the secret of the atom bomb?

One would avoid these problems if what I call the chronology protection conjecture holds.

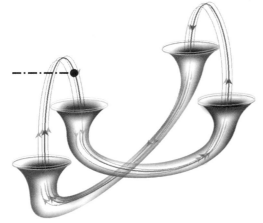

Passing a given point on the loop increases the energy density of that point.

Fig. 10.12 *In space-times that allow time travel, virtual particles can become real. They will pass the same point of space-time many times and can cause the energy density to become very large.*

This says that the laws of physics conspire to prevent *macroscopic* bodies from carrying information into the past. Like the cosmic censorship conjecture, it has not been proved but there are reasons to believe it is true.

The reason to believe that chronology protection operates is that when space-time is warped enough to make travel into the past possible, virtual particles moving on closed loops in space-time can become real particles traveling forward in time at or below the speed of light. As these particles can go round the loop any number of times, they pass each point on their route many times (Fig. 10.12). Thus their energy is counted over and over again and the energy density will become very large. This could give space-time a positive curvature which would not allow travel into the past. It is not yet clear whether these particles would cause positive or negative curvature or whether the curvature produced by some kinds of virtual particles might cancel that produced by other kinds. Thus the possibility of time travel remains open. But I'm not going to bet on it. My opponent might have the unfair advantage of knowing the future.

211

11

The Unification of Physics

A S WAS EXPLAINED IN THE FIRST CHAPTER, it would be very difficult to construct a complete unified theory of everything in the universe all at one go. So instead we have made progress by finding partial theories that describe a limited range of happenings and by neglecting other effects or approximating them by certain numbers. (Chemistry, for example, allows us to calculate the interactions of atoms, without knowing the internal structure of an atom's nucleus.) Ultimately, however, one would hope to find a complete, consistent, unified theory that would include all these partial theories as approximations, and that did not need to be adjusted to fit the facts by picking the values of certain arbitrary numbers in the theory. The quest for such a theory is known as "the unification of physics." Einstein spent most of his later years unsuccessfully searching for a unified theory, but the time was not ripe: there were partial theories for gravity and the electromagnetic force, but very little was known about the nuclear forces. Moreover, Einstein refused to

believe in the reality of quantum mechanics, despite the important role he had played in its development. Yet it seems that the uncertainty principle is a fundamental feature of the universe we live in. A successful unified theory must, therefore, necessarily incorporate this principle.

As I shall describe, the prospects for finding such a theory seem to be much better now because we know so much more about the universe. But we must beware of overconfidence — we have had false dawns before! At the beginning of this century, for example, it was thought that everything could be explained in terms of the properties of continuous matter, such as elasticity and heat conduction. The discovery of atomic structure and the uncertainty principle put an emphatic end to that. Then again, in 1928, physicist and Nobel prize winner Max Born told a group of visitors to Göttingen University, "Physics, as we know it, will be over in six months." His confidence was based on the recent discovery by Dirac of the equation that

Fig. 11.1 *The pairs of virtual particles and antiparticles would give even "empty" space an infinite energy density and would curve it up infinitely small. This infinite energy has to be subtracted out or canceled.*

governed the electron. It was thought that a similar equation would govern the proton, which was the only other particle known at the time, and that would be the end of theoretical physics. However, the discovery of the neutron and of nuclear forces knocked that one on the head too. Having said this, I still believe there are grounds for cautious optimism that we may now be near the end of the search for the ultimate laws of nature.

In previous chapters I have described general relativity, the partial theory of gravity, and the partial theories that govern the weak, the strong, and the electromagnetic forces. The last three may be combined in so-called grand unified theories, or GUTs, which are not very satisfactory because they do not include gravity and because they contain a number of quantities, like the relative masses of different particles, that cannot be predicted from the theory but have to be chosen to fit observations. The main difficulty in finding a theory that unifies gravity with the other forces is that general relativity is a "classical" theory; that is, it does not incorporate the uncertainty principle of quantum mechanics. On the other hand, the other partial theories depend on quantum mechanics in an essential way. A necessary first step, therefore, is to combine general relativity with the uncertainty principle. As we have seen, this can produce

213

filled with pairs of virtual particles and antiparticles. These pairs would have an infinite amount of energy and, therefore, by Einstein's famous equation $E = mc^2$, they would have an infinite amount of mass. Their gravitational attraction would thus curve up the universe to infinitely small size (Fig. 11.1).

Rather similar, seemingly absurd infinities occur in the other partial theories, but in all these cases the infinities can be canceled out by a process called renormalization. This involves canceling the infinities by introducing other infinities. Although this technique is rather dubious mathematically, it does seem to work in practice, and has been used with these theories to make predictions that agree with observations to an extraordinary degree of accuracy. Renormalization, however, does have a serious drawback from the point of view of trying to find a complete theory, because it means that the actual values of the masses and the strengths of the forces cannot be predicted from the theory, but have to be chosen to fit the observations.

In attempting to incorporate the uncertainty principle into general relativity, one has only two quantities that can be adjusted: the strength of gravity and the value of the cosmological constant. But adjusting these is not sufficient to remove all the infinities (Fig. 11.2). One there-

Fig. 11.2 *In general relativity one can adjust only the strength of gravity and the cosmological constant. These two adjustments are not enough to cancel all the infinities.*

some remarkable consequences, such as black holes not being black, and the universe not having any singularities but being completely self-contained and without a boundary. The trouble is, as explained in Chapter 7, that the uncertainty principle means that even "empty" space is

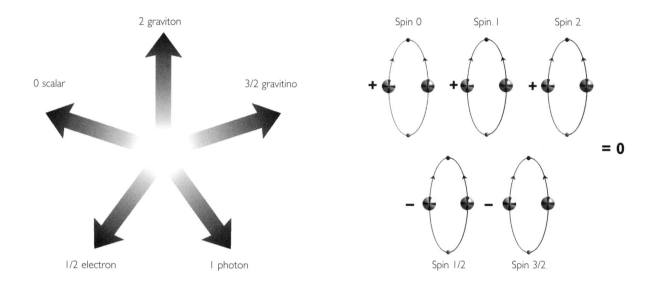

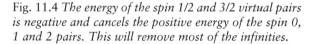

Fig. 11.3 *In supergravity, particles of different spin are regarded as different aspects of a single super-particle.*

Fig. 11.4 *The energy of the spin 1/2 and 3/2 virtual pairs is negative and cancels the positive energy of the spin 0, 1 and 2 pairs. This will remove most of the infinities.*

fore has a theory that seems to predict that certain quantities, such as the curvature of space-time, are really infinite, yet these quantities can be observed and measured to be perfectly finite! This problem in combining general relativity and the uncertainty principle had been suspected for some time, but was finally confirmed by detailed calculations in 1972. Four years later, a possible solution, called "supergravity," was suggested. The idea was to combine the spin-2 particle called the graviton, which carries the gravitational force, with certain other particles of spin 3/2, 1, 1/2, and 0. In a sense, all these

particles could then be regarded as different aspects of the same "superparticle," thus unifying the matter particles with spin 1/2 and 3/2 with the force-carrying particles of spin 0, 1, and 2 (Fig. 11.3). The virtual particle/antiparticle pairs of spin 1/2 and 3/2 would have negative energy, and so would tend to cancel out the positive energy of the spin 2, 1, and 0 virtual pairs. This would cause many of the possible infinities to cancel out (Fig. 11.4), but it was suspected that some infinities might still remain. However, the calculations required to find out whether or not there were any infinities left

Fig. 11.5

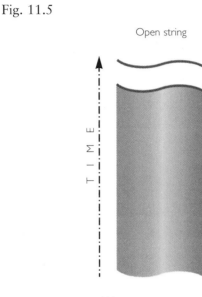

Open string

TIME

WORLD-SHEET OF OPEN STRING

Fig. 11.6

Closed string

TIME

WORLD-SHEET OF CLOSED STRING

uncanceled were so long and difficult that no one was prepared to undertake them. Even with a computer it was reckoned it would take at least four years, and the chances were very high that one would make at least one mistake, probably more. So one would know one had the right answer only if someone else repeated the calculation and got the same answer, and that did not seem very likely!

Despite these problems, and the fact that the particles in the supergravity theories did not seem to match the observed particles, most scientists believed that supergravity was probably the right answer to the problem of the unification of physics. It seemed the best way of unify-

ing gravity with the other forces. However, in 1984 there was a remarkable change of opinion in favor of what are called string theories. In these theories the basic objects are not particles, which occupy a single point of space, but things that have a length but no other dimension, like an infinitely thin piece of string. These strings may have ends (the so-called open strings) or they may be joined up with themselves in closed loops (closed strings). A particle occupies one point of space at each instant of time. Thus its history can be represented by a line in space-time (the "world-line"). A string, on the other hand, occupies a line in space at each moment of time. So its history in space-time is a two-dimen-

Fig. 11.7   Fig. 11.8

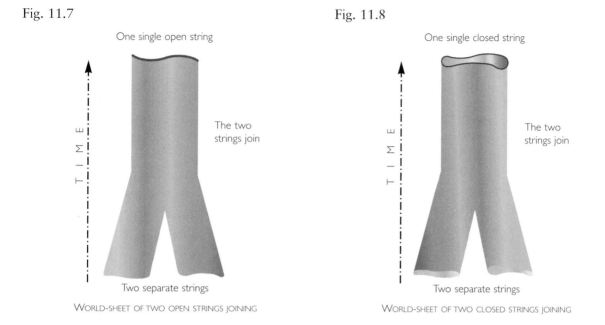

WORLD-SHEET OF TWO OPEN STRINGS JOINING   WORLD-SHEET OF TWO CLOSED STRINGS JOINING

sional surface called the world-sheet. (Any point on such a world-sheet can be described by two numbers, one specifying the time and the other the position of the point on the string.) The world-sheet of an open string is a strip: its edges represent the paths through space-time of the ends of the string (Fig. 11.5). The world-sheet of a closed string is a cylinder or tube (Fig. 11.6): a slice through the tube is a circle, which represents the position of the string at one particular time.

Two pieces of string can join together to form a single string; in the case of open strings they simply join at the ends (Fig. 11.7), while in the case of closed strings it is like the two legs

joining on a pair of trousers (Fig. 11.8). Similarly, a single piece of string can divide into two strings. In string theories, what were previously thought of as particles are now pictured as waves traveling down the string, like waves on a vibrating kite string. The emission or absorption of one particle by another corresponds to the dividing or joining together of strings. For example, the gravitational force of the sun on the earth was pictured in particle theories as being caused by the emission of a graviton by a particle in the sun and its absorption by a particle in the earth (Fig. 11.9). In string theory, this process corresponds to an H-shaped tube or pipe (Fig. 11.10) (string theory is rather like

Fig. 11.9

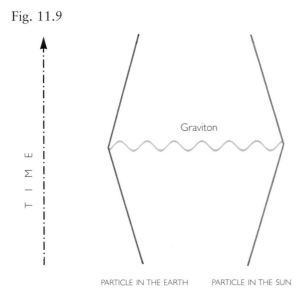

Graviton

TIME

PARTICLE IN THE EARTH   PARTICLE IN THE SUN

Fig. 11.10

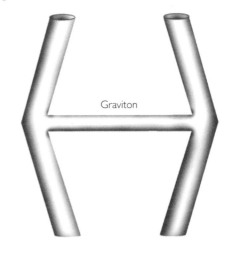

Graviton

PARTICLE IN THE EARTH   PARTICLE IN THE SUN

Figs. 11.9, 10 *In particle theories, long-range forces are pictured as being caused by the exchange of a force-carrying particle, but in string theory they are viewed as being caused by connecting tubes.*

---

plumbing, in a way). The two vertical sides of the H correspond to the particles in the sun and the earth and the horizontal crossbar corresponds to the graviton that travels between them.

String theory has a curious history. It was originally invented in the late 1960s in an attempt to find a theory to describe the strong force. The idea was that particles like the proton and the neutron could be regarded as waves on a string. The strong forces between the particles

would correspond to pieces of string that went between other bits of string, as in a spider's web. For this theory to give the observed value of the strong force between particles, the strings had to be like rubber bands with a pull of about ten tons.

In 1974 Joël Scherk from Paris and John Schwarz from the California Institute of Technology published a paper in which they showed that string theory could describe the gravitational force, but only if the tension in the string were very much higher, about a thousand million million million million million million tons (1 with thirty-nine zeros after it). The predictions of the string theory would be just the same as those of general relativity on normal length scales, but they would differ at very small distances, less than a thousand million million million million millionth of a centimeter (a centimeter divided by 1 with thirty-three zeros after it). Their work did not receive much attention, however, because at just about that time most people abandoned the original string theory of the strong force in favor of the theory based on quarks and gluons, which seemed to fit much better with observations. Scherk died in tragic circumstances (he suffered from diabetes and went into a coma when no one was around to give him an injection of insulin). So Schwarz was left alone as almost the only supporter of string theory, but now with the much higher proposed value of the string tension.

In 1984 interest in strings suddenly revived, apparently for two reasons. One was that people were not really making much progress toward showing that supergravity was finite or that it could explain the kinds of particles that we observe. The other was the publication of a paper by John Schwarz and Mike Green of Queen Mary College, London, that showed that string theory might be able to explain the existence of particles that have a built-in left-handedness, like some of the particles that we observe. Whatever the reasons, a large number

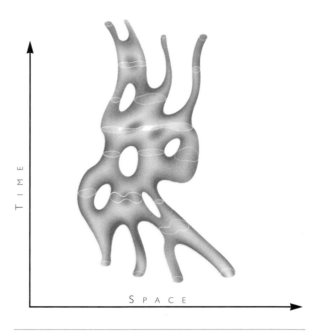

Fig. 11.11 *Closed strings combining to form sheets in space-time. If all elementary particles are treated as strings, a consistent quantum theory might be possible that accounts for all four fundamental forces.*

of people soon began to work on string theory and a new version was developed, the so-called heterotic string, which seemed as if it might be able to explain the types of particles that we observe.

String theories also lead to infinities, but it is thought they will all cancel out in versions like the heterotic string (though this is not yet known for certain). String theories, however, have a bigger problem: they seem to be consistent only if space-time has either ten or twenty-

Shortest path from A to B in two dimensions

Shortest path from A to B in three dimensions

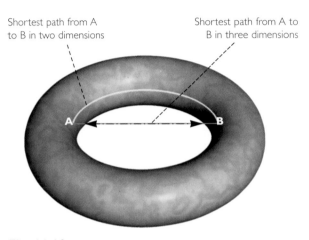

Fig. 11.12

six dimensions, instead of the usual four! Of course, extra space-time dimensions are a commonplace of science fiction indeed, they provide an ideal way of overcoming the normal restriction of general relativity that one can not travel faster than light or back in time (see Chapter 10). The idea is to take a shortcut through the extra dimensions. One can picture this in the following way. Imagine that the space we live in has only two dimensions and is curved like the surface of an anchor ring or torus (Fig. 11.12). If you were on one side of the inside edge of the ring and you wanted to get to a point on the other side, you would have to go round the inner edge of the ring. However, if you were able to travel in the third dimension, you could cut straight across.

Why don't we notice all these extra dimensions, if they are really there? Why do we see only three space dimensions and one time dimension? The suggestion is that the other dimensions are curved up into a space of very small size, something like a million million million million millionth of an inch. This is so small that we just don't notice it: we see only one time dimension and three space dimensions, in which space-time is fairly flat. It is like the surface of a straw. If you look at it closely, you see it is two-dimensional (the position of a point on the straw is described by two numbers, the length along the straw and the distance round the circular direction). But if you look at it from a distance, you don't see the thickness of the straw (Fig. 11.13) and it looks one-dimensional (the position of a point is specified only by the length along the straw). So it is with space-time: on a very small scale it is ten-dimensional and highly curved, but on bigger scales you don't see the curvature or the extra dimensions. If this picture is correct, it spells bad news for would-be space travelers: the extra dimensions would be far too small to allow a spaceship through. However, it raises another major problem. Why should some, but not all, of the dimensions be curled up into a small ball? Presumably, in the very early universe all the dimensions would have been very curved. Why did one time dimension and three space dimensions flatten out, while the other dimensions remain tightly curled up?

One possible answer is the anthropic principle. Two space dimensions do not seem to be enough to allow for the development of complicated beings like us. For example, two-dimensional animals living on a one-dimensional earth would have to climb over each other in order to get past each other. If a two-dimensional creature ate something it could not digest completely, it

Fig. 11.14

Fig. 11.14 *A two-dimensional animal with a digestive tract would fall apart.*
Fig. 11.13 *A straw looks like a two-dimensional cylinder at close range, but from a distance it looks like a one-dimensional line.*

would have to bring up the remains the same way it swallowed them, because if there were a passage right through its body, it would divide the creature into two separate halves: our two-dimensional being would fall apart (Fig. 11.14). Similarly, it is difficult to see how there could be any circulation of the blood in a two-dimensional creature.

There would also be problems with more than three space dimensions. The gravitational force between two bodies would decrease more

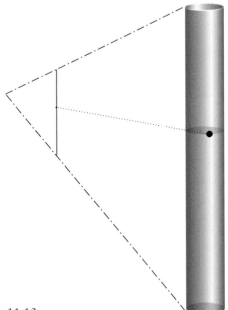

Fig. 11.13

rapidly with distance than it does in three dimensions. (In three dimensions, the gravitational force drops to 1/4 if one doubles the distance. In four dimensions it would drop to 1/8, in five dimensions to 1/16 and so on.) The significance of this is that the orbits of planets, like the earth, around the sun would be unstable: the least disturbance from a circular orbit (such as would be caused by the gravitational attraction of other planets) would result in the earth spiraling away from or into the sun. We would either freeze or be burned up. In fact, the same behavior of gravity with distance in more than three space dimensions means that the sun would not be able to exist in a stable state with pressure balancing gravity. It would either fall apart or it would collapse to form a black hole. In either case, it would not be of much use as a source of heat and light for life on earth. On a smaller scale, the electrical forces that cause the electrons to orbit round the nucleus in an atom would behave in the same way as gravitational forces. Thus the electrons would either escape from the atom altogether or would spiral into the nucleus. In either case, one could not have atoms as we know them.

It seems clear then that life, at least as we know it, can exist only in regions of space-time in which one time dimension and three space dimensions are not curled up small. This would mean that one could appeal to the weak anthropic principle, provided one could show that string theory does at least allow there to be such regions of the universe — and it seems that indeed string theory does. There may well be other regions of the universe, or other universes (whatever *that* may mean), in which all the dimensions are curled up small or in which more than four dimensions are nearly flat, but there would be no intelligent beings in such regions to observe the different number of effective dimensions.

Another problem is that there are at least four different string theories (open strings and three different closed string theories) and millions of ways in which the extra dimensions predicted by string theory could be curled up. Why should just one string theory and one kind of curling up be picked out? For a time there seemed no answer, and progress got bogged down. Then, from about 1994, people started discovering what are called dualities: different string theories and different ways of curling up the extra dimensions could lead to the same results in four dimensions. Moreover, as well as particles, which occupy a single point of space, and strings, which are lines, there were found to be other objects called p-branes, which occupied two-dimensional or higher-dimensional volumes in space. (A particle can be regarded as a 0-brane and a string as a 1-brane but there were also p-branes for p=2 to p=9.) What this seems to indicate is that there is a sort of democracy among supergravity, string, and p-brane theories: they seem to fit together but none can be said to be more fundamental than the others. They appear to be different approximations to some fundamental theory that are valid in different situations.

People have searched for this underlying theory, but without any success so far. However, I believe there may not be any single formulation of the fundamental theory any more than, as Gödel showed, one could formulate arithmetic in terms of a single set of axioms. Instead it may be like maps — you can't use a single map to describe the surface of the earth or an anchor ring: you need at least two maps in the case of the earth and four for the anchor ring to cover every point. Each map is valid only in a limited region, but different maps will have a region of overlap. The collection of maps provides a complete description of the surface (Fig. 11.15). Similarly, in physics it may be necessary to use different formulations in different situations, but

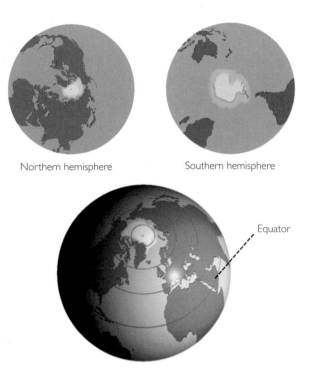

Northern hemisphere   Southern hemisphere

Equator

Fig. 11.15 *From a mathematical point of view the surface of the earth cannot be covered by a single map — one needs at least two overlapping maps. Similarly, it may not be possible to give a single fundamental formulation of theoretical physics: it may be necessary to use different formulations in different situations.*

two different formulations would agree in situations where they can both be applied. The whole collection of different formulations could be regarded as a complete unified theory, though one that could not be expressed in terms of a single set of postulates.

But can there really be such a unified theory? Or are we perhaps just chasing a mirage? There seem to be three possibilities:

1) There really is a complete unified theory, (or a collection of overlapping formulations) which we will someday discover if we are smart enough.

2) There is no ultimate theory of the universe, just an infinite sequence of theories that describe the universe more and more accurately.

3) There is no theory of the universe: events cannot be predicted beyond a certain extent but occur in a random and arbitrary manner.

Some would argue for the third possibility on the grounds that if there were a complete set of laws, that would infringe God's freedom to change his mind and intervene in the world. It's a bit like the old paradox: can God make a stone so heavy that he can't lift it? But the idea that God might want to change his mind is an example of the fallacy, pointed out by St. Augustine, of imagining God as a being existing in time: time is a property only of the universe that God created. Presumably, he knew what he intended when he set it up!

With the advent of quantum mechanics, we have come to recognize that events cannot be predicted with complete accuracy but that there is always a degree of uncertainty. If one likes,

Can God make a stone so heavy that he can't lift it?

one could ascribe this randomness to the intervention of God, but it would be a very strange kind of intervention: there is no evidence that it is directed toward any purpose. Indeed, if it were, it would by definition not be random. In modern times, we have effectively removed the third possibility above by redefining the goal of science: our aim is to formulate a set of laws that enables us to predict events only up to the limit set by the uncertainty principle.

The second possibility, that there is an infinite sequence of more and more refined theories, is in agreement with all our experience so far. On many occasions we have increased the sensitivity of our measurements or made a new class of observations, only to discover new phenomena that were not predicted by the existing theory, and to account for these we have had to develop a more advanced theory. It would therefore not be very surprising if the present generation of grand unified theories was wrong in claiming that nothing essentially new will happen between the electroweak unification energy of about 100 GeV and the grand unification energy of about a thousand million million GeV. We might indeed expect to find several new layers of structure more basic than the quarks and electrons that we now regard as "elementary" particles.

However, it seems that gravity may provide a limit to this sequence of "boxes within boxes." If one had a particle with an energy above what is called the Planck energy, ten million million million GeV (1 followed by nineteen zeros), its mass would be so concentrated that it would cut itself off from the rest of the universe and form a little black hole. Thus it does seem that the sequence of more and more refined theories should have some limit as we go to higher and

higher energies, so that there should be some ultimate theory of the universe (Fig. 11.16). Of course, the Planck energy is a very long way from the energies of around a hundred GeV, which are the most that we can produce in the laboratory at the present time. We shall not bridge that gap with particle accelerators in the foreseeable future! The very early stages of the universe, however, are an arena where such energies must have occurred. I think that there is a good chance that the study of the early universe and the requirements of mathematical consistency will lead us to a complete unified theory within the lifetime of some of us who are around today, always presuming we don't blow ourselves up first.

What would it mean if we actually did discover the ultimate theory of the universe? As was explained in Chapter 1, we could never be quite sure that we had indeed found the correct theory, since theories can't be proved. But if the theory was mathematically consistent and always gave predictions that agreed with observations, we could be reasonably confident that it was the right one. It would bring to an end a long and glorious chapter in the history of humanity's intellectual struggle to understand the universe. But it would also revolutionize the ordinary person's understanding of the laws

Fig. 11.16 *Observations on smaller and smaller scales have led to a sequence of physical theories valid at higher and higher energies, up to quantum chromodynamics (QCD) and possibly beyond, to grand unified theories (GUT). However, the Planck energy may provide a cutoff and suggests that there is an ultimate theory.*

that govern the universe. In Newton's time it was possible for an educated person to have a grasp of the whole of human knowledge, at least in outline. But since then, the pace of the development of science has made this impossible. Because theories are always being changed to account for new observations, they are never properly digested or simplified so that ordinary people can understand them. You have to be a specialist, and even then you can only hope to have a proper grasp of a small proportion of the scientific theories. Further, the rate of progress is so rapid that what one learns at school or university is always a bit out of date. Only a few people can keep up with the rapidly advancing frontier of knowledge, and they have to devote their whole time to it and specialize in a small area. The rest of the population has little idea of the advances that are being made or the excitement they are generating. Seventy years ago, if Eddington is to be believed, only two people understood the general theory of relativity. Nowadays tens of thousands of university graduates do, and many millions of people are at least familiar with the idea. If a complete unified theory was discovered, it would only be a matter of time before it was digested and simplified in the same way and taught in schools, at least in outline. We would then all be able to have some understanding of the laws that govern the universe and are responsible for our existence.

Even if we do discover a complete unified theory, it would not mean that we would be able to predict events in general, for two reasons. The first is the limitation that the uncertainty principle of quantum mechanics sets on our powers of prediction. There is nothing we can do to get around that. In practice, however, this first limitation is less restrictive than the second one. It arises from the fact that we could not solve the equations of the theory exactly, except in very simple situations. (We cannot even solve exactly for the motion of three bodies in Newton's theory of gravity, and the difficulty increases with the number of bodies and the complexity of the theory.) We already know the laws that govern the behavior of matter under all but the most extreme conditions. In particular, we know the basic laws that underlie all of chemistry and biology. Yet we have certainly not reduced these subjects to the status of solved problems: we have, as yet, had little success in predicting human behavior from mathematical equations! So even if we do find a complete set of basic laws, there will still be in the years ahead the intellectually challenging task of developing better approximation methods, so that we can make useful predictions of the probable outcomes in complicated and realistic situations. A complete, consistent, unified theory is only the first step: our goal is a complete *understanding* of the events around us, and of our own existence.

12

Conclusion

WE FIND OURSELVES in a bewildering world. We want to make sense of what we see around us and to ask: what is the nature of the universe? What is our place in it and where did it and we come from? Why is it the way it is?

To try to answer these questions we adopt some "world picture." Just as an infinite tower of tortoises supporting the flat earth is such a picture, so is the theory of superstrings. Both are theories of the universe, though the latter is much more mathematical and precise than the former. Both theories lack observational evidence: no one has ever seen a giant tortoise with the earth on its back, but then, no one has seen a superstring either. However, the tortoise theory fails to be a good scientific theory because it predicts that people should be able to fall off the edge of the world. This has not been found to agree with experience, unless that turns out to be the explanation for the people who are supposed to have disappeared in the Bermuda Triangle!

The earliest theoretical attempts to describe and explain the universe involved the idea that events and natural phenomena were controlled by spirits with human emotions who acted in a very humanlike and unpredictable manner. These spirits inhabited natural objects, like rivers and mountains, including celestial bodies, like the sun and moon. They had to be placated and their favors sought in order to ensure the fertility of the soil and the rotation of the seasons. Gradually, however, it must have been noticed that there were certain regularities: the sun always rose in the east and set in the west, whether or not a sacrifice had been made to the sun god. Further, the sun, the moon, and the planets followed precise paths across the sky that could be predicted in advance with considerable accuracy. The sun and the moon might still be gods, but they were gods who obeyed strict laws, apparently without any exceptions,

Fig. 12.1 *Some of the theoretical models noted in this book that attempt to explain the universe.*

The tortoise universe

The atom of Democritus

The flat earth model

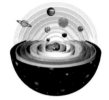

The Ptolemaic system

The Copernican system

The Rutherford atom

The atom of Niels Bohr

The strong anthropic model

The Friedmann closed universe

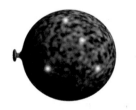

The expanding balloon theory

The black hole theory

The no-boundary proposal

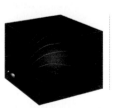

The sum over histories model

The string theory

The wormhole model

The inflationary universe

if one discounts stories like that of the sun stopping for Joshua.

At first, these regularities and laws were obvious only in astronomy and a few other situations. However, as civilization developed, and particularly in the last 300 years, more and more regularities and laws were discovered. The success of these laws led Laplace at the beginning of the nineteenth century to postulate scientific determinism; that is, he suggested that there would be a set of laws that would determine the evolution of the universe precisely, given its configuration at one time.

Laplace's determinism was incomplete in two ways. It did not say how the laws should be chosen and it did not specify the initial configuration of the universe. These were left to God. God would choose how the universe began and what laws it obeyed, but he would not intervene in the universe once it had started. In effect, God was confined to the areas that nineteenth-century science did not understand.

We now know that Laplace's hopes of determinism cannot be realized, at least in the terms he had in mind. The uncertainty principle of quantum mechanics implies that certain pairs of quantities, such as the position and velocity of a particle, cannot both be predicted with complete accuracy. Quantum mechanics deals with this situation via a class of quantum theories in which particles don't have well-defined positions and velocities but are represented by a wave. These quantum theories are deterministic

Left: *"The Creation of Adam" by Michelangelo. Laplace theorized that God chose how the universe began and what laws it would obey, but did not intervene thereafter.*

in the sense that they give laws for the evolution of the wave with time. Thus if one knows the wave at one time, one can calculate it at any other time. The unpredictable, random element comes in only when we try to interpret the wave in terms of the positions and velocities of particles. But maybe that is our mistake: maybe there are no particle positions and velocities, but only waves. It is just that we try to fit the waves to our preconceived ideas of positions and velocities. The resulting mismatch is the cause of the apparent unpredictability.

In effect, we have redefined the task of science to be the discovery of laws that will enable us to predict events up to the limits set by the uncertainty principle. The question remains, however: how or why were the laws and the initial state of the universe chosen?

In this book I have given special prominence to the laws that govern gravity, because it is gravity that shapes the large-scale structure of the universe, even though it is the weakest of the four categories of forces. The laws of gravity were incompatible with the view held until quite recently that the universe is unchanging in time: the fact that gravity is always attractive implies that the universe must be either expanding or contracting. According to the general theory of relativity, there must have been a state of infinite density in the past, the big bang, which would have been an effective beginning of time. Similarly, if the whole universe recollapsed, there must be another state of infinite density in the future, the big crunch, which would be an end of time. Even if the whole universe did not recollapse, there would be singularities in any localized regions that collapsed to form black holes. These singularities would be an end of time for anyone who fell into the black hole. At the big bang and other singularities, all the laws would have broken down, so God would still have had complete freedom to choose what happened and how the universe began.

When we combine quantum mechanics with general relativity, there seems to be a new possibility that did not arise before: that space and time together might form a finite, four-dimensional space without singularities or boundaries, like the surface of the earth but with more dimensions. It seems that this idea could explain many of the observed features of the universe, such as its large-scale uniformity and also the smaller-scale departures from homogeneity, like galaxies, stars, and even human beings. It could even account for the arrow of time that we observe. But if the universe is completely self-contained, with no singularities or boundaries, and completely described by a unified theory, that has profound implications for the role of God as Creator.

Einstein once asked the question: "How much choice did God have in constructing the universe?" If the no boundary proposal is correct, he had no freedom at all to choose initial conditions. He would, of course, still have had the freedom to choose the laws that the universe obeyed. This, however, may not really have been all that much of a choice; there may well be only one, or a small number, of complete unified theories, such as the heterotic string theory, that are self-consistent and allow the existence of structures as complicated as human beings who can investigate the laws of the universe and ask about the nature of God.

Even if there is only one possible unified theory, it is just a set of rules and equations. What is it that breathes fire into the equations and makes a universe for them to describe? The usual approach of science of constructing a mathematical model cannot answer the questions of why there should be a universe for the model to describe. Why does the universe go to all the bother of existing? Is the unified theory so compelling that it brings about its own existence? Or does it need a creator, and, if so, does he have any other effect on the universe? And who created him?

Up to now, most scientists have been too occupied with the development of new theories that describe *what* the universe is to ask the question *why*. On the other hand, the people whose business it is to ask *why*, the philosophers, have not been able to keep up with the advance of scientific theories. In the eighteenth century, philosophers considered the whole of human knowledge, including science, to be their field and discussed questions such as: did the universe have a beginning? However, in the nineteenth and twentieth centuries, science became too technical and mathematical for the philosophers, or anyone else except a few specialists. Philosophers reduced the scope of their inquiries so much that Wittgenstein, the most famous philosopher of this century, said, "The sole remaining task for philosophy is the analysis of language." What a comedown from the great tradition of philosophy from Aristotle to Kant!

However, if we do discover a complete theory, it should in time be understandable in broad principle by everyone, not just a few scientists. Then we shall all, philosophers, scientists, and just ordinary people, be able to take part in the discussion of the question of why it is that we and the universe exist. If we find the answer to that, it would be the ultimate triumph of human reason — for then we would know the mind of God.

Albert Einstein

Einstein's connection with the politics of the nuclear bomb is well known: he signed the famous letter to President Franklin Roosevelt that persuaded the United States to take the idea seriously, and he engaged in postwar efforts to prevent nuclear war. But these were not just the isolated actions of a scientist dragged into the world of politics. Einstein's life was, in fact, to use his own words, "divided between politics and equations."

Einstein's earliest political activity came during the First World War, when he was a professor in Berlin. Sickened by what he saw as the waste of human lives, he became involved in antiwar demonstrations. His advocacy of civil disobedience and public encouragement of people to refuse conscription did little to endear him to his colleagues. Then, following the war, he directed his efforts toward reconciliation and improving international relations. This, too, did not make him popular, and soon his politics were making it difficult for him to visit the United States, even to give lectures.

Above: *Albert Einstein (1879-1955). This photograph was taken at the turn of the century.*
Opposite: *Einstein and his wife, Elsa, arriving on a visit to San Diego, California, on New Year's Eve 1930. He was to leave Germany for good three years later.*

Einstein's second great cause was Zionism. Although he was Jewish by descent, Einstein rejected the biblical idea of God. However, a growing awareness of anti-Semitism, both before and during the First World War, led him gradually to identify with the Jewish community, and later to become an outspoken supporter of Zionism. Once more unpopularity did not stop him from speaking his mind. His theories came under attack; an anti-Einstein organization was even set up. One man was convicted of inciting others to murder Einstein (and fined a mere six dollars). But Einstein was phlegmatic. When a book was published entitled *100 Authors Against Einstein*, he retorted, "If I were wrong, then one would have been enough!"

In 1933, Hitler came to power. Einstein was in America, and declared he would not return to Germany. Then, while Nazi militia raided his house and confiscated his bank account, a Berlin newspaper displayed the headline "Good News from Einstein — He's Not Coming Back." In the face of the Nazi threat, Einstein renounced pacifism, and eventually, fearing that German scientists would build a nuclear bomb, proposed that the United States should develop its own. But even before the first atomic bomb had been detonated, he was publicly warning of the dangers of nuclear war and proposing international control of nuclear weaponry.

Throughout his life, Einstein's efforts toward peace probably achieved little that would last — and certainly won him few friends. His vocal support of the Zionist cause, however, was duly recognized in 1952, when he was offered the presidency of Israel. He declined, saying he thought he was too naive in politics. But perhaps his real reason was different: to quote him again, "Equations are more important to me, because politics is for the present, but an equation is something for eternity."

Galileo Galilei

GALILEO, perhaps more than any other single person, was responsible for the birth of modern science. His renowned conflict with the Catholic Church was central to his philosophy, for Galileo was one of the first to argue that man could hope to understand how the world works, and, moreover, that we could do this by observing the real world.

Galileo had believed Copernican theory (that the planets orbited the sun) since early on, but it was only when he found the evidence needed to support the idea that he started to publicly support it. He wrote about Copernicus's theory in Italian (not the usual academic Latin), and soon his views became widely supported outside the universities. This annoyed the Aristotelian professors, who united against him seeking to persuade the Catholic Church to ban Copernicanism.

Galileo, worried by this, traveled to Rome to speak to the ecclesiastical authorities. He argued that the Bible was not intended to tell us anything about scientific theories, and that it was usual to assume that, where the Bible conflicted with common sense, it was being allegorical. But the Church was afraid of a scandal that might undermine its fight against Protestantism, and so took repressive measures. It declared Copernicanism "false and erroneous" in 1616, and commanded Galileo never again to "defend or hold" the doctrine. Galileo acquiesced.

In 1623, a longtime friend of Galileo's became the Pope. Immediately Galileo tried to get the 1616 decree revoked. He failed, but he did manage to get permission to write a book discussing both Aristotelian and Copernican theories, on two conditions: he would not take sides and would come to the conclusion that man could in any case not determine how the world worked because God could bring about the same effects in ways unimagined by man, who could not place restrictions on God's omnipotence.

The book, *Dialogue Concerning the Two Chief World Systems*, was completed and published in 1632, with the full backing of the censors — and was immediately greeted throughout Europe as a literary and philosophical masterpiece. Soon the Pope, realizing that people were seeing the book as a convincing argument in favor of Copernicanism, regretted having allowed its publication. The Pope argued that although the book had the official blessing of the censors, Galileo had nevertheless contravened the 1616 decree. He brought Galileo before the Inquisition, who sentenced him to house arrest for life and commanded him to publicly renounce Copernicanism. For a second time, Galileo acquiesced.

Galileo remained a faithful Catholic, but his belief in the independence of science had not been

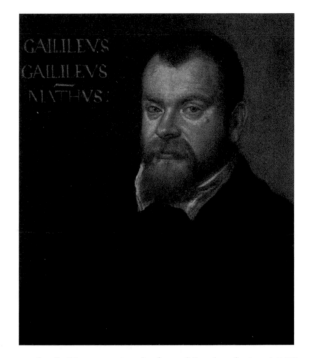

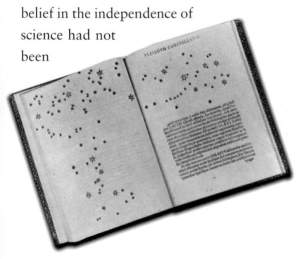

crushed. Four years before his death in 1642, while he was still under house arrest, the manuscript of his second major book was smuggled to a publisher in Holland. It was this work, referred to as *Two New Sciences*, even more than his support for Copernicus, that was to be the genesis of modern physics.

Opposite: *The telescope used by Galileo had a magnification of 30 x.* Above: *Galileo Galilei (1564-1642).*
Left: *Galileo's "Sidereus Nuncius," published in 1610, showed many stars revealed by his telescope.*

Isaac Newton

ISAAC NEWTON was not a pleasant man. His relations with other academics were notorious, with most of his later life spent embroiled in heated disputes. Following publication of *Principia Mathematica* — surely the most influential book ever written in physics — Newton had risen rapidly into public prominence. He was appointed president of the Royal Society and became the first scientist ever to be knighted.

Newton soon clashed with the Astronomer Royal, John Flamsteed, who had earlier provided Newton with much needed data for *Principia*, but was now withholding information that Newton wanted. Newton would not take no for an answer: he had himself appointed to the governing body of the Royal Observatory and then tried to force immediate publication of the data. Eventually he arranged for Flamsteed's work to be seized and prepared for publication by Flamsteed's mortal enemy, Edmond Halley. But Flamsteed took the case to

court and, in the nick of time, won a court order preventing distribution of the stolen work. Newton was incensed and sought his revenge by systematically deleting all references to Flamsteed in later editions of *Principia*.

A more serious dispute arose with the German philosopher Gottfried Leibniz. Both Leibniz and Newton had independently developed a branch of mathematics called calculus, which underlies most of modern physics. Although we now know that Newton discovered calculus years before Leibniz, he published his work much later. A major row ensued over who had been first, with scientists vigorously defending both contenders. It is remarkable, however, that most of the articles appearing in defense of Newton were originally written by his own hand — and only published in the name of friends! As the row grew, Leibniz made the mistake of appealing to the Royal Society to resolve the dispute. Newton, as president, appointed an "impartial" committee to investi-

Isaac Newton (1642-1727), by Vanderbank.

gate, coincidentally consisting entirely of Newton's friends! But that was not all: Newton then wrote the committee's report himself and had the Royal Society publish it, officially accusing Leibniz of plagiarism. Still unsatisfied, he then wrote an anonymous review of the report in the Royal Society's own periodical. Following the death of Leibniz, Newton is reported to have declared that he had taken great satisfaction in "breaking Leibniz's heart."

During the period of these two disputes, Newton had already left Cambridge and academe. He had been active in anti-Catholic politics at Cambridge, and later in Parliament, and was rewarded eventually with the lucrative post of Warden of the Royal Mint. Here he used his talents for deviousness and vitriol in a more socially acceptable way, successfully conducting a major campaign against counterfeiting, even sending several men to their death on the gallows.

Glossary

Absolute zero: The lowest possible temperature, at which substances contain no heat energy.

Acceleration: The rate at which the speed of an object is changing.

Anthropic principle: We see the universe the way it is because if it were different we would not be here to observe it.

Antiparticle: Each type of matter particle has a corresponding antiparticle. When a particle collides with its antiparticle, they annihilate, leaving only energy.

Atom: The basic unit of ordinary matter, made up of a tiny nucleus (consisting of protons and neutrons) surrounded by orbiting electrons.

Big bang: The singularity at the beginning of the universe.

Big crunch: The singularity at the end of the universe.

Black hole: A region of space-time from which nothing, not even light, can escape, because gravity is so strong.

Casimir effect: The attractive pressure between two flat, parallel metal plates placed very near to each other in a vacuum. The pressure is due to a reduction in the usual number of virtual particles in the space between the plates.

Chandrasekhar limit: The maximum possible mass of a stable cold star, above which it must collapse into a black hole.

Conservation of energy: The law of science that states that energy (or its equivalent in mass) can neither be created nor destroyed.

Coordinates: Numbers that specify the position of a point in space and time.

Cosmological constant: A mathematical device used by Einstein to give space-time an inbuilt tendency to expand.

Cosmology: The study of the universe as a whole.

Dark matter: Matter in galaxies, clusters, and possibly between clusters, that can not be observed directly but can be detected by its gravitational effect. As much as 90 percent of the mass of the universe may be in the form of dark matter.

Duality: A correspondence between apparently different theories that lead to the same physical results.

Einstein-Rosen bridge: A thin tube of space-time linking two black holes. *Also see* Wormhole.

Electric charge: A property of a particle by which it may repel (or attract) other particles that have a charge of similar (or opposite) sign.

Electromagnetic force: The force that arises between particles with electric charge; the second strongest of the four fundamental forces.

Electron: A particle with negative electric charge that orbits the nucleus of an atom.

Electroweak unification energy: The energy (around 100 GeV) above which the distinction between the electromagnetic force and the weak force disappears.

Elementary particle: A particle that, it is believed, cannot be subdivided.

Event: A point in space-time, specified by its time and place.

Event horizon: The boundary of a black hole.

Exclusion principle: The idea that two identical spin-1/2 particles cannot have (within the limits set by the uncertainty principle) both the same position and the same velocity.

Field: Something that exists throughout space and time, as opposed to a particle that exists at only one point at a time.

Frequency: For a wave, the number of complete cycles per second.

Gamma rays: Electromagnetic rays of very short wavelength, produced in radioactive decay or by collisions of elementary particles.

General relativity: Einstein's theory based on the idea that the laws of science should be the same for all observers, no matter how they are moving. It explains the force of gravity in terms of the curvature of a four-dimensional space-time.

Geodesic: The shortest (or longest) path between two points.

Grand unification energy: The energy above which, it is believed, the electromagnetic force, weak force, and strong force become indistinguishable from each other.

Grand unified theory (GUT): A theory which unifies the electromagnetic, strong, and weak forces.

Imaginary time: Time measured using imaginary numbers.

Light cone: A surface in space-time that marks out the possible directions for light rays passing through a given event.

Light-second (Light year): the distance traveled by light in one second (year).

Magnetic field: The field responsible for magnetic forces, now incorporated along with the electric field, into the electromagnetic field.

Mass: The quantity of matter in a body; its inertia, or resistance to acceleration.

Microwave background radiation: The radiation from the glowing of the hot early universe, now so greatly red-shifted that it appears not as light but as microwaves (radio waves with a wavelength of a few centimeters). See also COBE, on pages 180-181.

Naked singularity: A space-time singularity not surrounded by a black hole.

Neutrino: An extremely light (possibly massless) particle that is affected only by the weak force and gravity.

Neutron: An uncharged particle, very similar to the proton, which accounts for roughly half the particles in an atomic nucleus.

Neutron star: A cold star, supported by the exclusion principle repulsion between neutrons.

No boundary condition: The idea that the universe is finite but has no boundary (in imaginary time).

Nuclear fusion: The process by which two nuclei collide and coalesce to form a single, heavier nucleus.

Nucleus: The central part of an atom, consisting only of protons and neutrons, held together by the strong force.

Particle accelerator: A machine that, using electromagnets, can accelerate moving charged particles, giving them more energy.

Phase: For a wave, the position in its cycle at a specified time: a measure of whether it is at a crest, a trough, or somewhere in between.

Photon: A quantum of light.

Planck's quantum principle: The idea that light (or any other classical waves) can be emitted or absorbed only in discrete quanta, whose energy is proportional to their wavelength.

Positron: The (positively charged) antiparticle of the electron.

Primordial black hole: A black hole created in the very early universe.

Proportional: 'X is proportional to Y' means that when Y is multiplied by any number, so is X. 'X is inversely proportional to Y' means that when Y is multiplied by any number, X is divided by that number.

Proton: A positively charge particle, very similar to the neutron, that accounts for roughly half the particles in the nucleus of most atoms.

Pulsar: A rotating neutron star that emits regular pulses of radio waves.

Quantum: The indivisible unit in which waves may be emitted or absorbed.

Quantum chromodynamics (QCD): The theory that describes the interactions of quarks and gluons.

Quantum mechanics: The theory developed from Planck's quantum principle and Heisenberg's uncertainty principle.

Quark: A (charged) elementary particle that feels the strong force. Protons and neutrons are each composed of three quarks.

Radar: A system using pulsed radio waves to detect the position of objects by measuring the time it takes a single pulse to reach the object and be reflected back.

Radioactivity: The spontaneous breakdown of one type of atomic nucleus into another .

Red shift: The reddening of light from a star that is moving away from us, due to the Doppler effect.

Singularity: A point in space-time at which the space-time curvature becomes infinite.

Singularity theorem: A theorem that shows that a singularity must exist under certain circumstances — in particular, that the universe must have started with a singularity.

Space-time: The four-dimensional space whose points are events.

Spatial dimension: Any of the three dimensions that are spacelike — that is, any except the time dimension.

Special relativity: Einstein's theory based on the idea that the laws of science should be the same for all observers, no matter how they are moving.

Spectrum: The component frequencies that make up a wave. The visible part of the sun's spectrum can be seen in a rainbow.

Spin: An internal property of elementary particles, related to, but not identical to, the everyday concept of spin.

Stationary state: One that is not changing with time: a sphere spinning at a constant rate is stationary because it looks identical at any given instant.

String theory: A theory of physics in which particles are described as waves on strings. Strings have length but no other dimension.

Strong force: The strongest of the four fundamental forces, with the shortest range of all. It holds the quarks together within protons and neutrons, and holds the protons and neutrons together to form atoms.

Uncertainty principle: The principle, formulated by Heisenberg, that one can never be exactly sure of both the position and the velocity of a particle; the more accurately one knows the one, the less accurately one can know the other.

Virtual particle: In quantum mechanics, a particle that can never be directly detected, but whose existence does have measurable effects.

Wave/particle duality: The concept in quantum mechanics that there is no distinction between waves and particles; particles may sometimes behave like waves, and waves like particles.

Wavelength: For a wave, the distance between two adjacent troughs or two adjacent crests.

Weak force: The second weakest of the four fundamental forces, with a very short range. It affects all matter particles, but not force-carrying particles.

Weight: The force exerted on a body by a gravitational field. It is proportional to, but not the same as, its mass.

White dwarf: A stable cold star, supported by the exclusion principle repulsion between electrons.

Wormhole: A thin tube of space-time connecting distant regions of the Universe. Wormholes might also link to parallel or baby universes and could provide the possibility of timetravel.

Acknowledgments

Many people have helped me in writing this book. My scientific colleagues have without exception been inspiring. Over the years my principal associates and collaborators were Roger Penrose, Robert Geroch, Brandon Carter, George Ellis, Gary Gibbons, Don Page and Jim Hartle. I owe a lot to them, and to my research students, who have always given me help when needed.

One of my students, Brian Whitt, gave me a lot of help writing the first edition of this book. My editor at Bantam Books, Peter Guzzardi, made innumerable comments which improved the book considerably. In addition, for this illustrated edition, I would like to thank the people at Moon*Runner* Design, who did the illustrations, and Andrew Dunn who helped me revise the text and write the captions. I feel they did a good job.

I could not have written this book without my communication system. The software, called Equalizer, was donated by Walt Waltosz of Words Plus Inc., in Lancaster, California. My speech synthesiser was donated by Speech Plus, of Sunnyvale, California. The synthesiser and laptop computer were mounted on my wheelchair by David Mason, of Cambridge Adaptive Communication Ltd. With this system I can communicate better now than before I lost my voice.

I have had a number of secretaries and assistants over the years in which I wrote and revised this book. On the secretarial side, I'm very grateful to Judy Fella, Ann Ralph, Laura Gentry, Cheryl Billington and Sue Masey. My assistants have been Colin Williams, David Thomas, and Raymond Laflamme, Nick Phillips, Andrew Dunn, Stuart Jamieson, Jonathan Brenchley, Tim Hunt, Simon Gill, Jon Rogers and Tom Kendall. They, my nurses, colleagues, friends and family have enabled me to live a very full life and to pursue my research despite my disability.

Stephen Hawking

Photo credits:

AKG Photo, London: 3, 12, 156, 232. Ann Ronan Picture Library: 2, 3, 4, 6, 7, 8, 9, 14, 21, 22, 28, 29, 30, 50, 68, 71, 79, 83, 99, 121, 174. Image Select: 6, 9, 46, 72, 108, 146, 152, 153, 181, 192, 193, 241. Manni Masons Pictures: back cover, 67, 141, 235. NASA: 24. National Maritime Museum, Greenwich, UK: 182, 238, 239. Royal Astronomical Society: 6. Science Photo Library: 14, 16, 30, 31, 40, 54, 62, 64, 65, 71, 74, 77, 85, 89, 95, 97, 98, 109, 110, 120, 152, 183, 236, 237. Space Telescope Science Institute: 20, 126. Spectrum Colour Library: 50, 94. Ralph Alpher: 147. Subrahmanyan Chandrasekhar: 108. Thomas Gold: 62. Stephen Hawking: 125, 144. Fred Hoyle: 62. Andrei Linde: 166. Ron Miller (concepts of original diagrams): 111, 112, 128, 129, 176.

*All original illustrations not credited above have been created for this book by Malcolm Godwin and Jerome Grasdijk of Moon*Runner *Design, U.K.*

Index

The Universe in a Nutshell

The Universe in a Nutshell

Stephen Hawking

Bantam Books

New York   Toronto   London   Sydney   Auckland

CONTENTS

Stephen Hawking in 2001, © *Stewart Cohen.*

FOREWORD

I HADN'T EXPECTED MY POPULAR BOOK, *A Brief History of Time*, to be such a success. It was on the London *Sunday Times* bestseller list for over four years, which is longer than any other book has been, and remarkable for a book on science that was not easy going. After that, people kept asking when I would write a sequel. I resisted because I didn't want to write *Son of Brief History* or *A Slightly Longer History of Time*, and because I was busy with research. But I have come to realize that there is room for a different kind of book that might be easier to understand. *A Brief History of Time* was organized in a linear fashion, with most chapters following and logically depending on the preceding chapters. This appealed to some readers, but others got stuck in the early chapters and never reached the more exciting material later on. By contrast, the present book is more like a tree: Chapters 1 and 2 form a central trunk from which the other chapters branch off.

The branches are fairly independent of each other and can be tackled in any order after the central trunk. They correspond to areas I have worked on or thought about since the publication of *A Brief History of Time*. Thus they present a picture of some of the most active fields of current research. Within each chapter I have also tried to avoid a single linear structure. The illustrations and their captions provide an alternative route to the text, as in *The Illustrated Brief History of Time*, published in 1996; and the boxes, or sidebars, provide the opportunity to delve into certain topics in more detail than is possible in the main text.

In 1988, when *A Brief History of Time* was first published, the ultimate Theory of Everything seemed to be just over the horizon. How has the situation changed since then? Are we any closer to our goal? As will be described in this book, we have advanced a long way since then. But it is an ongoing journey still and the end is not yet in sight. According to the old saying, it is better to travel hopefully than to arrive. Our quest for discovery fuels our creativity in all fields, not just science. If we reached the end of the line, the human spirit would shrivel and die. But I don't think we will ever stand still: we shall increase in complexity, if not in depth, and shall always be the center of an expanding horizon of possibilities.

I want to share my excitement at the discoveries that are being made and the picture of reality that is emerging. I have concentrated on areas I have worked on myself for a greater feeling of immediacy. The details of the work are very technical but I believe the broad ideas can be conveyed without a lot of mathematical baggage. I just hope I have succeeded.

I have had a lot of help with this book. I would mention in particular Thomas Hertog and Neel Shearer, for assistance with the figures, captions, and boxes, Ann Harris and Kitty Ferguson, who edited the manuscript (or, more accurately, the computer files, because everything I write is electronic), Philip Dunn of the Book Laboratory and Moonrunner Design, who created the illustrations. But beyond that, I want to thank all those who have made it possible for me to lead a fairly normal life and carry on scientific research. Without them this book could not have been written.

Stephen Hawking
Cambridge, May 2, 2001.

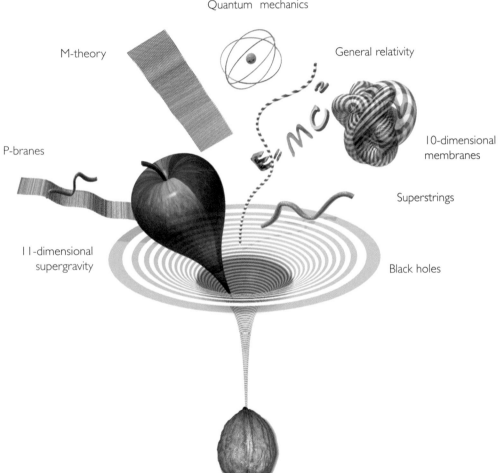

Quantum mechanics

M-theory

General relativity

P-branes

10-dimensional
membranes

Superstrings

11-dimensional
supergravity

Black holes

CHAPTER 1

A BRIEF HISTORY OF RELATIVITY

*How Einstein laid the foundations of the two fundamental theories
of the twentieth century: general relativity and quantum theory.*

Professor Einstein

Albert Einstein™

Low

A. Einstein

ALBERT EINSTEIN, THE DISCOVERER OF THE SPECIAL AND general theories of relativity, was born in Ulm, Germany, in 1879, but the following year the family moved to Munich, where his father, Hermann, and uncle, Jakob, set up a small and not very successful electrical business. Albert was no child prodigy, but claims that he did poorly at school seem to be an exaggeration. In 1894 his father's business failed and the family moved to Milan. His parents decided he should stay behind to finish school, but he did not like its authoritarianism, and within months he left to join his family in Italy. He later completed his education in Zurich, graduating from the prestigious Federal Polytechnical School, known as the ETH, in 1900. His argumentative nature and dislike of authority did not endear him to the professors at the ETH and none of them offered him the position of assistant, which was the normal route to an academic career. Two years later, he finally managed to get a junior post at the Swiss patent office in Bern. It was while he held this job that in 1905 he wrote three papers that both established him as one of the world's leading scientists and started two conceptual revolutions—revolutions that changed our understanding of time, space, and reality itself.

Toward the end of the nineteenth century, scientists believed they were close to a complete description of the universe. They imagined that space was filled by a continuous medium called the "ether." Light rays and radio signals were waves in this ether, just as sound is pressure waves in air. All that was needed for a complete theory were careful measurements of the elastic properties of the ether. In fact, anticipating such measurements, the Jefferson Lab at Harvard University was built entirely without iron nails so as not to interfere with delicate magnetic measurements. However, the planners forgot that the reddish brown bricks of which the lab and most of Harvard are built contain large amounts of iron. The building is still in use today, although Harvard is still not sure how much weight a library floor without iron nails will support.

Albert Einstein in 1920.

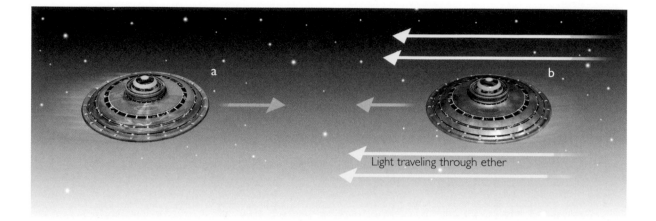

Light traveling through ether

(FIG. 1.1, above)
THE FIXED ETHER THEORY

If light were a wave in an elastic material called ether, the speed of light should appear higher to someone on a spaceship (a) moving toward it, and lower on a spaceship (b) traveling in the same direction as the light.

(FIG. 1.2, opposite)
No difference was found between the speed of light in the direction of the Earth's orbit and in a direction at right angles to it.

By the century's end, discrepancies in the idea of an all-pervading ether began to appear. It was expected that light would travel at a fixed speed through the ether but that if you were traveling through the ether in the same direction as the light, its speed would appear lower, and if you were traveling in the opposite direction of the light, its speed would appear higher (Fig. 1.1).

Yet a series of experiments failed to support this idea. The most careful and accurate of these experiments was carried out by Albert Michelson and Edward Morley at the Case School of Applied Science in Cleveland, Ohio, in 1887. They compared the speed of light in two beams at right angles to each other. As the Earth rotates on its axis and orbits the Sun, the apparatus moves through the ether with varying speed and direction (Fig. 1.2). But Michelson and Morley found no daily or yearly differences between the two beams of light. It was as if light always traveled at the same speed relative to where one was, no matter how fast and in which direction one was moving (Fig. 1.3, page 8).

Based on the Michelson-Morley experiment, the Irish physicist George FitzGerald and the Dutch physicist Hendrik Lorentz suggested that bodies moving through the ether would contract and that clocks would slow down. This contraction and the slowing down of clocks would be such that people would all measure the same speed for light, no matter how they were moving with respect to the ether. (FitzGerald and Lorentz still regarded ether as a real substance.) However, in a paper written in June 1905, Einstein

Earth's spin from west to east

Light at right angles to the orbit of
the Earth around the sun

Light beams at right angles to
one another following the
spin of the Earth also show
no difference in speed

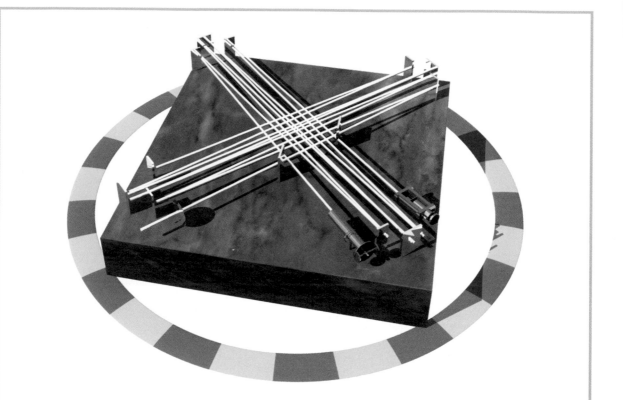

(FIG. 1.3) MEASURING THE SPEED OF LIGHT

In the Michelson-Morley interferometer, light from a source is split into two beams by a half-silvered mirror. The two beams of light travel at right angles to each other and are then combined into a single beam by hitting the half-silvered mirror again. A difference in the speed of light traveling in the two directions could mean that the wave crests in one beam arrived at the same time as the wave troughs of the other and canceled them out.

Right: Diagram of the experiment reconstructed from that which appeared in the *Scientific American* of 1887.

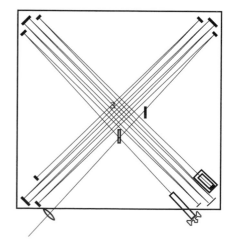

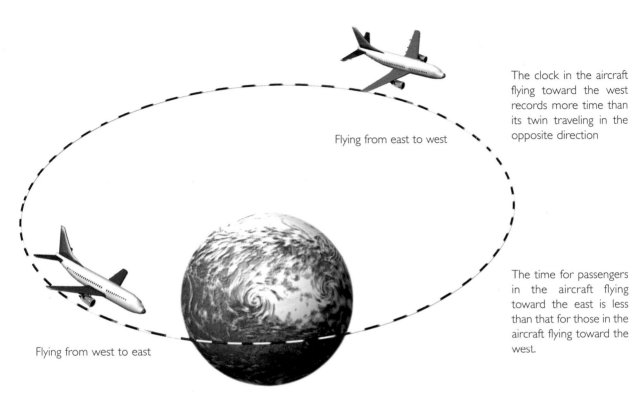

Flying from east to west

The clock in the aircraft flying toward the west records more time than its twin traveling in the opposite direction

The time for passengers in the aircraft flying toward the east is less than that for those in the aircraft flying toward the west.

Flying from west to east

pointed out that if one could not detect whether or not one was moving through space, the notion of an ether was redundant. Instead, he started from the postulate that the laws of science should appear the same to all freely moving observers. In particular, they should all measure the same speed for light, no matter how fast they were moving. The speed of light is independent of their motion and is the same in all directions.

This required abandoning the idea that there is a universal quantity called time that all clocks would measure. Instead, everyone would have his or her own personal time. The times of two people would agree if the people were at rest with respect to each other, but not if they were moving.

This has been confirmed by a number of experiments, including one in which two accurate clocks were flown in opposite directions around the world and returned showing very slightly different times (Fig. 1.4). This might suggest that if one wanted to live longer, one should keep flying to the east so that the plane's speed is added to the earth's rotation. However, the tiny fraction of a second one would gain would be more than canceled by eating airline meals.

(FIG. 1.4)
One version of the twins paradox (Fig. 1.5, page 10) has been tested experimentally by flying two accurate clocks in opposite directions around the world.

When they met up again the clock that flew toward the east had recorded slightly less time.

9

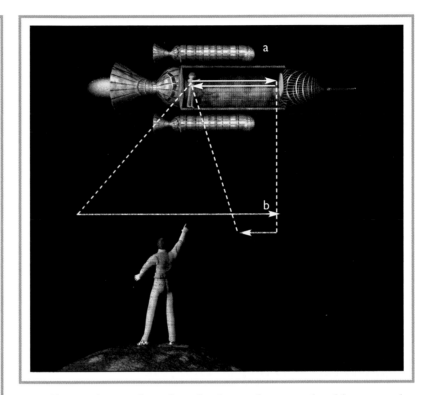

THE TWINS PARADOX

In the theory of relativity each observer has his own measure of time. This can lead to the so-called twins paradox.

One of a pair of twins **(a)** leaves on a space journey during which he travels close to the speed of light **(c)**, while his brother **(b)** remains on Earth.

Because of (a)'s motion, time runs more slowly in the space-craft as seen by the earthbound twin. So on his return the space traveler **(a2)** will find that his brother **(b2)** has aged more than himself.

Although it seems against common sense, a number of experiments have implied that in this scenario the traveling twin would indeed be younger.

(Fig. 1.6, right).
A spaceship passes Earth from left to right at four-fifths the speed of light. A pulse of light is emitted at one end of the cabin and reflected at the other end **(a)**.

The light is observed by people on Earth and on the spaceship. Because of the motion of the spaceship, they will disagree about the distance the light has traveled in reflecting back **(b)**.

They must therefore also disagree about the time the light has taken, because according to Einstein's postulate the speed of light is the same for all freely moving observers.

Einstein's postulate that the laws of nature should appear the same to all freely moving observers was the foundation of the theory of relativity, so called because it implied that only relative motion was important. Its beauty and simplicity convinced many thinkers, but there remained a lot of opposition. Einstein had overthrown two of the absolutes of nineteenth-century science: absolute rest, as represented by the ether, and absolute or universal time that all clocks would measure. Many people found this an unsettling concept. Did it imply, they asked, that *everything* was relative, that there were no absolute moral standards? This unease continued throughout the 1920s and 1930s. When Einstein was awarded the Nobel Prize in 1921, the citation was for important but (by his standard) comparatively minor work also carried out in 1905. It made no mention of relativity, which was considered too controversial. (I still get two or three letters a week telling me Einstein was wrong.) Nevertheless, the theory of relativity is now completely accepted by the scientific community, and its predictions have been verified in countless applications.

FIG. 1.7

A very important consequence of relativity is the relation between mass and energy. Einstein's postulate that the speed of light should appear the same to everyone implied that nothing could be moving faster than light. What happens is that as one uses energy to accelerate anything, whether a particle or a spaceship, its mass increases, making it harder to accelerate it further. To accelerate a particle to the speed of light would be impossible because it would take an infinite amount of energy. Mass and energy are equivalent, as is summed up in Einstein's famous equation $E = mc^2$ (Fig. 1.7). This is probably the only equation in physics to have recognition on the street. Among its consequences was the realization that if the nucleus of a uranium atom fissions into two nuclei with slightly less total mass, this will release a tremendous amount of energy (see pages 14-15, Fig. 1.8).

In 1939, as the prospect of another world war loomed, a group of scientists who realized these implications persuaded Einstein to overcome his pacifist scruples and add his authority to a letter to

President Roosevelt urging the United States to start a program of nuclear research.

This led to the Manhattan Project and ultimately to the bombs that exploded over Hiroshima and Nagasaki in 1945. Some people have blamed the atom bomb on Einstein because he discovered the relationship between mass and energy; but that is like blaming Newton for causing airplanes to crash because he discovered gravity. Einstein himself took no part in the Manhattan Project and was horrified by the dropping of the bomb.

After his groundbreaking papers in 1905, Einstein's scientific reputation was established. But it was not until 1909 that he was offered a position at the University of Zurich that enabled him to leave the Swiss patent office. Two years later, he moved to the German University in Prague, but he came back to Zurich in 1912, this time to the ETH. Despite the anti-Semitism that was common in much of Europe, even in the universities, he was now an academic hot property. Offers came in from Vienna and Utrecht, but he chose to

EINSTEIN'S PROPHETIC LETTER TO PRESIDENT ROOSEVELT IN 1939

"In the course of the last four months it has been made probable —through the work of Joliot in France as well as Fermi and Szilard in America— that it may become possible to set up a nuclear chain reaction in a large mass of uranium, by which vast amounts of power and large quantities of new radium-like elements would be generated. Now it appears almost certain that this could be achieved in the immediate future.

This new phenomenon would also lead to the construction of bombs, and it is conceivable —though much less certain—that extremely powerful bombs of a new type may thus be constructed."

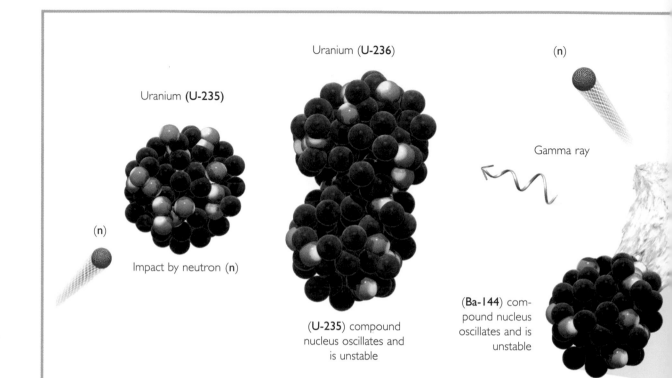

Uranium (**U-235**)

Uranium (**U-236**)

(**n**)

Gamma ray

(**n**)

Impact by neutron (**n**)

(**U-235**) compound nucleus oscillates and is unstable

(**Ba-144**) compound nucleus oscillates and is unstable

(FIG. 1.8)

NUCLEAR BINDING ENERGY

Nuclei are made up of protons and neutrons held together by a strong force. But the mass of the nucleus is always less than the sum of the individual masses of the protons and neutrons that make it up. The difference is a measure of the nuclear binding energy that holds the nucleus together. This binding energy can be calculated from the Einstein relationship: nuclear binding energy = Δmc^2 where Δm is the difference between the mass of the nucleus and the sum of the individual masses.

It is the release of this potential energy that creates the devastating explosive force of a nuclear device.

accept a research position with the Prussian Academy of Sciences in Berlin because it freed him from teaching duties. He moved to Berlin in April 1914 and was joined shortly after by his wife and two sons. The marriage had been in a bad way for some time, however, and his family soon returned to Zurich. Although he visited them occasionally, he and his wife were eventually divorced. Einstein later married his cousin Elsa, who lived in Berlin. The fact that he spent the war years as a bachelor, without domestic commitments, may be one reason why this period was so productive for him scientifically.

Although the theory of relativity fit well with the laws that governed electricity and magnetism, it was not compatible with Newton's law of gravity. This law said that if one changed the distribution of matter in one region of space, the change in the gravitational field would be felt instantaneously everywhere else in the universe. Not only would this mean one could send signals faster than light (something that was forbidden by relativity); in order to know what instantaneous meant, it also required the existence of absolute or universal time, which relativity had abolished in favor of personal time.

(**Kr-89**) compound nucleus
oscillates and is unstable

Fission yields an average
of 2.4 neutrons and an
energy of 215MeV

*Einstein's equation between
energy* (E), *mass* (m), *and
the speed of light* (c) *is such
that a small amount of mass
is equivalent to an enormous
amount of energy:* **E=mc²**.

Bound neutron

Proton

Free neutron

(**n**) neutrons can
initiate a chain reaction

Gamma ray

(n)

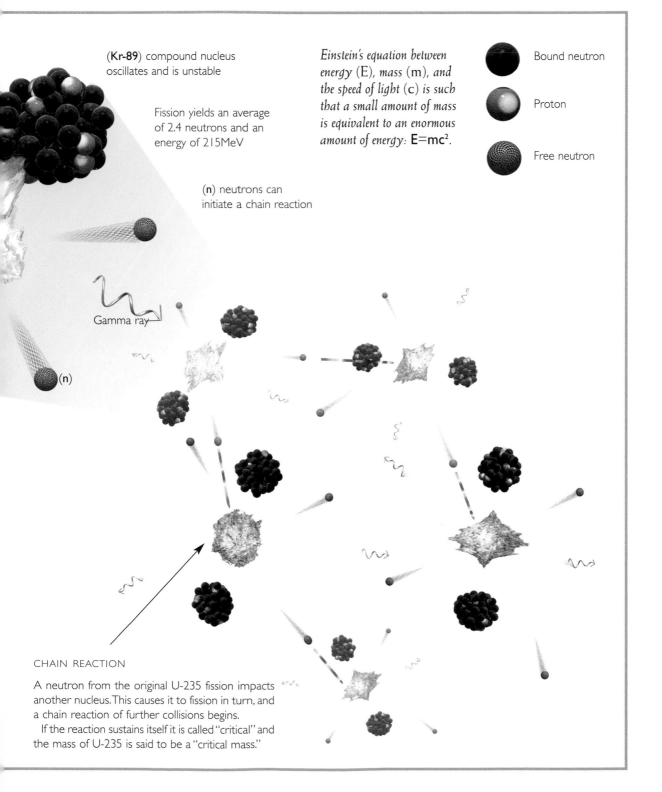

CHAIN REACTION

A neutron from the original U-235 fission impacts
another nucleus. This causes it to fission in turn, and
a chain reaction of further collisions begins.
    If the reaction sustains itself it is called "critical" and
the mass of U-235 is said to be a "critical mass."

(FIG. 1.9)

An observer in a box cannot tell the difference between being in a stationary elevator on Earth **(a)** and being accelerated by a rocket in free space **(b)**.

If the rocket motor is turned off **(c)**, it feels as if the elevator is in free fall to the bottom of the shaft **(d)**.

Einstein was aware of this difficulty in 1907, while he was still at the patent office in Bern, but it was not until he was in Prague in 1911 that he began to think seriously about the problem. He realized that there is a close relationship between acceleration and a gravitational field. Someone inside a closed box, such as an elevator, could not tell whether the box was at rest in the Earth's gravitational field or was being accelerated by a rocket in free space. (Of course, this was before the age of *Star Trek*, and so Einstein thought of people in elevators rather than spaceships.) But one cannot accelerate or fall freely very far in an elevator before disaster strikes (Fig. 1.9).

Fig. 1.10

Fig. 1.11

If the Earth were flat, one could equally well say that the apple fell on Newton's head because of gravity or because Newton and the surface of the Earth were accelerating upward (Fig. 1.10). This equivalence between acceleration and gravity didn't seem to work for a round Earth, however—people on the opposite sides of the world would have to be accelerating in opposite directions but staying at a constant distance from each other (Fig. 1.11).

But on his return to Zurich in 1912 Einstein had the brain wave of realizing that the equivalence would work if the geometry of spacetime was curved and not flat, as had been assumed hitherto.

If the Earth were flat (FIG. 1.10) one could say that either the apple fell on Newton's head because of gravity or that the Earth and Newton were accelerating upward. This equivalence didn't work for a spherical Earth (FIG. 1.11) because people on opposite sides of the world would be getting farther away from each other. Einstein overcame this difficulty by making space and time curved.

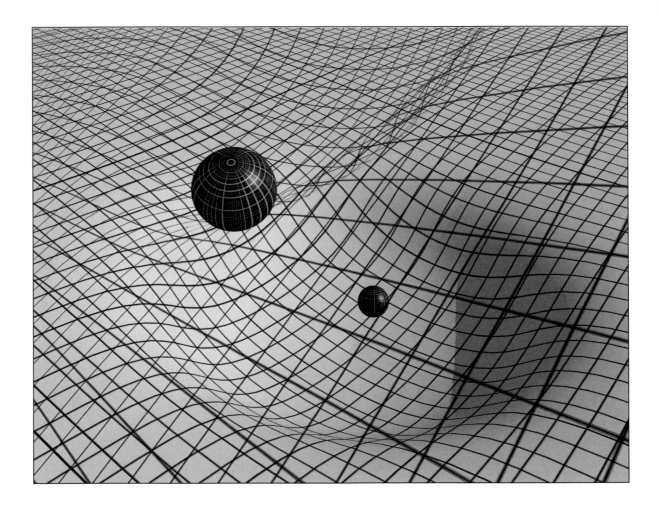

(FIG. 1.12) SPACETIME CURVES

Acceleration and gravity can be equivalent only if a massive body curves spacetime, thereby bending the paths of objects in its neighborhood.

His idea was that mass and energy would warp spacetime in some manner yet to be determined. Objects such as apples or planets would try to move in straight lines through spacetime, but their paths would appear to be bent by a gravitational field because spacetime is curved (Fig. 1.12).

With the help of his friend Marcel Grossmann, Einstein studied the theory of curved spaces and surfaces that had been developed earlier by Georg Friedrich Riemann. However, Riemann thought only of space being curved. It took Einstein to realize that it is spacetime which is curved. Einstein and Grossmann wrote a joint paper in 1913 in which they put forward the idea that what we think of as gravitational forces are just an expression of the fact that

Professor Einstein

spacetime is curved. However, because of a mistake by Einstein (who was quite human and fallible), they weren't able to find the equations that related the curvature of spacetime to the mass and energy in it. Einstein continued to work on the problem in Berlin, undisturbed by domestic matters and largely unaffected by the war, until he finally found the right equations in November 1915. He had discussed his ideas with the mathematician David Hilbert during a visit to the University of Göttingen in the summer of 1915, and Hilbert independently found the same equations a few days before Einstein. Nevertheless, as Hilbert himself admitted, the credit for the new theory belonged to Einstein. It was his idea to relate gravity to the warping of spacetime. It is a tribute to the civilized state of Germany at this period that such scientific discussions and exchanges could go on undisturbed even in wartime. It was a sharp contrast to the Nazi era twenty years later.

Albert Einstein™

Low

The new theory of curved spacetime was called general relativity to distinguish it from the original theory without gravity, which was now known as special relativity. It was confirmed in a spectacular fashion in 1919 when a British expedition to West Africa observed a slight bending of light from a star passing near

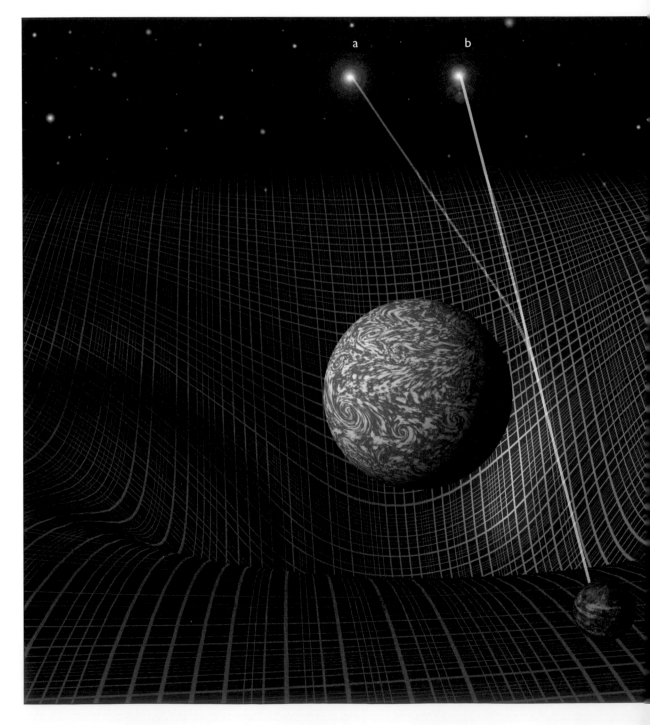

(FIG. 1.13) LIGHT CURVES

Light from a star passing near the Sun is deflected by the way the mass of the Sun curves spacetime **(a)**. This produces a slight shift in the apparent position of the star as seen from the Earth **(b)**. This can be observed during an eclipse.

the sun during an eclipse (Fig. 1.13). Here was direct evidence that space and time are warped, and it spurred the greatest change in our perception of the universe in which we live since Euclid wrote his *Elements of Geometry* around 300 B.C.

Einstein's general theory of relativity transformed space and time from a passive background in which events take place to active participants in the dynamics of the universe. This led to a great problem that remains at the forefront of physics in the twenty-first century. The universe is full of matter, and matter warps spacetime in such a way that bodies fall together. Einstein found that his equations didn't have a solution that described a static universe, unchanging in time. Rather than give up such an everlasting universe, which he and most other people believed in, he fudged the equations by adding a term called the cosmological constant, which warped spacetime in the opposite sense, so that bodies move apart. The repulsive effect of the cosmological constant could balance the attractive effect of the matter, thus allowing a static solution for the universe. This was one of the great missed opportunities of theoretical physics. If Einstein had stuck with his original equations, he could have predicted that the universe must be either expanding or contracting. As it was, the possibility of a time-dependent universe wasn't taken seriously until observations in the 1920s by the 100-inch telescope on Mount Wilson.

These observations revealed that the farther other galaxies are from us, the faster they are moving away. The universe is expanding, with the distance between any two galaxies steadily increasing with time (Fig. 1.14, page 22). This discovery removed the need for a cosmological constant in order to have a static solution for the universe. Einstein later called the cosmological constant the greatest mistake of his life. However, it now seems that it may not have been a mistake after all: recent observations, described in Chapter 3, suggest that there may indeed be a small cosmological constant.

(FIG. 1.14)

Observations of galaxies indicate that the universe is expanding: the distance between almost any pair of galaxies is increasing.

General relativity completely changed the discussion of the origin and fate of the universe. A static universe could have existed forever or could have been created in its present form at some time in the past. However, if galaxies are moving apart now, it means that they must have been closer together in the past. About fifteen billion years ago, they would all have been on top of each other and the density would have been very large. This state was called the "primeval atom" by the Catholic priest Georges Lemaître, who was the first to investigate the origin of the universe that we now call the big bang.

Einstein seems never to have taken the big bang seriously. He apparently thought that the simple model of a uniformly expanding universe would break down if one followed the motions of the galaxies back in time, and that the small sideways velocities of the galaxies would cause them to miss each other. He thought the universe might have had a previous contracting phase, with a bounce into the present expansion at a fairly moderate density. However, we now know that in order for nuclear reactions in the early universe to

The 100-inch Hooker telescope at Mount Wilson Observatory.

produce the amounts of light elements we observe around us, the density must have been at least ten tons per cubic inch and the temperature ten billion degrees. Further, observations of the microwave background indicate that the density was probably once a trillion trillion trillion trillion trillion trillion (1 with 72 zeros after it) tons per cubic inch. We also now know that Einstein's general theory of relativity does not allow the universe to bounce from a contracting phase to the present expansion. As will be discussed in Chapter 2, Roger Penrose and I were able to show that general relativity predicts that the universe began in the big bang. So Einstein's theory does imply that time has a beginning, although he was never happy with the idea.

Einstein was even more reluctant to admit that general relativity predicted that time would come to an end for massive stars when they reached the end of their life and no longer generated enough heat to balance the force of their own gravity, which was trying to make them smaller. Einstein thought that such stars would settle down to some

(FIG. 1.15)
When a massive star exhausts its nuclear fuel, it will lose heat and contract. The warping of spacetime will become so great that a black hole will be created from which light cannot escape. Inside the black hole time will come to an end.

final state, but we now know that there are no final-state configurations for stars of more than twice the mass of the sun. Such stars will continue to shrink until they become black holes, regions of spacetime that are so warped that light cannot escape from them (Fig. 1.15).

Penrose and I showed that general relativity predicted that time would come to an end inside a black hole, both for the star and for any unfortunate astronaut who happened to fall into it. But both the beginning and the end of time would be places where the equations of general relativity could not be defined. Thus the theory could not predict what should emerge from the big bang. Some saw this as an indication of God's freedom to start the universe off in any way God wanted, but others (including myself) felt that the beginning of the universe should be governed by the same laws that held at other times. We have made some progress toward this goal, as will be described in Chapter 3, but we don't yet have a complete understanding of the origin of the universe.

The reason general relativity broke down at the big bang was that it was not compatible with quantum theory, the other great conceptual revolution of the early twentieth century. The first step toward quantum theory had come in 1900, when Max Planck in Berlin discovered that the radiation from a body that was glowing red-hot was explainable if light could be emitted or absorbed only if it came in discrete packets, called quanta. In one of his groundbreaking papers, written in 1905 when he was at the patent office, Einstein showed that Planck's quantum hypothesis could explain what is called the photoelectric effect, the way certain metals give off electrons when light falls on them. This is the basis of modern light detectors and television cameras, and it was for this work that Einstein was awarded the Nobel Prize for physics.

Einstein continued to work on the quantum idea into the 1920s, but he was deeply disturbed by the work of Werner Heisenberg in Copenhagen, Paul Dirac in Cambridge, and Erwin Schrödinger in Zurich, who developed a new picture of reality called quantum mechanics. No longer did tiny particles have a definite position and

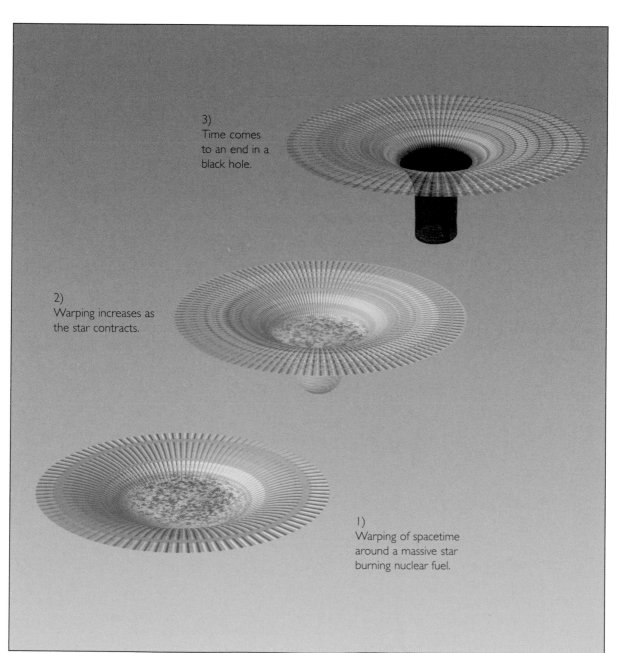

3)
Time comes
to an end in a
black hole.

2)
Warping increases as
the star contracts.

1)
Warping of spacetime
around a massive star
burning nuclear fuel.

Albert Einstein™

Albert Einstein with a puppet of himself shortly after arriving in America for good.

speed. Instead, the more accurately one determined a particle's position, the less accurately one could determine its speed, and vice versa. Einstein was horrified by this random, unpredictable element in the basic laws and never fully accepted quantum mechanics. His feelings were expressed in his famous dictum "God does not play dice." Most other scientists, however, accepted the validity of the new quantum laws because of the explanations they gave for a whole range of previously unaccounted-for phenomena and their excellent agreement with observations. They are the basis of modern developments in chemistry, molecular biology, and electronics, and the foundation for the technology that has transformed the world in the last fifty years.

In December 1932, aware that the Nazis and Hitler were about to come to power, Einstein left Germany and four months later renounced his citizenship, spending the last twenty years of his life at the Institute for Advanced Study in Princeton, New Jersey.

In Germany, the Nazis launched a campaign against "Jewish science" and the many German scientists who were Jews; this is part of the reason that Germany was not able to build an atomic bomb. Einstein and relativity were principal targets of this campaign. When told of the publication of a book entitled 100 *Authors Against Einstein*, he replied: "Why one hundred? If I were wrong, one would have been enough." After the Second World War, he urged the Allies to set up a world government to control the atomic bomb. In 1948, he was offered the presidency of the new state of Israel but turned it down. He once said: "Politics is for the moment, but an equation is for eternity." The Einstein equations of general relativity are his best epitaph and memorial. They should last as long as the universe.

The world has changed far more in the last hundred years than in any previous century. The reason has not been new political or economic doctrines but the vast developments in technology made possible by advances in basic science. Who better symbolizes those advances than Albert Einstein?

Albert Einstein™

CHAPTER 2

THE SHAPE OF TIME

Einstein's general relativity gives time a shape.
How this can be reconciled with quantum theory.

Are the loops complex
or simply impossible?

Main-line railroad heading
from past to future

Can time take a branch
line that loops back?

(FIG. 2.1) THE MODEL OF TIME AS A RAILROAD TRACK

But is it a main line that only operates in one direction
—toward the future—or can it loop back to rejoin the
main line at an earlier junction?

W HAT IS TIME? IS IT AN EVER-ROLLING STREAM THAT bears all our dreams away, as the old hymn says? Or is it a railroad track? Maybe it has loops and branches, so you can keep going forward and yet return to an earlier station on the line (Fig. 2.1).

The nineteenth-century author Charles Lamb wrote: "Nothing puzzles me like time and space. And yet nothing troubles me *less* than time and space, because I never think of them." Most of us don't worry about time and space most of the time, whatever that may be; but we all do wonder sometimes what time is, how it began, and where it is leading us.

Any sound scientific theory, whether of time or of any other concept, should in my opinion be based on the most workable philosophy of science: the positivist approach put forward by Karl Popper and others. According to this way of thinking, a scientific theory is a mathematical model that describes and codifies the observations we make. A good theory will describe a large range of phenomena on the basis of a few simple postulates and will make definite predictions that can be tested. If the predictions agree with the observations, the theory survives that test, though it can never be proved to be correct. On the other hand, if the observations disagree with the predictions, one has to discard or modify the theory. (At least, that is what is supposed to happen. In practice, people often question the accuracy of the observations and the reliability and moral character of those making the observations.) If one takes the positivist position, as I do, one cannot say what time actually is. All one can do is describe what has been found to be a very good mathematical model for time and say what predictions it makes.

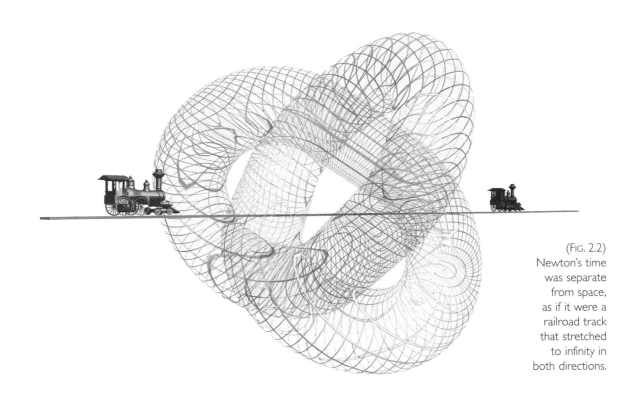

(FIG. 2.2)
Newton's time
was separate
from space,
as if it were a
railroad track
that stretched
to infinity in
both directions.

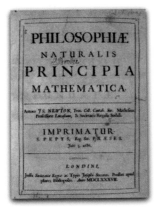

*Isaac Newton published his
mathematical model of time
and space over 300 years ago.*

Isaac Newton gave us the first mathematical model for time and space in his *Principia Mathematica*, published in 1687. Newton occupied the Lucasian chair at Cambridge that I now hold, though it wasn't electrically operated in his time. In Newton's model, time and space were a background in which events took place but which weren't affected by them. Time was separate from space and was considered to be a single line, or railroad track, that was infinite in both directions (Fig. 2.2). Time itself was considered eternal, in the sense that it had existed, and would exist, forever. By contrast, most people thought the physical universe had been created more or less in its present state only a few thousand years ago. This worried philosophers such as the German thinker Immanuel Kant. If the universe had indeed been created, why had there been an infinite wait before the creation? On the other hand, if the universe had existed forever, why hadn't everything that was going to happen already happened, meaning that history was over? In particular, why hadn't the universe reached thermal equilibrium, with everything at the same temperature?

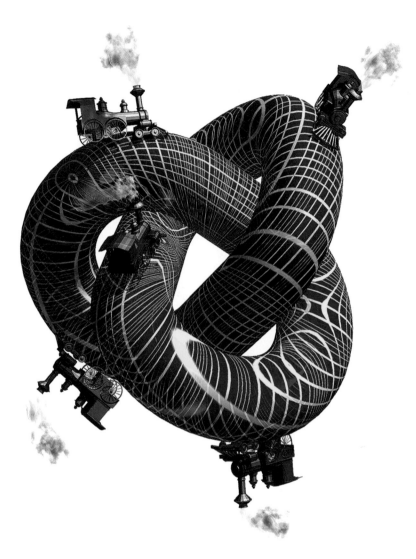

(FIG. 2.3) THE SHAPE AND DIRECTION OF TIME

Einstein's theory of relativity, which agrees with a large number of experiments, shows that time and space are inextricably interconnected.

One cannot curve space without involving time as well. Thus time has a shape. However, it appears to also have a one-way direction, as the locomotives in the illustration show.

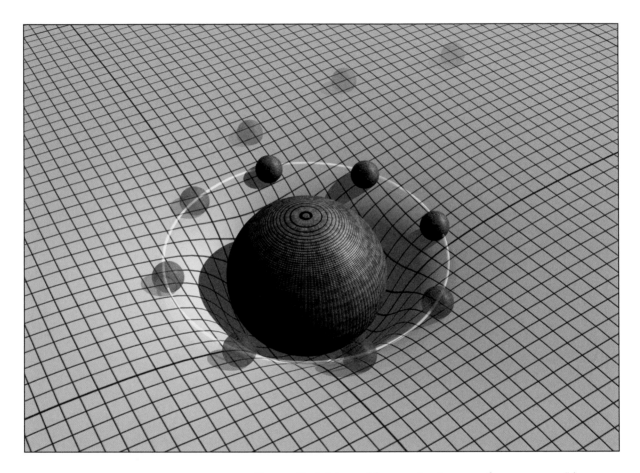

(FIG. 2.4)
THE RUBBER SHEET ANALOGY

The large ball in the center represents a massive body such as a star.

Its weight curves the sheet near it. The ball bearings rolling on the sheet are deflected by this curvature and go around the large ball, in the same way that planets in the gravitational field of a star can orbit it.

Kant called this problem an "antinomy of pure reason," because it seemed to be a logical contradiction; it didn't have a resolution. But it was a contradiction only within the context of the Newtonian mathematical model, in which time was an infinite line, independent of what was happening in the universe. However, as we saw in Chapter 1, in 1915 a completely new mathematical model was put forward by Einstein: the general theory of relativity. In the years since Einstein's paper, we have added a few ribbons and bows, but our model of time and space is still based on what Einstein proposed. This and the following chapters will describe how our ideas have developed in the years since Einstein's revolutionary paper. It has been a success story of the work of a large number of people, and I'm proud to have made a small contribution.

General relativity combines the time dimension with the three dimensions of space to form what is called spacetime (see page 33, Fig. 2.3). The theory incorporates the effect of gravity by saying that the distribution of matter and energy in the universe warps and distorts spacetime, so that it is not flat. Objects in this spacetime try to move in straight lines, but because spacetime is curved, their paths appear bent. They move as if affected by a gravitational field.

As a rough analogy, not to be taken too literally, imagine a sheet of rubber. One can place a large ball on the sheet to represent the Sun. The weight of the ball will depress the sheet and cause it to be curved near the Sun. If one now rolls little ball bearings on the sheet, they won't roll straight across to the other side but instead will go around the heavy weight, like planets orbiting the Sun (Fig. 2.4).

The analogy is incomplete because in it only a two-dimensional section of space (the surface of the rubber sheet) is curved, and time is left undisturbed, as it is in Newtonian theory. However, in the theory of relativity, which agrees with a large number of experiments, time and space are inextricably tangled up. One cannot curve space without involving time as well. Thus time has a shape. By curving space and time, general relativity changes them from being a passive background against which events take place to being active, dynamic participants in what happens. In Newtonian theory, where time existed independently of anything else, one could ask: What did God do before He created the universe? As Saint Augustine said, one should not joke about this, as did a man who said, "He was preparing Hell for those who pry too deep." It is a serious question that people have pondered down the ages. According to Saint Augustine, before God made heaven and earth, He did not make anything at all. In fact, this is very close to modern ideas.

In general relativity, on the other hand, time and space do not exist independently of the universe or of each other. They are defined by measurements within the universe, such as the number of vibrations of a quartz crystal in a clock or the length of a ruler. It is quite conceivable that time defined in this way, within the universe, should have a minimum or maximum value—in other words, a beginning or an end. It would make no sense to ask what happened before the beginning or after the end, because such times would not be defined.

St. Augustine, the fifth-century thinker who held that time did not exist before the beginning of the world.

Page from De Civitate Dei, *twelfth century. Biblioteca Laurenziana, Firenze.*

It was clearly important to decide whether the mathematical model of general relativity *predicted* that the universe, and time itself, should have a beginning or end. The general prejudice among theoretical physicists, including Einstein, held that time should be infinite in both directions. Otherwise, there were awkward questions about the creation of the universe, which seemed to be outside the realm of science. Solutions of the Einstein equations were known in which time had a beginning or end, but these were all very special, with a large amount of symmetry. It was thought that in a real body, collapsing under its own gravity, pressure or sideways velocities would prevent all the matter falling together to the same point, where the density would be infinite. Similarly, if one traced the expansion of the universe back in time, one would find that the matter of the universe didn't all emerge from a point of infinite density. Such a point of infinite density was called a singularity and would be a beginning or an end of time.

In 1963, two Russian scientists, Evgenii Lifshitz and Isaac Khalatnikov, claimed to have proved that solutions of the Einstein equations with a singularity all had a special arrangement of matter and velocities. The chances that the solution representing the universe would have this special arrangement were practically zero. Almost all solutions that could represent the universe would avoid having a singularity of infinite density: Before the era during which the universe has been expanding, there must have been a previous contracting phase during which matter fell together but missed colliding with itself, moving apart again in the present expanding phase. If this were the case, time would continue on forever, from the infinite past to the infinite future.

Not everyone was convinced by the arguments of Lifshitz and Khalatnikov. Instead, Roger Penrose and I adopted a different approach, based not on a detailed study of solutions but on the global structure of spacetime. In general relativity, spacetime is curved not only by massive objects in it but also by the energy in it. Energy is always positive, so it gives spacetime a curvature that bends the paths of light rays toward each other.

Now consider our past light cone (Fig. 2.5), that is, the paths through spacetime of the light rays from distant galaxies that reach

Observer looking back through time _____

Galaxies as they appeared recently _____

Galaxies as they appeared 5 _____
billion years ago

The background radiation _____

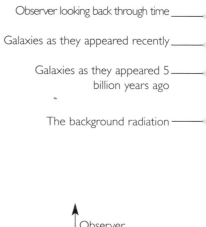

(FIG. 2.5) OUR PAST LIGHT CONE

When we look at distant galaxies, we are looking at the universe at an earlier time because light travels at a finite speed. If we represent time by the vertical direction and represent two of the three space directions horizontally, the light now reaching us at the point at the top has traveled toward us on a cone.

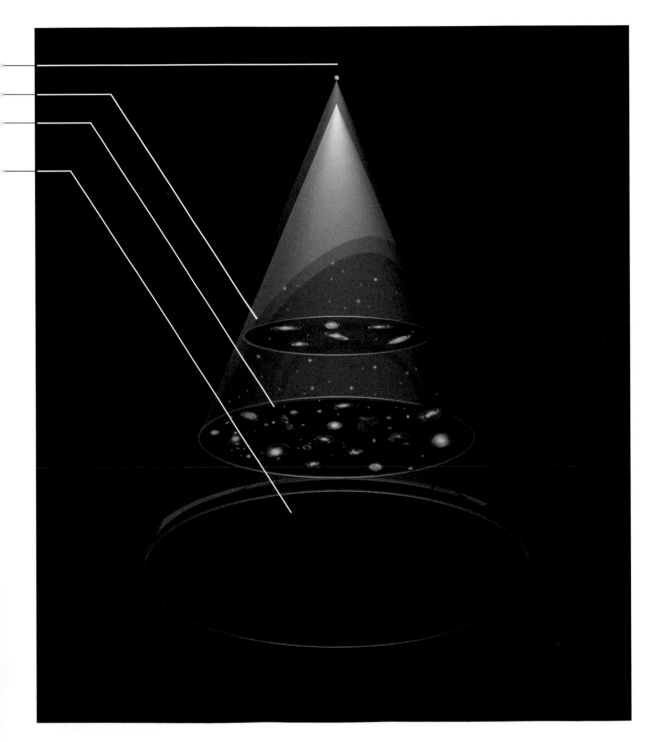

COSMIC MICROWAVE BACKGROUND SPECTRUM FROM COBE

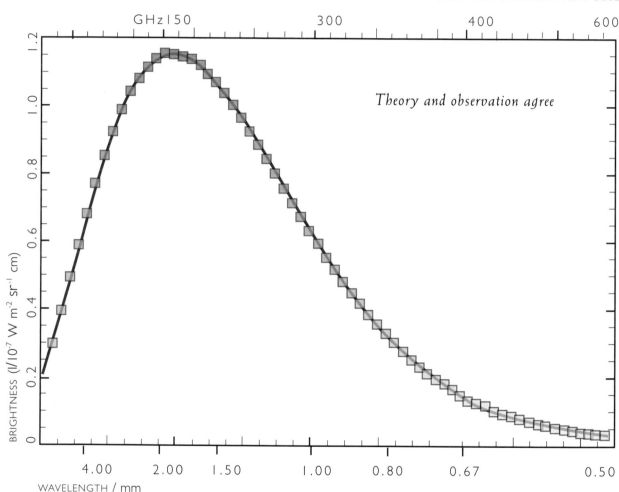

Theory and observation agree

GHz 150   300   400   600

BRIGHTNESS (I/10^{-7} W m^{-2} sr^{-1} cm)

WAVELENGTH / mm

4.00   2.00   1.50   1.00   0.80   0.67   0.50

(FIG. 2.6)

MEASUREMENT OF THE SPECTRUM OF MICROWAVE BACKGROUND

The spectrum—the distribution of intensity with frequency—of the cosmic microwave background radiation is characteristic of that from a hot body. For the radiation to be in thermal equilibrium, matter must have scattered it many times. This indicates that there must have been sufficient matter in our past light cone to cause it to bend in.

us at the present time. In a diagram with time plotted upward and space plotted sideways, this is a cone with its vertex, or point, at us. As we go toward the past, down the cone from the vertex, we see galaxies at earlier and earlier times. Because the universe has been expanding and everything used to be much closer together, as we look back further we are looking back through regions of higher matter density. We observe a faint background of microwave radiation that propagates to us along our past light cone from a much earlier time, when the universe was much denser and hotter than it is now. By tuning receivers to different frequencies of microwaves, we can measure the spectrum (the distribution of power arranged

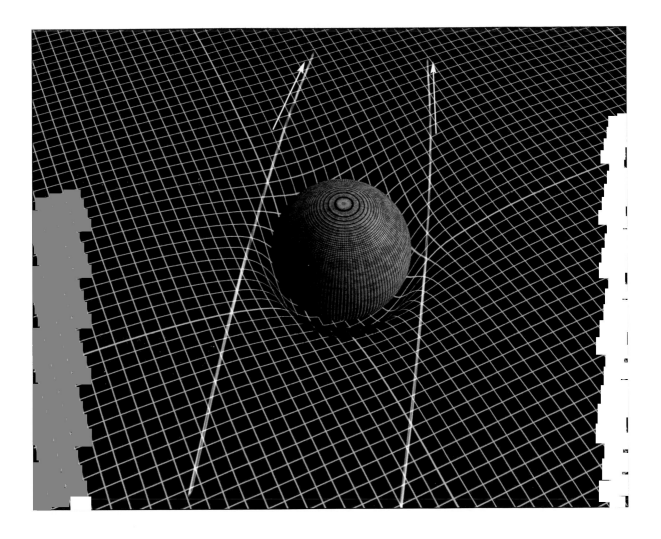

by frequency) of this radiation. We find a spectrum that is characteristic of radiation from a body at a temperature of 2.7 degrees
above absolute zero. This microwave radiation is not much good
for defrosting frozen pizza, but the fact that the spectrum agrees so
exactly with that of radiation from a body at 2.7 degrees tells us that
the radiation must have come from regions that are opaque to
microwaves (Fig. 2.6).

Thus we can conclude that our past light cone must pass
through a certain amount of matter as one follows it back. This
amount of matter is enough to curve spacetime, so the light rays in
our past light cone are bent back toward each other (Fig. 2.7).

(FIG. 2.7) WARPING SPACETIME

Because gravity is attractive, matter
always warps spacetime so that light
rays bend toward each other.

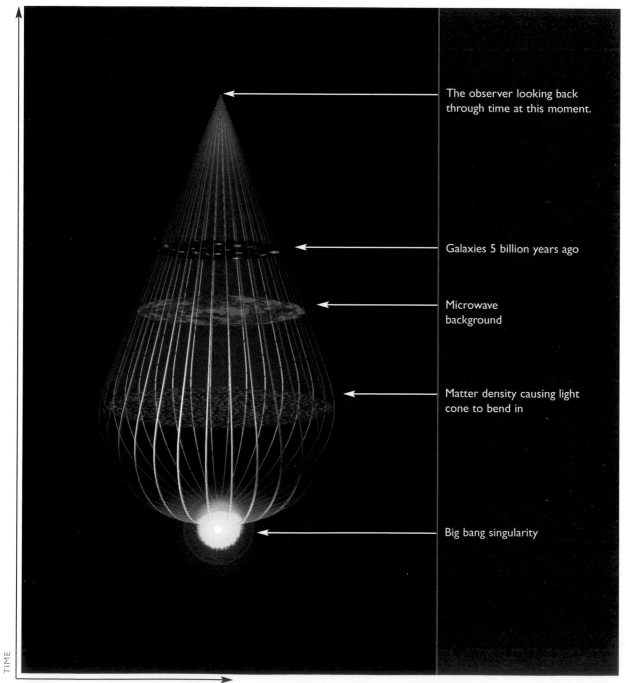

The observer looking back through time at this moment.

Galaxies 5 billion years ago

Microwave background

Matter density causing light cone to bend in

Big bang singularity

TIME

SPACE

As one goes back in time, the cross sections of our past light cone reach a maximum size and begin to get smaller again. Our past is pear-shaped (Fig. 2.8).

As one follows our past light cone back still further, the positive energy density of matter causes the light rays to bend toward each other more strongly. The cross section of the light cone will shrink to zero size in a finite time. This means that all the matter inside our past light cone is trapped in a region whose boundary shrinks to zero. It is therefore not very surprising that Penrose and I could prove that in the mathematical model of general relativity, time must have a beginning in what is called the big bang. Similar arguments show that time would have an end, when stars or galaxies collapse under their own gravity to form black holes. We had sidestepped Kant's antinomy of pure reason by dropping his implicit assumption that time had a meaning independent of the universe. Our paper, proving time had a beginning, won the second prize in the competition sponsored by the Gravity Research Foundation in 1968, and Roger and I shared the princely sum of $300. I don't think the other prize essays that year have shown much enduring value.

There were various reactions to our work. It upset many physicists, but it delighted those religious leaders who believed in an act of creation, for here was scientific proof. Meanwhile, Lifshitz and Khalatnikov were in an awkward position. They couldn't argue with the mathematical theorems that we had proved, but under the Soviet system they couldn't admit they had been wrong and Western science had been right. However, they saved the situation by finding a more general family of solutions with a singularity, which weren't special in the way their previous solutions had been. This enabled them to claim singularities, and the beginning or end of time, as a Soviet discovery.

(FIG. 2.8) TIME IS PEAR-SHAPED

If one follows our past light cone back in time, it will be bent back by the matter in the early universe. The whole universe we observe is contained within a region whose boundary shrinks to zero at the big bang. This would be a singularity, a place where the density of matter would be infinite and classical general relativity would break down.

THE UNCERTAINTY PRINCIPLE

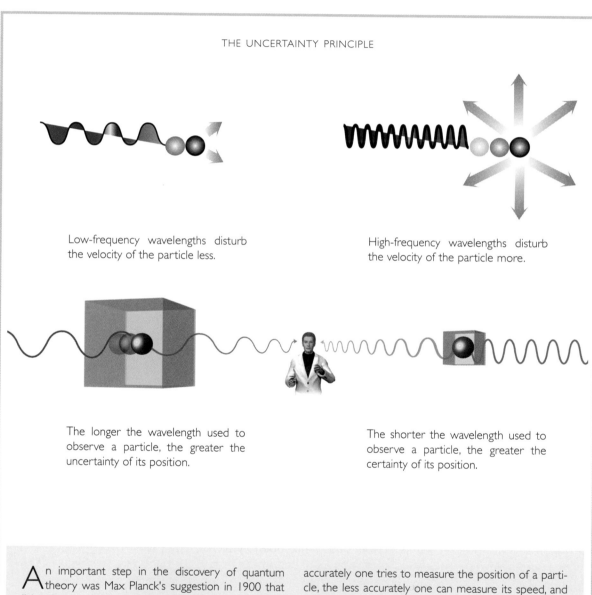

Low-frequency wavelengths disturb the velocity of the particle less.

High-frequency wavelengths disturb the velocity of the particle more.

The longer the wavelength used to observe a particle, the greater the uncertainty of its position.

The shorter the wavelength used to observe a particle, the greater the certainty of its position.

An important step in the discovery of quantum theory was Max Planck's suggestion in 1900 that light always comes in little packets he called quanta. But while Planck's quantum hypothesis clearly explained observations of the rate of radiation from hot bodies, the full extent of its implications wasn't realized until the mid-1920s, when the Germanphysicist Werner Heisenberg formulated his famous uncertainty principle. He noted that Planck's hypothesis implies that the more accurately one tries to measure the position of a particle, the less accurately one can measure its speed, and vice versa.

More precisely, he showed that the uncertainty in the position of a particle times the uncertainty in its momentum must always be larger than Planck's constant, which is a quantity that is closely related to the energy content of one quantum of light.

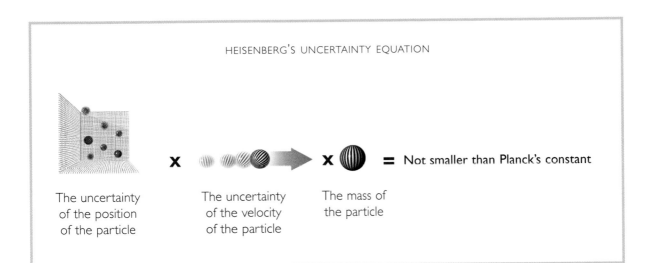

HEISENBERG'S UNCERTAINTY EQUATION

The uncertainty of the position of the particle

The uncertainty of the velocity of the particle

The mass of the particle

= Not smaller than Planck's constant

Most physicists still instinctively disliked the idea of time having a beginning or end. They therefore pointed out that the mathematical model might not be expected to be a good description of spacetime near a singularity. The reason is that general relativity, which describes the gravitational force, is a classical theory, as noted in Chapter 1, and does not incorporate the uncertainty of quantum theory that governs all other forces we know. This inconsistency does not matter in most of the universe most of the time, because the scale on which spacetime is curved is very large and the scale on which quantum effects are important is very small. But near a singularity, the two scales would be comparable, and quantum gravitational effects would be important. So what the singularity theorems of Penrose and myself really established is that our classical region of spacetime is bounded to the past, and possibly to the future, by regions in which quantum gravity is important. To understand the origin and fate of the universe, we need a quantum theory of gravity, and this will be the subject of most of this book.

Quantum theories of systems such as atoms, with a finite number of particles, were formulated in the 1920s, by Heisenberg, Schrödinger, and Dirac. (Dirac was another previous holder of my chair in Cambridge, but it still wasn't motorized.) However, people encountered difficulties when they tried to extend quantum ideas to the Maxwell field, which describes electricity, magnetism, and light.

THE MAXWELL FIELD

In 1865 the British physicist James Clerk Maxwell combined all the known laws of electricity and magnetism. Maxwell's theory rests on the existence of "fields" that transmit actions from one place to another. He recognized that the fields that transmit electric and magnetic disturbances are dynamical entities: they can oscillate and move through space.

Maxwell's synthesis of electromagnetism can be condensed into two equations that prescribe the dynamics of these fields. He himself derived the first great conclusion from these equations: that electromagnetic waves of all frequencies travel through space at the same fixed speed—the speed of light.

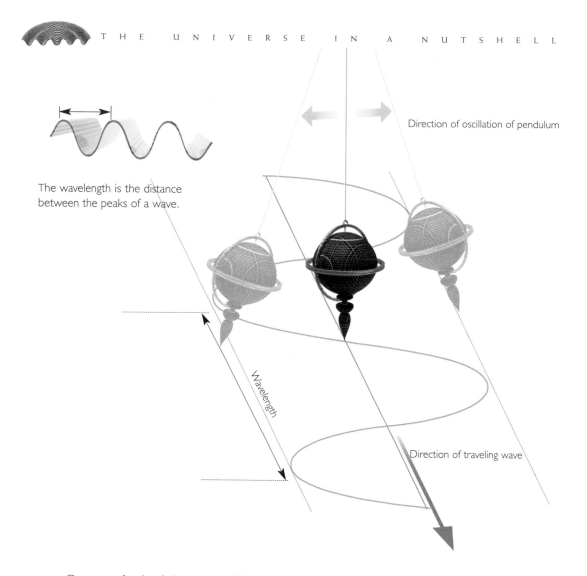

The wavelength is the distance between the peaks of a wave.

Direction of oscillation of pendulum

Wavelength

Direction of traveling wave

One can think of the Maxwell field as being made up of waves of different wavelengths (the distance between one wave crest and the next). In a wave, the field will swing from one value to another like a pendulum (Fig. 2.9).

According to quantum theory, the ground state, or lowest energy state, of a pendulum is not just sitting at the lowest energy point, pointing straight down. That would have both a definite position and a definite velocity, zero. This would be a violation of the uncertainty principle, which forbids the precise measurement of both position and velocity at the same time. The uncertainty in the position multiplied by the uncertainty in the momentum must be greater than a certain quantity, known as Planck's constant—a number that is too long to keep writing down, so we use a symbol for it: ℏ

(FIG. 2.9)

TRAVELING WAVE WITH OSCILLAT-
ING PENDULUM

Electromagnetic radiation travels through space as a wave, with its electric and magnetic fields oscillating, like a pendulum, in directions transverse to the wave's direction of motion. The radiation can be made up of fields of different wavelengths.

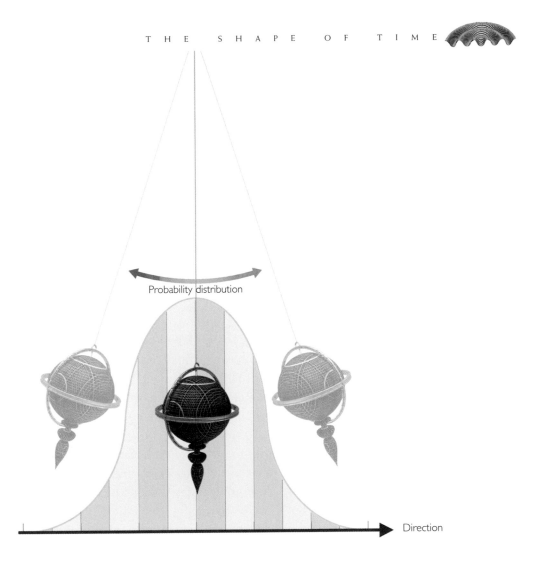

Probability distribution

Direction

So the ground state, or lowest energy state, of a pendulum does not have zero energy, as one might expect. Instead, even in its ground state a pendulum or any oscillating system must have a certain minimum amount of what are called zero point fluctuations. These mean that the pendulum won't necessarily be pointing straight down but will also have a probability of being found at a small angle to the vertical (Fig. 2.10). Similarly, even in the vacuum or lowest energy state, the waves in the Maxwell field won't be exactly zero but can have small sizes. The higher the frequency (the number of swings per minute) of the pendulum or wave, the higher the energy of the ground state.

Calculations of the ground state fluctuations in the Maxwell and electron fields made the apparent mass and charge of the electron infinite, which is not what observations show. However, in the

(Fig. 2.10)
PENDULUM WITH PROBABLITY DISTRIBUTION

According to the Heisenberg principle it is impossible for a pendulum to absolutely point straight down, with zero velocity. Instead quantum theory predicts that, even in its lowest energy state, the pendulum must have a minimum amount of fluctuations.

This means that the pendulum's position will be given by a probability distribution. In its ground state, the most likely position is pointing straight down, but it has also a probability of being found at a small angle to the vertical.

1940s the physicists Richard Feynman, Julian Schwinger, and Shin'ichiro Tomonaga developed a consistent way of removing or "subtracting out" these infinities and dealing only with the finite observed values of the mass and charge. Nevertheless, the ground state fluctuations still caused small effects that could be measured and that agreed well with experiment. Similar subtraction schemes for removing infinities worked for the Yang-Mills field in the theory put forward by Chen Ning Yang and Robert Mills. Yang-Mills theory is an extension of Maxwell theory that describes interactions in two other forces called the weak and strong nuclear forces. However, ground state fluctuations have a much more serious effect in a quantum theory of gravity. Again, each wavelength would have a ground state energy. Since there is no limit to how short the wavelengths of the Maxwell field can be, there are an infinite number of different wavelengths in any region of spacetime and an infinite amount of ground state energy. Because energy density is, like matter, a source of gravity, this infinite energy density ought to mean there is enough gravitational attraction in the universe to curl spacetime into a single point, which obviously hasn't happened.

One might hope to solve the problem of this seeming contradiction between observation and theory by saying that the ground state fluctuations have no gravitational effect, but this would not work. One can detect the energy of ground state fluctuations by the Casimir effect. If you place a pair of metal plates parallel to each other and close together, the effect of the plates is to reduce slightly the number of wavelengths that fit between the plates relative to the number outside. This means that the energy density of ground state fluctuations between the plates, although still infinite, is less than the energy density outside by a finite amount (Fig. 2.11). This difference in energy density gives rise to a force pulling the plates together, and this force has been observed experimentally. Forces are a source of gravity in general relativity, just as matter is, so it would not be consistent to ignore the gravitational effect of this energy difference.

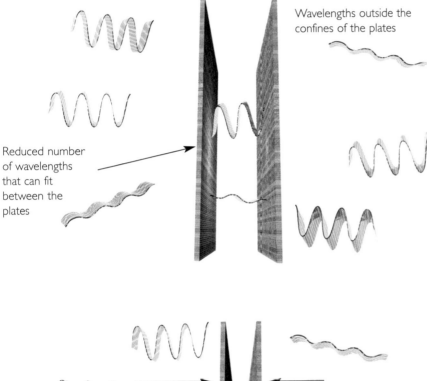

Reduced number of wavelengths that can fit between the plates

Wavelengths outside the confines of the plates

(FIG. 2.11)
THE CASIMIR EFFECT

The existence of ground state fluctuations has been confirmed experimentally by the Casimir effect, a slight force between parallel metal plates.

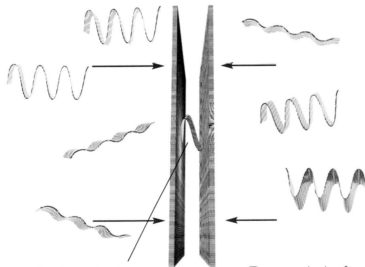

The energy density of ground state fluctuations between the plates is less than the density outside, causing the plates to draw together.

The energy density of ground state fluctuations is greater outside the plates.

47

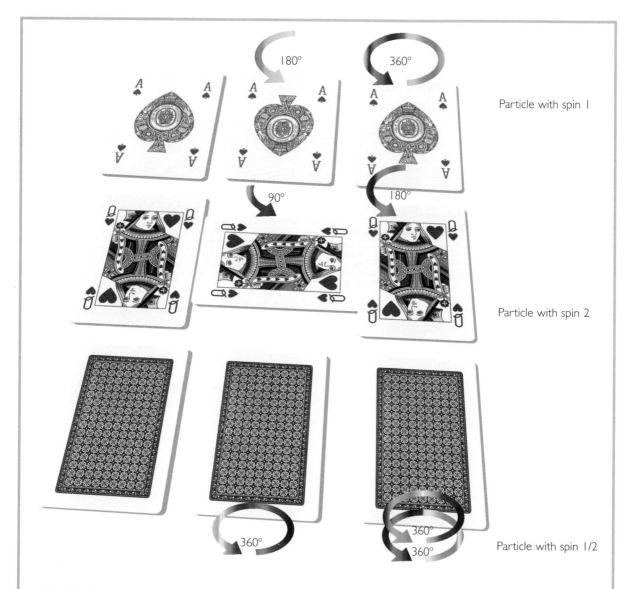

(FIG. 2.12) SPIN

All particles have a property called spin, having to do with what the particle looks like from different directions. One can illustrate this with a pack of playing cards. Consider first the ace of spades. This looks the same only if you turn it through a complete revolution, or 360 degrees. It is therefore said to have spin 1.

On the other hand, the queen of hearts has two heads. It is therefore the same under only half a revolution, 180 degrees. It is said to have spin 2. Similarly, one could imagine objects with spin 3 or higher that would look the same under smaller fractions of a revolution.

The higher the spin, the smaller the fraction of a complete revolution necessary to have the particle look the same. But the remarkable fact is that there are particles that look the same only if you turn them through two complete revolutions. Such particles are said to have spin 1/2.

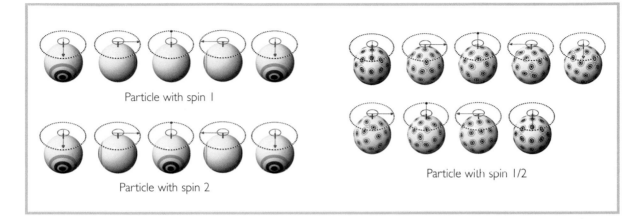

Particle with spin 1

Particle with spin 2

Particle with spin 1/2

Another possible solution to the problem might be to suppose there was a cosmological constant such as Einstein introduced in an attempt to have a static model of the universe. If this constant had an infinite negative value, it could exactly cancel the infinite positive value of the ground state energies in free space, but this cosmological constant seems very ad hoc, and it would have to be tuned to extraordinary accuracy.

Fortunately, a totally new kind of symmetry was discovered in the 1970s that provides a natural physical mechanism to cancel the infinities arising from ground state fluctuations. Supersymmetry is a feature of our modern mathematical models that can be described in various ways. One way is to say that spacetime has extra dimensions besides the dimensions we experience. These are called Grassmann dimensions, because they are measured in numbers known as Grassmann variables rather than in ordinary real numbers. Ordinary numbers commute; that is, it does not matter in which order you multiply them: 6 times 4 is the same as 4 times 6. But Grassmann variables *anti*commute: x times y is the same as −y times x.

Supersymmetry was first considered for removing infinities in matter fields and Yang-Mills fields in a spacetime where both the ordinary number dimensions and the Grassmann dimensions were flat, not curved. But it was natural to extend it to ordinary numbers and Grassmann dimensions that were curved. This led to a number of theories called supergravity, with different amounts of supersymmetry. One consequence of supersymmetry is that every field or particle should have a "superpartner" with a spin that is either 1/2 greater than its own or 1/2 less (Fig 2.12).

ORDINARY NUMBERS

A × B = B × A

GRASSMANN NUMBERS

A × B = −B × A

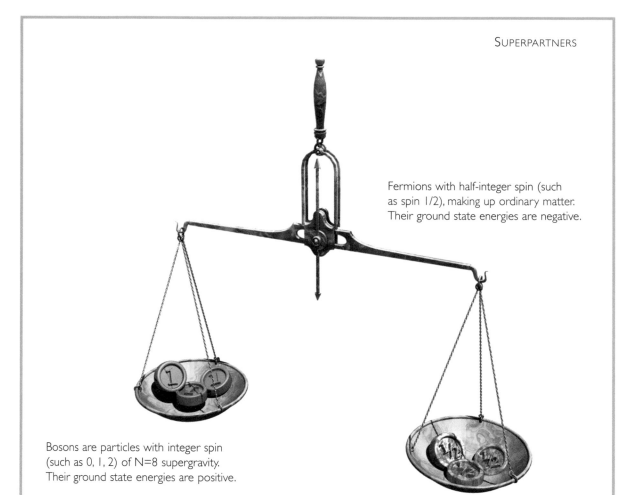

Fermions with half-integer spin (such as spin 1/2), making up ordinary matter. Their ground state energies are negative.

Bosons are particles with integer spin (such as 0, 1, 2) of N=8 supergravity. Their ground state energies are positive.

(FIG. 2.13)

All known particles in the universe belong to one of two groups, fermions or bosons. Fermions are particles with half-integer spin (such as spin 1/2), and they make up ordinary matter. Their ground state energies are negative.

Bosons are particles with integer spin (such as 0, 1, 2), and these give rise to forces between the fermions, such as the gravitational force and light. Their ground state energies are positive. Supergravity theory supposes that every fermion and every boson has a superpartner with a spin that is either 1/2 greater than its own or 1/2 less.

For example, a photon (which is a boson) has a spin of 1. Its ground state energy is positive. The photon's superpartner, the photino, has a spin of 1/2, making it a fermion. Hence, its ground state energy is negative.

In this supergravity scheme we end up with equal numbers of bosons and fermions. With the ground state energies of the bosons weighing in on the positive side and the fermions weighing in on the negative side, the ground state energies cancel one another out, eliminating the biggest infinities.

MODELS OF PARTICLE BEHAVIOR

1 If point particles actually existed as discrete elements like pool balls, then when two collided their path would be deflected into two new trajectories.

2 This is what appears to happen when two particles interact, although the effect is far more dramatic.

3 Quantum field theory shows two particles, like an electron and its antiparticle, a positron, colliding. In doing so they briefly annihilate one another in a frantic burst of energy, creating a photon. This then releases its energy, producing another electron-positron pair. This still appears as if they are just deflected into new trajectories.

4 If particles are not zero points but one-dimensional strings in which the oscillating loops vibrate as an electron and positron. Then, when they collide and annihilate one another, they create a new string with a different vibrational pattern. Releasing energy, it divides into two strings continuing along new trajectories.

5 If those original strings are viewed not as discrete moments but as an uninterrupted history in time, then the resulting strings are seen as a string world sheet.

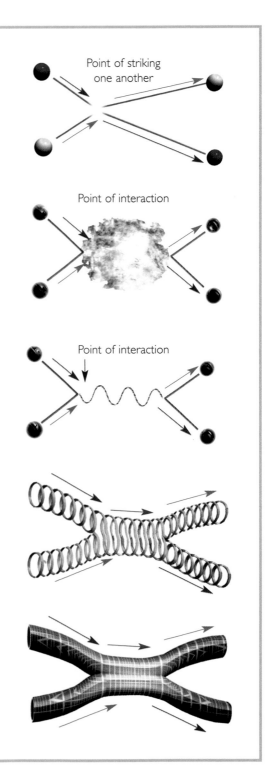

Point of striking
one another

Point of interaction

Point of interaction

(FIG. 2.14, opposite)
STRING OSCILLATIONS

In string theory the basic objects are not particles, which occupy a single point in space, but one-dimensional strings. These strings may have ends or they may join up with themselves in closed loops.

Just like the strings on a violin, the strings in string theory support certain vibrational patterns, or resonant frequencies, whose wavelengths fit precisely between the two ends.

But while the different resonant frequencies of a violin's strings give rise to different musical notes, the different oscillations of a string give rise to different masses and force charges, which are interpreted as fundamental particles. Roughly speaking, the shorter the wavelength of the oscillation on the string, the greater the mass of the particle.

The ground state energies of bosons, fields whose spin is a whole number (0, 1, 2 , etc.), are positive. On the other hand, the ground state energies of fermions, fields whose spin is a half number (1/2, 3/2 , etc.), are negative. Because there are equal numbers of bosons and fermions, the biggest infinities cancel in supergravity theories (see Fig 2.13, page 50).

There remained the possibility that there might be smaller but still infinite quantities left over. No one had the patience needed to calculate whether these theories were actually completely finite. It was reckoned it would take a good student two hundred years, and how would you know he hadn't made a mistake on the second page? Still, up to 1985, most people believed that most supersymmetric supergravity theories would be free of infinities.

Then suddenly the fashion changed. People declared there was no reason not to expect infinities in supergravity theories, and this was taken to mean they were fatally flawed as theories. Instead, it was claimed that a theory named supersymmetric string theory was the only way to combine gravity with quantum theory. Strings, like their namesakes in everyday experience, are one-dimensional extended objects. They have only length. Strings in string theory move through a background spacetime. Ripples on the string are interpreted as particles (Fig. 2.14).

If the strings have Grassmann dimensions as well as their ordinary number dimensions, the ripples will correspond to bosons and fermions. In this case, the positive and negative ground state energies will cancel so exactly that there will be no infinities even of the smaller sort. Superstrings, it was claimed, were the TOE, the Theory of Everything.

Historians of science in the future will find it interesting to chart the changing tide of opinion among theoretical physicists. For a few years, strings reigned supreme and supergravity was dismissed as just an approximate theory, valid at low energy. The qualification "low energy" was considered particularly damning, even though in this context low energies meant particles with energies of

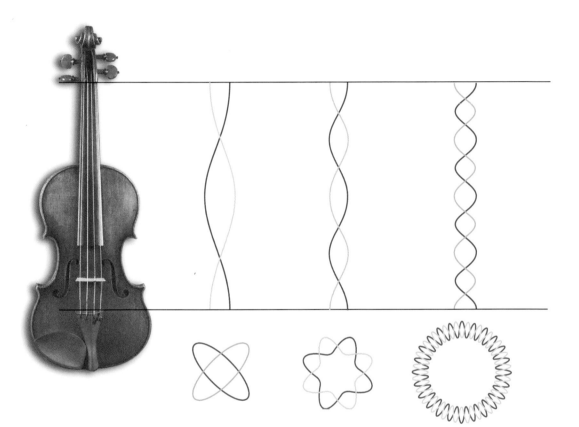

less than a billion billion times those of particles in a TNT explosion. If supergravity was only a low energy approximation, it could not claim to be the fundamental theory of the universe. Instead, the underlying theory was supposed to be one of five possible superstring theories. But which of the five string theories described our universe? And how could string theory be formulated, beyond the approximation in which strings were pictured as surfaces with one space dimension and one time dimension moving through a flat background spacetime? Wouldn't the strings curve the background spacetime?

In the years after 1985, it gradually became apparent that string theory wasn't the complete picture. To start with, it was realized that strings are just one member of a wide class of objects that can be extended in more than one dimension. Paul Townsend, who, like me, is a member of the Department of Applied Mathematics and Theoretical Physics at Cambridge, and who did much of the fundamental work on these objects, gave them the name "p-branes." A p-brane has length in p directions. Thus a p=1 brane is a string, a p=2 brane is a surface or membrane, and so on (Fig. 2.15). There seems no reason to favor the p=1 string case over other possible values of p. Instead, we should adopt the principle of p-brane democracy: all p-branes are created equal.

All the p-branes could be found as solutions of the equations of supergravity theories in 10 or 11 dimensions. While 10 or 11 dimensions doesn't sound much like the spacetime we experience, the idea was that the other 6 or 7 dimensions are curled up so small that we don't notice them; we are only aware of the remaining 4 large and nearly flat dimensions.

I must say that personally, I have been reluctant to believe in extra dimensions. But as I am a positivist, the question "Do extra dimensions really exist?" has no meaning. All one can ask is whether mathematical models with extra dimensions provide a good description of the universe. We do not yet have any observations that require extra dimensions for their explanation. However, there is a possibility we may observe them in the Large Hadron Collider

(FIG. 2.15) P-BRANES

P-branes are objects that are extended in p dimensions. Special cases are strings, which are p=1, and membranes, which are p=2, but higher values of p are possible in ten- or eleven-dimensional spacetime. Often, some or all of the p-dimensions are curled up like a torus.

*We hold these truths
to be self-evident:
All p-branes
are created equal!*

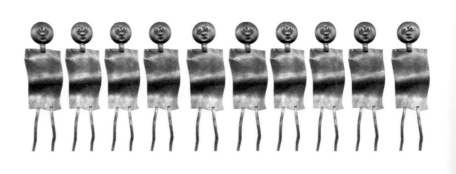

Paul Townsend, the egghead of p-branes

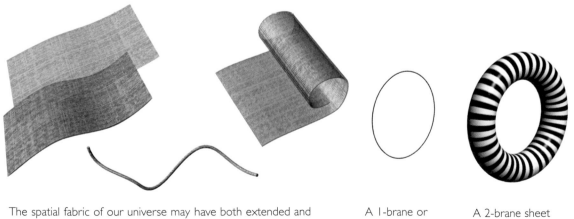

The spatial fabric of our universe may have both extended and curled-up dimensions. The membranes can be seen better if they are curled up.

A 1-brane or string curled up

A 2-brane sheet curled up into a torus

(Fig. 2.16) A UNIFIED FRAMEWORK?

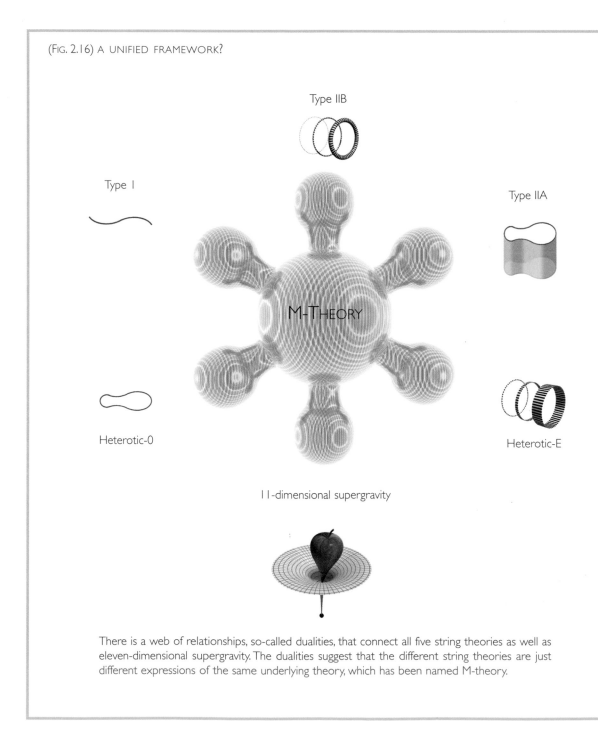

Type IIB

Type I

Type IIA

M-Theory

Heterotic-O

Heterotic-E

11-dimensional supergravity

There is a web of relationships, so-called dualities, that connect all five string theories as well as eleven-dimensional supergravity. The dualities suggest that the different string theories are just different expressions of the same underlying theory, which has been named M-theory.

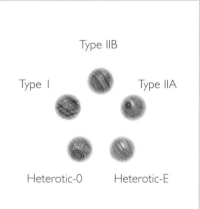

Type IIB

Type I   Type IIA

Heterotic-0   Heterotic-E

Prior to the mid-nineties it appeared that there were five distinct string theories, each separate and uncon- nected.

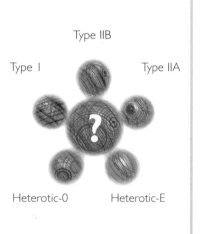

Type IIB

Type I   Type IIA

Heterotic-0   Heterotic-E

M-theory unites the five string theories within a single theoretical framework, but many of its prop- erties have yet to be understood.

in Geneva. But what has convinced many people, including myself, that one should take models with extra dimensions seriously is that there is a web of unexpected relationships, called dualities, between the models. These dualities show that the models are all essentially equivalent; that is, they are just different aspects of the same under- lying theory, which has been given the name M-theory. Not to take this web of dualities as a sign we are on the right track would be a bit like believing that God put fossils into the rocks in order to mis- lead Darwin about the evolution of life.

These dualities show that the five superstring theories all describe the same physics and that they are also physically equiva- lent to supergravity (Fig. 2.16). One cannot say that superstrings are more fundamental than supergravity, or vice versa. Rather, they are different expressions of the same underlying theory, each useful for calculations in different kinds of situations. Because string theo- ries don't have any infinities, they are good for calculating what happens when a few high energy particles collide and scatter off each other. However, they are not of much use for describing how the energy of a very large number of particles curves the universe or forms a bound state, like a black hole. For these situations, one needs supergravity, which is basically Einstein's theory of curved spacetime with some extra kinds of matter. It is this picture that I shall mainly use in what follows.

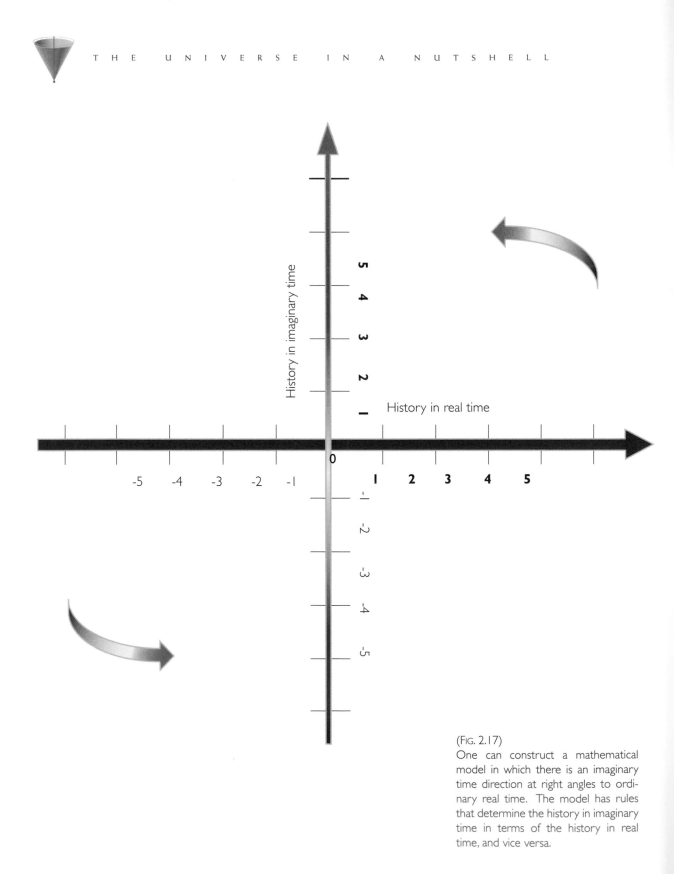

History in imaginary time

History in real time

5
4
3
2
1

0

-5   -4   -3   -2   -1

1   2   3   4   5

-1
-2
-3
-4
-5

(FIG. 2.17)
One can construct a mathematical
model in which there is an imaginary
time direction at right angles to ordinary real time. The model has rules
that determine the history in imaginary
time in terms of the history in real
time, and vice versa.

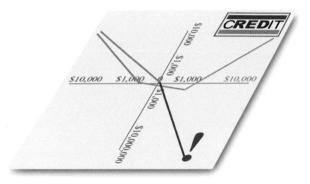

To describe how quantum theory shapes time and space, it is helpful to introduce the idea of imaginary time. Imaginary time sounds like something from science fiction, but it is a well-defined mathematical concept: time measured in what are called imaginary numbers. One can think of ordinary real numbers such as 1, 2, -3.5, and so on as corresponding to positions on a line stretching from left to right: zero in the middle, positive real numbers on the right, and negative real numbers on the left (Fig. 2.17).

Imaginary numbers can then be represented as corresponding to positions on a vertical line: zero is again in the middle, positive imaginary numbers plotted upward, and negative imaginary numbers plotted downward. Thus imaginary numbers can be thought of as a new kind of number at right angles to ordinary real numbers. Because they are a mathematical construct, they don't need a physical realization; one can't have an imaginary number of oranges or an imaginary credit card bill (Fig. 2.18).

One might think this means that imaginary numbers are just a mathematical game having nothing to do with the real world. From the viewpoint of positivist philosophy, however, one cannot determine what is real. All one can do is find which mathematical models describe the universe we live in. It turns out that a mathematical model involving imaginary time predicts not only effects we have already observed but also effects we have not been able to measure yet nevertheless believe in for other reasons. So what is real and what is imaginary? Is the distinction just in our minds?

(FIG. 2.18)
Imaginary numbers are a mathematical construction. You can't have an imaginary number credit card bill.

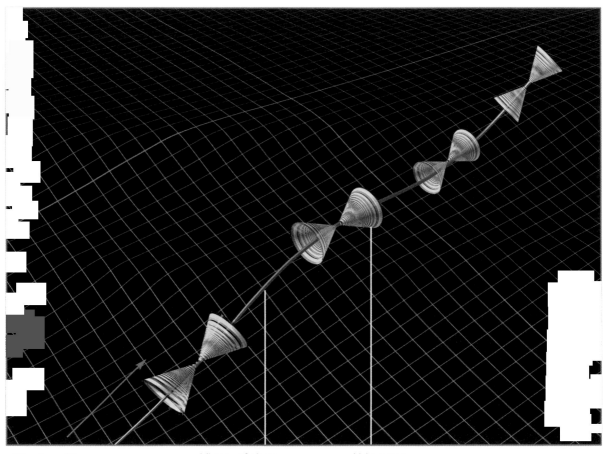

Direction of time   History of observer   Light cones

(FIG. 2.19)

In the real time spacetime of classical general relativity, time is distinguished from the space directions because it increases only along the history of an observer, unlike the space directions, which can increase or decrease along that history. The imaginary time direction of quantum theory, on the other hand, is like another space direction, so can increase or decrease.

Einstein's classical (i.e., nonquantum) general theory of relativity combined real time and the three dimensions of space into a four-dimensional spacetime. But the real time direction was distinguished from the three spatial directions; the world line or history of an observer always increased in the real time direction (that is, time always moved from past to future), but it could increase *or* *decrease* in any of the three spatial directions. In other words, one could reverse direction in space, but not in time (Fig. 2.19).

On the other hand, because imaginary time is at right angles to real time, it behaves like a fourth spatial direction. It can therefore

(Fig. 2.20) IMAGINARY TIME

In an imaginary spacetime that is a sphere, the imaginary time direction could represent the distance from the South Pole. As one moves north, the circles of latitude at constant distances from the South Pole become bigger, corresponding to the universe expanding with imaginary time. The universe would reach maximum size at the equator and then contract again with increasing imaginary time to a single point at the North Pole. Even though the universe would have zero size at the poles, these points would not be singularities, just as the North and South Poles on the Earth's surface are perfectly regular points. This suggests that the origin of the universe in imaginary time can be a regular point in spacetime.

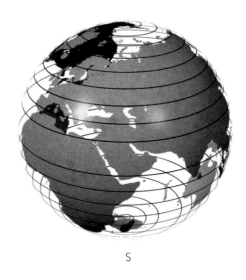

S

Imaginary time as degrees of latitude

N

(Fig. 2.21)

Instead of degrees of latitude, the imaginary time direction in a spacetime that is a sphere could also correspond to degrees of longitude. Because all the lines of longitude meet at the North and South Poles, time is standing still at the poles; an increase of imaginary time leaves one on the same spot, just as going west on the North Pole of the Earth still leaves one on the North Pole.

Imaginary time as degrees of longitude which meet at the North and South Poles

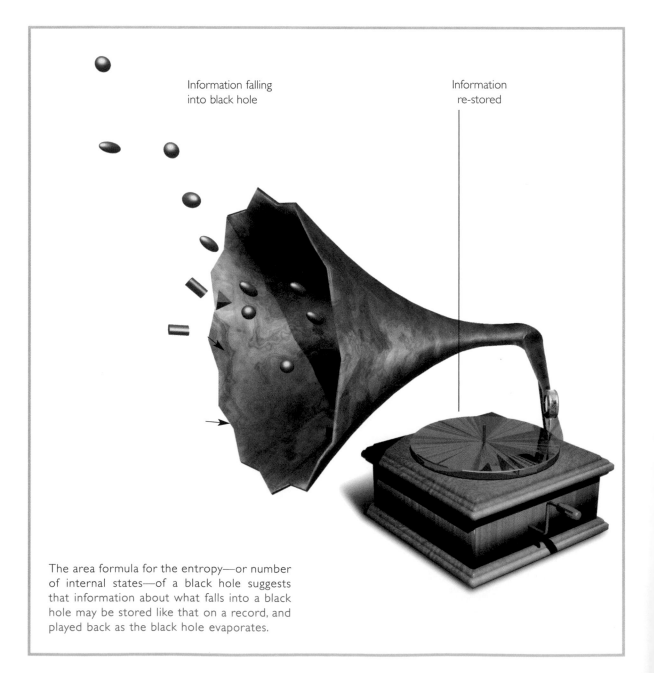

Information falling
into black hole

Information
re-stored

The area formula for the entropy—or number
of internal states—of a black hole suggests
that information about what falls into a black
hole may be stored like that on a record, and
played back as the black hole evaporates.

have a much richer range of possibilities than the railroad track of ordinary real time, which can only have a beginning or an end or go around in circles. It is in this imaginary sense that time has a shape.

To see some of the possibilities, consider an imaginary time spacetime that is a sphere, like the surface of the Earth. Suppose that imaginary time was degrees of latitude (Fig. 2.20, see page 61). Then the history of the universe in imaginary time would begin at the South Pole. It would make no sense to ask, "What happened before the beginning?" Such times are simply not defined, any more than there are points south of the South Pole. The South Pole is a perfectly regular point of the Earth's surface, and the same laws hold there as at other points. This suggests that the beginning of the universe in imaginary time can be a regular point of spacetime, and that the same laws can hold at the beginning as in the rest of the universe. (The quantum origin and evolution of the universe will be discussed in the next chapter.)

Another possible behavior is illustrated by taking imaginary time to be degrees of longitude on the Earth. All the lines of longitude meet at the North and South Poles (Fig. 2.21, see page 61) Thus time stands still there, in the sense that an increase of imaginary time, or of degrees of longitude, leaves one in the same spot. This is very similar to the way that ordinary time appears to stand still on the horizon of a black hole. We have come to recognize that this standing still of real and imaginary time (either both stand still or neither does) means that the spacetime has a temperature, as I discovered for black holes. Not only does a black hole have a temperature, it also behaves as if it has a quantity called entropy. The entropy is a measure of the number of internal states (ways it could be configured on the inside) that the black hole could have without looking any different to an outside observer, who can only observe its mass, rotation, and charge. This black hole entropy is given by a very simple formula I discovered in 1974. It equals the area of the horizon of the black hole: there is one bit of information about the internal state of the black hole for each fundamental unit of area of

$$S = \frac{Akc^3}{4\,\hbar G}$$

THE BLACK HOLE ENTROPY
FORMULA

A the area of the event horizon of the black hole

$\hbar$ Planck's constant

k Boltzmann's constant

G Newton's gravitational constant

c Speed of light

S Entropy

Even a tiny fragment of the 2-D holographic plate contains enough information to reconstruct the whole 3-D image of the apple.

THE HOLOGRAPHIC PRINCIPLE

The realization that the surface area of the horizon surrounding a black hole measures the black hole's entropy has led people to advocate that the maximum entropy of any closed region of space can never exceed a quarter of the area of the circumscribing surface. Since entropy is nothing more than a measure of the total information contained in a system, this suggests that the information associated with all phenomena in the three-dimensional world can be stored on its two-dimensional boundary, like a holographic image. In a certain sense the world would be two-dimensional.

the horizon. This shows that there is a deep connection between quantum gravity and thermodynamics, the science of heat (which includes the study of entropy). It also suggests that quantum gravity may exhibit what is called holography (Fig. 2.22).

Information about the quantum states in a region of spacetime may be somehow coded on the boundary of the region, which has two dimensions less. This is like the way that a hologram carries a three-dimensional image on a two-dimensional surface. If quantum gravity incorporates the holographic principle, it may mean that we can keep track of what is inside black holes. This is essential if we are to be able to predict the radiation that comes out of black holes. If we can't do that, we won't be able to predict the future as fully as we thought. This is discussed in Chapter 4. Holography is discussed again in Chapter 7. It seems we may live on a 3-brane—a four-dimensional (three space plus one time) surface that is the boundary of a five-dimensional region, with the remaining dimensions curled up very small. The state of the world on a brane encodes what is happening in the five-dimensional region.

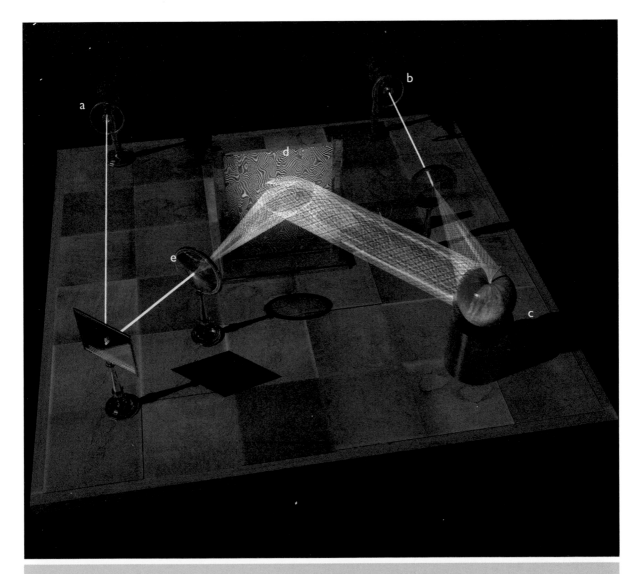

(FIG. 2.22) Holography is essentially a phenomenon of interference of wave patterns. Holograms are created when the light from a single laser is split into two separate beams (a) and (b). One (b) bounces off the object (c) onto a photo-sensitized plate (d). The other (a) passes through a lens (e) and collides with the reflected light of (b), creating an interference pattern on the plate.

When a laser is shone through the developed plate a fully *three-dimensional* image of the original object appears. An observer can move around this holographic image, being able to see all the hidden faces that a normal photo could not show.

The two-dimensional surface of the plate on the left, unlike a normal photo, has the remarkable property that any tiny fragment of its surface contains all the information needed to reconstruct the whole image.

CHAPTER 3

THE UNIVERSE IN A NUTSHELL

The universe has multiple histories, each of which is determined by a tiny nut.

I could be bounded in a nutshell
and count myself a king of infinite space...

—Shakespeare,
Hamlet, Act 2, Scene 2

HAMLET MAY HAVE MEANT THAT ALTHOUGH WE HUMAN beings are very limited physically, our minds are free to explore the whole universe, and to go boldly where even *Star Trek* fears to tread—bad dreams permitting.

Is the universe actually infinite or just very large? And is it everlasting or just long-lived? How could our finite minds comprehend an infinite universe? Isn't it presumptuous of us even to make the attempt? Do we risk the fate of Prometheus, who in classical mythology stole fire from Zeus for human beings to use, and was punished for his temerity by being chained to a rock where an eagle picked at his liver?

Despite this cautionary tale, I believe we can and should try to understand the universe. We have already made remarkable progress in understanding the cosmos, particularly in the last few years. We don't yet have a complete picture, but this may not be far off.

The most obvious thing about space is that it goes on and on and on. This has been confirmed by modern instruments such as the Hubble telescope, which allows us to probe deep into space. What we see are billions and billions of galaxies of various shapes and sizes (see page 70, Fig. 3.1). Each galaxy contains uncounted billions of stars, many of which have planets around them. We live on a planet orbiting a star in an outer arm of the spiral Milky Way

Above: *Prometheus. Etruscan vase painting, 6th century* B.C.

Left: *Hubble space telescope lens and mirrors being upgraded by a space shuttle mission. Australia can be seen below.*

69

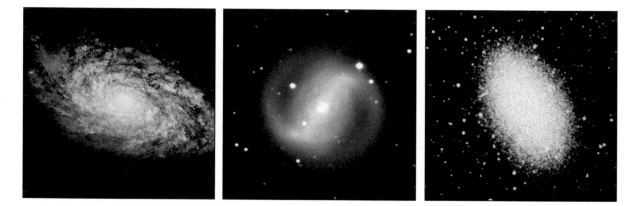

Spiral galaxy NGC 4414   *Spiral bar galaxy NGC 4314*   *Elliptical galaxy NGC 147*

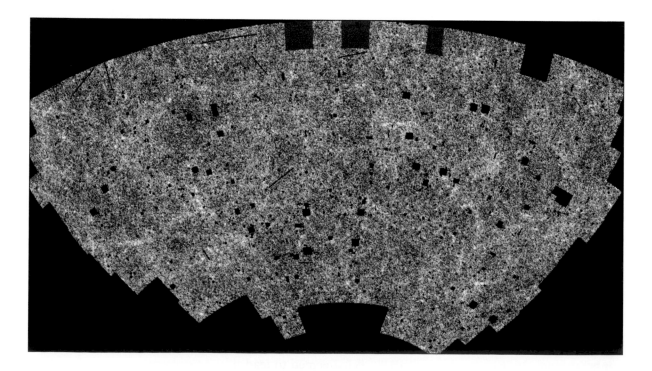

(FIG. 3.1) When we look deep into the universe, we see billions and billions of galaxies.
Galaxies can have various shapes and sizes; they can be either elliptical or spiral, like our own Milky Way.

galaxy. The dust in the spiral arms blocks our view of the universe in the plane of the galaxy, but we have a clear line of sight in cones of directions on each side of the plane, and we can plot the positions of distant galaxies (Fig. 3.2). We find that the galaxies are distributed roughly uniformly throughout space, with some local concentrations and voids. The density of galaxies appears to drop off at very large distances, but that seems to be because they are so far away and faint that we can't make them out. As far as we can tell, the universe goes on in space forever (see page 72, Fig. 3.3).

Although the universe seems to be much the same at each position in space, it is definitely changing in time. This was not realized until the early years of the twentieth century. Up to then, it was thought the universe was essentially constant in time. It might have existed for an infinite time, but that seemed to lead to absurd conclusions. If stars had been radiating for an infinite time, they would have heated up the universe to their temperature. Even

(FIG. 3.2)

Our planet Earth **(E)** orbits the Sun in the outer region of the spiral Milky Way galaxy. The stellar dust in the spiral arms blocks our view within the plane of the galaxy but we have a clear view on either side of that plane.

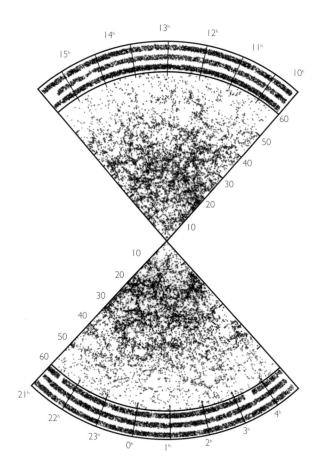

(FIG. 3.3)
Apart from some local concentrations, we find that galaxies are distributed roughly uniformly throughout space.

at night, the whole sky would be as bright as the sun, because every line of sight would end either on a star or on a cloud of dust that had been heated up until it was as hot as the stars (Fig. 3.4).

The observation that we have all made, that the sky at night is dark, is very important. It implies that the universe cannot have existed forever in the state we see today. Something must have happened in the past to make the stars light up a finite time ago, which means that the light from very distant stars has not had time to reach us yet. This would explain why the sky at night isn't glowing in every direction.

If the stars had just been sitting there forever, why did they suddenly light up a few billion years ago? What was the clock that told them it was time to shine? As we've seen, this puzzled those philosophers, much like Immanuel Kant, who believed that the universe had existed forever. But for most people, it was consistent with the idea that the universe had been created, much as it is now, only a few thousand years ago.

However, discrepancies with this idea began to appear with the observations by Vesto Slipher and Edwin Hubble in the second decade of the twentieth century. In 1923, Hubble discovered that

(FIG. 3.4)
If the universe was static and infinite in every direction, every line of sight would end in a star, which would make the night sky as bright as the sun.

73

THE DOPPLER EFFECT

The relationship between speed and wavelength, which is called the Doppler effect, is an everyday experience.

Listen to a plane that passes overhead; as it approaches, its engine sounds at a higher pitch, and when it passes and disappears, it sounds at a lower pitch.

The higher pitch corresponds to sound waves with a shorter wavelength (the distance between one wave crest and the next) and a higher frequency (the number of waves per second).

This is because, as the plane moves toward you, it will be nearer to you when it emits the next wave crest, lessening the distance between wave crests.

Similarly, as the plane moves away the wavelengths increase and the pitch you perceive is lower.

many faint patches of light, called nebulae, were in fact other galaxies, vast collections of stars like our sun but at a great distance. In order for them to appear so small and faint, the distances had to be so great that light from them would have taken millions or even billions of years to reach us. This indicated that the beginning of the universe couldn't have been just a few thousand years ago.

But the second thing Hubble discovered was even more remarkable. Astronomers had learned that by analyzing the light from other galaxies, it was possible to measure whether they are moving toward us or away from us (Fig. 3.5). To their great surprise, they had found that nearly all galaxies are moving away. Moreover, the farther they are from us, the faster they are moving away. It was Hubble who recognized the dramatic implications of this discovery:

(FIG. 3.5)

The Doppler effect is also true of light waves. If a galaxy were to remain at a constant distance from Earth, characteristic lines in the spectrum would appear in a normal or standard position. However, if the galaxy is moving away from us, the waves will appear elongated or stretched and the characteristic lines will be shifted toward the red (*right*). If the galaxy is moving toward us then the waves will appear to be compressed, and the lines will be blue-shifted (*left*).

Our galactic neighbor, Andromeda, measured by Hubble and Slipher.

CHRONOLOGY OF DISCOVERIES MADE BY SLIPHER AND HUBBLE, BETWEEN 1910 AND 1930.

1912 —Slipher measured light from four nebulae, finding three of them red-shifted but Andromeda blue-shifted. His interpretation was that Andromeda is moving toward us while the other nebulae move away from us.

1912-1914 —Slipher measured 12 more nebulae. All except one were red-shifted.

1914 —Slipher presented his findings to the American Astronomical Society. Hubble heard the presentation.

1918 —Hubble began to investigate the nebulae.

1923 —Hubble determined that the spiral nebulae (including Andromeda) are other galaxies.

1914-1925 —Slipher and others kept measuring Doppler shifts. The score in 1925 was 43 red shifts to 2 blue shifts.

1929 —Hubble and Milton Humason—after continuing to measure Doppler shifts and finding that on the large scale every galaxy appears to be receding from every other—announced their discovery that the universe is expanding.

on the large scale, every galaxy is moving away from every other galaxy. The universe is expanding (Fig. 3.6).

The discovery of the expansion of the universe was one of the great intellectual revolutions of the twentieth century. It came as a total surprise, and it completely changed the discussion of the origin of the universe. If the galaxies are moving apart, they must have been closer together in the past. From the present rate of expansion, we can estimate that they must have been very close together indeed ten to fifteen billion years ago. As described in the last chapter, Roger Penrose and I were able to show that Einstein's general theory of relativity implied that the universe and time itself must have had a beginning in a tremendous explosion. Here was the explanation of

Edwin Hubble at the 100-inch Mount Wilson telescope in 1930.

(FIG. 3.6) HUBBLE'S LAW

By analyzing the light from other galaxies, Edwin Hubble discovered in the 1920s that nearly all galaxies are moving away from us, at a velocity V that is proportional to their distance R from the Earth, so V = H × R.

This important observation, known as Hubble's law, established that the universe is expanding, with the Hubble constant H setting the rate of expansion.

The graph below shows recent observations of the red-shift of galaxies, confirming Hubble's law to vast distances away from us.

The slight upward bend in the graph at large distances indicates that the expansion is speeding up, which may be caused by vacuum energy.

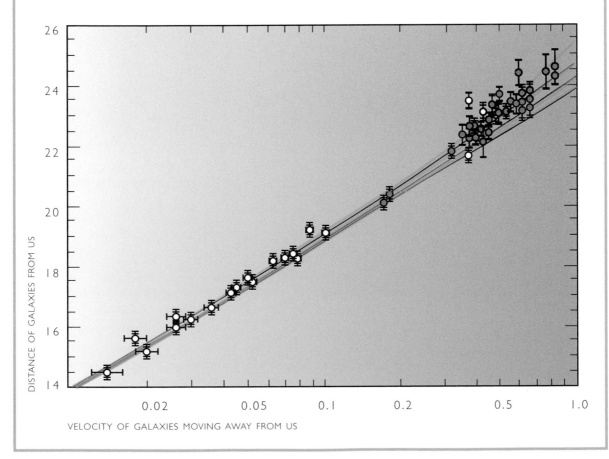

DISTANCE OF GALAXIES FROM US

VELOCITY OF GALAXIES MOVING AWAY FROM US

Big bang singularity

Planck era. Unknown, exotic laws of physics

Grand Unification Theory (GUT) epoch. The balance of matter/antimatter tips in the balance of matter.

Electro-weak era dominated by quarks and antiquarks.

Hadron and lepton era. Quarks confined in the formation of protons, neutrons, mesons, and baryons.

Protons and neutrons bind as nuclei of hydrogen, helium, lithium, and deuterium.

Matter and radiation couple together and the first stable nuclei form.

Decoupling of matter and energy. The optically dense universe becomes transparent to the cosmic background radiation.

Clusters of matter form quasars, stars, and proto-galaxies. Stars begin to synthesize heavier nuclei.

New galaxies form with solar systems condensing around stars. Atoms link to form complex molecules of life-forms.

10^{-43} seconds 10^{-35} seconds 10^{-10} seconds 1 second 3 minutes 300,000 years 1,000 million years 15,000 million years

THE HOT BIG BANG

If general relativity were correct, the universe started with an infinite temperature and density at the big bang singularity. As the universe expanded, the temperature of the radiation decreased. At about a hundredth of a second after the big bang, the temperature would have been 100 billion degrees, and the universe would have contained mostly photons, electrons, and neutrinos (extremely light particles), and their antiparticles, together with some protons and neutrons. For the next three minutes, as the universe cooled to about one billion degrees, protons and neutrons would have begun combining to form the nuclei of helium, hydrogen, and other light elements.

Hundreds of thousands of years later, when the temperature had dropped to a few thousand degrees, the electrons would have slowed down to the point where the light nuclei could capture them to form atoms. However, the heavier elements of which we are made, such as carbon and oxygen, would not form until billion of years later from the burning of helium in the center of stars.

This picture of a dense, hot early stage of the universe was first put forward by the scientist George Gamow in 1948, in a paper he wrote with Ralph Alpher, which made the remarkable prediction that radiation from this very hot early stage should still be around today. Their prediction was confirmed in 1965, when the physicists Arno Penzias and Robert Wilson observed the cosmic microwave background radiation.

why the sky at night is dark: no star could have been shining longer than ten to fifteen billion years, the time since the big bang.

We are used to the idea that events are caused by earlier events, which in turn are caused by still earlier events. There is a chain of causality stretching back into the past. But suppose this chain has a beginning. Suppose there was a first event. What caused *it*? This was not a question that many scientists wanted to address. They tried to avoid it, either by claiming, like the Russians, that the universe didn't have a beginning or by maintaining that the origin of the universe did not lie within the realm of science but belonged to metaphysics or religion. In my opinion, this is not a position any true scientist should take. If the laws of science are suspended at the beginning of the universe, might not they fail at other times also? A law is not a law if it only holds sometimes. *We must try to understand the beginning of the universe on the basis of science. It may be a task beyond our powers, but we should at least make the attempt.*

While the theorems that Penrose and I proved showed that the universe must have had a beginning, they didn't give much information about the nature of that beginning. They indicated that the universe began in a big bang, a point where the whole universe, and everything in it, was scrunched up into a single point of infinite density. At this point, Einstein's general theory of relativity would have broken down, so it cannot be used to predict in what manner the universe began. One is left with the origin of the universe apparently being beyond the scope of science.

This was not a conclusion that scientists should be happy with. As Chapters 1 and 2 point out, the reason general relativity broke down near the big bang is that it did not incorporate the uncertainty principle, the random element of quantum theory that Einstein had objected to on the grounds that God does not play dice. However, all the evidence is that God is quite a gambler. One can think of the universe as being like a giant casino, with dice being rolled or wheels being spun on every occasion (Fig. 3.7). You might think that operating a casino is a very chancy business, because you risk losing money each time dice are thrown or the wheel is spun. But over a large number of bets, the gains and losses average out to a result that *can* be predicted, even though the result of any particular bet cannot be predicted (Fig. 3.8). The casino operators make sure the odds average out in their favor. That is why casino operators are so rich. The only chance you have of winning against them is to stake all your money on a few rolls of the dice or spins of the wheel.

It is the same with the universe. When the universe is big, as it is today, there are a very large number of rolls of the dice, and the results average out to something one can predict. That is why classical laws work for large systems. But when the universe is very small, as it was near in time to the big bang, there are only a small number of rolls of the dice, and the uncertainty principle is very important.

Because the universe keeps on rolling the dice to see what happens next, it doesn't have just a single history, as one might have thought. Instead, the universe must have every possible history, each with its own probability. There must be a history of the universe in which Belize won every gold medal at the Olympic Games, though maybe the probability is low.

This idea that the universe has multiple histories may sound like science fiction, but it is now accepted as science fact. It was formulated by Richard Feynman, who was both a great physicist and quite a character.

We are now working to combine Einstein's general theory of relativity and Feynman's idea of multiple histories into a complete unified theory that will describe everything that happens in the universe. This unified theory will enable us to calculate how the universe will develop if we know how the histories started. But the unified theory will not in itself tell us how the universe began or what its initial state was. For that, we need what are called boundary conditions, rules that tell us what happens on the frontiers of the universe, the edges of space and time.

If the frontier of the universe was just at a normal point of space and time, we could go past it and claim the territory beyond as part of the universe. On the other hand, if the boundary of the

(Fig. 3.7, above, and Fig. 3.8, opposite) If a gambler bets on red for a large number of spins of the wheel, one can fairly accurately predict his return because the results of the single spins average out.

On the other hand, it is impossible to predict the outcome of any particular bet.

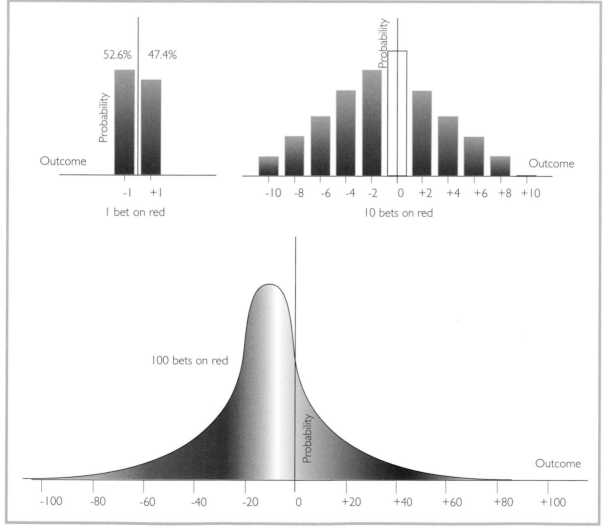

52.6%   47.4%

Probability

Outcome

-1   +1

1 bet on red

Probability

Outcome

-10 -8 -6 -4 -2 0 +2 +4 +6 +8 +10

10 bets on red

100 bets on red

Probability

Outcome

-100   -80   -60   -40   -20   0   +20   +40   +60   +80   +100

If the boundary of the universe was simply a point of spacetime, we could keep extending frontiers.

universe was at a jagged edge where space and time were scrunched up and the density was infinite, it would be very difficult to define meaningful boundary conditions.

However, a colleague named Jim Hartle and I realized there was a third possibility. Maybe the universe has no boundary in space and time. At first sight, this seems to be in direct contradiction with the theorems that Penrose and I proved, which showed that the universe must have had a beginning, a boundary in time. However, as explained in Chapter 2, there is another kind of time, called imaginary time, that is at right angles to the ordinary real time that we feel going by. The history of the universe in real time determines its history in imaginary time, and vice versa, but the two kinds of history can be

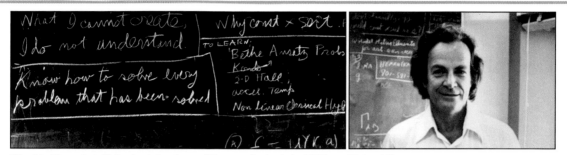

The blackboard at Caltech at the time of Feynman's death in 1988.   Richard Feynman.

FEYNMAN STORIES

Born in Brooklyn, New York, in 1918, Richard Feynman completed his Ph.D. under John Wheeler at Princeton University in 1942. Shortly afterward, he was drawn into the Manhattan Project. There he was known for both his exuberant personality and practical jokes—at the Los Alamos labs, he enjoyed cracking the top-secret safes—and for being an exceptional physicist: he became a key contributor to atomic bomb theory. Feynman's perpetual curiosity about the world was the very root of his being. It was not only the engine for his scientific success, it led him to numerous astonishing exploits, such as deciphering Mayan hieroglyphics.

In the years following World War II, Feynman found a powerful new way of thinking about quantum mechanics, for which he was awarded the Nobel Prize in 1965. He challenged the basic classical assumption that each particle has one particular history. Instead, he suggested that particles travel from one location to another along every possible path through spacetime. With each trajectory Feynman associated two numbers, one for the size—the amplitude—of a wave and one for its phase—whether it is at a crest or a trough. The probability of a particle going from A to B is found by adding up the waves associated with every possible path that passes through A and B.

Nevertheless, in the everyday world it seems to us that objects follow a single path between their origin and their final destination. This agrees with Feynman's multiple history (or sum-over-histories) idea, because for large objects his rule for assigning numbers to each path ensures that all paths but one cancel out when their contributions are combined. Only one of the infinity of paths matters as far as the motion of macroscopic objects is concerned, and this trajectory is precisely the one emerging from Newton's classical laws of motion.

very different. In particular, the universe need have no beginning or end in imaginary time. Imaginary time behaves just like another direction in space. Thus, the histories of the universe in imaginary time can be thought of as curved surfaces, like a ball, a plane, or a saddle shape, but with four dimensions instead of two (see Fig. 3.9, page 84).

If the histories of the universe went off to infinity like a saddle or a plane, one would have the problem of specifying what the boundary conditions were at infinity. But one can avoid having to specify boundary conditions at all if the histories of the universe in imaginary time are closed surfaces, like the surface of the Earth. The surface of the Earth doesn't have any boundaries or edges. There are no reliable reports of people falling off.

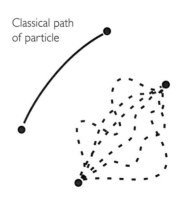

Classical path of particle

In Feynman's path integral a particle takes every possible path.

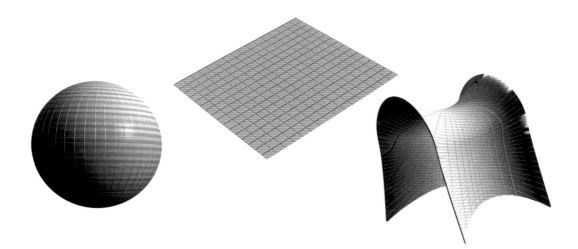

(FIG. 3.9) HISTORIES OF THE UNIVERSE

If the histories of the universe went off to infinity like a saddle, one would have the problem of specifying what the boundary conditions were at infinity. If all the histories of the universe in imaginary time are closed surfaces like that of the Earth, one would not have to specify boundary conditions at all.

EVOLUTION LAWS AND INITIAL CONDITIONS

The laws of physics prescribe how an initial state evolves with time. For instance, if we throw a stone in the air, the laws of gravity will accurately prescribe the stone's subsequent motion.

But we cannot predict where the stone will land exclusively from those laws. For this, we must also know its speed and direction as it left our hand. In other words, we must know the initial conditions —the boundary conditions—of the stone's motion.

Cosmology attempts to describe the evolution of the entire universe using these laws of physics. Hence we must ask what the initial conditions of the universe were to which we should apply these laws.

The initial state may have had a profound impact on basic features of the universe, perhaps even the properties of elementary particles and forces that were crucial for the development of biological life.

One proposal is the *no boundary* condition, the proposal that time and space are finite, forming a closed surface without boundary, just as the surface of the Earth is finite in size but has no boundary. The no boundary proposal is based on Feynman's multiple history idea, but the history of a particle in Feynman's sum is now replaced by a complete spacetime that represents the history of the entire universe. The no boundary condition is precisely the restriction on the possible histories of the universe to those spacetimes that have no boundary in imaginary time. In other words, the boundary condition of the universe is that it has no boundary.

Cosmologists are currently investigating whether initial configurations that are favored by the no boundary proposal, perhaps together with weak anthropic arguments, are likely to evolve to a universe like the one we observe.

If the histories of the universe in imaginary time are indeed closed surfaces, as Hartle and I proposed, it would have fundamental implications for philosophy and our picture of where we came from. The universe would be entirely self-contained; it wouldn't need anything outside to wind up the clockwork and set it going. Instead, everything in the universe would be determined by the laws of science and by rolls of the dice within the universe. This may sound presumptuous, but it is what I and many other scientists believe.

Even if the boundary condition of the universe is that it has no boundary, it won't have just a single history. It will have multiple histories, as suggested by Feynman. There will be a history in imaginary time corresponding to every possible closed surface, and each history in imaginary time will determine a history in real time. Thus we have a superabundance of possibilities for the universe. What picks out the particular universe that we live in from the set of all possible universes? One point we can notice is that many of the possible histories of the universe won't go through the sequence of forming galaxies and stars that was essential to our own development. While it may be that intelligent beings can evolve without galaxies and stars, this seems unlikely. Thus, the very fact that we exist as beings who can ask the question "Why is the universe the way it is?" is a restriction on the history we live in. It implies it is one of the minority of histories that have galaxies and stars. This is an example of what is called the anthropic principle. The anthropic principle says that the universe has to be more or less as we see it, because if it were

The surface of the Earth doesn't have any boundaries or edges. Reports of people falling off are thought to be exaggerations.

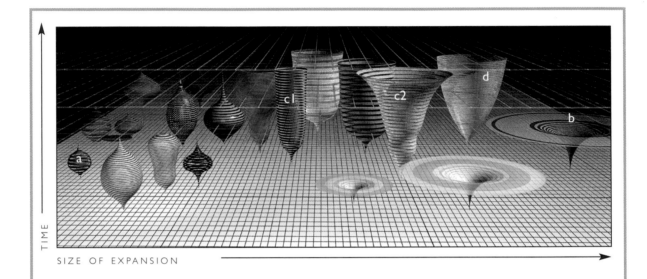

TIME

SIZE OF EXPANSION

THE ANTHROPIC PRINCIPLE

Roughly speaking, the anthropic principle says that we see the universe the way it is, at least in part, because we exist. It is a perspective that is diametrically opposed to the dream of a fully predictive, unified theory in which the laws of nature are complete and the world is the way it is because it could not be otherwise. There are a number of different versions of the anthropic principle, ranging from those that are so weak as to be trivial to those that are so strong as to be absurd. Although most scientists are reluctant to adopt a strong version of the anthropic principle, few people would quarrel with the utility of some weak anthropic arguments.

The weak anthropic principle amounts to an explanation of which of the various possible eras or parts of the universe we *could* inhabit. For instance, the reason why the big bang occurred about ten thousand million years ago is that the universe must be old enough so that some stars will have completed their evolution to produce elements like oxygen and carbon, out of which we are made, and young enough so that some stars would still be providing energy to sustain life.

Within the framework of the no boundary proposal, one can use Feynman's rule for assigning numbers to each history of the universe to find which properties of the universe are likely to occur. In this context, the anthropic principle is implemented by requiring that the histories contain intelligent life. One would feel happier about the anthropic principle, of course, if one could show that a number of different initial configurations for the universe are likely to have evolved to produce a universe like the one we observe. This would imply that the initial state of the part of the universe that we inhabit did not have to be chosen with great care.

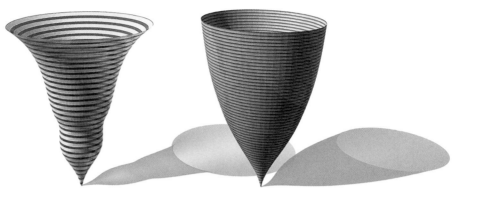

(FIG. 3.10, opposite)
On the far left of the illustration are those universes **(a)** that collapsed on themselves, becoming closed. On the far right are those open universes **(b)** that will continue expanding forever.

Those critical universes that are balanced between falling back on themselves and continuing to expand like **(c1)** or the double inflation of **(c2)** might harbor intelligent life. Our own universe **(d)** is poised to continue expanding for now.

The double inflation could harbor intelligent life.

The inflation of our own universe continues to expand for now.

different, there wouldn't be anyone here to observe it (Fig. 3.10). Many scientists dislike the anthropic principle because it seems rather vague and does not appear to have much predictive power. But the anthropic principle can be given a precise formulation, and it seems to be essential when dealing with the origin of the universe. M-theory, described in Chapter 2, allows a very large number of possible histories for the universe. Most of these histories are not suitable for the development of intelligent life; either they are empty, last for too short a time, are too highly curved, or wrong in some other way. Yet according to Richard Feynman's idea of multiple histories, these uninhabited histories can have quite a high probability (see page 84).

In fact, it doesn't really matter how many histories there may be that don't contain intelligent beings. We are interested only in the subset of histories in which intelligent life develops. This intelligent life need not be anything like humans. Little green aliens would do as well. In fact, they might do rather better. The human race does not have a very good record of intelligent behavior.

As an example of the power of the anthropic principle, consider the number of directions in space. It is a matter of common experience that we live in three-dimensional space. That is to say, we can represent the position of a point in space by three

(FIG. 3.11)

From a distance, a drinking straw looks like a one-dimensional line.

numbers, for example, latitude, longitude, and height above sea level. But why is space three-dimensional? Why isn't it two, or four, or some other number of dimensions, as in science fiction? In M-theory, space has nine or ten dimensions, but it is thought that six or seven of the directions are curled up very small, leaving three dimensions that are large and nearly flat (Fig. 3.11).

Why don't we live in a history in which eight of the dimensions are curled up small, leaving only two dimensions that we notice? A two-dimensional animal would have a hard job digesting food. If it had a gut that went right through it, it would divide the animal in two, and the poor creature would fall apart. So two flat directions are not enough for anything as complicated as intelligent life. On the other hand, if there were four or more nearly flat directions, the gravitational force between two bodies would increase more rapidly as they approached each other. This would mean that planets would not have stable orbits about their suns. They would either fall into the sun (Fig. 3.12A) or escape to the outer darkness and cold (Fig. 3.12B).

FIG. 3.12A

FIG. 3.12B

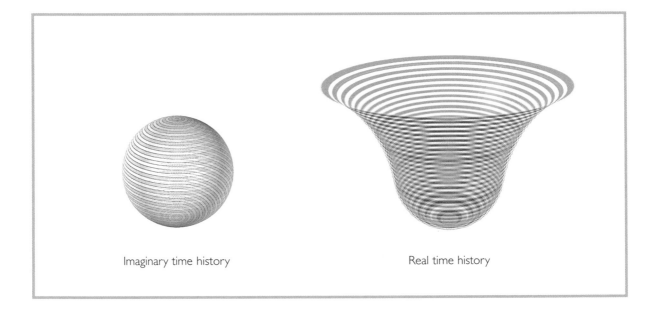

Imaginary time history   Real time history

(FIG. 3.13)

The simplest imaginary time history without boundary is a sphere.

This determines a history in real time that expands in an inflationary manner.

Similarly, the orbits of electrons in atoms would not be stable, so matter as we know it would not exist. Thus, although the idea of multiple histories would allow any number of nearly flat directions, only histories with three flat directions will contain intelligent beings. Only in such histories will the question be asked, "Why does space have three dimensions?"

The simplest history of the universe in imaginary time is a round sphere, like the surface of the Earth, but with two more dimensions (Fig. 3.13). It determines a history of the universe in the real time that we experience, in which the universe is the same at every point of space and is expanding in time. In these respects, it is like the universe we live in. But the rate of expansion is very rapid, and it keeps on getting faster. Such accelerating expansion is called inflation, because it is like the way prices go up and up at an ever-increasing rate.

FIG. 3.14   MATTER ENERGY   GRAVITATION ENERGY

Inflation in prices is generally held to be a bad thing, but in the case of the universe, inflation is very beneficial. The large amount of expansion smoothes out any lumps and bumps there may have been in the early universe. As the universe expands, it borrows energy from the gravitational field to create more matter. The positive matter energy is exactly balanced by the negative gravitational energy, so the total energy is zero. When the universe doubles in size, the matter and gravitational energies both double— so twice zero is still zero. If only the banking world were so simple (Fig. 3.14).

If the history of the universe in imaginary time were a perfectly round sphere, the corresponding history in real time would be a universe that continued to expand in an inflationary manner forever. While the universe is inflating, matter could not fall

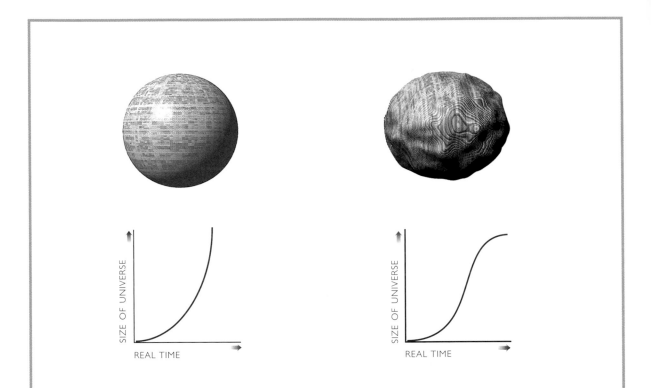

(FIG. 3.15) THE INFLATIONARY UNIVERSE

In the hot big bang model, there was not enough time in the early universe for heat to flow from one region to another. Nevertheless we observe that regardless of which direction we look, the temperature of the microwave background radiation is the same. This means that the initial state of the universe must have had exactly the same temperature everywhere.

In an attempt to find a model in which many different initial configurations could have evolved to something like the present universe, it was suggested that the early universe may have been through a period of very rapid expansion. This expansion is said to be inflationary, meaning it takes place at an ever-increasing rate, rather than the decreasing rate of expansion we observe today. Such an inflationary phase could provide an explanation for the problem of why the universe looks the same in every direction, because there would be enough time for light to travel from one region to another in the early universe.

The corresponding history in imaginary time of a universe that continues to expand in an inflationary manner forever is a perfectly round sphere. But in our own universe, the inflationary expansion slowed down after a fraction of a second, and galaxies could form. In imaginary time, this means that the history of our universe is a sphere with a slightly flattened South Pole.

WHOLESALE PRICE INDEX - INFLATION AND HYPERINFLATION		
July 1914	1.0	
January 1919	2.6	One German mark in 1914
July 1919	3.4	
January 1920	12.6	Ten thousand marks 1923
January 1921	14.4	
July 1921	14.3	Two million marks 1923
January 1922	**36.7**	
July 1922	**100.6**	Ten million marks 1923
January 1923	**2,785.0**	
July 1923	**194,000.0**	One milliard marks 1923
November 1923	**726,000,000,000.0**	

together to form galaxies and stars, and life, let alone intelligent life like us, could not develop. Thus although histories of the universe in imaginary time that are perfectly round spheres are allowed by the notion of multiple histories, they are not of much interest. However, histories in imaginary time that are slightly flattened at the south pole of the spheres are much more relevant (Fig. 3.15).

In this case, the corresponding history in real time will expand in an accelerated, inflationary manner at first. But then the expansion will begin to slow down, and galaxies can form. In order for intelligent life to be able to develop, the flattening at the South Pole must be very slight. This will mean that the universe will expand initially by an enormous amount. The record level of monetary inflation occurred in Germany between the world wars, when prices rose billions of times—but the amount of inflation that must have occurred in the universe is at least a billion billion billion times that (Fig. 3.16).

(FIG. 3.16)
INFLATION MAY BE A LAW OF NATURE

Inflation in Germany rose after the peace until by February 1920 the price level was five times as high as it had been in 1918. After July 1922 the phase of hyperinflation began. All confidence in money vanished and the price index rose faster and faster for fifteen months, outpacing the printing presses, which could not produce money as fast as it was depreciating. By late 1923, 300 paper mills were working at top speed and 150 printing companies had 2,000 presses running day and night turning out currency.

a   b   c

(FIG. 3.17)

PROBABLE AND IMPROBABLE
HISTORIES

Smooth histories like **(a)** are the most
probable, but there are only a small
number of them.

Although slightly irregular histories
(b) and **(c)** are each less probable,
there are such a large number of
them that the likely histories of the
universe will have small departures
from smoothness.

Because of the uncertainty principle, there won't be just one history of the universe that contains intelligent life. Instead, the histories
in imaginary time will be a whole family of slightly deformed
spheres, each of which corresponds to a history in real time in which
the universe inflates for a long time but not indefinitely. We can then
ask which of these allowable histories is the most probable. It turns
out that the most probable histories are not completely smooth but
have tiny ups and downs (Fig. 3.17). The ripples on the most probable histories really are minuscule. The departures from smoothness
are of the order of one part in a hundred thousand. Nevertheless,
although they are extremely small, we have managed to observe
them as small variations in the microwaves that come to us from different directions in space. The Cosmic Background Explorer satellite
was launched in 1989 and made a map of the sky in microwaves.

The different colors indicate different temperatures, but the whole
range from red to blue is only about a ten-thousandth of a degree. Yet

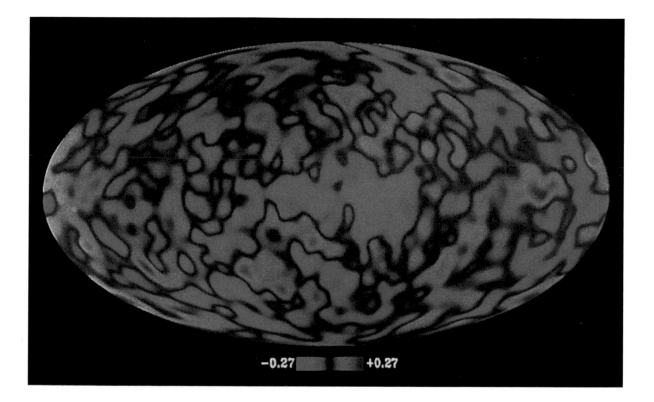

−0.27   +0.27

this is enough variation between different regions of the early universe for the extra gravitational attraction in the denser regions to stop them expanding eventually, and to cause them to collapse again under their own gravity to form galaxies and stars. So in principle, at least, the COBE map is the blueprint for all the structures in the universe.

What will be the future behavior of the most probable histories of the universe that are compatible with the appearance of intelligent beings? There seem to be various possibilities, depending on the amount of matter in the universe. If there is more than a certain critical amount, the gravitational attraction between the galaxies will slow them down and will eventually stop them from flying apart. They will then start falling toward each other and will all come together in a big crunch that will be the end of the history of the universe in real time (see Fig. 3.18, page 96).

If the density of the universe is below the critical value, gravity is too weak to stop the galaxies from flying apart forever.

The full sky map made by the COBE satellite DMR instrument, showing evidence for the wrinkles in time.

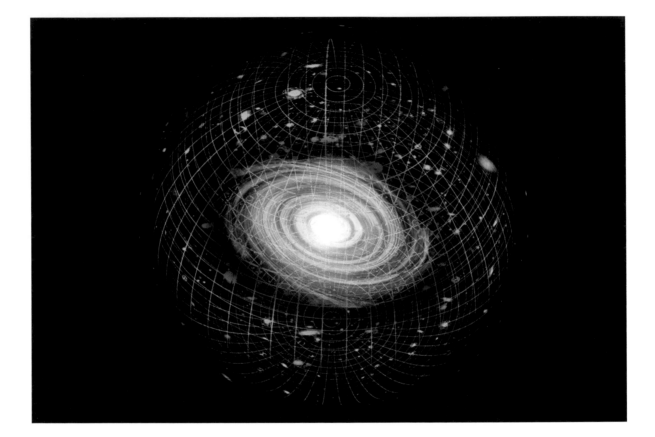

(Fig. 3.18, above)
One possible end of the universe is the big crunch in which all matter will be sucked back into a vast cataclysmic gravity well.

(Fig. 3.19, opposite)
The long cold whimper in which everything runs down and the last stars flicker out, having exhausted their fuel.

All the stars will burn out, and the universe will get increasingly emptier and colder. So, again, things will come to an end, but in a less dramatic way. Either way, the universe will last a good few billion years more (Fig. 3.19).

As well as matter, the universe may contain what is called "vacuum energy," energy that is present even in apparently empty space. By Einstein's famous equation, $E = mc^2$, this vacuum energy has mass. This means that it has a gravitational effect on the expansion of the universe. But, remarkably enough, the effect of vacuum energy is the opposite of that of matter. Matter causes the expansion to slow down and can eventually stop and reverse it. On the other hand, vacuum energy causes the expansion to accelerate, as in inflation. In fact, vacuum energy acts just like the cosmological constant mentioned in Chapter 1 that Einstein added to his original equations

in 1917, when he realized that they didn't admit a solution representing a static universe. After Hubble's discovery of the expansion
of the universe, this motivation for adding a term to the equations
disappeared, and Einstein rejected the cosmological constant as a
mistake.

However, it may not have been a mistake at all. As described
in Chapter 2, we now realize that quantum theory implies that
spacetime is filled with quantum fluctuations. In a supersymmetric
theory, the infinite positive and negative energies of these ground
state fluctuations cancel out between particles of different spin. But
we wouldn't expect the positive and negative energies to cancel so
completely that there wasn't a small, finite amount of vacuum energy left over, because the universe is not in a supersymmetric state.
The only surprise is that the vacuum energy is so nearly zero that it

> THE
> COSMOLOGICAL
> CONSTANT
> WAS MY
> GREATEST
> MISTAKE?
>
> *Albert Einstein*

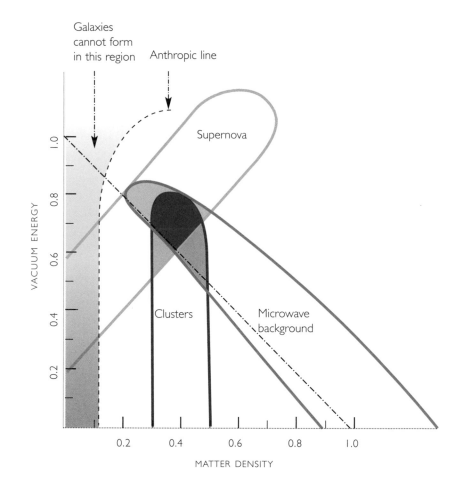

Galaxies cannot form in this region

Anthropic line

Supernova

VACUUM ENERGY

1.0
0.8
0.6
0.4
0.2

Clusters

Microwave background

0.2   0.4   0.6   0.8   1.0

MATTER DENSITY

(FIG. 3.20)
By combining observations from distant supernovae, the cosmic microwave background radiation, and the distribution of matter in the universe, the vacuum energy and matter density in the universe can be fairly well estimated.

was not obvious some time ago. Maybe this is another example of the anthropic principle. A history with a larger vacuum energy would not have formed galaxies, so would not contain beings who could ask the question: "Why is the vacuum energy the value we observe?"

We can try to determine the amounts of matter and vacuum energy in the universe from various observations. We can show the results in a diagram in which the matter density is the horizontal direction and vacuum energy is the vertical direction. The dotted line shows the boundary of the region in which intelligent life could develop (Fig. 3.20).

*"I could be bounded in a nutshell
and count myself a king
of infinite space."*

—Shakespeare,
Hamlet, Act 2, Scene 2

Observations of supernovae, clustering, and the microwave background each mark out regions in this diagram. Fortunately, all three regions have a common intersection. If the matter density and vacuum energy lie in this intersection, it means that the expansion of the universe has begun to speed up again, after a long period of slowing down. It seems that inflation may be a law of nature.

In this chapter we have seen how the behavior of the vast universe can be understood in terms of its history in imaginary time, which is a tiny, slightly flattened sphere. It is like Hamlet's nutshell, yet this nut encodes everything that happens in real time. So Hamlet was quite right. We could be bounded in a nutshell and still count ourselves kings of infinite space.

CHAPTER 4

PREDICTING THE FUTURE

*How the loss of information in black holes may reduce our ability
to predict the future.*

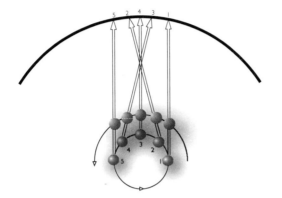

(FIG. 4.1)
An observer on Earth (blue) orbiting the sun watches Mars (red) against a backdrop of constellations.

The complicated apparent motion of the planets in the sky can be explained by Newton's laws and has no influence on personal fortunes.

THE HUMAN RACE HAS ALWAYS WANTED TO CONTROL THE future, or at least to predict what will happen. That is why astrology is so popular. Astrology claims that events on Earth are related to the motions of the planets across the sky. This is a scientifically testable hypothesis, or would be if astrologers stuck their necks out and made definite predictions that could be tested. However, wisely enough, they make their forecasts so vague that they can apply to any outcome. Statements such as "Personal relations may become intense" or "You will have a financially rewarding opportunity" can never be proved wrong.

But the real reason most scientists don't believe in astrology is not scientific evidence or the lack of it but because it is not consistent with other theories that have been tested by experiment. When Copernicus and Galileo discovered that the planets orbit the Sun rather than the Earth, and Newton discovered the laws that govern their motion, astrology became extremely implausible. Why should the positions of other planets against the background sky as seen from Earth have any correlations with the macromolecules on a minor planet that call themselves intelligent life (Fig. 4.1)? Yet this is what astrology would have us believe. There is no more experimental evidence for some of the theories described in this book

"Mars occupies Sagittarius this month and for you it will be a time to seek self-knowledge. Mars asks you to live life according to what feels right as opposed to what others think is right. And this will happen.

On the 20th Saturn arrives in the area of your solar chart related to commitment and career and you will be learning to take responsibilities and deal with difficult relationships.

However, at the time of the full moon you will gain a wonderful insight and overview of your entire life which will transform you."

103

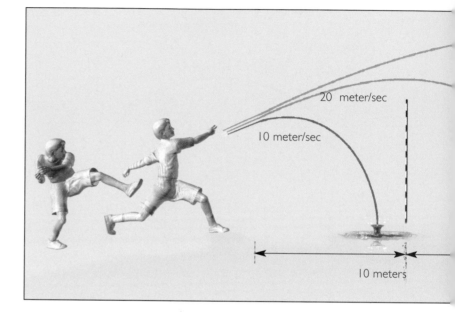

20 meter/sec

10 meter/sec

10 meters

(FIG. 4.2)
If you know where and at what speed a baseball is thrown, you can predict where it will go.

than there is for astrology, but we believe them because they are consistent with theories that have survived testing.

The success of Newton's laws and other physical theories led to the idea of scientific determinism, which was first expressed at the beginning of the nineteenth century by the French scientist the Marquis de Laplace. Laplace suggested that if we knew the positions and velocities of all the particles in the universe at one time, the laws of physics should allow us to predict what the state of the universe would be at any other time in the past or in the future (Fig. 4.2).

In other words, if scientific determinism holds, we should in principle be able to predict the future and wouldn't need astrology. Of course, in practice even something as simple as Newton's theory of gravity produces equations that we can't solve exactly for more than two particles. Furthermore, the equations often have a property known as chaos, so that a small change in position or velocity at one time can lead to completely different behavior at later times. As those who have seen *Jurassic Park* know, a tiny disturbance in one place can cause a major change in another. A butterfly flapping its wings in Tokyo can cause rain in New York's Central Park (Fig. 4.3). The trouble is the sequence of events is not repeatable. The next time the butterfly flaps its wings, a host of other factors will be different

(FIG. 4.3)

104

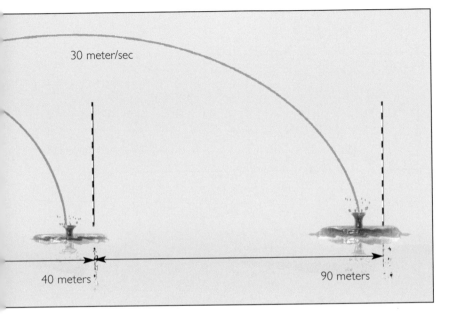

30 meter/sec

40 meters

90 meters

and will also influence the weather. That is why weather forecasts are so unreliable.

Thus, although in principle the laws of quantum electrodynamics should allow us to calculate everything in chemistry and biology, we have not had much success in predicting human behavior from mathematical equations. Nevertheless, despite these practical difficulties most scientists have comforted themselves with the idea that, again in principle, the future is predictable.

IN

?!

At first sight, determinism would also seem to be threatened by the uncertainty principle, which says that we cannot measure accurately both the position and the velocity of a particle at the same time. The more accurately we measure the position, the less accurately we can determine the velocity, and vice versa. The Laplace version of scientific determinism held that if we knew the positions and velocities of particles at one time, we could determine their positions and velocities at any time in the past or future. But how could we even get started if the uncertainty principle prevented us from knowing accurately both the positions and the velocities at one time? However good our computer is, if we put lousy data in, we will get lousy predictions out.

OUT

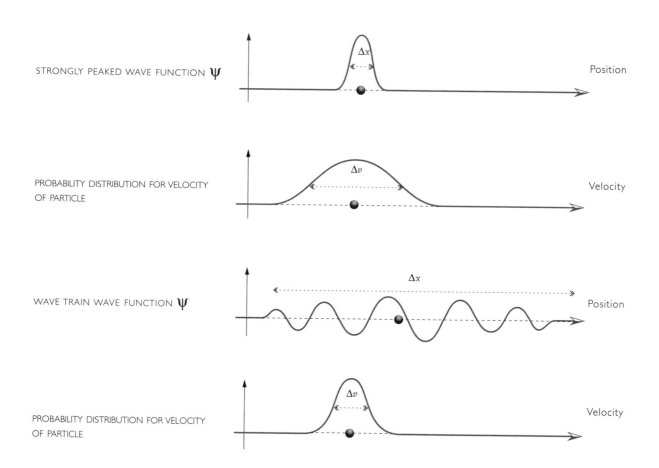

STRONGLY PEAKED WAVE FUNCTION Ψ

Position

PROBABILITY DISTRIBUTION FOR VELOCITY OF PARTICLE

Velocity

WAVE TRAIN WAVE FUNCTION Ψ

Position

PROBABILITY DISTRIBUTION FOR VELOCITY OF PARTICLE

Velocity

(FIG. 4.4)

The wave function determines the probabilities that the particle will have different positions and velocities in such a way that Δx and Δv obey the uncertainty principle.

However, determinism *was* restored in a modified form in a new theory called quantum mechanics, which incorporated the uncertainty principle. In quantum mechanics, one can, roughly speaking, accurately predict half of what one would expect to predict in the classical Laplace point of view. In quantum mechanics, a particle does not have a well-defined position or velocity, but its state *can* be represented by what is called a wave function (Fig. 4.4).

A wave function is a number at each point of space that gives the probability that the particle is to be found at that position. The rate at which the wave function changes from point to point tells how probable different particle velocities are. Some wave functions are sharply peaked at a particular point in space. In these cases, there is only a small amount of uncertainty in the position of the particle. But we can also see in the diagram that in such cases, the wave function changes rapidly near the point, up on one side and

(Fig. 4.5)
THE SCHRÖDINGER EQUATION

The evolution in time of the wave function ψ is determined by the Hamiltonian operator H, which is associated with the energy of the physical system under consideration.

down on the other. That means the probability distribution for the velocity is spread over a wide range. In other words, the uncertainty in the velocity is large. Consider, on the other hand, a continuous train of waves. Now there is a large uncertainty in position but a small uncertainty in velocity. So the description of a particle by a wave function does not have a well-defined position or velocity. It satisfies the uncertainty principle. We now realize that the wave function is *all* that can be well defined. We cannot even suppose that the particle has a position and velocity that are known to God but are hidden from us. Such "hidden-variable" theories predict results that are not in agreement with observation. Even God is bound by the uncertainty principle and cannot know the position and velocity; He can only know the wave function.

The rate at which the wave function changes with time is given by what is called the Schrödinger equation (Fig. 4.5). If we know the

(FIG. 4.6)
In the flat spacetime of special relativity observers moving at different speeds will have different measures of time, but we can use the Schrödinger equation in any of these times to predict what the wave function will be in the future.

wave function at one time, we can use the Schrödinger equation to calculate it at any other time, past or future. Therefore, there is still determinism in quantum theory, but it is on a reduced scale. Instead of being able to predict both the positions and the velocities, we can predict only the wave function. This can allow us to predict either the positions or the velocities, but not both accurately. Thus in quantum theory the ability to make exact predictions is just half what it was in the classical Laplace worldview. Nevertheless, within this restricted sense it is still possible to claim that there is determinism.

However, the use of the Schrödinger equation to evolve the wave function forward in time (that is, to predict what it will be at future times) implicitly assumes that time runs on smoothly everywhere, forever. This was certainly true in Newtonian physics. Time was assumed to be absolute, meaning that each event in the history of the universe was labeled by a number called time, and that a series of time labels ran smoothly from the infinite past to the infinite future. This is what might be called the commonsense view of time, and it is the view of time that most people and even most physicists have at the back of their minds. However, in 1905, as we have seen, the concept of absolute time was overthrown by the special theory of relativity, in which time was no longer an independent quantity on its own but was just one direction in a four-dimensional continuum called spacetime. In special relativity, different observers traveling at

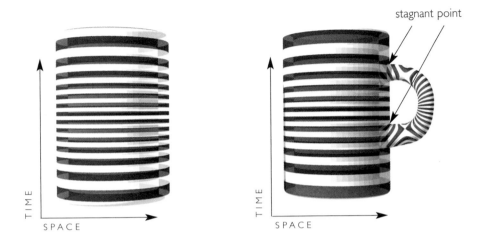

stagnant point

TIME

SPACE

TIME

SPACE

different velocities move through spacetime on different paths. Each observer has his or her own measure of time along the path he or she is following, and different observers will measure different intervals of time between events (Fig. 4.6).

Thus in special relativity there is no unique absolute time that we can use to label events. However, the spacetime of special relativity is flat. This means that in special relativity, the time measured by any freely moving observer increases smoothly in spacetime from minus infinity in the infinite past to plus infinity in the infinite future. We can use any of these measures of time in the Schrödinger equation to evolve the wave function. In special relativity, therefore, we still have the quantum version of determinism.

The situation was different in the general theory of relativity, in which spacetime was not flat but curved, and distorted by the matter and energy in it. In our solar system, the curvature of spacetime is so slight, at least on a macroscopic scale, that it doesn't interfere with our usual idea of time. In this situation, we could still use this time in the Schrödinger equation to get a deterministic evolution of the wave function. However, once we allow spacetime to be curved, the door is opened to the possibility that it may have a structure that doesn't admit a time that increases smoothly for every observer, as we would expect for a reasonable measure of time. For example, suppose that spacetime was like a vertical cylinder (Fig. 4.7).

(FIG. 4.7) TIME STANDS STILL

A measure of time would necessarily have stagnation points where the handle joined the main cylinder: points where time stood still. At these points, time would not increase in any direction. Therefore, one could not use the Schrödinger equation to predict what the wave function will be in the future.

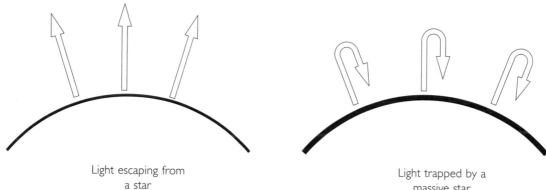

Light escaping from
a star

Light trapped by a
massive star

Fig. 4.9

Fig. 4.8

Height up the cylinder would be a measure of time that increased for every observer and ran from minus infinity to plus infinity. However, imagine instead that spacetime was like a cylinder with a handle (or "wormhole") that branched off and then joined back on. Then any measure of time would necessarily have stagnation points where the handle joined the main cylinder: points where time stood still. At these points, time would not increase for any observer. In such a spacetime, we could not use the Schrödinger equation to get a deterministic evolution for the wave function. Watch out for wormholes: you never know what may come out of them.

Black holes are the reason we think time will not increase for every observer. The first discussion of black holes appeared in 1783. A former Cambridge don, John Michell, presented the following argument. If one fires a particle, such as a cannonball, vertically upward, its ascent will be slowed by gravity, and eventually the particle will stop moving upward and will fall back (Fig. 4.8). However, if the initial upward velocity is greater than a critical value called the escape velocity, gravity will never be strong enough to stop the particle, and it will get away. The escape velocity is about 12 kilometers per second for the Earth, and about 618 kilometers per second for the Sun.

THE SCHWARZSCHILD BLACK HOLE

In 1916 the German astronomer Karl Schwarzschild found a solution to Einstein's theory of relativity that represents a spherical black hole. Schwarzschild's work revealed a stunning implication of general relativity. He showed that if the mass of a star is concentrated in a small enough region, the gravitational field at the surface of the star becomes so strong that even light can no longer escape. This is what we now call a black hole, a region of spacetime bounded by a so-called event horizon, from which it is impossible for anything, including light, to reach a distant observer.

For a long time most physicists, including Einstein, were skeptical whether such extreme configurations of matter could actually ever occur in the real universe. However,

we now understand that when any sufficiently heavy nonrotating star, however complicated its shape and internal structure, runs out of nuclear fuel, it will necessarily collapse to a perfectly spherical Schwarzschild black hole. The radius **(R)** of the black hole's event horizon depends only on its mass; it is given by the formula:

$$R = \frac{2GM}{c^2}$$

In this formula the symbol **(c)** stands for the speed of light, **(G)** for Newton's constant, and **(M)** for the mass of the black hole. A black hole with the same mass as the Sun, for instance, would have a radius of only two miles!

Both of these escape velocities are much higher than the speed of real cannonballs, but they are small compared to the speed of light, which is 300,000 kilometers per second. Thus, light can get away from the Earth or Sun without much difficulty. However, Michell argued that there could be stars that are much more massive than the Sun and have escape velocities greater than the speed of light (Fig. 4.9). We would not be able to see these stars, because any light they sent out would be dragged back by the gravity of the star. Thus they would be what Michell called dark stars and we now call black holes.

Michell's idea of dark stars was based on Newtonian physics, in which time was absolute and went on regardless of what happened. Thus they didn't affect our ability to predict the future in the classical Newtonian picture. But the situation was very different in the general theory of relativity, in which massive bodies curve spacetime.

In 1916, shortly after the theory was first formulated, Karl Schwarzschild (who died soon after of an illness contracted on the Russian front in the First World War) found a solution of the field equations of general relativity that represented a black hole. What Schwarzschild had found wasn't understood or its importance recognized for many years. Einstein himself never believed in black

(FIG. 4.10)
The quasar 3C273, the first quasi-stellar radio source to be discovered, produces a large amount of power in a small region. Matter falling into a black hole seems to be the only mechanism that can account for such a high luminosity.

JOHN WHEELER

John Archibald Wheeler was born in 1911 in Jacksonville, Florida. He earned his Ph.D. from Johns Hopkins University in 1933 for his work on the scattering of light by the helium atom. In 1938 he worked with the Danish physicist Niels Bohr to develop the theory of nuclear fission. For a while thereafter Wheeler, together with his graduate student Richard Feynman, concentrated on the study of electrodynamics; but shortly after America entered World War II, both went on to contribute to the Manhattan Project.

In the early 1950s, inspired by Robert Oppenheimer's work in 1939 on the gravitational collapse of a massive star, Wheeler turned his attention to Einstein's theory of general relativity. At that time most physicists were caught up in the study of nuclear physics and general relativity was not really regarded as relevant to the physical world. But almost single-handedly Wheeler transformed the field, both through his research and through his teaching of Princeton's first course on relativity.

Much later, in 1969, he coined the term *black hole* for the collapsed state of matter, which few yet believed was real. Inspired by the work of Werner Israel, he conjectured that black holes have no hair, which meant that the collapsed state of any nonrotating massive star could in fact be described by Schwarzschild's solution.

holes, and his attitude was shared by most of the old guard in general relativity. I remember going to Paris to give a seminar on my discovery that quantum theory means that black holes aren't completely black. My seminar fell rather flat because at that time almost no one in Paris believed in black holes. The French also felt that the name as they translated it, *trou noir,* had dubious sexual connotations and should be replaced by *astre occlu,* or "hidden star." However, neither this nor other suggested names caught the public imagination like the term *black hole,* which was first introduced by John Archibald Wheeler, the American physicist who inspired much of the modern work in this field.

The discovery of quasars in 1963 brought forth an outburst of theoretical work on black holes and observational attempts to detect them (Fig. 4.10). Here is the picture that has emerged. Consider what we believe would be the history of a star with a mass twenty times that of the Sun. Such stars form from clouds of gas, like those in the Orion Nebula (Fig. 4.11). As clouds of gas contract under their own gravity, the gas heats up and eventually becomes hot enough to start the nuclear fusion reaction that converts hydrogen into helium. The heat generated by this process creates a pressure that supports the star against its own gravity and stops it from contracting further. A star will stay in this state for a long time, burning hydrogen and radiating light into space.

(Fɪɢ. 4.11)
Stars form in clouds of gas and dust like the Orion Nebula.

The gravitational field of the star will affect the paths of light rays coming from it. One can draw a diagram with time plotted upward and distance from the center of the star plotted horizontally (see Fig. 4.12, page 114). In this diagram, the surface of the star is represented by two vertical lines, one on either side of the center. One can choose that time be measured in seconds and distance in light-seconds—the distance light travels in a second. When we use these units, the speed of light is 1; that is, the speed of light is 1 light-second per second. This means that far from the star and its gravitational field, the path of a light ray on the diagram is a line at a 45-degree angle to the vertical. However, nearer the star, the curvature of space-time produced by the mass of the star will change the paths of the light rays and cause them to be at a smaller angle to the vertical.

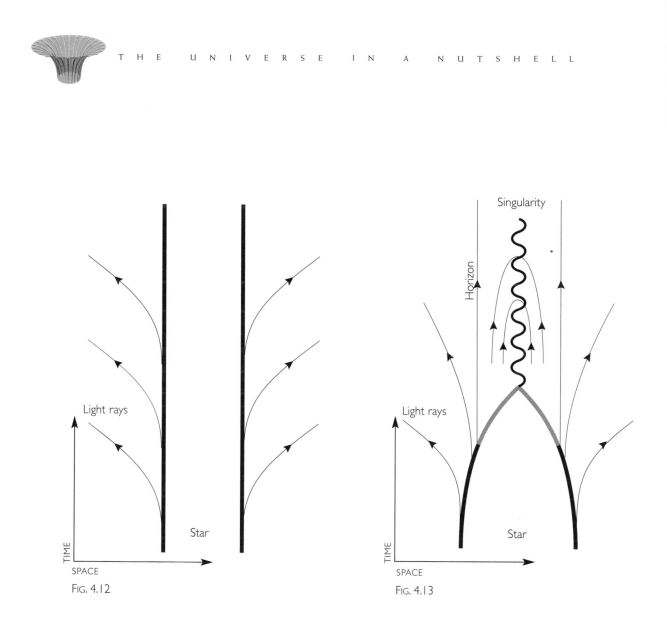

FIG. 4.12

FIG. 4.13

(FIG. 4.12) Spacetime around a non-collapsing star. Light rays can escape from the surface of the star (the red vertical lines). Far from the star, the light rays are at 45 degrees to the vertical, but near the star the warping of space-time by the mass of the star causes light rays to be at a smaller angle to the vertical.

(FIG. 4.13) If the star collapses (the red lines meeting at a point) the warping becomes so large that light rays near the surface move inward. A black hole is formed, a region of spacetime from which it is not possible for light to escape.

Massive stars will burn their hydrogen into helium much faster than the Sun does. This means they can run out of hydrogen in as little as a few hundred million years. After that, such stars face a crisis. They can burn their helium into heavier elements such as carbon and oxygen, but these nuclear reactions do not release much energy, so the stars lose heat and the thermal pressure that supports them against gravity. Therefore they begin to get smaller. If they are more than about twice the mass of the Sun, the pressure will never be sufficient to stop the contraction. They will collapse to zero size and infinite density to form what is called a singularity (Fig. 4.13). In the diagram of time against distance from the center, as a star shrinks, the paths of light rays from its surface will start out

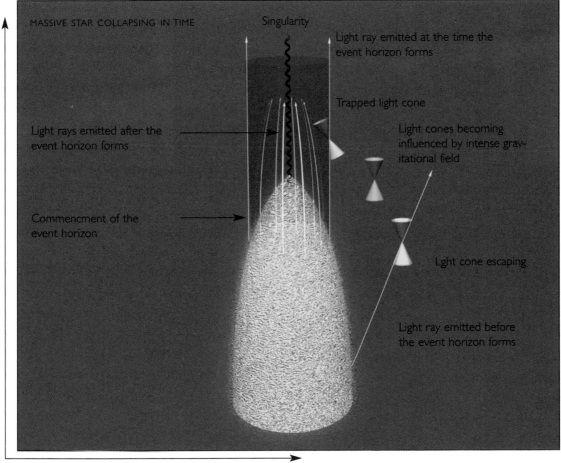

MASSIVE STAR COLLAPSING IN TIME

Singularity

Light ray emitted at the time the
event horizon forms

Trapped light cone

Light rays emitted after the
event horizon forms

Light cones becoming
influenced by intense gravitational field

Commencment of the
event horizon

Lght cone escaping

Light ray emitted before
the event horizon forms

TIME

SPACE

at smaller and smaller angles to the vertical. When the star reaches a certain critical radius, the path will be vertical on the diagram, which means that the light will hover at a constant distance from the center of the star, never getting away. This critical path of light will sweep out a surface called the event horizon, which separates the region of spacetime from which light can escape from the region from which it cannot. Any light emitted by the star after it passes the event horizon will be bent back inward by the curvature of spacetime. The star will have become one of Michell's dark stars, or, as we say now, a black hole.

How can you detect a black hole if no light can get out of it? The answer is that a black hole still exerts the same gravitational

The horizon, the outer boundary of a black hole, is formed by light rays that just fail to get away from the black hole, but stay hovering at a constant distance from the center.

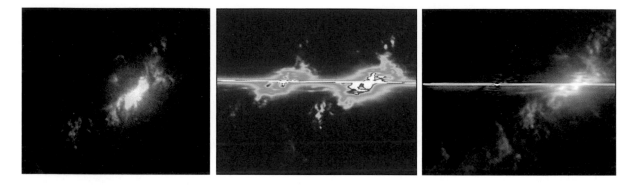

(FIG. 4.15)

A BLACK HOLE AT THE CENTER OF
A GALAXY

Left: The galaxy NGC 4151 revealed
by the wide-field planetary camera.

Center: The horizontal line passing
through the image is from light generated by the black hole at the center of
4151.

Right: Image showing the velocity of
oxygen emissions. All the evidence
indicates that NGC 4151 contains a
black hole about a hundred million
times the mass of the Sun.

(FIG. 4.14)

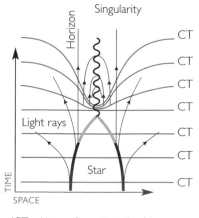

(CT—Lines of constant time)

pull on neighboring objects as did the body that collapsed. If the
Sun were a black hole and had managed to become one without losing any of its mass, the planets would still orbit as they do now.

One way of searching for a black hole is therefore to look for
matter that is orbiting what seems to be an unseen compact massive
object. A number of such systems have been observed. Perhaps the
most impressive are the giant black holes that occur in the centers
of galaxies and quasars (Fig. 4.15).

The properties of black holes that have been discussed thus far
don't raise any great problems with determinism. Time will come to
an end for an astronaut who falls into a black hole and hits the singularity. However, in general relativity, one is free to measure time at
different rates in different places. One could therefore speed up the
astronaut's watch as he or she approached the singularity, so that it
still registered an infinite interval of time. On the time-and-distance
diagram (Fig. 4.14), the surfaces of constant values of this new time
would be all crowded together at the center, below the point where
the singularity appeared. But they would agree with the usual measure of time in the nearly flat spacetime far away from the black hole.

One could use this time in the Schrödinger equation and calculate the wave function at later times if one knew it initially. Thus
one still has determinism. It is worth noting, however, that at late
times, part of the wave function is inside the black hole, where it
can't be observed by someone outside. Thus an observer who is sen-
sible enough not to fall into a black hole cannot run the
Schrödinger equation backward and calculate the wave function at
early times. To do that, he or she would need to know the part of
the wave function that is inside the black hole. This contains the

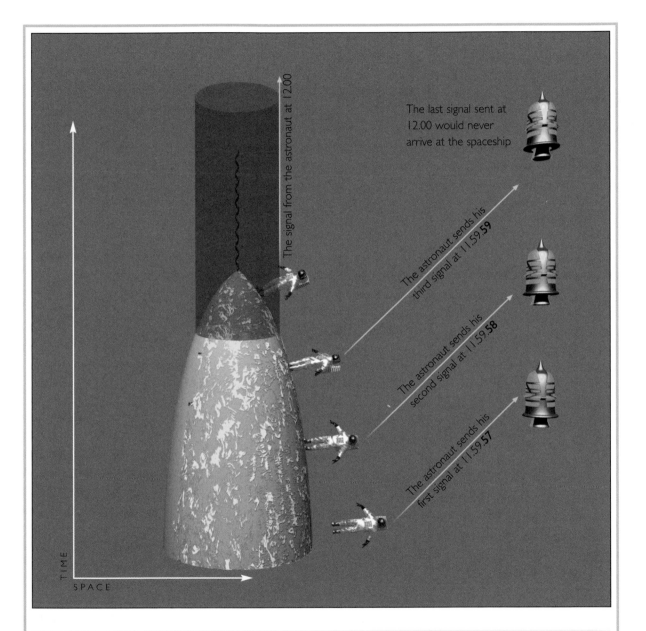

The signal from the astronaut at 12.00

The last signal sent at 12.00 would never arrive at the spaceship

The astronaut sends his third signal at 11.59.**59**

The astronaut sends his second signal at 11.59.**58**

The astronaut sends his first signal at 11.59.**57**

TIME

SPACE

The illustration above shows an astronaut who lands on a collapsing star at 11.59.57 and joins the star as it shrinks below the critical radius where gravity is so strong that no signal can escape. He sends signals from his watch to a spaceship orbiting the star at regular intervals.

Someone watching the star at a distance will never see it cross the event horizon and enter the black hole. Instead, the star will appear to hover just outside the critical radius, and a clock on the surface of the star will seem to slow down and stop.

The no-hair result.

BLACK HOLE TEMPERATURE

A black hole emits radiation as if it were a hot body with a temperature (T) that depends only on its mass. More precisely, the temperature is given by the following formula:

$$T = \frac{\hbar c^3}{8\pi\, k\, G\, M}$$

In this formula the symbol (c) stands for the speed of light, ($\hbar$) for Planck's constant, (G) for Newton's gravitational constant, and (k) for Boltzmann's constant.

Finally, (M) represents the mass of the black hole, so the smaller the black hole, the higher its temperature. This formula tells us that the temperature of a black hole of a few solar masses is only about a millionth of a degree above absolute zero.

information about what fell into the hole. This is potentially a very large amount of information, because a black hole of a given mass and rate of rotation can be formed from a very large number of different collections of particles; a black hole does not depend on the nature of the body that had collapsed to form it. John Wheeler called this result "a black hole has no hair." For the French, this just confirmed their suspicions.

The difficulty with determinism arose when I discovered that black holes aren't completely black. As we saw in Chapter 2, quantum theory means that fields can't be exactly zero even in what is called the vacuum. If they were zero, they would have both an exact value or position at zero and an exact rate of change or velocity that was also zero. This would be a violation of the uncertainty principle, which says that the position and velocity can't both be well defined. All fields must instead have a certain amount of what are called vacuum fluctuations (in the same way that the pendulum in Chapter 2 had to have zero point fluctuations). Vacuum fluctuations can be interpreted in several ways that seem different but are in fact mathematically equivalent. From a positivist viewpoint, one is free to use whatever picture is most useful for the problem in question. In this case it is helpful to think of vacuum fluctuations as pairs of virtual particles that appear together at some point of spacetime, move apart, and come back together and annihilate each other. "Virtual" means that these particles cannot be observed directly, but their indirect effects *can* be measured, and they agree with theoretical predictions to a remarkable degree of accuracy (Fig. 4.16).

If a black hole is present, one member of a pair of particles may fall into the black hole, leaving the other member free to escape to infinity (Fig. 4.17). To someone far from the black hole, the escaping particles appear to have been radiated by the black hole. The spectrum of a black hole is exactly what we would expect from a hot body, with a temperature proportional to the gravitational field on the horizon—the boundary—of the black hole. In other words, the temperature of a black hole depends on its size.

A black hole of a few solar masses would have a temperature of about a millionth of a degree above absolute zero, and a larger black hole would have an even lower temperature. Thus any quantum

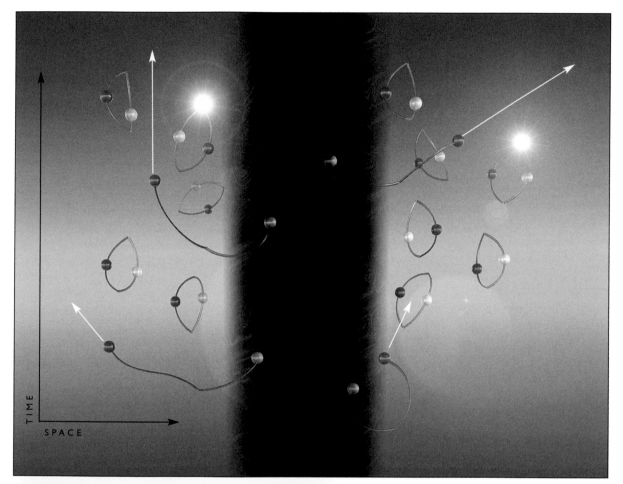

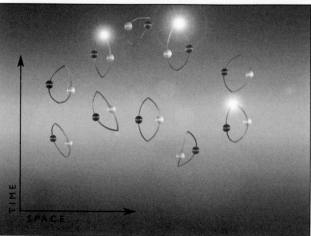

(Fig. 4.17)
Above: Virtual particles appearing and annihilating one another, close to the event horizon of a black hole.

One of the pair falls into the black hole while its twin is free to escape. From outside the event horizon it appears that the black hole is radiating the particles that escape.

(Fig. 4.16)
Left: In empty space particle pairs appear, lead a brief existence, and then annihilate one another.

Events that will never be seen by the observer

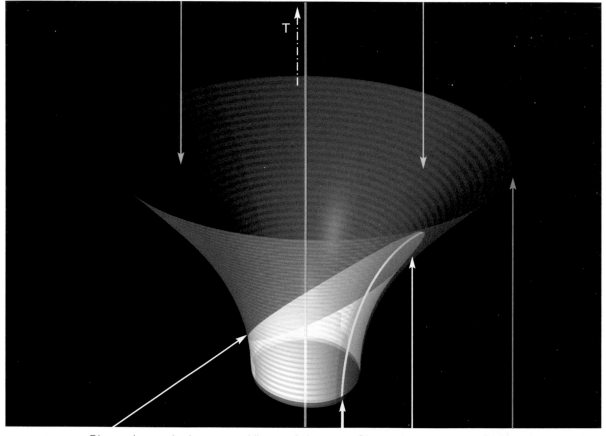

T

Observer's event horizon   History of observer   Observer's event horizon Surface of constant time

(Fig. 4.18)
The de Sitter solution of the field equations of general relativity represents a universe that expands in an inflationary manner. In the diagram time is shown in the upward and the size of the universe in the horizontal direction. Spatial distances increase so rapidly that light from distant galaxies never reaches us, and there is an event horizon, a boundary of the region we cannot observe, as in a black hole.

radiation from such black holes would be utterly swamped by the 2.7-degree radiation left over from the hot big bang—the cosmic background radiation that we discussed in Chapter 2. It would be possible to detect the radiation from much smaller and hotter black holes, but there don't seem to be many of them around. That is a pity. If one were discovered, I would get a Nobel Prize. However, we have indirect observational evidence for this radiation, and that evidence comes from the early universe. As described in Chapter 3, it is thought that very early in its history, the universe went through an inflationary period during which it expanded at an ever-increasing rate. The expansion during this period would have been so rapid that some objects would be too distant from us for their light ever to reach us; the universe would have expanded too much and too rapidly while that light was traveling toward us. Thus there would be a horizon in the universe like the horizon of a black hole, separating the region from which light can reach us and the region from which it cannot (Fig. 4.18).

Very similar arguments show that there should be thermal radiation from this horizon, as there is from a black hole horizon. In thermal radiation, we have learned to expect a characteristic spectrum of density fluctuations. In this case, these density fluctuations would have expanded with the universe. When their length scale became longer than the size of the event horizon, they would have become frozen in, so that we can observe them today as small variations in the temperature of the cosmic background radiation left over from the early universe. The observations of those variations agree with the predictions of thermal fluctuations with remarkable accuracy.

Even if the observational evidence for black hole radiation is a bit indirect, everyone who has studied the problem agrees it must occur in order to be consistent with our other observationally tested theories. This has important implications for determinism. The radiation from a black hole will carry away energy, which must mean that the black hole will lose mass and get smaller. In turn, this will mean that its temperature will rise and the rate of radiation will increase. Eventually the black hole will get down to zero mass. We don't know how to calculate what happens at this point, but the only natural, reasonable outcome would seem to be that the black hole disappears completely. So what happens then to the part of the wave function inside the black hole and the information it contains about what had fallen into the black hole? The first guess might be that this part of the wave function, and the information it carries, would emerge when the black hole finally disappears. However, information cannot be carried for free, as one realizes when one gets a telephone bill.

Information requires energy to carry it, and there's very little energy left in the final stages of a black hole. The only plausible way the information

(FIG. 4.19)

The positive energy carried away by the thermal radiation from its horizon reduces the black hole's mass. As it loses mass, the temperature of the black hole rises and its rate of radiation increases, so it loses mass more and more quickly. We don't know what happens if the mass becomes extremely small, but the most likely outcome seems to be that the black hole would disappear completely.

inside could get out would be if it emerged continuously with the radiation, rather than waiting for this final stage. However, according to the picture of one member of a virtual-particle pair falling in and the other member escaping, one would not expect the escaping particle to be related to what fell in, or to carry away information about it. So the only answer would seem to be that the information in the part of the wave function inside the black hole gets lost (Fig. 4.19).

Such loss of information would have important implications for determinism. To start with, we have noted that even if you knew the wave function after the black hole disappeared, you could not run the Schrödinger equation backward and calculate what the wave function was before the black hole formed. What that was would depend in part on the bit of the wave function that got lost in the black hole. We are used to thinking we can know the past exactly. However, if information gets lost in black holes, this is not the case. Anything could have happened.

In general, however, people such as astrologers and those who consult them are more interested in predicting the future than in retrodicting the past. At first glance, it might seem that the loss of part of the wave function down the black hole would not prevent us from predicting the wave function outside the black hole. But it turns out that this loss does interfere with such a prediction, as we can see when we consider a thought experiment proposed by Einstein, Boris Podolsky, and Nathan Rosen in the 1930s.

Imagine that a radioactive atom decays and sends out two particles in opposite directions and with opposite spins. An observer who looks only at one particle cannot predict whether it will be spinning to the right or left. But if the observer measures it to be spinning to the right, then he or she can predict with certainty that the other particle will be spinning to the left, and vice versa (Fig. 4.20). Einstein thought that this proved that quantum theory was ridiculous: the other particle might be at the other side of the

(FIG. 4.20)

In the Einstein-Podolsky-Rosen thought experiment, the observer who has measured the spin of one particle will know the direction of the spin of the second particle.

(FIG. 4.21)
A virtual-particle pair has a wave function that predicts that both particles will have opposite spins. But if one particle falls into the black hole, it is impossible to predict with certainty the spin of the remaining particle.

galaxy by now, yet one would instantaneously know which way it was spinning. However, most other scientists agree that it was Einstein who was confused, not quantum theory. The Einstein-Podolsky-Rosen thought experiment does not show that one is able to send information faster than light. That would be the ridiculous part. One cannot *choose* that one's own particle will be measured to be spinning to the right, so one cannot prescribe that the distant observer's particle should be spinning to the left.

In fact, this thought experiment is exactly what happens with black hole radiation. The virtual-particle pair will have a wave function that predicts that the two members will definitely have opposite spins (Fig. 4.21). What we would like to do is predict the spin and wave function of the outgoing particle, which we could do if we could observe the particle that has fallen in. But that particle is now inside the black hole, where its spin and wave function cannot be

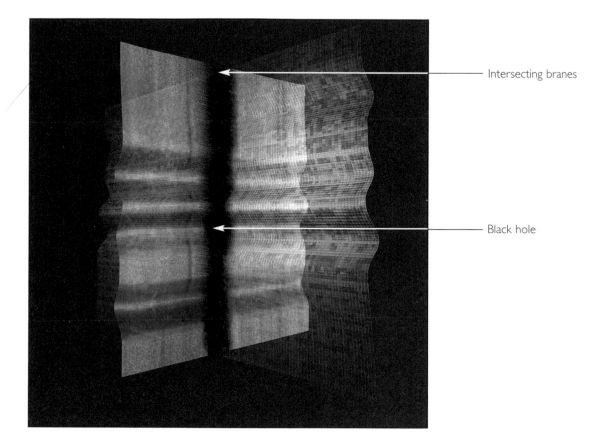

Intersecting branes

Black hole

(Fig. 4.22)

Black holes can be thought of as the intersections of p-branes in the extra dimensions of spacetime. Information about the internal states of black holes would be stored as waves on the p-branes.

measured. Because of this, it is not possible to predict the spin or the wave function of the particle that escapes. It can have different spins and different wave functions, with various probabilities, but it doesn't have a unique spin or wave function. Thus it would seem that our power to predict the future would be further reduced. The classical idea of Laplace, that one could predict both the positions and the velocities of particles, had to be modified when the uncertainty principle showed that one could not accurately measure both positions and velocities. However, one could still measure the wave function and use the Schrödinger equation to predict what it should be in the future. This would allow one to predict with certainty one combination of position and velocity—which is half of what one could predict according to Laplace's ideas. We can predict with certainty that the particles have opposite spins, but if one particle falls into the black hole, there is no prediction we can make with certainty about the

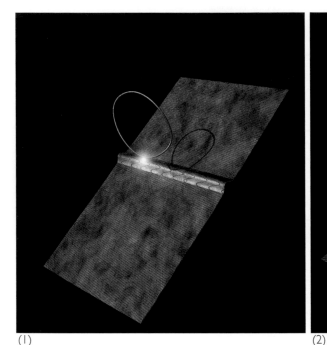

(1)

(2)

(FIG. 4.23)
A particle falling into a black hole can be thought of as a closed loop of string hitting a p-brane (1). It will excite waves in the p-brane (2). Waves can come together and cause part of the p-brane to break off as a closed string (3). This would be a particle emitted by the black hole.

remaining particle. This means that there isn't *any* measurement outside the black hole that can be predicted with certainty: our ability to make definite predictions would be reduced to zero. So maybe astrology is no worse at predicting the future than the laws of science.

Many physicists didn't like this reduction in determinism and therefore suggested that information about what is inside can somehow get out of a black hole. For years it was just a pious hope that some way to save the information would be found. But in 1996 Andrew Strominger and Cumrun Vafa made an important advance. They chose to regard a black hole as being made up of a number of building blocks, called p-branes (see page 54).

Recall that one way of thinking about p-branes is as sheets that move through the three dimensions of space and also through seven extra dimensions that we don't notice (see Fig. 4.22, page 125). In certain cases, one can show that the number of waves on the p-branes is the same as the amount of information one would expect the black hole to contain. If particles hit the p-branes, they excite extra waves on the branes. Similarly, if waves moving in different

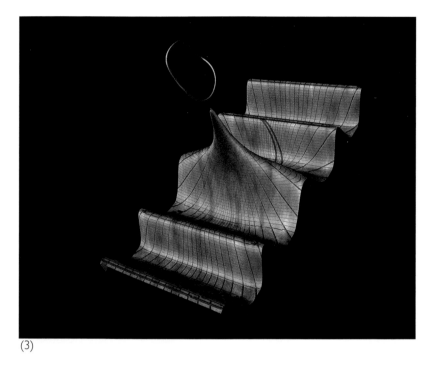

(3)

directions on the p-branes come together at some point, they can create a peak so great that a bit of the p-brane breaks away and goes off as a particle. Thus the p-branes can absorb and emit particles like black holes (Fig. 4.23).

Once can regard the p-branes as an effective theory; that is, while we don't need to believe that there actually are little sheets moving through a flat spacetime, black holes can behave as if they were made up of such sheets. It is like water, which is made up of billions and billions of H_2O molecules with complicated interactions. But a smooth fluid is a very good effective model. The mathematical model of black holes as made of p-branes gives results similar to the virtual-particle pair picture described earlier. Thus from a positivist viewpoint, it is an equally good model, at least for certain classes of black hole. For these classes, the p-brane model predicts exactly the same rate of emission that the virtual-particle pair model predicts. However, there is one important difference: in the p-brane model, information about what falls into the black hole will be stored in the wave function for the waves on the p-branes. The p-branes are

regarded as sheets in *flat* spacetime, and for that reason, time will flow forward smoothly, the paths of light rays won't be bent, and the information in the waves won't be lost. Instead, the information will eventually emerge from the black hole in the radiation from the p-branes. Thus, according to the p-brane model, we can use the Schrödinger equation to calculate what the wave function will be at later times. Nothing will get lost, and time will roll smoothly on. We will have complete determinism in the quantum sense.

So which of these pictures is correct? Does part of the wave function get lost down black holes, or does all the information get out again, as the p-brane model suggests? This is one of the outstanding questions in theoretical physics today. Many people believe that recent work shows that information is not lost. The world is safe and predictable, and nothing unexpected will happen. But it's not clear. If one takes Einstein's general theory of relativity seriously, one must allow the possibility that spacetime ties itself in a knot and information gets lost in the folds. When the starship *Enterprise* went through a wormhole, something unexpected happened. I know, because I was on board, playing poker with Newton, Einstein, and Data. I had a big surprise. Just look what appeared on my knee.

Courtesy of Paramount Pictures.
STAR TREK: THE NEXT GENERATION
Copyright © 2001 by Paramount Pictures.
All Rights Reserved

CHAPTER 5

PROTECTING THE PAST

Is time travel possible?
Could an advanced civilization go back and change the past?

Whereas Stephen W. Hawking (having lost a previous bet on this subject by not demanding genericity) still firmly believes that naked singularities are an anathema and should be prohibited by the laws of classical physics,

And whereas John Preskill and Kip Thorne (having won the previous bet) still regard naked singularities as quantum gravitational objects that might exist, unclothed by horizons, for all the Universe to see,

Therefore Hawking offers, and Preskill/Thorne accept, a wager that

> When any form of classical matter or field that is incapable of becoming singular in flat spacetime is coupled to general relativity via the classical Einstein equations, then

A dynamical evolution from generic initial conditions (*i.e., from an open set of initial data*) **can never produce a naked singularity** (*a past-incomplete null geodesic from* $\mathcal{I}_+$).

The loser will reward the winner with clothing to cover the winner's nakedness. The clothing is to be embroidered with a suitable, truly concessionary message.

Stephen W. Hawking   John P. Preskill & Kip S. Thorne

Pasadena, California, 5 February 1997

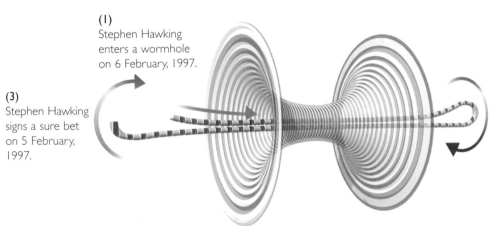

(1)
Stephen Hawking enters a wormhole on 6 February, 1997.

(3)
Stephen Hawking signs a sure bet on 5 February, 1997.

(2)
In the future it is proved that the dynamical evolution from generic initial conditions can never produce a naked singularity.

M Y FRIEND AND COLLEAGUE KIP THORNE, WITH WHOM I have had a number of bets (left), is not one to follow the accepted line in physics just because everyone else does. This led him to have the courage to be the first serious scientist to discuss time travel as a practical possibility.

It is tricky to speculate openly about time travel. One risks either an outcry at the waste of public money being spent on something so ridiculous or a demand that the research be classified for military purposes. After all, how could we protect ourselves against someone with a time machine? They might change history and rule the world. There are only a few of us foolhardy enough to work on a subject that is so politically incorrect in physics circles. We disguise the fact by using technical terms that are code for time travel.

Kip Thorne

133

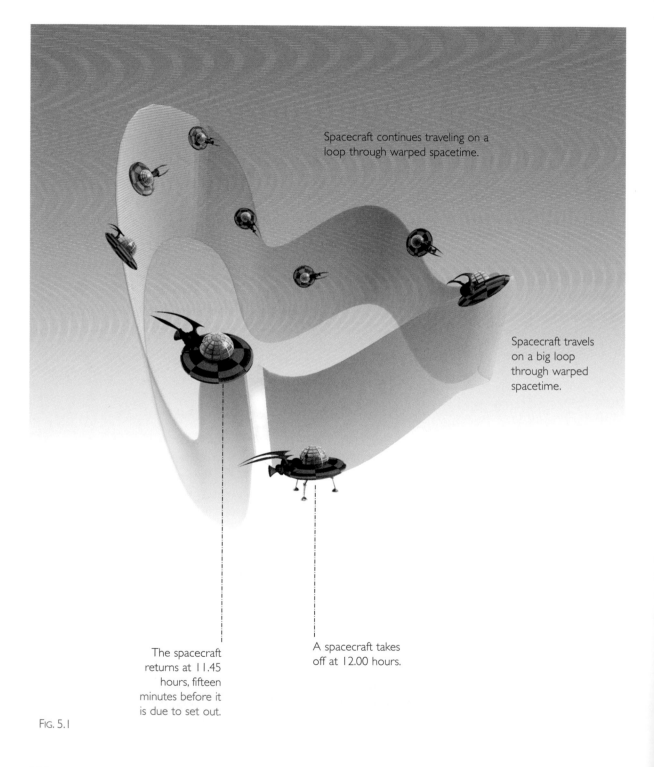

Spacecraft continues traveling on a loop through warped spacetime.

Spacecraft travels on a big loop through warped spacetime.

The spacecraft returns at 11.45 hours, fifteen minutes before it is due to set out.

A spacecraft takes off at 12.00 hours.

FIG. 5.1

The basis of all modern discussions of time travel is Einstein's general theory of relativity. As we have seen in earlier chapters, the Einstein equations made space and time dynamic by describing how they were curved and distorted by the matter and energy in the universe. In general relativity someone's personal time as measured by their wristwatch would always increase, just as it did in Newtonian theory or the flat spacetime of special relativity. But there was now the possibility that spacetime could be warped so much that you could go off in a spaceship and come back before you set out (Fig. 5.1).

One way this could happen is if there were wormholes, tubes of spacetime mentioned in Chapter 4 that connect different regions of space and time. The idea is that you steer your spaceship into one mouth of the wormhole and come out of the other mouth in a different place and at a different time (Fig. 5.2, see page 136).

Wormholes, if they exist, would be the solution to the speed limit problem in space: it would take tens of thousands of years to cross the galaxy in a spaceship that traveled at less than the speed of light, as relativity demands. But you might go through a wormhole to the other side of the galaxy and be back in time for dinner. However, one can show that if wormholes exist, you could also use them to get back before you set out. So you might think that you could do something like blowing up the rocket on its launch pad to prevent your setting out in the first place. This is a variation of the grandfather paradox: what happens if you go back and kill your grandfather before your father was conceived? (see Fig. 5.3, page 138)

Of course, this is a paradox only if you believe you have free will to do what you like when you go back in time. This book will

SHALLOW WORMHOLE

Enters at 12.00 hours

Exits at 12.00 hours

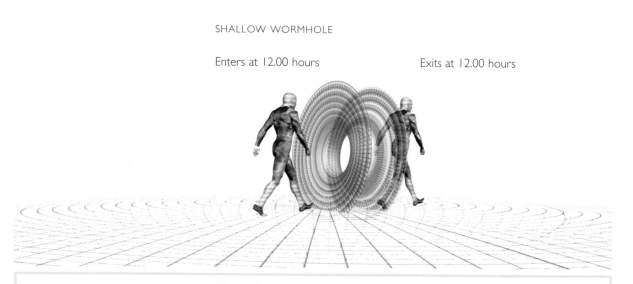

(FIG. 5.2) A SECOND VARIATION ON THE TWINS PARADOX

(I)
If there was a wormhole with its two ends close together,
you could walk through the wormhole and come out at the same time.

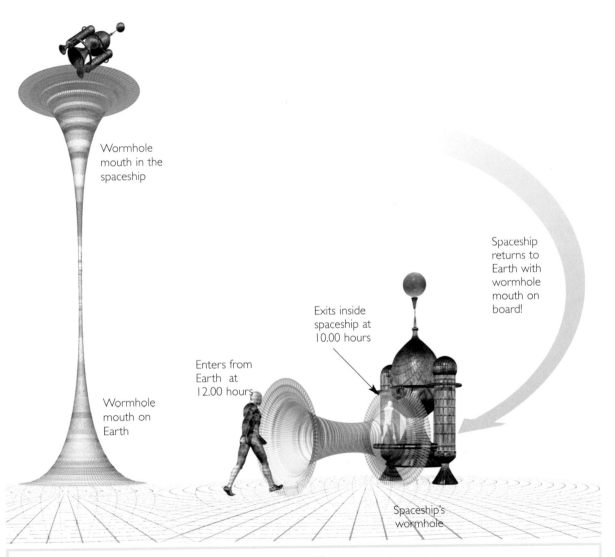

Wormhole mouth in the spaceship

Wormhole mouth on Earth

Enters from Earth at 12.00 hours

Exits inside spaceship at 10.00 hours

Spaceship returns to Earth with wormhole mouth on board!

Spaceship's wormhole

(2)
One can imagine taking one end of the wormhole on a long journey on a spaceship while the other end remains on Earth.

(3)
Because of the twins paradox effect, when the spaceship returns, less time has elapsed for the mouth it contains than for the mouth that stays on earth. This would mean that if you step into the Earth mouth, you could come out of the spaceship at an earlier time.

(FIG. 5.3)

Can a bullet fired through a wormhole into an earlier time affect the one who fires it?

COSMIC STRINGS

Cosmic strings are long, heavy objects with a tiny cross section that may have been produced during the early stages of the universe. Once cosmic strings formed, they were further stretched by the expansion of the universe, and by now a single cosmic string could cross over the entire length of our observable universe.

The occurrence of cosmic strings is suggested by modern theories of particles, which predict that in the hot early stages of the universe, matter was in a symmetric phase, much like liquid water—which is symmetrical: the same at every point in every direction—rather than like ice crystals, which have a discrete structure.

When the universe cooled, the symmetry of the early phase could have been broken in different ways in distant regions. Consequently, the cosmic matter would have settled into different ground states in those regions. Cosmic strings are the configurations of matter at the boundaries between these regions. Their formation was therefore an inevitable consequence of the fact that different regions could not agree on their ground states.

not go into a philosophical discussion of free will. Instead it will concentrate on whether the laws of physics allow spacetime to be so warped that a macroscopic body such as a spaceship can return to its own past. According to Einstein's theory, a spaceship necessarily travels at less than the local speed of light and follows what is called a timelike path through spacetime. Thus one can formulate the question in technical terms: does spacetime admit timelike curves that are closed—that is, that return to their starting point again and again? I shall refer to such paths as "time loops."

There are three levels on which we can try to answer this question. The first is Einstein's general theory of relativity, which assumes that the universe has a well-defined history without any uncertainty. For this classical theory we have a fairly complete picture. However, as we have seen, this theory can't be quite right, because we observe that matter is subject to uncertainty and quantum fluctuations.

We can therefore ask the question about time travel on a second level, that of semiclassical theory. In this, we consider matter to behave according to quantum theory, with uncertainty and quantum fluctuations, but spacetime to be well defined and classical. Here the picture is less complete, but at least we have some idea of how to proceed.

(FIG. 5.4)
Does spacetime admit timelike curves that are closed, returning to their starting point again and again?

Finally, there is the full quantum theory of gravity, whatever that may be. In this theory, where not just matter but also time and space themselves are uncertain and fluctuate, it is not even clear how to pose the question of whether time travel is possible. Maybe the best we can do is to ask how people in regions where spacetime is nearly classical and free from uncertainty would interpret their measurements. Would they think that time travel had taken place in regions of strong gravity and large quantum fluctuations?

To start with the classical theory: the flat spacetime of special relativity (relativity without gravity) doesn't allow time travel, nor do the curved spacetimes that were known early on. It was therefore a great shock to Einstein when in 1949 Kurt Gödel, of Gödel's theorem (see box), discovered a spacetime that was a universe full of rotating matter, with time loops through every point (Fig. 5.4).

The Gödel solution required a cosmological constant, which may or may not exist in nature, but other solutions were subsequently found without a cosmological constant. A particularly interesting case is one in which two cosmic strings move at high speed past each other.

Cosmic strings should not be confused with the strings of

GÖDEL'S INCOMPLETENESS THEOREM

In 1931 the mathematician Kurt Gödel proved his famous incompleteness theorem about the nature of mathematics. The theorem states that within any formal system of axioms, such as present-day mathematics, questions always persist that can neither be proved nor disproved on the basis of the axioms that define the system. In other words, Gödel showed that there are problems that cannot be solved by any set of rules or procedures.

Gödel's theorem set fundamental limits on mathematics. It came as a great shock to the scientific community, since it overthrew the widespread belief that mathematics was a coherent and complete system based on a single logical foundation. Gödel's theorem, Heisenberg's uncertainty principle, and the practical impossibility of following the evolution of even a deterministic system that becomes chaotic, form a core set of limitations to scientific knowledge that only came to be appreciated during the twentieth century.

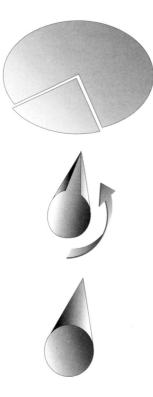

FIG. 5.5

string theory, though they are not entirely unrelated. They are objects with length but a tiny cross section. Their occurrence is predicted in some theories of elementary particles. The spacetime outside a single cosmic string is flat. However, it is flat spacetime with a wedge cut out, with the sharp end of the wedge at the string. It is like a cone: take a large circle of paper and cut out a segment like a slice of pie, a wedge with its corner at the center of the circle. Then discard the piece you have cut out and glue the cut edges of the remaining piece together so that you have a cone. This represents the spacetime in which the cosmic string exists (Fig. 5.5).

Notice that because the surface of the cone is the same flat sheet of paper with which you started (minus the wedge), you can still call it "flat" except at the apex. You can recognize that there is curvature at the apex by the fact that a circle around the apex has a smaller circumference than a circle drawn at the same distance around the center of the original round sheet of paper. In other words, a circle around the apex is shorter than one would expect for a circle of that radius in flat space because of the missing segment (Fig. 5.6).

Similarly, in the case of a cosmic string, the wedge that is removed from flat spacetime shortens circles around the string but does not affect time or distances along the string. This means that the spacetime around a single cosmic string does not contain any time loops, so it is not possible to travel into the past. However, if there is a second cosmic string that is moving relative to the first, its time direction will be a combination of the time and space directions of the first. This means that the wedge that is cut out for the second string will shorten both distances in space and time intervals as seen by someone moving with the first string (Fig. 5.7). If the cosmic strings are moving at nearly the speed of light relative to each other, the saving of time going around both strings can be so great that one arrives back before one set out. In other words, there are time loops that one can follow to travel into the past.

The cosmic string spacetime contains matter that has positive energy density and is consistent with the physics we know. However, the warping that produces the time loops extends all the way out to infinity in space and back to the infinite past in time. Thus these

FIG. 5.6

Wedges removed from
spacetime with sharp
edges not parallel

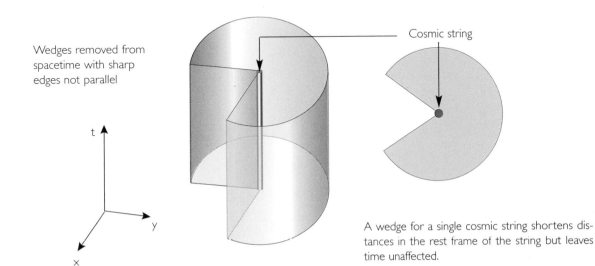

Cosmic string

A wedge for a single cosmic string shortens distances in the rest frame of the string but leaves time unaffected.

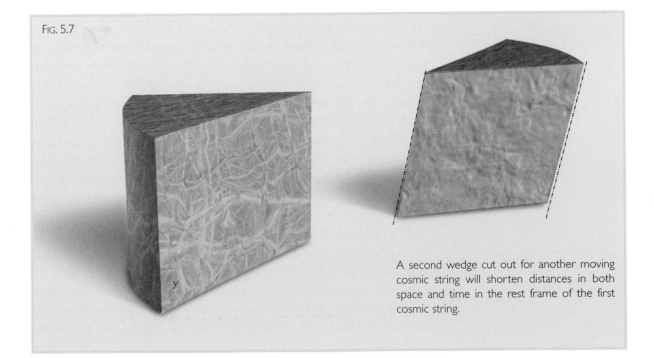

FIG. 5.7

A second wedge cut out for another moving cosmic string will shorten distances in both space and time in the rest frame of the first cosmic string.

FINITELY GENERATED TIME TRAVEL HORIZON

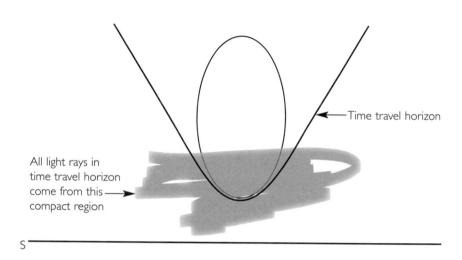

Time travel horizon

All light rays in
time travel horizon
come from this
compact region

S

(FIG. 5.8)
Even the most advanced civilization
could warp spacetime only in a finite
region. The time travel horizon, the
boundary of the part of spacetime in
which it is possible to travel into one's
past, would be formed by light rays
that emerge from finite regions.

spacetimes were created with time travel in them. We have no reason
to believe that our own universe was created in such a warped fashion,
and we have no reliable evidence of visitors from the future. (I'm dis-
counting the conspiracy theory that UFOs are from the future and
that the government knows and is covering it up. Its record of cover-
ups is not that good.) I shall therefore assume that there were no time
loops in the distant past or, more precisely, in the past of some surface
through spacetime that I shall call S. The question then is: could some
advanced civilization build a time machine? That is, could it modify
the spacetime to the future of S (above the surface S in the diagram)
so that time loops appeared in a finite region? I say a finite region
because no matter how advanced the civilization becomes, it could
presumably control only a finite part of the universe.

In science, finding the right formulation of a problem is often
the key to solving it, and this was a good example. To define what
was meant by a finite time machine, I went back to some early work
of mine. Time travel is possible in a region of spacetime in which
there are time loops, paths that move at less than the speed of light
but which nevertheless manage to come back to the place and time
they started because of the warping of spacetime. Since I have

assumed there were no time loops in the distant past, there must be what I call a time travel "horizon," the boundary separating the region of time loops from the region without them (Fig.5.8).

Time travel horizons are rather like black hole horizons. While a black hole horizon is formed by light rays that just miss falling into the black hole, a time travel horizon is formed by light rays on the verge of meeting up with themselves. I then take as my criterion for a time machine what I call a finitely generated horizon—that is, a horizon that is formed by light rays that all emerge from a bounded region. In other words, they don't come in from infinity or from a singularity, but originate from a finite region containing time loops—the sort of region our advanced civilization is supposed to create.

The question then is: could some advanced civilization build a time machine?

In adopting this definition as the footprint of a time machine, we have the advantage of being able to use the machinery that Roger Penrose and I developed to study singularities and black holes. Even without using the Einstein equations, I can show that, in general, a finitely generated horizon will contain a light ray that actually meets up with itself—that is, a light ray that keeps coming back to the same point over and over again. Each time the light came around it would be more and more blue-shifted, so the images would get bluer and bluer. The wave crests of a pulse of light will get closer and closer together and the light will get around in shorter and shorter intervals of its time. In fact, a particle of light would have only a finite history, as defined by its own measure of time, even though it went around and around in a finite region and did not hit a curvature singularity.

(FIG. 5.9, above)
The danger of time travel.

(FIG. 5.10, opposite)
The prediction that black holes radiate and lose mass implies that quantum theory causes negative energy to flow into the black hole across the horizon. For the black hole to shrink in size, the energy density on the horizon must be negative, the sign that is required to build a time machine.

One might not care if a particle of light completed its history in a finite time. But I can also prove that there would be paths moving at less than the speed of light that had only finite duration. These could be the histories of observers who would be trapped in a finite region before the horizon and would go around and around faster and faster until they reached the speed of light in a finite time. So if a beautiful alien in a flying saucer invites you into her time machine, step with care. You might fall into one of these trapped repeating histories of only finite duration (Fig. 5.9).

These results do not depend on the Einstein equations but only on the way spacetime would have to warp to produce time loops in a finite region. However, we can now ask what kind of matter an advanced civilization would have to use to warp spacetime so as to build a finite-sized time machine. Can it have positive energy density everywhere, as in the cosmic string spacetime I described earlier? The cosmic string spacetime did not satisfy my requirement that the time loops appear in a finite region. However, one might think that this was just because the cosmic strings were infinitely long. One might imagine that one could build a finite time machine using finite loops of cosmic string and have the energy density positive everywhere. It is a pity to disappoint people such as Kip, who want to return to the past, but it can't be done with positive energy density everywhere. I can prove that to build a finite time machine, you need negative energy.

Energy density is always positive in classical theory, so time machines of finite size are ruled out on this level. However, the situation is different in the semiclassical theory, in which one considers matter to behave according to quantum theory but spacetime to be well defined and classical. As we have seen, the uncertainty principle of quantum theory means that fields are always fluctuating up and down even in apparently empty space, and have an energy density that is infinite. Thus one has to subtract an infinite quantity to get the finite energy density that we observe in the universe. This subtraction can leave the energy density negative, at least locally. Even in flat space, one can find quantum states in which the energy

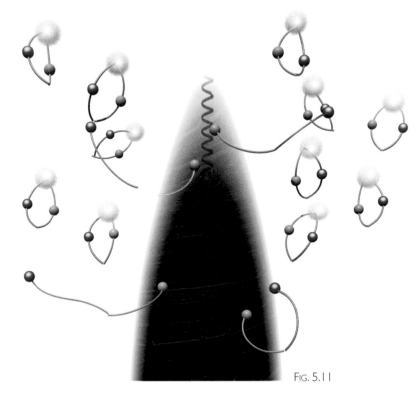

Fig. 5.11

density is negative locally although the total energy is positive. One might wonder whether these negative values actually cause spacetime to warp in the appropriate way to build a finite time machine, but it seems they must. As we saw in Chapter 4, quantum fluctuations mean that even apparently empty space is full of pairs of virtual particles that appear together, move apart, and then come back together and annihilate each other (Fig. 5.10). One member of a virtual-particle pair will have positive energy and the other negative energy. When a black hole is present, the negative-energy member can fall in and the positive-energy member can escape to infinity, where it appears as radiation that carries positive energy away from the black hole. The negative-energy particles falling in cause the black hole to lose mass and to evaporate slowly, with its horizon shrinking in size (Fig. 5.11).

Ordinary matter with positive energy density has an attractive gravitational effect and warps spacetime to bend light rays toward each other—just as the ball on the rubber sheet in Chapter 2 always makes the smaller ball bearings curve toward it, never away.

Annihilation

Antiparticle

Particle

Creation

Fig. 5.10

145

My grandson,
William Mackenzie Smith.

This would imply that the area of the horizon of a black hole could only increase with time, never shrink. For the horizon of a black hole to shrink in size, the energy density on the horizon must be negative and warp spacetime to make light rays diverge from each other. This was something I first realized when I was getting into bed soon after the birth of my daughter. I won't say how long ago that was, but I now have a grandson.

The evaporation of black holes shows that on the quantum level the energy density can sometimes be negative and warp spacetime in the direction that would be needed to build a time machine. Thus we might imagine that some very advanced civilization could arrange things so that the energy density is sufficiently negative to form a time machine that could be used by macroscopic objects such as spaceships. However, there's an important difference between a black hole horizon, which is formed by light rays that just keep going, and the horizon in a time machine, which contains closed light rays that keep going around and around. A virtual particle moving on such a closed path would bring its ground state energy back to the same point again and again. One would therefore expect the energy density to be infinite on the horizon—the boundary of the time machine, the region in which one can travel into the past. This is borne out by explicit calculations in a few backgrounds that are simple enough for exact calculations. It would mean that a person or a space probe that tried to cross the horizon to get into the time machine would get wiped out by a bolt of radiation (Fig. 5.12). So the future looks black for time travel—or should one say blindingly white?

The energy density of matter depends on the state it is in, so it is possible that an advanced civilization might be able to make the energy density finite on the boundary of the time machine by "freezing out" or removing the virtual particles that go around and around in a closed loop. It is not clear, however, that such a time machine would be stable: the least disturbance, such as someone crossing the horizon to enter the time machine, might set off circulating virtual particles and trigger a bolt of lightning. This is a

question that physicists should be free to discuss without being laughed to scorn. Even if it turns out that time travel is impossible, it is important that we understand why it is impossible.

To answer that question definitively, we need to consider quantum fluctuations not only of matter fields but of spacetime itself. One might expect that these would cause a certain fuzziness in the paths of light rays and in the whole concept of time ordering. Indeed, one can regard the radiation from black holes as leaking out because quantum fluctuations of spacetime mean that the horizon is not exactly defined. Because we don't yet have a complete theory of quantum gravity, it is difficult to say what the effects of spacetime fluctuations should be. Nevertheless, we can hope to get some pointers from the Feynman sum over histories described in Chapter 3.

(FIG. 5.12)
One might get wiped out by a bolt of radiation when crossing the time travel horizon.

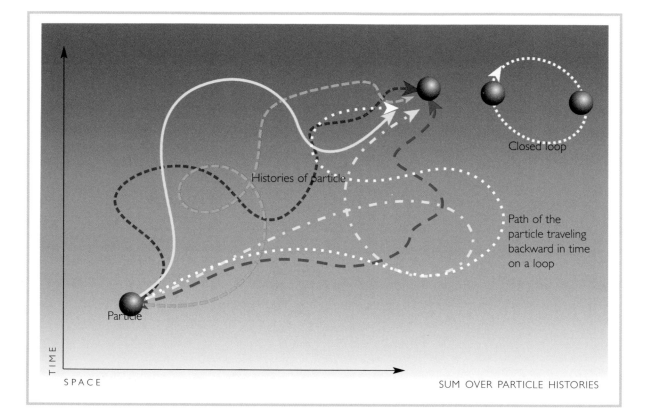

Closed loop

Histories of particle

Path of the
particle traveling
backward in time
on a loop

Particle

TIME

SPACE

SUM OVER PARTICLE HISTORIES

(FIG. 5.13)
The Feynman sum over histories has to include histories in which particles travel back in time, and even histories that are closed loops in time and space.

Each history will be a curved spacetime with matter fields in it. Since we are supposed to sum over all possible histories, not just those that satisfy some equations, the sum must include spacetimes that are warped enough for travel into the past (Fig. 5.13). So the question is, why isn't time travel happening everywhere? The answer is that time travel is indeed taking place on a microscopic scale, but we don't notice it. If one applies the Feynman sum-over-histories idea to a particle, one has to include histories in which the particle travels faster than light and even backward in time. In particular, there will be histories in which the particle goes around and around on a closed loop in time and space. It would be like the film *Groundhog Day*, in which a reporter has to live the same day over and over again (Fig. 5.14).

One cannot observe particles with such closed-loop histories directly with a particle detector. However, their indirect effects have been measured in a number of experiments. One is a small shift in the

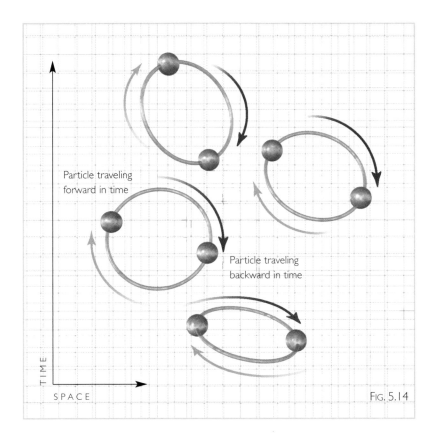

Particle traveling
forward in time

Particle traveling
backward in time

TIME

SPACE

FIG. 5.14

light given out by hydrogen atoms, caused by electrons moving in closed loops. Another is a small force between parallel metal plates, caused by the fact that there are slightly fewer closed-loop histories that can fit between the plates compared to the region outside—another equivalent interpretation of the Casimir effect. Thus the existence of closed-loop histories is confirmed by experiment (Fig. 5.15).

One might dispute whether closed-loop particle histories have anything to do with the warping of spacetime, because they occur even in fixed backgrounds such as flat space. But in recent years we have found that phenomena in physics often have dual, equally valid descriptions. One can equally well say that a particle moves on a closed loop in a given fixed background, or that the particle stays fixed and space and time fluctuate around it. It is just a question of whether you do the sum over particle paths first and then the sum over curved spacetimes, or vice versa.

FIG. 5.15

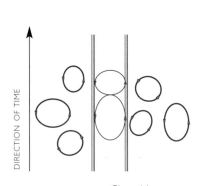

DIRECTION OF TIME

Closed loops

149

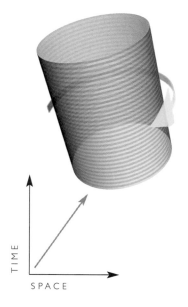

TIME

SPACE

(FIG. 5.16)
The Einstein universe is like a cylinder: it is finite in space and constant in time. Because of its finite size, it can rotate at less than the speed of light everywhere.

It seems, therefore, that quantum theory allows time travel on a microscopic scale. However, this is not much use for science fiction purposes, such as going back and killing your grandfather. The question therefore is: can the probability in the sum over histories be peaked around spacetimes with macroscopic time loops?

One can investigate this question by studying the sum over histories of matter fields in a series of background spacetimes that get closer and closer to admitting time loops. One would expect something dramatic to happen when time loops first appear, and this is borne out in a simple example that I studied with my student Michael Cassidy.

The background spacetimes in the series we studied were closely related to what is called the Einstein universe, the spacetime that Einstein proposed when he believed that the universe was static and unchanging in time, neither expanding nor contracting (see Chapter 1). In the Einstein universe time runs from the infinite past to the infinite future. The space directions, however, are finite and close on themselves, like the surface of the Earth but with one more dimension. One can picture this spacetime as a cylinder with the long axis being the time direction and the cross section being the three space directions (Fig. 5.16).

The Einstein universe does not represent the universe we live in because it is not expanding. Nevertheless, it is a convenient background to use when discussing time travel, because it is simple enough that one can do the sum over histories. Forgetting about time travel for the moment, consider matter in an Einstein universe that is rotating about some axis. If you were on the axis, you could remain at the same point of space, just as you do when standing at the center of a children's carousel. But if you were not on the axis, you would be moving through space as you rotated about the axis. The further you were from the axis, the faster you would be moving (Fig. 5.17). So if the universe were infinite in space, points sufficiently far from the axis would have to be rotating faster than light. However, because the Einstein universe is finite in the space directions, there is a critical rate of rotation below which no part of the universe is rotating faster than light.

ROTATING IN FLAT SPACE

Rotating at less than
the speed of light

Axis of rotation

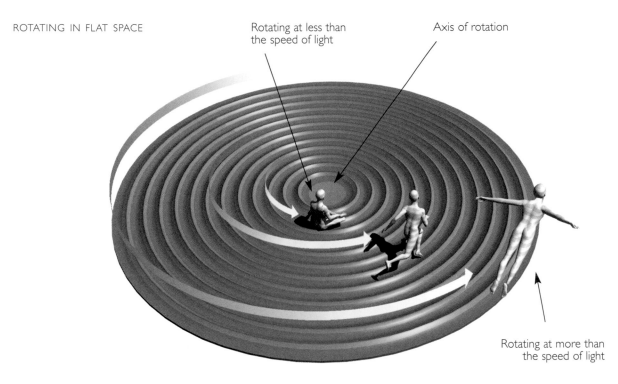

Rotating at more than
the speed of light

Now consider the sum over particle histories in a rotating Einstein universe. When the rotation is slow, there are many paths a particle can take using a given amount of energy. Thus the sum over all particle histories in this background gives a large amplitude. This means that the probability of this background would be high in the sum over all curved spacetime histories—that is, it is among the more probable histories. However, as the rate of rotation of the Einstein universe approaches the critical value, so that its outer edges are moving at a speed approaching the speed of light, there is only one particle path that is classically allowed on that edge, namely, one that is moving at the speed of light. This means that the sum over particle histories will be small. Thus the probability of these backgrounds will be low in the sum over all curved spacetime histories. That is, they are the least probable.

(FIG. 5.17)
In flat space a rigid rotation will move faster than the speed of light far from its axis.

(FIG. 5.18) BACKGROUND WITH CLOSED TIME-LIKE CURVES

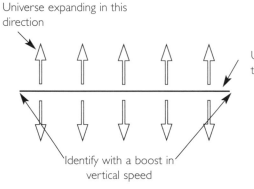

Universe expanding in this direction

Universe *not* expanding in this direction

Identify with a boost in vertical speed

What do rotating Einstein universes have to do with time travel and time loops? The answer is that they are mathematically equivalent to other backgrounds that do admit time loops. These other backgrounds are universes that are expanding in two space directions. The universes are not expanding in the third space direction, which is periodic. That is to say, if you go a certain distance in this direction, you get back to where you started. However, each time you do a circuit of the third space direction, your speed in the first or second directions is increased (Fig. 5.18).

If the boost is small, there are no time loops. However, consider a sequence of backgrounds with increasing boosts in speed. At a certain critical boost, time loops will appear. Not surprisingly, this critical boost corresponds to the critical rate of rotation of the Einstein universes. Since the sum-over-histories calculations in these backgrounds are mathematically equivalent, one can conclude that the probability of these backgrounds goes to zero as they approach the warping needed for time loops. In other words, the probability of having sufficient warping for a time machine is zero. This supports what I have called the Chronology Protection Conjecture: that the laws of physics conspire to prevent time travel by macroscopic objects.

Although time loops are allowed by the sum over histories, the probabilities are extremely small. Based on the duality arguments I mentioned earlier, I estimate the probability that Kip Thorne could go back and kill his grandfather as less than one in ten with a trillion trillion trillion trillion trillion zeroes after it.

That's a pretty small probability, but if you look closely at the picture of Kip, you may see a slight fuzziness around the edges. That corresponds to the faint possibility that some bastard from the future came back and killed his grandfather, so he's not really there.

As gambling men, Kip and I would bet on odds like that. The trouble is, we can't bet each other because we are now both on the same side. On the other hand, I wouldn't take a bet with anyone else. He might be from the future and know that time travel worked.

You might wonder if this chapter is part of a government cover-up on time travel. You might be right.

The probability that Kip could go back and kill his grandfather is $1/10^{10^{60}}$.

In other words less than 1 in 10 —with a trillion trillion trillion trillion trillion zeroes after it.

CHAPTER 6

OUR FUTURE? STAR TREK OR NOT?

*How biological and electronic life
will go on developing in complexity at an ever-increasing rate.*

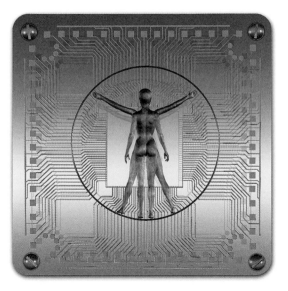

(FIG. 6.1) GROWTH OF POPULATION

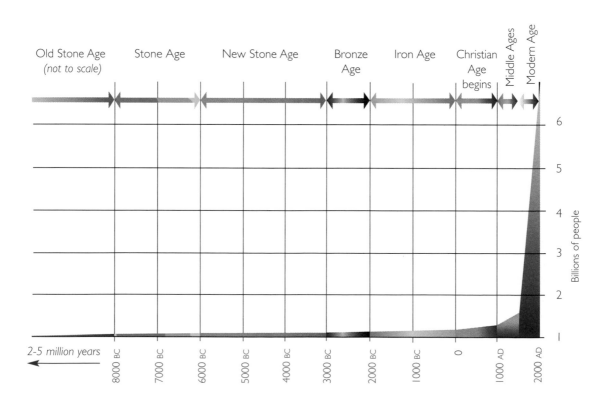

| Old Stone Age *(not to scale)* | Stone Age | New Stone Age | Bronze Age | Iron Age | Christian Age begins | Middle Ages | Modern Age |

2-5 million years

8000 BC 7000 BC 6000 BC 5000 BC 4000 BC 3000 BC 2000 BC 1000 BC 0 1000 AD 2000 AD

Billions of people

Newton, Einstein, Commander Data, and myself playing poker in a scene from Star Trek.

T HE REASON *STAR TREK* IS SO POPULAR IS BECAUSE IT IS A safe and comforting vision of the future. I'm a bit of a *Star Trek* fan myself, so I was easily persuaded to take part in an episode in which I played poker with Newton, Einstein, and Commander Data. I beat them all, but unfortunately there was a red alert, so I never collected my winnings.

Star Trek shows a society that is far in advance of ours in science, in technology, and in political organization. (The last might not be difficult.) There must have been great changes, with their accompanying tensions and upsets, in the time between now and then, but in the period we are shown, science, technology, and the organization of society are supposed to have achieved a level of near perfection.

I want to question this picture and ask if we will ever reach a final steady state in science and technology. At no time in the ten thousand years or so since the last ice age has the human race been in a state of constant knowledge and fixed technology. There have been a few setbacks, like the Dark Ages after the fall of the Roman Empire. But the world's population, which is a measure of our technological ability to preserve life and feed ourselves, has risen steadily, with only a few hiccups such as the Black Death (Fig. 6.1).

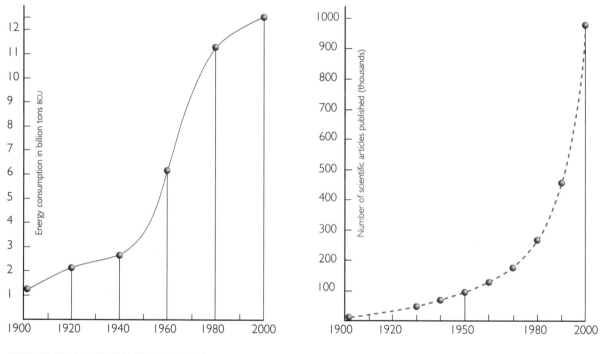

WORLDWIDE ELECTRICITY CONSUMPTION

WORLDWIDE PUBLICATION OF SCIENTIFIC ARTICLES

(FIG 6.2)

Left: The total worldwide energy consumption in billions of tons BCU, where 1 ton ~Bituminous Coal Unit = 8.13 MW-hr.

Right: The number of scientific articles published each year. The vertical scale is in thousands. In 1900 there were 9,000. By 1950 there were 90,000 and by the year 2000 there were 900,000.

In the last two hundred years, population growth has become exponential; that is, the population grows by the same percentage each year. Currently, the rate is about 1.9 percent a year. That may not sound like very much, but it means that the world population doubles every forty years (Fig. 6.2).

Other measures of technological development in recent times are electricity consumption and the number of scientific articles. They too show exponential growth, with doubling times of less than forty years. There is no sign that scientific and technological development will slow down and stop in the near future—certainly not by the time of *Star Trek*, which is supposed to be not that far in the future. But if the population growth and the increase in the consumption of electricity continue at their current rates, by 2600 the world's population will be standing shoulder to shoulder, and electricity use will make the Earth glow red-hot (see illustration opposite).

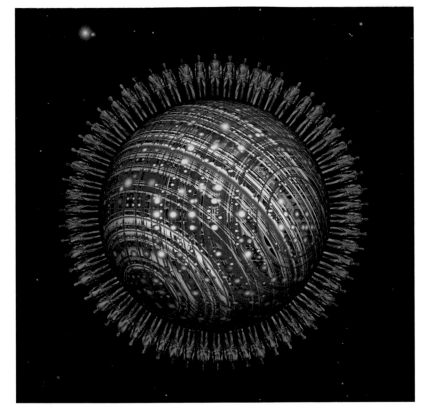

By the year 2600 the world's population would be standing shoulder to shoulder, and the electricity consumption would make the Earth glow red-hot.

If you stacked all the new books being published next to each other, you would have to move at ninety miles an hour just to keep up with the end of the line. Of course, by 2600 new artistic and scientific work will come in electronic forms, rather than as physical books and papers. Nevertheless, if the exponential growth continued, there would be ten papers a second in my kind of theoretical physics, and no time to read them.

Clearly, the present exponential growth cannot continue indefinitely. So what will happen? One possibility is that we will wipe ourselves out completely by some disaster, such as a nuclear war. There is a sick joke that the reason we have not been contacted by extraterrestrials is that when a civilization reaches our stage of development, it becomes unstable and destroys itself. However, I'm an optimist. I don't believe the human race has come so far just to snuff itself out when things are getting interesting.

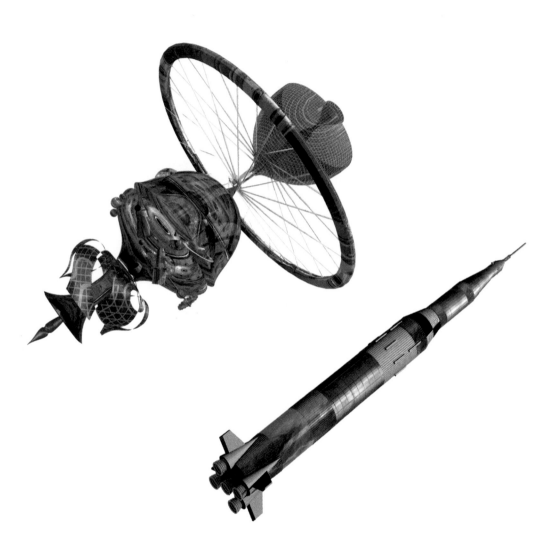

(FIG. 6.3)

Star Trek's story line depends on the *Enterprise*, and starships like the one above, being able to travel at warp speed, which is much faster than light. However, if the Chronology Protection Conjecture is correct, we shall have to explore the galaxy using rocket-propelled spaceships that travel slower than light.

The *Star Trek* vision of the future—that we achieve an advanced but essentially static level—may come true in respect of our knowledge of the basic laws that govern the universe. As I shall describe in the next chapter, there may be an ultimate theory that we will discover in the not-too-distant future. This ultimate theory, if it exists, will determine whether the *Star Trek* dream of warp drive can be realized. According to present ideas, we shall have to explore the galaxy in a slow and tedious manner, using spaceships traveling slower than light, but since we don't yet have a complete unified theory, we can't quite rule out warp drive (Fig. 6.3).

On the other hand, we already know the laws that hold in all but the most extreme situations: the laws that govern the crew of the *Enterprise,* if not the spaceship itself. Yet it doesn't seem that we will ever reach a steady state in the uses we make of these laws or in the complexity of the systems that we can produce with them. It is with this complexity that the rest of this chapter will be concerned.

By far the most complex systems that we have are our own bodies. Life seems to have originated in the primordial oceans that covered the Earth four billion years ago. How this happened we don't know. It may be that random collisions between atoms built up macromolecules that could reproduce themselves and assemble themselves into more complicated structures. What we do know is that by three and a half billion years ago, the highly complicated DNA molecule had emerged.

DNA is the basis for all life on Earth. It has a double helix structure, like a spiral staircase, which was discovered by Francis Crick and James Watson in the Cavendish lab at Cambridge in 1953. The two strands of the double helix are linked by pairs of bases, like the treads in a spiral staircase. There are four bases in DNA: adenine, guanine, thymine, and cytosine. The order in which they occur along the spiral staircase carries the genetic information that enables the DNA to assemble an organism around it and reproduce itself. As it makes copies of itself, there are occasional errors in the proportion or order of the bases along the spiral. In most cases, the mistakes in copying make the DNA either unable or less likely to reproduce itself, meaning that such genetic errors, or mutations, as they are called, will die out. But in a few cases, the error or mutation will increase the chances of the DNA surviving and reproducing. Such changes in the genetic code will be favored. This is how the information contained in the sequence of DNA gradually evolves and increases in complexity (see Fig. 6.4, page 162).

Because biological evolution is basically a random walk in the

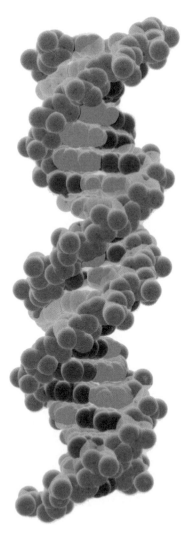

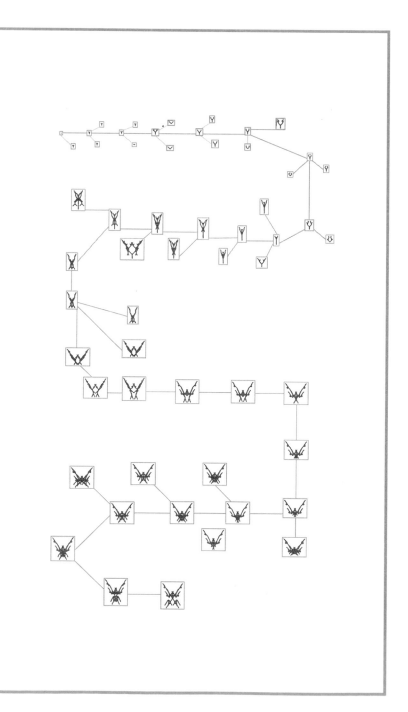

(FIG. 6.4) EVOLUTION IN ACTION

On the right are computer-generated biomorphs that evolved in a program devised by the biologist Richard Dawkins.

Survival of a particular strain depended upon simple qualities like being "interesting," "different," or "insect-like."

Starting from a single pixel, the early random generations developed through a process similar to natural selection. Dawkins bred an insect-like form in a remarkable 29 generations (with a number of evolutionary dead ends).

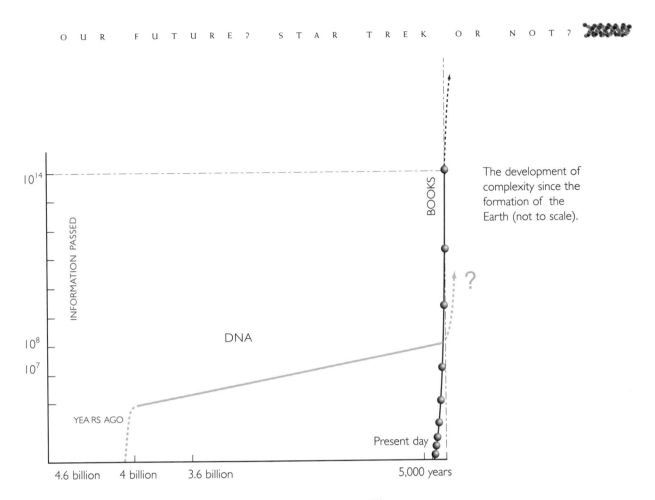

The development of complexity since the formation of the Earth (not to scale).

space of all genetic possibilities, it has been very slow. The complexity, or number of bits of information, that is coded in DNA is roughly the number of bases in the molecule. For the first two billion years or so, the rate of increase in complexity must have been of the order of one bit of information every hundred years. The rate of increase of DNA complexity gradually rose to about one bit a year over the last few million years. But then, about six or eight thousand years ago, a major new development occurred. We developed written language. This meant that information could be passed from one generation to the next without having to wait for the very slow process of random mutations and natural selection to code it into the DNA sequence. The amount of complexity increased enormously. A single paperback romance could hold as much information as the difference in DNA between apes and humans, and a thirty-volume encyclopedia could describe the entire sequence of human DNA (Fig. 6.5).

Even more important, the information in books can be

← Entire human DNA sequence in 30 volumes →

FIG 6.5

Growing embryos outside the human body will allow bigger brains and greater intelligence.

updated rapidly. The current rate at which human DNA is being updated by biological evolution is about one bit a year. But there are two hundred thousand new books published each year, a new-information rate of over a million bits a second. Of course, most of this information is garbage, but even if only one bit in a million is useful, that is still a hundred thousand times faster than biological evolution.

This transmission of data through external, nonbiological means has led the human race to dominate the world and to have an exponentially increasing population. But now we are at the beginning of a new era, in which we will be able to increase the complexity of our internal record, the DNA, without having to wait for the slow process of biological evolution. There has been no significant change in human DNA in the last ten thousand years, but it is likely that we will be able to completely redesign it in the next thousand. Of course, many people will say that genetic engineering of humans should be banned, but it is doubtful we will be able to prevent it. Genetic engineering of plants and animals will be allowed for economic reasons, and someone is bound to try it on humans. Unless we have a totalitarian world order, someone somewhere will design improved humans.

Clearly, creating improved humans will create great social and political problems with respect to unimproved humans. My intention is not to defend human genetic engineering as a desirable development, but just to say it is likely to happen whether we want it or not. This is the reason why I don't believe science fiction like *Star Trek*, where people four hundred years into the future are essentially the same as we are today. I think the human race, and its DNA, will increase its complexity quite rapidly. We should recognize that this is likely to happen and consider how we will deal with it.

In a way, the human race needs to improve its mental and physical qualities if it is to deal with the increasingly complex world around it and meet new challenges such as space travel. Humans also need to increase their complexity if biological systems are to keep ahead of electronic ones. At the moment, computers have the advantage of speed, but they show no sign of intelligence. This is not surprising, because our present computers are less complex than the brain of an earthworm, a species not noted for its intellectual powers.

But computers obey what is known as Moore's law: their speed

At present our computers remain outstripped in computational power by the brain of a humble earthworm.

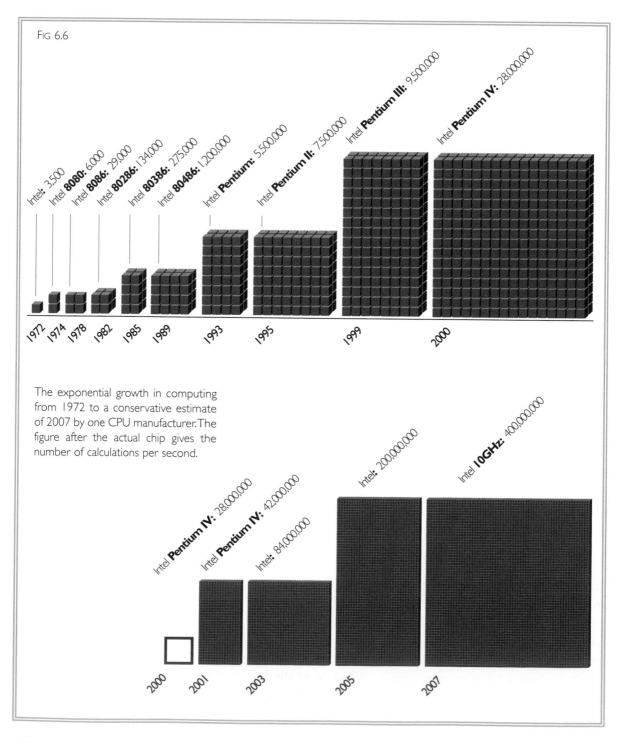

FIG 6.6

Intel: 3,500

Intel **8080:** 6,000

Intel **8086:** 29,000

Intel **80286:** 134,000

Intel **80386:** 275,000

Intel **80486:** 1,200,000

Intel **Pentium:** 5,500,000

Intel **Pentium II:** 7,500,000

Intel **Pentium III:** 9,500,000

Intel **Pentium IV:** 28,000,000

1972 1974 1978 1982 1985 1989 1993 1995 1999 2000

The exponential growth in computing from 1972 to a conservative estimate of 2007 by one CPU manufacturer. The figure after the actual chip gives the number of calculations per second.

Intel **Pentium IV:** 28,000,000

Intel **Pentium IV:** 42,000,000

Intel: 84,000,000

Intel: 200,000,000

Intel **10GHz:** 400,000,000

2000 2001 2003 2005 2007

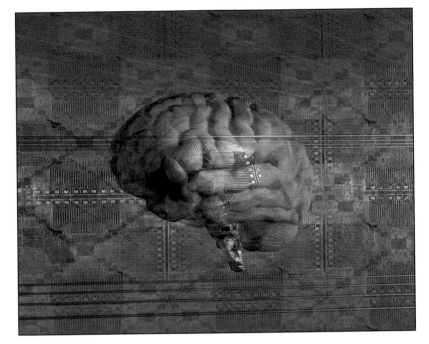

and complexity double every eighteen months (Fig. 6.6). It is one of those exponential growths that clearly cannot continue indefinitely. However, it will probably continue until computers have a complexity similar to that of the human brain. Some people say that computers can never show true intelligence, whatever that may be. But it seems to me that if very complicated chemical molecules can operate in humans to make them intelligent, then equally complicated electronic circuits can also make computers act in an intelligent way. And if they are intelligent, they can presumably design computers that have even greater complexity and intelligence.

Will this increase of biological and electronic complexity go on forever, or is there a natural limit? On the biological side, the limit on human intelligence up to now has been set by the size of the brain that will pass through the birth canal. Having watched my three children being born, I know how difficult it is for the head to get out. But within the next hundred years, I expect we will be able to grow babies outside the human body, so this limitation will be removed. Ultimately, however, increases in the size of the human brain through genetic engineering will come up against the problem that the body's chemical messengers responsible for our mental

Neural implants will offer enhanced memory and complete packages of information, such as an entire language or the contents of this book learned within minutes. Such enhanced humans will bear little resemblance to ourselves.

A BRIEF HISTORY OF THE UNIVERSE

EVENTS *(not to scale)*

0.00003 billion years.
The big bang and a fiery, optically dense, inflationary universe.

Matter/energy decouple.
The universe is transparent.

1 billion years.
Clusters of matter form protogalaxies synthesizing heavier nuclei.

3 billion years.
Galaxies recorded by Hubble Space Telescope in its Deep Field exploration.

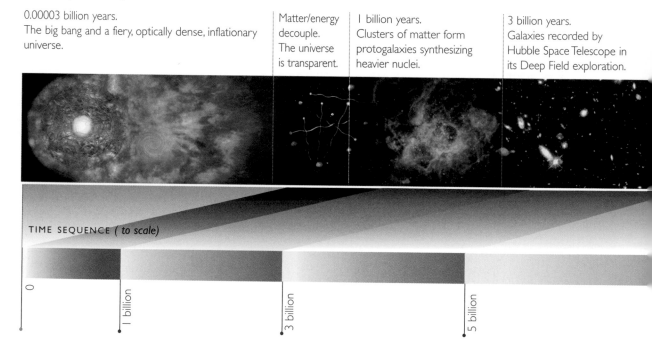

TIME SEQUENCE (*to scale*)

0

1 billion

3 billion

5 billion

(FIG. 6.7)
The human race has been in existence for only a tiny fraction of the history of the universe. (If this chart was to scale and the length that human beings have been around was 7cm, then the whole history of the universe would be over a kilometer.) Any alien life we meet is likely to be much more primitive or much more advanced than we are.

activity are relatively slow-moving. This means that further increases in the complexity of the brain will be at the expense of speed. We can be quick-witted or very intelligent, but not both. Still, I think we can become a lot more intelligent than most of the people in *Star Trek*, not that that might be difficult.

Electronic circuits have the same complexity-versus-speed problem as the human brain. In this case, however, the signals are electrical, not chemical, and travel at the speed of light, which is much higher. Nevertheless, the speed of light is already a practical limit on the design of faster computers. One can improve the situation by making the circuits smaller, but ultimately there will be a limit set by the atomic nature of matter. Still, we have some way to go before we meet that barrier.

Another way in which electronic circuits can increase their

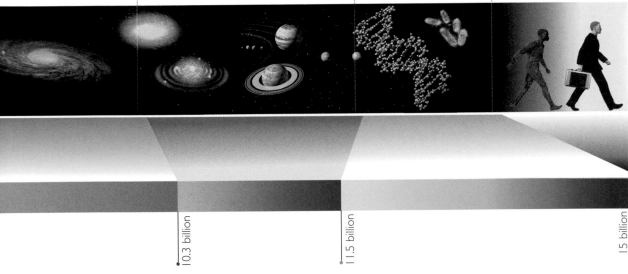

New galaxies, like our own, with heavier nuclei, are formed.

Formation of our solar system with orbiting planets.

3.5 billion years ago life-forms begin to appear.

0.0005 billion years ago early humans appear.

10.3 billion

11.5 billion

15 billion

complexity while maintaining speed is to copy the human brain. The brain does not have a single CPU—central processing unit—that processes each command in sequence. Rather, it has millions of processors working together at the same time. Such massively parallel processing will be the future for electronic intelligence as well.

Assuming we don't destroy ourselves in the next hundred years, it is likely that we will spread out first to the planets in the solar system and then to the nearby stars. But it won't be like *Star Trek* or *Babylon 5*, with a new race of nearly human beings in almost every stellar system. The human race has been in its present form for only two million years out of the fifteen billion years or so since the big bang (Fig. 6.7).

So even if life develops in other stellar systems, the chances of

169

THE BIOLOGICAL-ELECTRONIC INTERFACE

Within two decades a thousand-dollar computer may be as complex as the human brain. Parallel processors could mimic the way our brain works and make computers act in intelligent and conscious ways.

Neural implants may allow a much faster interface between the brain and computers, dissolving the distance between biological and electronic intelligence.

In the near future, most business transactions will probably be made between cyberpersonalities via the World Wide Web.

Within a decade, many of us may even choose to live a virtual existence on the Net, forming cyberfriendships and relationships.

Our understanding of the human genome will undoubtedly create great medical advances, but it will also enable us to increase the complexity of the human DNA structure significantly. In the next few hundred years, human genetic engineering may replace biological evolution, redesigning the human race and posing entirely new ethical questions.

Space travel beyond our solar system will probably require either genetically engineered humans or unmanned computer-controlled probes.

catching it at a recognizably human stage are very small. Any alien life we encounter will likely be either much more primitive or much more advanced. If it is more advanced, why hasn't it spread through the galaxy and visited Earth? If aliens had come here, it should have been obvious: more like the film *Independence Day* than *E.T.*

So how does one account for our lack of extraterrestrial visitors? It could be that there is an advanced race out there which is aware of our existence but is leaving us to stew in our own primitive juices. However, it is doubtful it would be so considerate to a lower life-form: do most of us worry how many insects and earthworms we squash underfoot? A more reasonable explanation is that there is a very low probability either of life developing on other planets or of that life developing intelligence. Because we claim to be intelligent, though perhaps without much ground, we tend to see intelligence as an inevitable consequence of evolution. However, one can question that. It is not clear that intelligence has much survival value. Bacteria do very well without intelligence and will survive us if our so-called intelligence causes us to wipe ourselves out in a nuclear war. So as we explore the galaxy we may find primitive life, but we are not likely to find beings like us.

The future of science won't be like the comforting picture painted in *Star Trek*: a universe populated by many humanoid races, with an advanced but essentially static science and technology. Instead, I think we will be on our own, but rapidly developing in biological and electronic complexity. Not much of this will happen in the next hundred years, which is all we can reliably predict. But by the end of the next millennium, if we get there, the difference from *Star Trek* will be fundamental.

Does intelligence have much long-term survival value?

CHAPTER 7

BRANE NEW WORLD

Do we live on a brane or are we just holograms?

Here be dragons

(FIG. 7.1)

M-theory is like a jigsaw. It is easy to identify and fit together the pieces around the edges but we don't have much idea of what happens in the middle, where we can't make the approximation that some quantity or other will be small.

H OW WILL OUR JOURNEY OF DISCOVERY PROCEED IN THE
future? Will we succeed in our quest for a complete unified
theory that will govern the universe and everything that it
contains? In fact, as described in Chapter 2, we may have already
identified the Theory of Everything (ToE) as M-theory. This theory doesn't have a single formulation, at least as far as we know.
Instead we have discovered a network of apparently different
theories that all seem to be approximations to the same underlying fundamental theory in different limits, just as Newton's
Theory of Gravity is an approximation to Einstein's General
Theory of Relativity in the limit that the gravitational field is
weak. M-theory is like a jigsaw: it is easiest to identify and fit
together the pieces round the edges of the jigsaw, the limits of
M-theory where some quantity or other is small. We now have a
fairly good idea of these edges but there is still a gaping hole at
the center of the M-theory jigsaw where we don't know what is
going on (Fig. 7.1). We can't really claim to have found the
Theory of Everything until we have filled that hole.

What is in the center of M-theory? Will we discover dragons (or
something equally strange) like on old maps of unexplored lands?
Our experience in the past suggests we are likely to find unexpected new phenomena whenever we extend the range of our observations to smaller scales. At the begining of the twentieth century, we
understood the workings of nature on the scales of classical physics,
which is good from interstellar distances down to about a hundredth of a millimeter. Classical physics assumes that matter is a

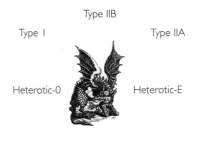

Type IIB

Type I   Type IIA

Heterotic-O   Heterotic-E

11-dimensional supergravity

(FIG. 7.2)

Right: The classical indivisible atom. *Far right:* An atom showing electrons orbiting a nucleus of protons and neutrons.

(FIG. 7.3)

Top: A proton consists of two up quarks, each with a positive two-thirds electrical charge, and one down quark, having a negative one-third charge. *Bottom:* A neutron consists of two down quarks, each with a negative one-third electrical charge, and one up quark, having a positive two-thirds charge.

continuous medium with properties like elasticity and viscosity, but evidence began to emerge that matter is not smooth but grainy: it is made of tiny building blocks called atoms. The word atom comes from Greek and means indivisible, but it was soon found that atoms consisted of electrons orbiting a nucleus made up of protons and neutrons (Fig. 7.2).

The work on atomic physics in the first thirty years of the century took our understanding down to lengths of a millionth of a millimeter. Then we discovered that protons and neutrons are made of even smaller particles called quarks (Fig. 7.3).

Our recent research on nuclear and high-energy physics has taken us to length scales that are smaller by a further factor of a billion. It might seem that we could go on forever, discovering structures on smaller and smaller length scales. However, there is a limit to this series, as there is to the series of Russian dolls within Russian dolls (Fig. 7.4).

Eventually, one gets down to a smallest doll, which can't be taken apart any more. In physics, the smallest doll is called the Planck length. To probe to shorter distances would require particles of such high energy that they would be inside black holes. We don't know exactly what the fundamental Planck length is in M-theory, but it might be as small as a millimeter divided by a hundred thousand billion billion billion. We are not about to build particle accelerators that can probe to distances that small. They would have to

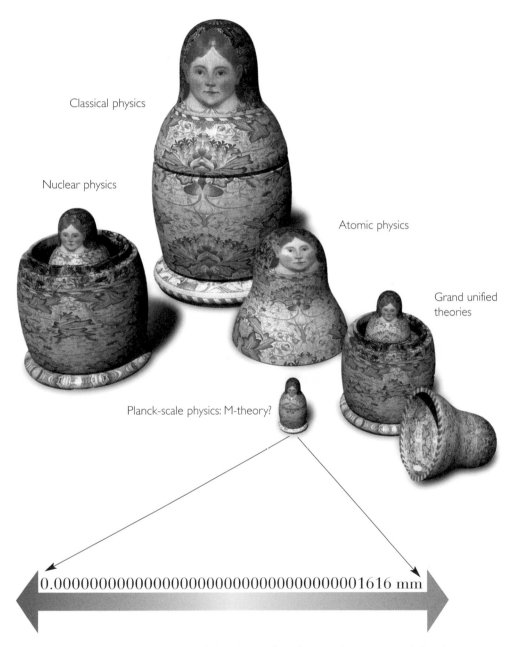

Classical physics

Nuclear physics

Atomic physics

Grand unified theories

Planck-scale physics: M-theory?

0.00000000000000000000000000000001616 mm

(FIG. 7.4) Each doll represents a theoretical understanding of nature down to a certain length scale. Each contains a smaller doll that corresponds to a theory that describes nature on shorter scales. But there exists a smallest fundamental length in physics, the Planck length, a scale at which nature may be described by M-theory.

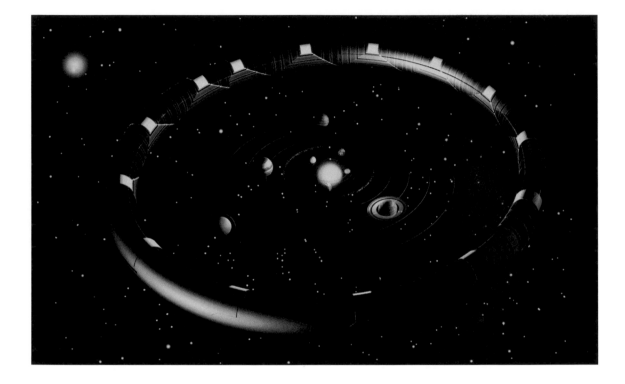

(FIG. 7.5)

The size of an accelerator needed to probe distances as small as a Planck length would be greater than the diameter of the solar system.

be larger than the solar system, and they are not likely to be approved in the present financial climate (Fig. 7.5).

However, there has been an exciting new development that means we might discover at least some of the dragons of M-theory more easily (and cheaply). As explained in Chapters 2 and 3, in the M-theory network of mathematical models, spacetime has ten or eleven dimensions. Up to recently it was thought that the six or seven extra dimensions would all be curled up very small. It would be like a human hair (Fig.7.6).

If you look at a hair under a magnifying glass, you can see it has thickness, but to the naked eye it just appears like a line with length but no other dimension. Spacetime may be similar: on human, atomic, or even nuclear physics length scales, it may appear four-dimensional and nearly flat. On the other hand if we probe to very short distances using extremely high energy particles, we should see that spacetime was ten- or eleven-dimensional.

When probes have a high enough energy, they could reveal that spacetime is multidimensional.

(FIG. 7.6)
To the naked eye a hair looks like a line; its only dimension appears to be length. Similarly, spacetime may look four-dimensional to us, but appear ten- or eleven-dimensional when probed with very high-energy particles.

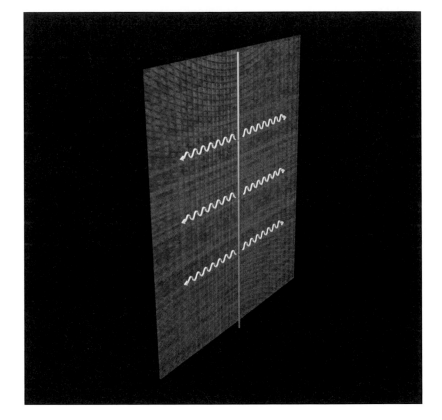

(FIG. 7.7) BRANE WORLDS

The electric force would be confined to the brane and would fall off at the right rate for electrons to have stable orbits about the nuclei of atoms.

If all the additional dimensions were very small, it would be very difficult to observe them. However, there has recently been the suggestion that one or more of the extra dimensions might be comparitively large or even infinite. This idea has the great advantage (at least to a positivist like me) that it may be testable by the next generation of particle accelerators or by sensitive short-range measurements of the gravitational force. Such observations could either falsify the theory or experimentally confirm the presence of other dimensions.

Large extra dimensions are an exciting new development in our search for the ultimate model or theory. They would imply that we lived in a brane world, a four-dimensional surface or brane in a higher-dimensional spacetime.

Matter and nongravitational forces like the electric force would be confined to the brane. Thus everything not involving gravity would

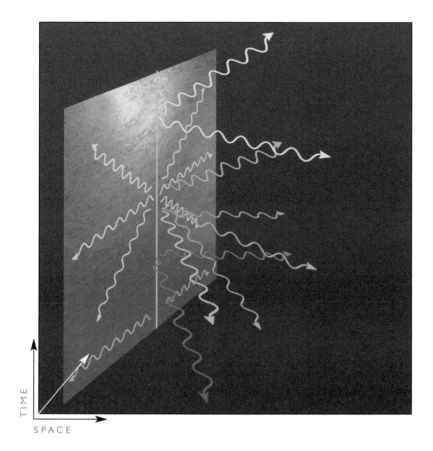

behave as it would in four dimensions. In particular, the electric force between the nucleus of an atom and the electrons orbiting around it would fall off with distance at the right rate for atoms to be stable against the electrons falling into the nucleus (Fig. 7.7).

This would be in accordance with the anthropic principle that the universe must be suitable for intelligent life: if atoms weren't stable, we wouldn't be here to observe the universe and ask why it appears four-dimensional.

On the other hand, gravity in the form of curved space would permeate the whole bulk of the higher-dimensional spacetime. This would mean that gravity would behave differently from other forces we experience: because gravity would spread out in the extra dimensions, it would fall off more rapidly with distance than one would expect (Fig. 7.8).

(FIG. 7.8)
Gravity would spread into the extra dimensions as well as acting along the brane, and would fall off faster with distance than it would in four dimensions.

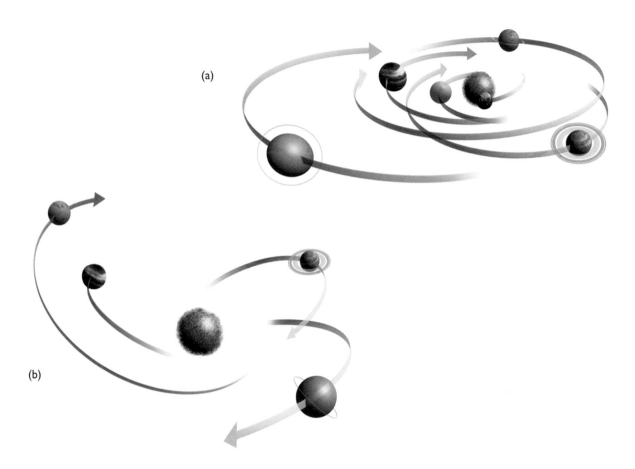

(a)

(b)

(FIG. 7.9)
A faster falloff of the gravitational force at large distances would mean that planetary orbits would be unstable. Planets would either fall into the Sun **(a)** or escape its attraction altogether **(b)**.

If this more rapid falloff of the gravitational force extended to astronomical distances, we would have noticed its effect on the orbits of the planets. In fact they would be unstable, as was remarked in Chapter 3: the planets would either fall into the Sun or escape to the dark and cold of interstellar space (Fig. 7.9).

However, this would not happen if the extra dimensions ended on another brane not that far away from the brane on which we live. Then for distances greater than the separation of the branes, gravity would not be able to spread out freely but would effectively be confined to the brane, like the electric forces, and fall off at the right rate for planetary orbits (Fig. 7.10).

On the other hand, for distances less than the separation of the branes, gravity would vary more rapidly. The very small gravitational force between heavy objects has been measured accurately in

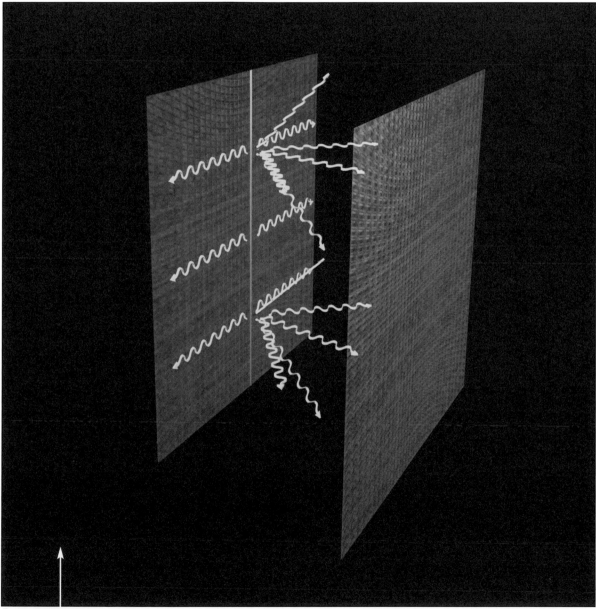

Extra dimensions

(FIG. 7.10) A second brane near our brane world would prevent gravity from spreading far into the extra dimensions and would mean that at distances greater than the brane separation, gravity would fall off at the rate one would expect for four dimensions.

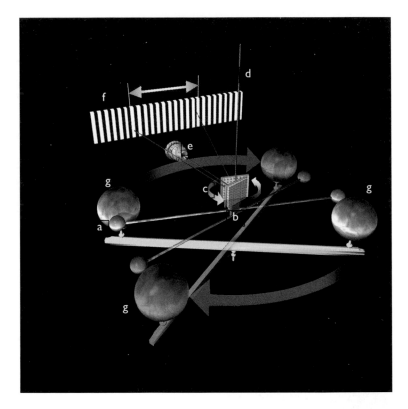

(FIG. 7.11)

THE CAVENDISH EXPERIMENT

A laser beam (e) determines any twist of the dumbbell as it is projected on a calibrated screen (f). Two small lead spheres (a) attached to the dumbbell (b) with a small mirror (c) are freely suspended by a torsion fiber.

Two large lead spheres (g) are placed near the small ones on a rotating bar. As the larger lead spheres rotate to the opposite position, the dumbbell oscillates and then settles to a new position.

the lab but the experiments so far would not have detected the effects of branes separated by less than a few millimeters. New measurements are now being made at shorter distances (Fig. 7.11).

In this brane world, we would live on one brane but there would be another "shadow" brane nearby. Because light would be confined to the branes and would not propagate through the space between, we could not see the shadow world. But we would feel the gravitational influence of matter on the shadow brane. In our brane such gravitational forces would appear to be produced by sources that were truly "dark" in that the only way we could detect them is through their gravity (Fig. 7.12). In fact in order to explain the rate at which stars orbit the center of our galaxy, it seems there must be more mass than is accounted for by the matter we observe.

(FIG. 7.12) In the brane world scenario, planets may orbit a dark mass on a shadow brane because the gravitational force propagates into the extra dimensions.

EVIDENCE FOR DARK MATTER

Various cosmological observations strongly suggest that there should be much more matter in our galaxy and other galaxies than we see. The most convincing of these observations is that stars on the outskirts of spiral galaxies like our own Milky Way orbit far too fast to be held in their orbits only by the gravitational attraction of all the stars that we observe (see opposite).

We have known since the 1970s that there is a discrepancy between the observed rotational velocities of stars in the outer regions of spiral galaxies (indicated by the dots on the diagram) and the orbit velocities that one would expect according to Newton's laws from the distribution of the visible stars in the galaxy (the solid curve on the diagram). This discrepancy indicates that there should be much more matter in the outer parts of the spiral galaxies.

ROTATION CURVE FOR SPIRAL GALAXY NGC 3198

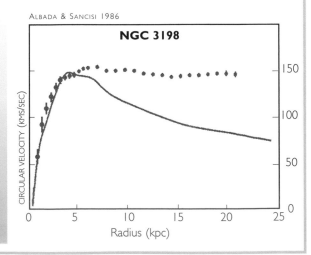

Albada & Sancisi 1986

THE NATURE OF DARK MATTER

Cosmologists now believe that while the central parts of spiral galaxies consist largely of ordinary stars, their outskirts are dominated by dark matter that we cannot see directly. But one of the fundamental problems is to discover the nature of the dominant form of dark matter in these outer regions of galaxies. Before the 1980s it was usually assumed that this dark matter was ordinary matter comprised of protons, neutrons, and electrons in some not readily detectable form: perhaps gas clouds, or MACHOs—"massive compact halo objects" like white dwarfs or neutron stars, or even black holes.

However, recent study of the formation of galaxies has led cosmologists to believe that a significant fraction of the dark matter must be in a different form from ordinary matter. Perhaps it arises from the masses of very light elementary particles such as axions or neutrinos. It may even consist of more exotic species of particles, such as WIMPs—"weakly interacting massive particles"—that are predicted by modern theories of elementary particles but have not yet been detected experimentally.

The no man's land of extra dimensions that lies between branes.

(FIG. 7.13)
We would not see a shadow galaxy on a shadow brane because light would not propagate through the extra dimensions. But gravity would, so the rotation of our galaxy would be affected by dark matter, matter we cannot see.

This missing mass might arise from some exotic species of particle in our world such as WIMPs (weakly interacting massive particles) or axions (very light elementary particles). But missing mass could also be evidence of the existence of a shadow world with matter in it. Maybe it contains shallow human beings wondering about the mass that seems to be missing from their world to account for the orbits of shadow stars around the center of the shadow galaxy (Fig. 7.13).

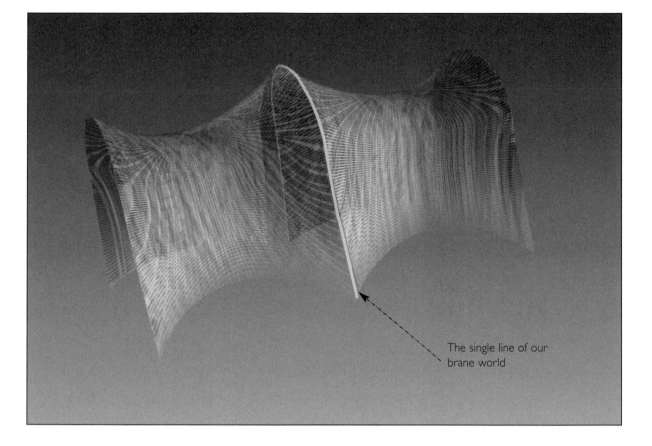

The single line of our brane world

Instead of the extra dimensions ending on a second brane, another possibility is that they are infinite but highly curved, like a saddle (Fig. 7.14). Lisa Randall and Raman Sundrum showed that this kind of curvature would act rather like a second brane: the gravitational influence of an object on the brane would be confined to a small neighborhood of the brane and not spread out to infinity in the extra dimensions. As in the shadow brane model, the gravitational field would have the right long-distance falloff to explain planetary orbits and lab measurements of the gravitational force, but gravity would vary more rapidly at short distances.

There is however an important difference between this Randall-Sundrum model and the shadow brane model. Bodies that move under the influence of gravity will produce gravitational waves, ripples of curvature that travel through spacetime at the speed of light.

(FIG. 7.14)

In the Randall-Sundrum model there is only one brane (shown here in only one dimension). The extra dimensions extend to infinity, but are curved like a saddle. This curvature prevents the gravitational field of matter on the brane from spreading far into the extra dimensions.

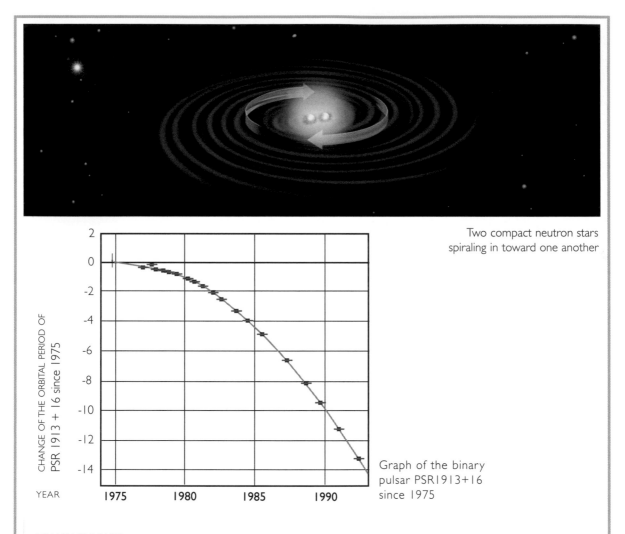

Two compact neutron stars spiraling in toward one another

Graph of the binary pulsar PSR1913+16 since 1975

BINARY PULSARS

General relativity predicts that heavy bodies moving under the influence of gravity emit gravitational waves. Like light waves, gravitational waves carry energy away from the objects that emit them. However, the rate of energy loss is usually extremely low, hence very difficult to observe. For instance, the emission of gravitational waves is causing the Earth to slowly spiral in toward the Sun, but it would take another 10^{27} years for them to collide!

But in 1975 Russell Hulse and Joseph Taylor discovered the binary pulsar PSR1913+16, a system consisting of two compact neutron stars orbiting each other with a maximum separation of only one solar radius. According to general relativity, the rapid motion means that the orbital period of this system should decrease on a much shorter time scale because of the emission of a strong gravitational wave signal. The change predicted by general relativity is in excellent agreement with careful observations by Hulse and Taylor of the orbital parameters, which indicate that since 1975 the period has shortened by more than ten seconds. In 1993 they were awarded the Nobel Prize for this confirmation of general relativity.

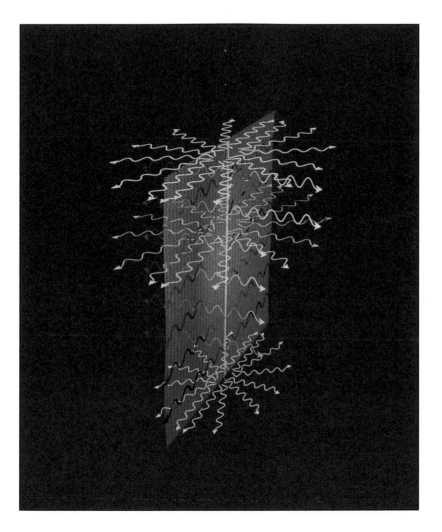

Like the electromagnetic waves of light, gravitational waves should carry energy, a prediction that has been confirmed by observations of the binary pulsar PSR1913+16.

If we indeed live on a brane in a spacetime with extra dimensions, gravitational waves generated by the motion of bodies on the brane would travel off into the other dimensions. If there were a second shadow brane, gravitational waves would be reflected back and trapped between the two branes. On the other hand, if there was only a single brane and the extra dimensions went on forever, as in the Randall-Sundrum model, gravitational waves could escape altogether and carry away energy from our brane world (Fig. 7.15).

(FIG. 7.15)
In the Randall-Sundrum model, short wavelength gravitational waves can carry energy away from sources on the brane, causing apparent violation of the law of conservation of energy.

191

This would seem to breach one of the fundamental principles of physics: the Law of Conservation of Energy. The total amount of energy remains the same. However, it appears to be a violation only because our view of what is happening is restricted to the brane. An angel who could see the extra dimensions would know that the energy was the same, just more spread out.

The gravitational waves produced by two stars orbiting each other would have a wavelength which would be much longer than the radius of the saddle-shaped curvature in the extra dimensions. This would mean they would tend to be confined to a small neighborhood of the brane—like gravitational force—and would not spread out much into the extra dimensions or carry away much energy from the brane. On the other hand, gravitational waves that were shorter than the scale on which the extra dimensions are curved would escape easily from the vicinity of the brane.

The only sources of significant amounts of short gravitational waves are likely to be black holes. A black hole on the brane will extend to a black hole in the extra dimensions. If the black hole is small, it will be almost round; that is, it will reach about as far into the extra dimensions as its size on the brane. On the other hand, a large black hole on the brane will extend to a "black pancake," which is confined to a vicinity of the brane and which is much less thick (in the extra dimensions) than it is wide (on the brane) (Fig. 7.16).

As explained in Chapter 4, quantum theory means that black holes won't be completely black: they will emit particles and radiation of all kinds like hot bodies. The particles and radiation-like light would be emitted along the brane because matter and nongravitational forces like electricity would be confined to the brane. However, black holes also emit gravitational waves. These would not be confined to the brane but would travel in the extra dimension as well. If the black hole was large and pancake-like, the gravitational waves would stay near the brane. This would mean that the black hole would lose energy (and therefore mass by $E=mc^2$) at the rate one would expect for a black hole in four-dimensional spacetime. The black hole would therefore slowly evaporate and shrink in size until

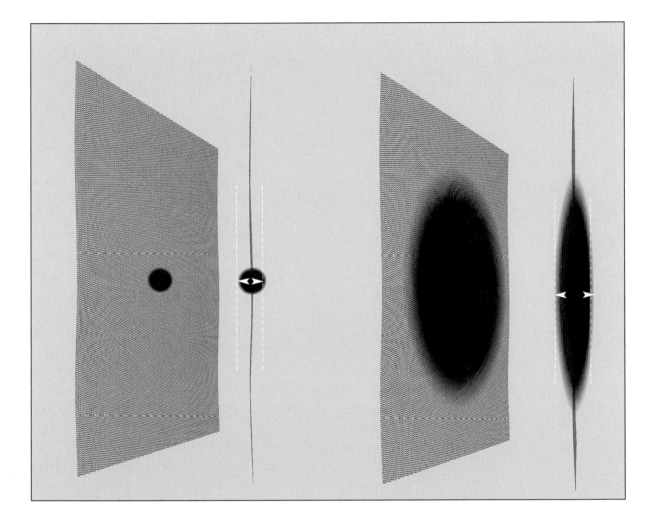

it became smaller than the radius of curvature of the saddle-like extra dimensions. At this point the gravitational waves emitted by the black hole would begin to escape freely into the extra dimensions. To someone on the brane, the black hole—or dark star as Michell called it (see Chapter 4)—would appear to be emitting dark radiation, radiation that cannot be observed directly on the brane but whose existence could be inferred from the fact that the black hole was losing mass.

(FIG. 7.16)

A black hole in our world on the brane would extend into the extra dimensions. If the black hole is small, it would be almost round, but a large black hole on the brane would extend to a pancake-shaped black hole in the extra dimension.

(FIG. 7.17) The formation of a brane world could be like the formation of a bubble of steam in boiling water.

It would mean that the final burst of radiation from an evaporating black hole would appear less powerful than it actually was. This could be why we have not observed bursts of gamma rays that can be ascribed to dying black holes, though the other, more prosaic explanation would be that there aren't many black holes with mass low enough to evaporate in the age of the universe thus far.

The radiation from brane-world black holes arises from quantum fluctuations of particles on and off a brane but branes, like everything else in the universe, will be subject to quantum fluctuations themselves. These can cause branes to appear and disappear spontaneously. The quantum creation of a brane would be a bit like the formation of bubbles of steam in boiling water. Liquid water consists of billions and billions of H_2O molecules packed together with couplings between nearest neighbors. As the water is heated up, the molecules move faster and bounce off each other. Occasionally these collisions will give molecules such high velocities that a group of them will break free of their bonds and form a little bubble of steam surrounded by water. The bubble will then grow or shrink in a random manner with more molecules from the liquid joining the steam or vice versa. Most small bubbles of steam will collapse to liquid again but a few will grow to a certain critical size beyond which the bubbles are almost certain to continue to grow. It is these large expanding bubbles that one observes when water boils (Fig. 7.17).

The behavior of brane worlds would be similar. The uncertainty principle would allow brane worlds to appear from nothing as bubbles, with the brane forming the surface of the bubble and the interior being the higher-dimensional space. Very small bubbles would tend to collapse again to nothing, but a bubble that grew by quantum fluctuations beyond a certain critical size would be likely to keep on growing. People (such as us) living on the brane, the surface of the bubble, would think the universe was expanding. It would be like painting galaxies on the surface of a balloon and blowing it up. The galaxies would move apart but no galaxy would be picked out as the center of expansion. Let's hope there's no one with a cosmic pin to deflate the bubble.

According to the no boundary proposal described in Chapter 3, the spontaneous creation of a brane world would have a history in imaginary time which was like a nutshell: that is, it would be a four-dimensional sphere, like the surface of the Earth but with two more dimensions. The important difference is that the nutshell described in Chapter 3 was essentially hollow: the four-dimensional sphere wouldn't have been the boundary of anything and the other six or seven dimensions of spacetime that M-theory predicts would all be curled up even smaller than the nutshell. On the new brane world picture, however, the nutshell would be filled: the history in imaginary time of the brane on which we live would be a four-dimensional sphere that would be the boundary of a five-dimensional bubble with the remaining five or six dimensions curled up very small (Fig. 7.18).

This history of the brane in imaginary time would determine its history in real time. In real time the brane would expand in an accelerated inflationary manner like that described in Chapter 3. A perfectly smooth and round nutshell would be the most probable history of the bubble in imaginary time. However, it would correspond to a brane that expanded forever in an inflationary way in real time. Galaxies would not form on such a brane and so intelligent life would not have developed. On the other hand, imaginary time histories that are not perfectly smooth and round would have somewhat lower probabilities but could correspond to real time behavior in which the brane had a phase of accelerating inflationary expansion at first but then began to slow down. During this decelerating expansion galaxies could have formed and intelligent life might have developed. Thus, according to the anthropic principle described in Chapter 3, it is only the slightly hairy nutshells which will be observed by intelligent beings asking why the origin of the universe wasn't perfectly smooth.

As the brane expanded, the volume of the higher-dimensional space inside would increase. Eventually there would be an enormous bubble surrounded by the brane on which we live. But do we really live on the brane? According to the idea of holography described in Chapter 2, information about what happens in a region

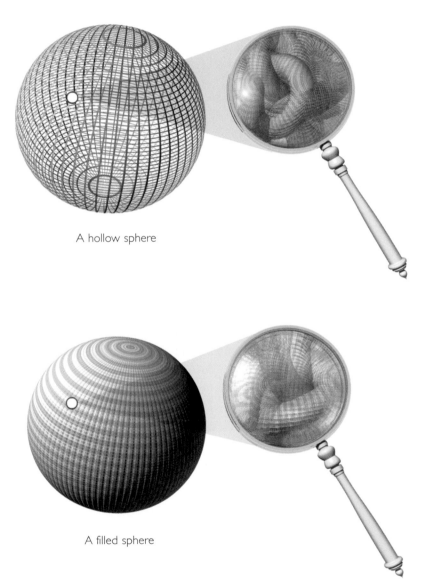

A hollow sphere

A filled sphere

(FIG. 7.18)
The brane world picture of the origin of the universe differs from that discussed in Chapter 3, because the slightly flattened four-dimensional sphere, or nutshell, is no longer hollow but is filled by a fifth dimension.

HOLOGRAPHY

Holography encodes the information in a region of space onto a surface one dimension lower. It seems to be a property of gravity, as is shown by the fact that the area of the event horizon measures the number of internal states of a black hole. In a brane world model, holography would be a one-to-one correspondence between states in our four-dimensional world and states in higher dimensions. From a positivist viewpoint, one cannot distinguish which description is more fundamental.

of spacetime can be encoded on its boundary. So maybe we think we live in a four-dimensional world because we are shadows cast on the brane by what is happening in the interior of the bubble. However, from a positivist viewpoint, one cannot ask: which is reality, brane or bubble?. They are both mathematical models that describe the observations. One is free to use whichever model is most convenient. What is outside the brane? There are several possibilities (Fig. 7.19):

1. There may be nothing outside. Although a bubble of steam has water outside it, this is just an analogy to help us visualize the origin of the universe. One could imagine a mathematical model that was just a brane with a higher-dimensional space inside but absolutely nothing outside, not even empty space. One can calculate what the mathematical model predicts without reference to what is outside.

2. One could have a mathematical model in which the outside of a bubble was glued to the outside of a similar bubble. This model is actually mathematically equivalent to the possibility discussed above that there is nothing outside the bubble but the difference is psychological: people feel happier being placed in the center of spacetime rather than on its edge; but for a positivist, possibilities 1 and 2 are the same.

3. The bubble might expand into a space that was not a mirror image of what was inside the bubble. This possibility is different from the two discussed above and is more like the case of boiling water. Other bubbles could form and expand. If they collided and merged with the bubble in which we lived, the results could be catastrophic. It has even been suggested that the big bang itself may have produced by a collision between branes.

Brane world models like this are a hot topic of research. They are highly speculative but they offer new kinds of behavior that can be tested by observation. They could explain why gravity seems to be so weak. Gravity might be quite strong in the fundamental theory but the spreading of the gravitational force in the extra dimensions would mean it would be weak at large distances on the brane on which we live.

A consequence of this would be that the Planck length, the smallest distance to which we can probe without creating a black hole, would be quite a lot larger than it would appear from the weakness of gravity on our four-dimensional brane. The smallest Russian doll wouldn't be so tiny after all and might be within the reach of particle accelerators of the future. In fact we might already have discovered the smallest doll, the fundamental Planck length, if the U.S. hadn't gone through a fit of feeling poor in 1994 and canceled the SSC (Superconducting Super Collider) even though it was half built. Other particle accelerators such as the LHC (Large

(FIG. 7.19)

1. A brane/bubble with a higher-dimensional space inside with nothing outside.

Identify

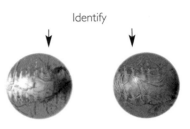

2. A possibility in which the outside of a brane/bubble is glued to the outside of another bubble.

3. A brane/bubble expands into a space which is not the mirror image of what is inside. Other bubbles could form and expand in such a scenario.

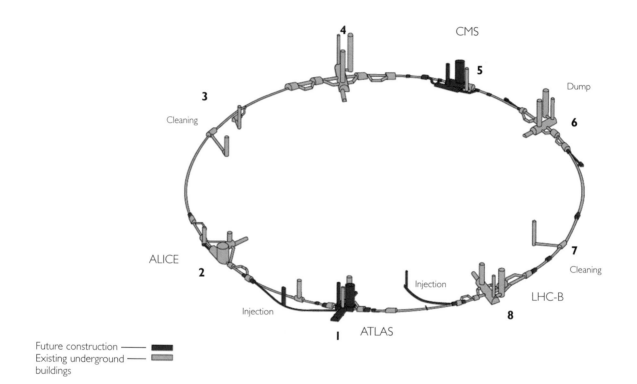

4   CMS

3

Cleaning

5

Dump

6

ALICE

2

Injection

Injection

7

Cleaning

LHC-B

Injection

8

I   ATLAS

Future construction ——— ▬

Existing underground ——— ▬
buildings

(FIG. 7.20)
Layout of the LEP tunnel showing the existing infrastructure and the future construction of the Large Hadron Collider in Geneva, Switzerland.

Hadron Collider) at Geneva are now being built (Fig. 7.20). With them and with other observations such as the cosmic microwave background radiation, we may be able to determine whether or not we live on a brane. If we do, it will presumably be because the anthropic principle picks out brane models from the vast zoo of universes allowed by M-theory. We could well paraphrase Miranda in Shakespeare's *The Tempest*:

> *O Brane new world.*
> *That has such creatures in't.*

That is the universe in a nutshell.

Glossary

Absolute time

The idea that there can be a universal clock. Einstein's theory of relativity showed that there could be no such concept.

Absolute zero

The lowest possible temperature at which substances contain no heat energy; about −273 degrees Centigrade or 0 on the Kelvin scale.

Acceleration

A change in an object's speed or direction. *Also see* velocity.

Amplitude

The maximum height of a wave peak or the maximum depth of a wave trough.

Anthropic principle

The idea that we see the universe the way it is because if it were any different, we wouldn't be here to see it.

Antiparticle

Each type of matter particle has a corresponding antiparticle. When a particle collides with its antiparticle, they annihilate, leaving only energy.

Atom

The basic unit of ordinary matter, made up of a tiny nucleus (consisting of protons and neutrons) surrounded by orbiting electrons.

Big bang

The singularity at the beginning of the universe, about fifteen billion years ago.

Big crunch

The name given to one possible scenario for the end of the universe, where all space and matter collapse to form a singularity.

Black hole

A region of spacetime from which nothing, not even light, can escape because gravity is so strong.

Blue shift

The shortening of the wavelength of radiation emitted by an object that is moving toward an observer, caused by the Doppler effect.

Boson

A particle or pattern of string vibration whose spin is a whole number.

Boundary conditions

The initial state of a physical system or, more generally, the state of the system at a boundary in time or space.

Brane

An object, which appears to be a fundamental ingredient of M-theory, that can have a variety of spatial dimensions. In general, a p-brane has length in p directions, a 1-brane is a string, a 2-brane is a surface or a membrane, etc.

Brane world

A four-dimensional surface or brane in a higher-dimensional spacetime.

Casimir effect

The attractive pressure between two flat, parallel metal plates placed very near to each other in a vacuum. The pressure is due to a reduction in the usual number of virtual particles in the space between the plates.

Chronology protection conjecture

The idea that the laws of physics conspire to prevent time travel by macroscopic objects.

Classical theory

A theory based on concepts established before relativity and quantum mechanics. It assumes that objects have well-defined positions and velocities. This is not true on very small scales, as the Heisenberg uncertainty principle shows.

Closed string

A type of string in the shape of a loop.

Conservation of energy

The law of science that states that energy (or its equivalent in mass) can neither be created or destroyed.

Cosmic string

A long, heavy object with a tiny cross section that may have been produced during the early stages of the universe. By now a single string could stretch across the entire universe.

Cosmological constant

A mathematical device used by Einstein to give the universe a built-in tendency to expand, allowing general relativity to predict a static universe.

Cosmology

The study of the universe as a whole.

Curled-up dimension

A spatial dimension that is curved up so small that it can escape detection.

Dark matter

Matter in galaxies and clusters, and possibly between clusters, that cannot be observed directly but that can be detected by its gravitational field. As much as ninety percent of the matter in the universe is dark matter.

DNA

Deoxyribonucleic acid, comprised of phosphate, a sugar, and four bases: adenine, guanine, thymine, and cytosine. Two strands of DNA form a double helix structure that resembles a spiral staircase. DNA encodes all the information cells require to reproduce and plays a vital part in heredity.

Doppler effect

The shift of frequency and wavelength of sound waves or light waves that an observer perceives if the source is moving relative to that observer.

Duality

A correspondence between apparently different theories that lead to the same physical results.

Electric charge

A property of a particle by which it may repel (or attract) other particles that have a charge of similar (or opposite) sign.

Electromagnetic force

The force that arises between particles with electric charge of a similar (or opposite) sign.

Electromagnetic wave

A wavelike disturbance in an electric field. All waves of the electromagnetic spectrum travel at the speed of light, e.g., visible light, x-rays, microwaves, infrared, etc.

Electron

A particle with negative charge that orbits the nucleus of an atom.

Elementary particle

A particle that it is believed cannot be subdivided.

Entropy

A measure of the disorder of a physical system; the number of different microscopic configurations of a system that leave its macroscopic appearance unchanged.

Ether

A hypothetical nonmaterial medium once supposed to fill all space. The idea that such a medium is required for the propagation of electromagnetic radiation is no longer tenable.

Event

A point in spacetime specified by its place and time.

Event horizon

The edge of a black hole; the boundary of the region from which it is not possible to escape to infinity.

Exclusion principle

The idea that two identical spin $-\frac{1}{2}$ particles cannot have (within the limits of the uncertainty principle) both the same position and the same velocity.

Fermion

A particle or a pattern of string vibration whose spin is half of a whole number.

Field

Something that exists throughout space and time, as opposed to a particle that exists only at one point at a time.

Force field

The means by which a force communicates its influence.

Free space

A portion of vacuum space completely free of fields, i.e., not acted on by any forces.

Frequency

For a wave, the number of complete cycles per second.

General Relativity

Einstein's theory based on the idea that the laws of science should be the same for all observers, no matter how they are moving. It explains the force of gravity in terms of the curvature of a four-dimensional spacetime.

Grand Unification Theory

A theory that unifies the electromagnetic, strong, and weak forces.

Grassman numbers

A class of numbers that do not commute. In ordinary real numbers, it does not matter in which order they are multiplied: A x B=C and B x A=C. However, Grassman numbers *anti*commute, so A x B is the same as -B x A.

Gravitational field

The means by which gravity communicates its influence.

Gravitational force

The weakest of the four fundamental forces of nature.

Gravitational wave

A wavelike disturbance in a gravitational field.

Ground state

The state of a system with minimum energy.

Holographic theory

The idea that the quantum states of a system in a region of spacetime may be encoded on the boundary of that region.

Imaginary number

An abstract mathematical construction. Real and imaginary numbers can be thought of as labelling the positions of points in a plane so that imaginary numbers are at right angles to ordinary real numbers.

Imaginary time

Time measured using imaginary numbers.

Infinity
> A boundless or endless extent or number.

Inflation
> A brief period of accelerated expansion during which the very early universe increased its size by an enormous factor.

Initial conditions
> The state of a physical system at its beginning.

Interference pattern
> The wave pattern that appears from the merging of two or more waves that are emitted from different locations or at different times.

Kelvin
> A temperature scale in which temperatures are quoted relative to absolute zero.

Light cone
> A surface in spacetime that marks out the possible direction for light rays passing through a given event.

Light second
> Distance traveled by light in one second.

Light year
> Distance traveled by light in one year.

Lorentz contraction
> The shortening of moving objects along their direction of motion, as predicted by special relativity.

Macroscopic
> Large enough to be seen by the naked eye; usually used for scales down to 0.01 mm. Scales below this size are referred to as microscopic.

Magnetic field
> The field responsible for magnetic forces.

Mass
> The quantity of matter in a body; its inertia or resistance to acceleration in free space.

Maxwell field
> The synthesis of electricity, magnetism, and light into dynamic fields that can oscillate and move through space.

Microwave background radiation
> The radiation from the glowing of the hot early universe; now so red-shifted that it appears not as light but as microwaves (radio waves with a wavelength of a few centimeters).

Moore's law
> A law stating that the power of computers will double every eighteen months. This clearly cannot continue indefinitely.

M-Theory
> A theory that unites all five string theories, as well as supergravity, within a single thoretical framework, but which is not yet fully understood.

Naked singularity
> A spacetime singularity, not surrounded by a black hole, which is visible to a distant observer.

Neutrino
> A chargeless species of particle subject only to the weak force.

Neutron
> An uncharged particle, very similar to the proton, which accounts for roughly half the particles in an atomic nucleus. Composed of three quarks (2 down, 1 up).

Newton's laws of motion
> Laws describing the motion of bodies based on the conception of absolute space and time. These held sway until Einstein's discovery of special relativity.

Newton's universal theory of gravity
> The theory that the strength of the attraction

205

between two bodies depends on the mass and separation of the bodies; it is proportional to the product of their masses and inversely proportional to the square of the distance between them.

No boundary condition
The idea that the universe is finite but has no boundary in imaginary time.

Nuclear fission
The process by which a nucleus breaks down into two or more smaller nuclei, releasing energy.

Nuclear fusion
The process by which two nuclei collide and join to form a larger, heavier nucleus.

Nucleus
The central part of an atom, consisting only of protons and neutrons held together by the strong force.

Observer
A person or piece of equipment that measures physical properties of a system.

Particle accelerator
A machine that can accelerate moving charged particles, increasing their energy.

P-brane
A brane with p dimensions. *Also see* Brane.

Photoelectric effect
The way in which certain metals give off electrons when light falls on them.

Photon
A quantum of light; the smallest packet of the electromagnetic field.

Planck length
About 10^{-35} centimeters. The size of a typical string in string theory.

Planck time
About 10^{-43} seconds; time it takes light to travel the distance of the Planck length.

Planck's constant
The cornerstone of the uncertainty principle—the product of the uncertainty in position and velocity must be greater than Planck's constant. It is represented by the symbol ℏ.

Planck's quantum principle
The idea that electromagnetic waves (e.g., light) can be emitted and absorbed only in discrete quanta.

Positivist approach
The idea that a scientific theory is a mathematical model that describes and codifies the observations we make.

Positron
The positively charged antiparticle of the electron.

Primordial black hole
A black hole created in the early universe.

Proton
A positively charged particle, very similar to the neutron, that accounts for roughly half the mass of an atomic nucleus. It is made of three quarks (2 up and 1 down).

Quantum (plural: quanta)
The indivisible unit in which waves may be absorbed or emitted.

Quantum gravity
A theory that merges quantum mechanics with general relativity.

Quantum mechanics
The physical laws that govern the realm of the very small, such as atoms, protons, and the like; developed from Planck's quantum principle and Heisenberg's uncertainty principle.

Quark
A charged elementary particle that feels the strong force. Quarks come in six "flavors": up, down, strange, charmed, bottom, and top, and each flavor in three "colors": red, green, and blue.

Radiation

The energy transmitted by waves or particles through space or some other medium.

Radioactivity

The spontaneous breakdown of one type of atomic nucleus into another.

Randall-Sundrum Model

The theory that we live on a brane in an infinite five-dimensional space of negative curvature, like a saddle.

Red shift

The reddening of radiation emitted by an object that is moving away from an observer, caused by the Doppler effect.

Schrödinger equation

Equation governing the evolution of the wave function in quantum theory.

Scientific determinism

A clockwork conception of the universe in which complete knowledge of the state of the universe enables the complete state to be predicted at earlier or future times; suggested by Laplace.

Second law of thermodynamics

The law stating that entropy always increases and can never decrease.

Singularity

A point in spacetime at which the spacetime curvature becomes infinite.

Singularity theorem

A theorem showing that a singularity, a point where general relativity breaks down, must exist under certain circumstances; in particular, that the universe must have started with a singularity.

Solar eclipse

A period of darkness that occurs when the moon passes between the Earth and the Sun, typically lasting a few minutes on Earth. In 1919 an eclipse viewed from West Africa proved special relativity beyond doubt.

Spacetime

The four-dimensional space whose points are events.

Spatial dimension

Any of the three spacetime dimensions that are spacelike.

Special relativity

Einstein's theory based on the idea that the laws of science should be the same for all observers, no matter how they are moving, in the absence of gravitational fields.

Spectrum

The component frequencies that make up a wave. The visible part of the sun's spectrum can sometimes be seen as a rainbow.

Spin

An internal property of elementary particles, related to but not identical to the everyday notion of spin.

Standard model of cosmology

Big bang theory together with an understanding of the standard model of particle physics.

Standard model of particle physics

A unifying theory for the three nongravitational forces and their effects on matter.

Stationary state

A state that is not changing with time.

String

A fundamental one-dimensional object in string theory that replaces the concept of structureless elementary particles. Different vibration patterns of a string give rise to elementary particles with different properties.

String theory

A theory of physics in which particles are described as waves on strings; unites quantum mechanics and general relativity. Also known as superstring theory.

Strong force

The strongest of the four fundamental forces, with the shortest range of all. It holds quarks together to form protons and neutrons and these particles together to form the atomic nucleus.

Supergravity

A set of theories unifying general relativity and supersymmetry.

Supersymmetry

A principle that relates the properties of particles of different spin.

Thermodynamics

The study of the relationship between energy, work, heat, and entropy in a dynamical physical system.

Time dilation

A feature of special relativity predicting that the flow of time will slow for an observer in motion, or in the presence of a strong gravitational field.

Time loop

Another name for a closed timelike curve.

Uncertainty principle

The principle formulated by Heisenberg that one can never be exactly sure of both the position and the velocity of a particle. The more accurately one knows the one, the less accurately one can know the other.

Unified theory

Any theory which describes all four forces and all of matter within a single framework.

Vacuum energy

Energy that is present even in apparently empty space. It has the curious property that unlike the presence of mass, the presence of vacuum energy would cause the expansion of the universe to speed up.

Velocity

A number describing the speed and direction of an object's motion.

Virtual particle

In quantum mechanics, a particle that can never be directly detected, but whose existence does have measurable effects. *Also see* Casimir effect.

Wave function

A fundamental concept in quantum mechanics; a number at each point in space associated with a particle, determining the probability that the particle is to be found at that position.

Wave/particle duality

The concept in quantum mechanics that there is no distinction between waves and particles; particles may behave like waves and vice versa.

Wavelength

The distance between two adjacent troughs or two adjacent peaks of a wave.

Weak force

The second weakest of the four fundamental forces, with a very short range. It affects all matter particles, but not force-carrying particles.

Weight

The force exerted on a body by a gravitational field. It is proportional to but not the same as its mass.

Wormhole

A thin tube of spacetime connecting distant regions of the universe. Wormholes may also link parallel or baby universes and could provide the possibility of time travel.

Yang-Mills theory

An extension to Maxwell's field theory that describes interactions between the weak and the strong force.

Suggested Further Readings

There are many popular books ranging from the very good, like *The Elegant Universe*, to the indifferent (which I won't identify). I have therefore restricted my list to authors who have made a significant contribution to the field in order to convey the authentic experience.

I apologize to those I have left out because of my ignorance. A second list, "Getting More Technical," is included for readers who want to pursue more advanced texts.

Einstein, Albert. *The Meaning of Relativity*, Fifth Edition.
Princeton: Princeton University Press, 1966.

Feynman, Richard. *The Character of Physical Law*.
Cambridge, Mass: MIT Press, 1967.

Greene, Brian. *The Elegant Universe: Superstrings, Hidden Dimensions, and the Quest for the Ultimate Theory*.
New York, W.W. Norton & Company, 1999.

Guth, Alan H. *The Inflationary Universe: The Quest for a New Theory of Cosmic Origins*.
New York: Perseus Books Group, 2000.

Rees, Martin J. *Our Cosmic Habitat*.
Princeton: Princeton University Press, 2001.

Rees, Martin J. *Just Six Numbers: The Deep Forces that Shape the Universe*.
New York: Basic Books, 2000.

Thorne, Kip. *Black Holes and Time Warps: Einstein's Outrageous Legacy*.
New York: W.W. Norton & Company, 1994.

Weinberg, Steven. *The First Three Minutes: A Modern View of the Origin of the Universe*, Second Edition.
New York: Basic Books, 1993.

Getting More Technical

Hartle, James. *Gravity: An Introduction to Einstein's General Relativity*.
Reading, Mass.: Addison-Wesley Longman, 2002.

Linde, Andrei D. *Particle Physics and Inflationary Cosmology*.
Chur, Switzerland: Harwood Academic Publishers, 1990.

Misner, Charles W., Kip S. Thorne, John A. Wheeler. *Gravitation*.
San Francisco: W. H. Freeman and Company, 1973.

Peebles, P. J. *Principles of Physical Cosmology*. Princeton, New Jersey: Princeton University Press, 1993.

Polchinski, Joseph. *String Theory: An Introduction to the Bosonic String*.
Cambridge: Cambridge University Press, 1998.

Wald, Robert M. *General Relativity*.
Chicago: University of Chicago Press, 1984.

Picture Acknowledgments

page 3, 19: Courtesy of the Archives, California Institute of Technology. Albert Einstein™ Licensed by The Hebrew University of Jerusalem, Represented by the Roger Richman Agency Inc., www.albert-einstein.net; **page 5**: AKG Photo, London; Albert Einstein™ Licensed by The Hebrew University of Jerusalem, Represented by the Roger Richman Agency Inc., www.albert-einstein.net; **page 13**: Courtesy Los Alamos National Laboratory; **page 23**: Courtesy Science Photo Library; **page 26**: Albert Einstein™ Licensed by The Hebrew University of Jerusalem, Represented by the Roger Richman Agency Inc., www.albert-einstein.net; **page 27**: Photo by Harry Burnett/courtesy of the Archives, California Institute of Technology. Albert Einstein™ Licensed by The Hebrew University of Jerusalem, Represented by the Roger Richman Agency Inc., www.albert-einstein.net; **page 55**: Courtesy Neel Shearer; **page 68**: Courtesy Space Telescope Science Institute (STScI)/NASA; **page 69**: Prometheus bound with an eagle picking out his liver, black-figure vase painting, Etruscan. Vatican Museums and Galleries, Vatican City, Italy/Bridgeman Art Library; **page 70**: Spiral galaxy NGC 4414 photo courtesy Hubble Heritage Team, STScI/NASA; Spiral bar galaxy NGC 4314 photo courtesy University of Texas et al., STScI/NASA; Elliptical galaxy NGC 147 photo courtesy STScI/NASA; Milky Way photo courtesy S.J. Maddox, G. Efstathiou, W. Sutherland, J. Loveday, Department of Astrophysics, Oxford University; **page 76**: Courtesy Jason Ware, galaxyphoto.com; **page 77**: Courtesy of The Observatories of the Carnegie Institution of Washington; **page 83**: Photo by Floyd Clark/courtesy of the Archives, California Institute of Technology; **page 107**: Courtesy Neel Shearer; **page 112**: Courtesy NASA/Chandra X-Ray Center/Smithsonian Astrophysical Observatory/H. Marshall et al.; **page 113**: Courtesy STScI/NASA; **page 116**: Courtesy STScI/NASA; **pages 133, 153**: Copyright California Institute of Technology; **page 147**: Courtesy Neel Shearer; **page 162**: From *The Blind Watchmaker* by Richard Dawkins, New York: W.W. Norton & Company, 1986; **page 168**: Hubble Deep Field courtesy R. Williams, STScI/NASA; **page 169**: "INDEPENDENCE DAY" ©1996 Twentieth Century Fox Film Corporation. All rights reserved.; E.T. still: Copyright © 2001 by Universal Studios Publishing Rights, a Division of Universal Studios Licensing, Inc. All rights reserved.; **page 195**: Courtesy Neel Shearer.

All original illustrations not credited above have been created for this book by
Malcolm Godwin of Moonrunner Design Ltd., UK.

Index

*) Page numbers in boldface refer to illustrations